# Structural Adjustment and Beyond in Sub-Saharan Africa

**Research and Policy Issues**

Edited by
ROLPH VAN DER HOEVEN
AND FRED VAN DER KRAAIJ

Ministry of Foreign Affairs (DGIS)
The Hague
*in association with*
JAMES CURREY
London
HEINEMANN
Portsmouth (N.H.)

021892

Ministry of Foreign Affairs (DGIS)
The Hague
The Netherlands

in association with

James Currey Ltd
54b Thornhill Square
Islington, London N1 1BE
England

Heinemann;
A Division of Reed Publishing (USA) Inc
361 Hanover Street, Portsmouth
New Hampshire 03801
USA

First published 1994

1 2 3 4 5 98 97 96 95 94

**British Library Cataloguing in Publication Data**

Structural Adjustment and Beyond in Sub-Saharan
Africa:
Research and Policy Issues
    I. Hoeven, Rolph van der    II. Kraaij,
    Fred van der
    338.967

ISBN 0-85255-150-9 Paper (James Currey)
ISBN 0-85255-151-7 Cloth (James Currey)

ISBN 0-435-08962-5 Cloth (Heinemann)
ISBN 0-435-08964-1 Paper (Heinemann)

Typeset in 10/11½pt Palatino by Colset Pte Ltd, Singapore
Printed in Great Britain by Villiers Publications, London N3

# Contents

## APPENDICES

# List of Tables

# List of Figures

# Acknowledgements

In December 1992 the Netherlands Minister for Development Co-operation, Jan Pronk, decided to organize an international seminar on structural adjustment in Sub-Saharan Africa. The seminar was to be held in June 1993 and was to bring together scholars, policy-makers and donor representatives to discuss (i) the methodologies used in doing research on the impact of structural adjustment in Sub-Saharan Africa, (ii) the results of this research, and (iii) the practical issues which policy-makers both in Sub-Saharan Africa and in donor organisations are facing.

The resulting challenge was considerable, given the relatively short period of time available and was only equalled by the Minister's desire to have the seminar's proceedings published as quickly as possible. Within a period of six months substance had to be given to the idea of holding a seminar on this topic by elaborating the main themes to be discussed. Furthermore, some sixty participants, ranging over the various groups, had to be selected and a number of researchers and policy-makers of international reputation had to be persuaded to prepare papers on specified subjects for presentation at the seminar. Last but not least, the logistical preparation and organization of the seminar had to be taken care of. It goes without saying that such an undertaking could never have been successful without the support and contribution of many people.

In the first place, we should like to acknowledge the active support which Minister Jan Pronk has given throughout the preparation of the seminar and the editing of its proceedings. He made useful suggestions for the structure of the seminar and the list of participants. His interest is well illustrated both by his personal participation in the seminar's discussions and by his contribution to this volume.

The seminar was organized by the Directorate-General for International Co-operation (DGIS) of the Netherlands Ministry of Foreign Affairs, in collaboration with the Institute of Social Studies (ISS), and a large number of staff of these two institutions were involved. Among the ISS staff Peter de Valk and Bert Helmsing in particular made substantial contributions. Bert Helmsing's bright ideas contributed much to the success of the undertaking, while Peter de Valk provided valuable input in the compilation of the Pre-Seminar Reader which was sent to the participants in preparation for the seminar. We also owe Peter de Valk our thanks for the contribution he made to the editing of Chapters 4, 7 and 9 of this book.

The overall responsibility for the organization of the seminar was in the hands of a Steering Group, energetically chaired by Marnix Krop, and consisting of Dick Bark, Bernard Berendsen, Bert Helmsing, Erik Jansonius, Fred van der Kraaij, Bengt van Loosdrecht, George Waardenburg and Wim Wessels, all, apart from Bert Helmsing, staff members of DGIS/Ministry of Foreign Affairs. We appreciate the good work they did.

A sub-committee, which put forward suggestions for the substance of the seminar, included Erik Ader, Gerben de Jong, Peter de Valk, Jan Willem Gunning, Marie Hulsman, Rolph van der Hoeven, Fred van der Kraaij and Marc Wuyts and was chaired by George Waardenburg. It is not possible to acknowledge each person individually. All participated enthusiastically and made valuable suggestions. The Pre-Seminar Reader, which was much appreciated by the seminar participants, was compiled by a small Editorial Group composed of George Waardenburg (chairman), Gerben de Jong, Peter de Valk and Fred van der Kraaij.

The day-to-day preparation for the seminar was organized and supervised by an Executive Secretariat manned by Bert Helmsing, Erik Jansonius and Fred van der Kraaij. In particular, our thanks are owed to Erik Jansonius whose combination of discretion and relentless energy ensured that agreements and planning schedules were respected.

During the three days of the seminar a Steering Committee consisting of Marnix Krop (chairman), Bert Helmsing, Fred van der Kraaij, George Waardenburg and Wim Wessels looked after the smooth execution of the programme. Chairpersons Malima, Toye and Waardenburg ably presided over the meetings and particularly warm thanks go to them for their commendable efforts. A particular word of thanks must be addressed to the rapporteurs as well as the translators who made their useful contribution behind the scenes. Hence, warm thanks to Gerben de Jong, Peter de Valk, Marie Hulsman, Fred van der Kraaij, Aart van der Laan and Howard White as well as to the many anonymous translators. The Conference Secretariat, composed of Erik Jansonius and ISS secretaries Liesbeth Rientjes and Mariëtte Puthaar, had a major role in the smooth running of the seminar and we are very grateful to them, in particular to the two ISS secretaries who also provided valuable secretarial and logistical support throughout the whole period of the organization of the seminar. We would also like to thank Gary Debus of the ISS for his co-ordination of the production of this book and Margaret Cornell for her copy-editing of the final manuscript.

Of course, without the participation of the numerous researchers, policy-makers, donor representatives and individual experts whose names are listed at the end of the volume, there would have been no seminar. Therefore our most sincere thanks go to them, for their willingness to accept the invitation, for their papers, comments, remarks and other reactions on the issues dealt with by the seminar, and for their interest in the well-being of the peoples of Sub-Saharan Africa. We sincerely hope that this book will contribute to a better understanding of the necessary processes of change and their effects on ordinary people as well as to better policy action by governments and donors.

Rolph van der Hoeven
Fred van der Kraaij

February, 1994

# Notes on Contributors

*The views expressed in this volume are those of the contributors and not necessarily of the organizations they represent. This list includes speakers and discussants at the seminar.*

**Simeon Ibi Ajayi** is a Professor of Economics at the University of Ibadan, Nigeria. His main research interests are macroeconomic and public policy, monetary economics and health economics. He has written over 60 publications. Areas of recent publications include debt and growth, exchange rates, structural adjustment, debt and capital flight, and the economics of capital flight. He has worked as a consultant, among others to the World Bank, WHO, the AERC and the Carnegie Corporation of New York.

**Brian van Arkadie** is an Extraordinary Professor of Economic Development at the Institute of Social Studies, The Hague, the Netherlands, presently working with the ACBI in Harare. His main areas of expertise include macroeconomic planning, development planning, industrialization and trade policies. He has written numerous articles and books on these subjects. He has worked as a consultant for UNDP, UNEP, UNIDO, UNCTAD, IFAD, OECD, the UK Government, the EC, IMF, World Bank and the Carnegie Endowment for International Peace.

**Jean-Paul Azam** is a Professor of Economics, University of Auvergne at Clermont-Ferrand, France and a member of CERDI. His research interests include both theory and econometric applications and cover the macroeconomics of developing countries, the functioning of markets, microeconomics and macroeconomics of agricultural supply response, the social consequences of macroeconomic policies and economic theory. He occupies several editorial and other research positions (among others, *Journal of African Economies*, *Revue d'économie du développement*), was consultant for the CFD (ex-CCCE), EC, OECD Development Centre, UNICEF, UNDP, World Bank and is a prolific writer of books, articles and reports.

**Boubacar Barry** is a Professor of History, Cheikh Anta Diop University, Dakar, Senegal and Founding Director of IRIS. He is co-ordinator of the GCA-ALF project on the democratic transition in Africa. His publications include books and articles on the Senegambia and on regional co-operation and integration in West Africa.

**Jacques Bugnicourt** is a political economist who worked with the Senegalese Government and who was a professor at IDEP, Dakar, Senegal. He also worked as a consultant for various UN organizations and agencies. He is currently Executive Secretary of ENDA, an international Third World NGO, and is based at the organization's headquarters in Dakar.

**Moustapha Deme** is an economist with a career in the civil service of the Republic of Mali. He served as First Secretary at the Malian Embassy in Bonn (Germany) and in Brussels (Belgium, EC), was the Director of Economic Affairs within the Ministry of Finance and Directeur de Cabinet to the Presidency of the Republic. Since 1991 he has been working as an independent consultant.

**Lionel Demery**, an economist, spent eight years with the ILO in Bangkok, Thailand and has held posts in the University of Wales, Overseas Development Institute (London) and the University of Warwick, UK. He is currently a staff member in the Educational and Social Policy Department, World Bank (Washington DC). He has written several articles in learned journals and is best known for his work on adjustment and income distribution. Among others he has written the monograph *Poverty Alleviation under Structural Adjustment* (1987). Recently, he has co-edited *Understanding the Social Effects of Policy Reform* (World Bank, forthcoming).

**Sébastien Dessus** holds a dual master's degree in economics and in econometrics and mathematical economics. He is currently Principal Research Assistant for the OECD Development Centre, where he has been working on agricultural trade liberalization and on the political feasibility of adjustment. He has published papers on export performance and adjustment, and on the consequences of trade liberalization.

**Diane Elson** is a Lecturer in Development Economics at the University of Manchester, UK. She has written many books, articles, reports and reviews on various subjects including gender and structural adjustment. She is the co-editor of *Women's Employment and Multinationals in Western Europe* (1989) and editor of *Male Bias in the Development Process* (1991).

**Willem van der Geest** is a Research Associate at the International Development Centre, Queen Elizabeth House, Oxford, UK. He has worked as a researcher and consultant in African and Asian countries for, among others, the World Bank, UNCTAD and the UN. His main areas of interest include trade diversification in developing countries, agricultural policy, food markets, and structural adjustment. He has written academic as well as other publications and is the editor of *Negotiating Structural Adjustment in Africa* (1994).

**Jane Harrigan** is currently Lecturer in Development Economics, University of Manchester, UK. Formerly Agricultural Pricing Economist, Government of Malawi (1985–87) and Research Fellow, Institute of Development Policy and Management, University of Manchester (1987–90). She is co-author of the two-volume book *Aid and Power: The World Bank and Policy-based Lending* (1991). Consultant to various international organizations including the World Bank, the FAO, and the Economist Intelligence Unit (London).

**Rolph van der Hoeven** is an economist and Interdepartmental Manager, Structural Adjustment Issues at the ILO, Geneva. He has previously worked as a Senior Economic Adviser to UNICEF in New York. He has published widely on economic planning, basic needs and structural adjustment. He is the author of *Planning for Basic Needs: A Soft Option or a Solid Policy?* (1988), co-author of *Basic Needs in Development Planning* (1983) and co-editor of *World Recession and Global Interdependence* (1987), *Africa's Recovery in the 1990s* (1992) and *Poverty Monitoring. An International Concern* (1994).

**Ishrat Husain** is currently Chief Economist for the Africa Region in the World Bank, Washington DC. He has previously worked as Chief, Debt and International Finance Division and the Bank's Resident Representative in Nigeria. Before joining the World Bank, he worked in various policy positions in the Government of Pakistan.

**Emmanuel Gabriel Kasonde**, an economist, combines the experiences of civil servant, businessman and politician. He is the founder of the Century Holdings Group of Companies (Zambia), has occupied various public offices (since 1959) and served as Zambia's Minister of Finance and Development Planning from 7 November 1991 till 15 April 1993.

**Fred van der Kraaij** is an economist in the Policy Planning Section of the Directorate-General for International Co-operation of the Ministry of Foreign Affairs, The Hague, the Netherlands. He previously taught at the University of Liberia, and worked in Mali (Office du Niger and Ministry of Planning), Burkina Faso and Senegal (Netherlands Embassy). He is the author of *The Open Door Policy of Liberia – An Economic History of Modern Liberia* (1983, two volumes) and other studies on Liberia. He has also written extensively on development in various West African countries where he worked from 1975 till 1991 and on Ethiopia.

**Jean-Dominique Lafay** is currently Professor of Economics at the University of Paris I (Panthéon-Sorbonne), France and in charge of courses for graduate students in public economics. He has published several books and articles (among others in *European Journal of Political Economy*, *Public Choice*, *Revue Economique*, *Soviet Studies*) on public choice, bureaucracy, politico-economic modelling and adjustment.

**Kighoma A. Malima** combines a career in academia, as a Professor of Economics at the University of Dar es Salaam, Tanzania, with one in the public sector. Since the 1980s he has been several times Tanzania's Minister of Planning, Finance and Planning and Minister of Finance, his current position. He has long and first-hand experience with structural adjustment, on which subject he has published on various occasions.

**Taye Mengistae** is Assistant Professor of Economics and was until October 1993 Chairman of the Department of Economics, Addis Ababa University, Ethiopia.

He is currently on leave of study at St. Antony's College, University of Oxford, UK. Areas of research and interest include structural adjustment in Africa, in particular the social dimensions of adjustment on which subject he has published on various occasions.

**Christian Morrisson** is Head of the Research Programme at the OECD Development Centre. He has published many books and articles (in *Economic Journal, European Economic Review, Journal of Comparative Economics, Review of Income and Wealth, Revue Economique, World Development*) on income distribution, adjustment, agriculture and education in developing countries.

**Paul Mosley** is a Professor of Economics at the University of Reading, UK. Previous employment includes the Ministry of Finance in Kenya and the University of Manchester's Institute for Development Policy and Management (Director). Among his numerous publications are books on the settler economies of Kenya and Zimbabwe, the making of economic policy and overseas aid. He is the co-author of *Aid and Power: The World Bank and Policy-based Lending* (1991) and co-editor of *Development Finance and Policy Reform* (1992).

**Harris Mule**, a former Permanent Secretary in the Ministry of Finance and Planning, Kenya, and a former Assistant President of IFAD, is currently working as a freelance economic consultant.

**Achola Pala Okeyo**, an anthropologist and educationalist, is currently Chief, Africa Section of UNIFEM, New York. She has a wide background in policy research and analysis and in project evaluation, particularly with regard to socio-economic development and cultural change with emphasis on agriculture, food systems, food security, the household economy, notably paying attention to the role of women, and to land ownership and land tenure. She is well known for her prolific writing in all these areas.

**Jan Pieter Pronk** is the Netherlands' Minister for Development Co-operation. His present term of office began in November 1989, and he held the same position from 1973 to 1977. He is Vice-Chairman of the Labour Party which he has represented in Parliament on several occasions. From 1965 to 1971 he lectured on development strategy and development economics, conducted research and published papers on development issues, economic planning and aspects of the international economic order. From 1978 to 1980 he lectured in development economics at the Institute of Social Studies in The Hague. Prior to his present position, Jan Pronk lectured on the international economic order at the University of Amsterdam. From 1980 to 1986 he served as Deputy Secretary-General of UNCTAD and was a member of the Independent Commission on International Development Issues (the Brandt Commission).

**Alexander Sarris** is Professor of Economics at the University of Athens, Greece and Senior Research Fellow at Cornell University, USA. He has previously taught at the University of California at Berkeley. He has held numerous consulting appointments with the World Bank, the FAO, IFAD, among others. He is the author of eight books and monographs and over forty professional articles, in the fields of agricultural and development economics, applied international economics, policy analysis, and macro-micro modelling. He has extensive field experience in developing countries.

**Venkatesh Seshamani** is Professor of Economics at the University of Zambia, having previously taught at Bombay and Dar es Salaam Universities. He is the co-author of several textbooks and has written research-based monographs, reports, and articles as well as many conference and seminar papers. His main research interests are in the areas of industrialization, structural adjustment and its economic and social impacts. He has been consultant to the ECA, World Bank, UNICEF, ILO, SIDA and other organizations. He also assisted in drafting the African Alternative Framework to Structural Adjustment Programmes.

**Frances Stewart** is a development economist and at present Director of the International Development Centre, Oxford, UK. She has worked at UNICEF as a Special Adviser on Adjustment. Her main areas of research and publications are adjustment and poverty, appropriate technology and basic needs. Her books include *Technology and Underdevelopment* (1977), *Planning to Meet Basic Needs* (1985), *Adjustment with a Human Face* (co-author) (1987) and *North-South and South-South: Essays on International Economics* (1992). She is a co-editor of *Alternative Development Strategies in Sub-Saharan Africa* (1992) and has contributed to recent editions of the *Human Development Report* (UNDP). She has also been consultant to various international organizations.

**John Toye** is currently Director of the Institute of Development Studies, Sussex, UK. His work has focused on public finance in developing countries, the role of foreign aid and the World Bank's use of programme aid in support of structural adjustment reforms in developing countries. He has published widely on his research findings. He is the co-author of *Does Aid Work In India?* (1990) and of *Aid and Power: The World Bank and Policy-based Lending* (1991).

**Peter de Valk** is Senior Lecturer in Economics at the Institute of Social Studies, The Hague, the Netherlands. He has lived and worked in several African countries for many years. Currently, his research on industrialization in Africa focuses on the relationship between macroeconomic variables and policies and microeconomic behaviour and outcomes. His latest book is *A General Framework for Evaluating the Performance of Textile Enterprises in LDCs – With an Application to Tanzania under Structural Adjustment* (1992). His previous work in Africa includes studies on decentralization in African countries, problems in project implementation, and rural industrialization.

**Samuel Wangwe** is Senior Research Fellow at UNU/INTECH, Maastricht, the Netherlands, on leave from the Economics Department at the University of Dar es Salaam, Tanzania, where he is Professor of Economics. He has contributed more than 80 papers and reports, and written and edited several books. His recent research has focused on industry, trade and technological development.

**Willi Wapenhans**, an agricultural economist and a former Senior Vice-President of the World Bank, served prior to his retirement at the end of 1992 as Special Adviser to the President of this institution and Chairman of the Task Force on Portfolio Management. He is currently serving as Senior Economic Adviser to the Republic of Belarus. He has published widely in both English and German. He is the recipient of several awards and honours.

**Marc Wuyts** is a Professor of Economics and Applied Statistics, Institute of Social Studies, The Hague, the Netherlands. He has extensive experience in teaching in Sub-Saharan Africa (University of Dar Es Salaam, University of Eduardo Mondlane). Areas of research are structural adjustment in Africa, macro-economy and rural development in Africa. Areas of particular interest are South Africa, Mozambique and Tanzania.

**Joseph Yao** is a Professor of Economics at the University of Abidjan, Côte d'Ivoire and the present Director of CIRES. His areas of research and publications include human resources economics, environmental economics and structural adjustment.

# List of Acronyms

AAF — African Alternative Framework
AERC — African Economic Research Consortium
ACBF — African Capacity Building Fund
ACBI — African Capacity Building Initiative
ACP — African, Caribbean, and Pacific
ADB — African Development Bank
ADLI — Agriculture Demand-Led Industrialization
AGE — Applied General Equilibrium
AIDS — Acquired Immunity Deficiency Syndrome
AL — Adjustment Lending
ALDEP — Arable Lands Development Programme
ALF — Africa Leadership Forum
BWI — Bretton Woods Institutions
CCCE — Caisse Centrale de Coopération Economique (lending agency of the French Government, now called CFD)
CDS — Centre for Development Studies
CEC — Commission of the European Communities
CEE — Central and Eastern Europe
CEPR — Centre for Economic Policy Research
CERDI — Centre d'Etude et de Recherche pour le Développement International (Study and research centre for international development)
CFA — Communauté Financière Africaine (franc zone, West African area)
CFAC — Coopération Financière en Afrique centrale (franc zone, Central African area)
CFD — Caisse Française de Développement (lending agency of the French Government, formerly CCCE)
CFNPP — Cornell Food and Nutrition Policy Program
CGE — Computable General Equilibrium
CIEREA — Conférence des Institutions d'Enseignement et de Recherche Economiques et de Gestion en Afrique (Organization of Educational, Economic Research and Management Institutions in Africa)
CIRES — Centre Ivoirien de Recherches Economiques et Sociales (Ivorian Centre for Economic and Social Research)

CMEA — Council for Mutual Economic Assistance (also Comecon)
CODESRIA — Council for the Development of Economic and Social Research in Africa
DGIS — Directorate-General for International Co-operation
DPT — Dyphtheria Polio Typhoid
D.W. — Durbin Watson (test)
EC — European Community
ECA — (United Nations) Economic Commission for Africa
ECDPM — European Centre for Development Policy Management
EDI — Economic Development Institute
EFF — Extended Fund Facility
EIAL — Early Intensive Adjustment Lending Countries
EIU — Economist Intelligence Unit
ENDA TW — Environmental Development Action in the Third World
EPU — European Payment Union
ERA — Exchange Rate Adjustment
ERP — Economic Recovery Programme
ERP — Economic Reform Programme
ESAF — Enhanced Structural Adjustment Facility
EXP — Exports
FAO — Food and Agricultural Organization
FAP — Financial Assistance Programme
FFW — Food For Work
FSU — Former Soviet Union
FY — Fiscal Year/Financial Year
G-10 — Group of Ten (Industrialized Countries)
GCA — Global Coalition for Africa
GDI — Gross Domestic Investment
GDP — Gross Domestic Product
GDS — Gross Domestic Savings
GNP — Gross National Product
GTZ — Gezellschaft für Technische Zusammenarbeit (German agency for technical cooperation)
HIV — Human Immunity Virus
IBRD — International Bank for Reconstruction and Development
IDA — International Development Association
IDC — International Development Centre
IDEP — Institut Africain de Développement Economique et de Planification (African Institute for Economic Development and Planning)
IDS — Institute of Development Studies

| | | | |
|---|---|---|---|
| IFAD | International Fund for Agricultural Development | PPMU | Programme Planning and Monitoring Unit |
| IFC | International Finance Corporation | PSD | Programme for Sustained Development |
| IFI | International Financial Institution | PUSH | Project Urban Self Help |
| IFPRI | International Food Policy Research Institute | RAL | Report on Adjustment Lending |
| | | RUNS | Rural Urban North South |
| ILO | International Labour Office | SADC | Southern African Development Community ( = former SADCC) |
| IMF | International Monetary Fund | | |
| INTECH | Institute for New Technologies | SADCC | Southern African Development Co-ordination Conference (now SADC) |
| IOC | Inward Oriented Country | | |
| IRIS | Institut de Recherche pour l'Intégration Sous-Régionale (Research Institute for Sub-regional Integration) | SAF | Structural Adjustment Facility |
| | | SAL | Structural Adjustment Loan |
| | | SAP | Structural Adjustment Programme |
| ISS | Institute of Social Studies | SAPROG | Social Action Programme |
| JICA | Japan International Co-operation Agency | SDA | Social Dimensions of Adjustment |
| | | SECAL | Sectoral Adjustment Loan |
| KfW | Kreditanstalt für Wiederaufbau (lending agency of the German Government) | SIDA | Swedish International Development Agency |
| | | SOCETEC | Societé d'études et d'applications techniques (consultancy firm for studies and technical applications) |
| LBRP | Labour Based Relief Programme | | |
| LDC | Least Developed Country | | |
| LIC | Low-Income Country | SPA | Special Programme of Assistance for Low-Income Debt-Distressed Countries of Africa |
| LSMS | Living Standards Measurement Survey | | |
| MADIA | Managing Agricultural Development In Africa | SSA | Sub-Saharan Africa |
| | | SSN | Social Safety Net |
| MFA | Ministry of Foreign Affairs | STF | Systemic Transition Facility |
| NAL | Non Adjustment Lending Countries | TPE | Targeted Public Expenditure |
| | | UDEAC | Union Douanière et Economique de l'Afrique Centrale (Central African Customs and Economic Union) |
| NAP | New Agricultural Policy | | |
| NEAP | National Environmental Action Plan | | |
| NGO | Non-Governmental Organization | UK | United Kingdom |
| NIC | Newly Industrialized Country | UN | United Nations |
| NPV | Net Present Value | UNO | United Nations Organization |
| OAL | Other Adjustment Lending Countries | UNCTAD | United Nations Conference on Trade and Development |
| OAU | Organization of African Unity | UNDP | United Nations Development Programme |
| ODA | Offical Development Assistance | | |
| ODA | Overseas Development Administration (UK) | UNICEF | United Nations Children's Fund |
| | | UNIDO | United Nations Industrial Development Organization |
| ODI | Overseas Development Institute (London, UK) | UNIFEM | United Nations Development Fund for Women |
| OECD | Organization for Economic Co-operation and Development | UNU | United Nations University |
| OECF | Overseas Economic Co-operation Fund | UMOA | Union Monétaire Ouest Africaine (West African Monetary Union) |
| OED | Operations Evaluation Department | USA | United States of America |
| OLS | Ordinary Least Square | USAID | United States Agency for International Development |
| OOC | Outward Oriented Country | | |
| OPEC | Organization of Petroleum Exporting Countries | VAT | Value Added Tax |
| | | WAS | Welfare Assistance Schemes |
| PAMSCAD | Programme of Action to Mitigate the Social Costs of Adjustment | WB | World Bank |
| | | WHO | World Health Organization |
| | | WIDER | World Institute for Development Economics Research |
| PAP | Poverty Alleviation Programme | | |
| PFP | Policy Framework Paper | ZK | Zambian Kwacha |

# STRUCTURAL ADJUSTMENT IN SUB-SAHARAN AFRICA

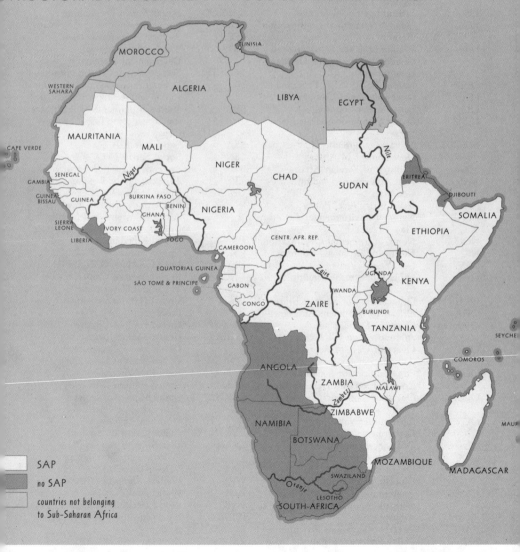

SAP

no SAP

countries not belonging
to Sub-Saharan Africa

# 1 Introduction and Overview

## ROLPH VAN DER HOEVEN and FRED VAN DER KRAAIJ

## Introduction

This volume brings together most of the papers presented at the seminar 'Structural Adjustment and Beyond – International Seminar on Structural Adjustment and Long-Term Development in Sub-Saharan Africa: Research and Policy Issues', which was held in The Hague in June 1993. It had been convened by the Netherlands Minister for Development Co-operation, Jan Pronk, and was organized by the Directorate General for International Co-operation of the Netherlands Ministry of Foreign Affairs, in collaboration with the Institute of Social Studies.

The major reason for the seminar was a very practical one. For a number of years, discussions on adjustment policies in international meetings like Round Table Conferences, Consultative Group Meetings or of the Special Programme of Assistance to the Low-Income Debt-Distressed Countries of Africa (SPA) had more often than not been fed by *ad hoc* evaluations or research activities which not infrequently happened to support the then current view of a government delegation or a bilateral donor or international agency which had financed or carried out the study or research. It was therefore considered important that researchers and policy-makers from Africa, from donor countries and from international organizations should meet, not merely to exchange quotations from papers, studies and evaluations, as usually happens at policy-making meetings, but to discuss the underlying assumptions, techniques, methodologies, shortcomings and merits of current research findings in order to improve the interaction between policy and research. Many people shared this opinion and in fact, some sixty people from Sub-Saharan Africa, Europe, North America and Japan participated in the seminar.

The two key questions to be addressed were, firstly, what is the state of the art with respect to research on the impact of structural adjustment in Sub-Saharan Africa? And secondly, how can current and future research on structural adjustment contribute better to policy-making in Sub-Saharan Africa and in donor organizations?

The organization of the seminar was very much influenced by two seemingly contradictory issues which often crop up in discussions on structural adjustment. The first is that the signals of whether structural adjustment policies in Sub-Saharan Africa are successful in reviving growth and combating poverty are not always clear; among researchers, a consensus on whether adjustment policies have contributed substantially to economic growth seems to be lacking.

1

The second issue is that, despite inconclusiveness regarding the result of past adjustment strategies, there is considerable consensus that in many Sub-Saharan African countries some kind of adjustment is necessary and that the long-term objectives of adjustment policies should be sustainable growth and the alleviation of poverty. There is also much consensus about the necessity of a number of policy instruments to be followed, such as sound fiscal balances, an appropriate exchange-rate policy, the development of human resources and infrastructure for the development of agriculture and small-scale industries.

However, controversy still continues about the relation between adjustment policies and broader societal questions of democracy, about the interaction between various classes in society, and about the appropriate public institutions for accountability and for governing development, as well as about a number of policy instruments in the light of the shared objectives of growth and poverty alleviation. To our mind, chief among these are the appropriate mix between price policies and more direct intervention in urban and rural development, the role of political factors and governance in restructuring the economy, the role of non-governmental organizations and labour unions in influencing societal acceptance of changes, the application of policies necessary to lead to structural changes and industrial development as well as the role of foreign aid and finance in the process of structural adjustment.

It would be quite unrealistic to expect a single seminar to deal exhaustively with all of these issues and others not mentioned here. The discussion and presentation of papers at the seminar were therefore grouped under four main themes in order to respond to the two principal questions. These themes were raised by both researchers and practitioners in order to arrive at a proper understanding of what has happened, why it has happened and which challenges for further policies and research this entails.

The four themes were:

- the rationale and origins of structural adjustment policies;
- an evaluation of the methodologies used in assessing the macroeconomic effectiveness of adjustment policies;
- the social consequences and political dimensions of adjustment policies;
- adjustment policies and long-term growth perspectives.

Given the interest shown in the seminar, we decided to present the contributions by the speakers in a volume which also contains a separate chapter on the discussion and the suggestions for further action. For this purpose we asked contributors to rework their papers as chapters for this volume, and we owe them our gratitude for their prompt reaction and respect for the deadline. The summary of the discussion, the conclusions and the suggestions for further action are based on the written contributions which most commentators had provided, on the comments of other participants and on our own impressions. In doing this, we have been guided more by the desire to provide a coherent chapter of reasonable proportions, than to present a comprehensive account of the discussion. Commentators may not therefore find all the points they made included. It goes without saying that the editors bear full responsibility for any omissions or misrepresentations of views.

The remainder of this Introduction provides an overview of the book.

# Overview

The *Keynote Address* by Kighoma A. Malima is presented in Chapter 2. Malima focuses on the African experience of structural adjustment, with special reference to Tanzania, and refers to the seminar's title, 'structural adjustment and beyond' to argue that the 'beyond' aspect may be quite distant for many countries of Sub-Saharan Africa. He recognizes both the inevitability and justification of economic reform programmes and the need for external support to realize their objectives, but he raises the fundamental question as to whether the structural adjustment programmes are a solution to the problems of the region, since *experimentation* appears to be the order of the day. He also refers to the terms-of-trade losses incurred by many Sub-Saharan African countries since the mid-1980s and to the debt problem. His pleas for structural adjustment in developed countries and for changes in restrictive practices, particularly in trade and resource flows which threaten the success of adjustment in developing countries, hardly come as a surprise.

He stresses the necessity of a correct preparation of Structural Adjustment Programmes, both for economic and political reasons and to enhance the ownership of the programme by the Sub-Saharan African countries concerned. In this context, Malima takes issue with the Bretton Woods institutions for dealing with all countries as though they are homogeneous. According to him the implementation of SAPs may compromise the future of Sub-Saharan African countries where these reform programmes (i) pose a serious threat to domestic industry by including total trade liberalization, (ii) indiscriminately eliminate subsidies and reduce too severely the role of the state, and (iii) marginalize indigenous entrepreneurs by enforcing too large and and too rapid programmes of privatization which necessitate having recourse to foreign capital and manpower. Failing to protect the long-term interests of the adjusting countries seriously endangers their sustainable development.

*Part One* covers the first theme of the seminar: the underlying rationale for the structural adjustment policies of the 1980s in Sub-Saharan Africa, in terms of both the theoretical debate and the empirical conditions leading to the crisis period.

In Chapter 3 John Toye presents the context, assumptions, origin and diversity of structural adjustment. He starts with the historical background of adjustment policies, defined in the past as the restructuring of certain economic sectors in the industrialized countries because of the increasing competition from emerging developing countries. He also elaborates on the deteriorating international economic environment, with the oil price shocks of 1973 and 1979/80, the evolution of interest rates on the international capital markets and the deflationary policies in the industrialized countries. The external factors are juxtaposed with internal factors, such as poor economic management, which according to some views is the major cause of the economic slowdown in Sub-Saharan Africa. Toye distinguishes between different categories of developing countries. The assumptions behind structural adjustment are explained by the decline of structuralism and the emergence of monoeconomics, but with some important qualifications, incorporating (i) a renewed role for monetarism, (ii) some insights of neo-Marxism, in particular with respect to the role of the (captured) state, and (iii) the theory of urban bias (the 'rent-seekers'). This, according to Toye, gave way to the acceptance of structural adjustment policies as a solution to the problems of the countries of Sub-Saharan Africa.

Toye describes the evolution of policy thinking within the World Bank starting in the mid-1960s, and raises the important question: 'What was it that changed a sporadic and covert practice into a publicly acknowledged policy with lending commitments of $6.5 billion by 1989 and 99 completed operations by 1991?' He gives three reasons for this, the most eye-catching of which is the reduced need for more project aid in developing countries. In this respect Toye also pays attention to the evolution of the Bank's anti-poverty programme. He discusses some misconceptions about structural adjustment, such as the idea that all SAPs are alike. Although he recognizes the existence of a kind of 'family resemblance', he stresses the diversity in implementation and in outcomes. He concludes by drawing attention to Sub-Saharan Africa's aid dependence and its debt problem which does not appear to him to be sustainable without further concessional aid or debt rescheduling.

Chapter 4 by Willi Wapenhans discusses the political economy of structural adjustment from an external perspective. Wapenhans' point of departure is the thesis that considerations of political economy at home and abroad no longer stop at international borders. In retrospect, structural adjustment, a term first used by the then World Bank President Robert McNamara in his concluding remarks to the Annual Meeting of the Board of Governors of the Bank in October 1979 in Belgrade, cannot be regarded as a quick fix to adapt to a changing external environment, but must be regarded as a process of transition. Thus, Wapenhans' second thesis is that structural adjustment policies as we now know them are inadequate for Sub-Saharan Africa, given the continent's institutional and policy deficiencies and the need to deal with its widespread poverty and the threatened environment as well as the need for economic growth and sustainable development. Wapenhans recalls the earlier approach of the IMF (the Polak Model) to analysing stabilization measures, and the two-gap model initially used by the World Bank to analyse external funding requirements. These two different approaches led to a collision in the early 1980s between the two institutions, which was followed, however, by increased collaboration as the decade advanced, leading to integration of the two approaches.

He further explains how the agenda for adjustment gradually changed, to include not only stabilization measures, but also measures for a better use of productive resources, for economic growth, for 'adjustment with a human face', for good governance, for political reforms and, most recently, for environmental concerns. He foresees that external support of economic reform programmes is going to be increasingly dependent on a number of conditions which he mentions. He emphasizes the importance of the political dimension of the domestic policy process and, especially, of policy change – both with respect to the design of SAPs and to the analysis of their implementation. SAPs therefore need to be country-specific. He further questions the relevance of empirical cross-country comparisons when evaluating the success of SAPs. Nevertheless, he asserts, despite his earlier criticism and scepticism, that structural adjustment will remain a useful tool. While drawing attention to a limited set of economic, political and institutional objectives that already exceeds the formal requirements of economic modelling, he calls for an integration of economic and political analyses – just as the IMF and World Bank models of stabilization and of growth were integrated in the 1980s.

*Part Two* deals with the state of research on the macroeconomic effectiveness of structural adjustment programmes in Sub-Saharan Africa.

Simeon Ibi Ajayi focuses in Chapter 5 on the methodological problems encountered when attempts are made to assess the impact of SAPs in Sub-Saharan Africa as well as on the outcome of recent research on the macroeconomic impact of these programmes. He rejects both the 'before-and-after' and the 'control-group' approaches as methodologies to measure the macroeconomic impact of SAPs. A third approach, the modified-control-group approach, is found to be more reliable. In discussing various country experiences and on the basis of the modified-control-group approach, he arrives at a number of lessons to be learnt from past experiences. Noticeable among them are the conclusions that (i) there is no 'quick fix', (ii) the negative effects of the hostile external environment faced by many Sub-Saharan African countries are persistent, and (iii) the external debt remains heavy. He concludes by arguing that there are not only differences between African countries, but that Africa itself is also different in significant ways from other developing regions.

In Chapter 6 Paul Mosley calls SAPs an improvization; recommendations attached to SAPs have a weak theoretical basis. He starts by reviewing the existing World Bank assessments of the effectiveness of adjustment in relation to the rest of the literature, reviewing both macroeconomic indicators such as the real growth rate of GDP, the investment/GDP ratio, the exports/GDP ratio and social consequences such as the effect on income distribution and on the incidence of poverty, and agrees with Ajayi in his rejection of the 'control-group' approach, which had been used in the past on various occasions by the World Bank to measure the impact of SAPs. According to Mosley this approach fails to explain the superior economic performance of certain 'non-adjusting' countries within the low-income and Sub-Saharan groups as compared with 'adjusting countries'. He argues that the best approach for evaluating the impact of an SAP seems to be to break it down into its different components and measure the effect of each of these. In this context he distinguishes various methods, two of which he treats in his contribution: regression analysis and simulation modelling methods. Noticeable among the outcomes of these two methods is the conclusion that tariff reductions and reductions in credit and agricultural input subsidies may have a negative effect in some Sub-Saharan African countries. Furthermore, it appears that price-based policy instruments can work only if certain 'catalysts' are also present, but that World Bank and IMF policies *can* undermine these catalysts. Mosley concludes that in this case the policy of emphasizing 'getting prices right' will not work.

*Part Three* concerns the social consequences and political dimensions of structural adjustment.

In Chapter 7 Jean-Paul Azam restricts his contribution on the social impact of SAPs to one aspect, namely, income distribution and does not analyse the changes in the provision of public goods. He raises, first, some measurement problems, since national accounts data are far from reliable and specific (household) survey data are available to only a limited extent. The seriousness of the data problem even leads him to state that GDP figures are probably unreliable and increasingly under-recorded due to the lack of knowledge of developments in the informal sector. He argues that there is uncertainty about the social impact of adjustment programmes, not only because of the theoretical ambiguity of the distributional impact of adjustment but also because this uncertainty is intrinsically rooted in the nature of structural adjustment programmes. He ends his lucid exposé with a section on the political economy, the bureaucratic vs. the predatory state, also paying attention to the process of political liberalization recently begun in Sub-Saharan Africa. In the light of this he pleads for an active role on the part of external agencies (donors) whom he urges to act in favour of the politically less vociferous in adjusting countries and thus to make adjustment work for the poor.

Venkatesh Seshamani questions the necessity and the nature of the set-up of social safety nets as well as the need for targeted public expenditures, in Chapter 8. He discusses the recent promotion of Poverty Alleviation Programmes (PAPs) in order to mitigate the adverse short-term effects of SAPs. These PAPs can take various forms, such as the Social Dimensions of Adjustment (SDA) components of SAPs, Social Action Programmes (SAPROGs), Social Safety Nets (SSNs) and Targeted Public Expenditures (TPEs). He argues that PAPs and SAPs should be integrated, but that it should be recognized that while economic growth is indeed a necessary condition, it is far from being a sufficient condition for addressing poverty. The rationale of PAPs is therefore much broader than the aim of mitigating the adverse consequences of SAPs. More specifically, the promotion of PAPs is only one of at least three approaches to alleviating poverty in Sub-Saharan Africa. Seshamani explains the reasons why he rejects universalistic transfer programmes and instead favours targeted transfers, though the latter have their own set of problems. He makes the notable recommendation of linking the pace of economic reform to the capacity to administer PAPs. The latter, however, face a similar problem to that of SAPs, namely a lack of reliable data describing the socio-economic conditions. His analysis of numerous examples of Poverty Alleviation Programmes and Targeted Public Expenditures, some of which are very critical, are illustrative of the practical problems encountered, notably in the countries of Southern Africa. In his concluding remarks he draws attention to the fact that sustained economic growth requires the development of human capital, hence the importance of human resources development.

The political dimension of adjustment was already partially raised by Wapenhans in Chapter 4. In Chapter 9, Christian Morrisson and his co-authors Jean-Dominique Lafay and Sébastien Dessus first briefly outline the state of research with respect to the issue. Then, on the basis of a simulation model they present the political consequences of IMF-supported adjustment programmes and in particular of a devaluation of the CFA franc, a very controversial but highly topical issue. The simulation is based on data originating from 23 Sub-Saharan African countries which experienced this type of adjustment programme during the 1980s. Their emphasis on a clear and close interaction between economics and politics fits well with the remarks made by other contributors to the seminar. Noteworthy is their conclusion that aid is a determining factor with respect to political stability, especially in the franc zone. One of their other major conclusions refers to the need for an integrated (political and economic) analysis of proposed stabilization and aid policies instead of the present approaches which either favour economic yardsticks without, consciously or unconsciously, taking such political considerations into account or rely on political considerations and disregard economic reality.

*Part Four* deals with structural adjustment and long-term development perspectives in Sub-Saharan Africa.

In Chapter 10 Ishrat Husain bases his assessment of adjustment policies on the agenda set by the World Bank's Long-Term Perspective Study on Sub-Saharan Africa (1989) which provides a consensus programme for sustainable and equitable development. Husain sees structural adjustment policies as essential to improving the incentive structure, the trade regime, the allocation of resources and their efficiency in stimulating growth-enhancing impulses in the economy. He cautions against labelling all structural adjustment measures as being an integral part of structural reform and argues that the adverse social consequences of adjustment are often the result of stabilization policies which are, by definition, contractionary, and not of adjustment policies. Husain singles out the successful turn-around of agriculture in Nigeria as a consequence of adjustment policies and argues that special attention should be given to the agricultural sector in adjustment. Improvement in agricultural performance will usually lead to poverty reduction according to Husain.

In order to achieve the objectives of long-term and sustainable growth, structural adjustment policies have to be accompanied by additional actions such as investment in infrastructure, building up human capital, and establishing an enabling environment for private initiatives. Husain stresses that poverty alleviation needs to be integrated into structural adjustment programmes, thus allying himself with Seshamani in this respect. This can be done by making greater use of the factors of production owned by the poor, i.e. labour and land. The latter implies priority in SAPs for the agricultural sector. Education, and human resources development more generally, also has an important role to play. However, even despite such actions being taken, Africa's weak administrative capacity and the elite's firm grip on the political system lead him to expect progress in poverty reduction to be limited. It is also argued that, especially in areas where some empirical basis has been established, environmental considerations ought increasingly to be reflected in the design of structural adjustment programmes, and this should eventually lead to the development of national environmental plans. External finance remains critical in Africa's adjustment efforts and, despite the important initiatives which have been taken in recent years to provide debt relief, their actual impact has been limited.

*Part Five* consists of the Discussion and Conclusions and an Epilogue.

In Chapter 11 the editors present the discussions at the seminar on the basis of the discussants' comments on the papers presented by the speakers (Chapters 3 to 10) as well as subsequent interventions by other participants. The discussions have been grouped together under five themes according to the seminar's main issues as follows:

(i) The context and goals of SAPs;
(ii) Macroeconomic perspectives and methodological questions;
(iii) Social consequences and political dimensions;

(iv) Long-term perspectives;
(v) The interaction between structural adjustment policies and research.

The main points arising from the discussion indicate that, although there appears to be consensus about the need for adjustment and for incorporating social and environmental concerns as well as equitable growth in the concept and design of adjustment policies, a large number of issues remained on which researchers amongst themselves as well as policy-makers from national and international organizations differed. Major pointers for further work and greater dialogue between researchers and practitioners related to the theoretical basis of adjustment policies, the evaluation of past processes, the role of households and the informal sector, the relation between macro and micro economic policy, trade, industrialization and structural change, the role of the state, external influences and the role of multilateral and bilateral capital and aid flows.

The Epilogue (Chapter 12) contains some concluding remarks by Jan Pronk and Fred van der Kraaij. It combines a retrospective view of the seminar based on some of their personal concerns with various policy implications for Dutch and multilateral action.

The Appendix consists of three documents. In the first, Willem van der Geest presents a review of research literature on the impact of structural adjustment in Sub-Saharan Africa. It is followed by a complementary review of research literature on industrialization by Peter de Valk. In the third, Fred van der Kraaij presents background material on Sub-Saharan Africa's current economic and political situation, as well as an overview of the Bretton Woods institutions' involvement in stabilization and structural adjustment programmes.

# KEYNOTE ADDRESS

# 2 Structural Adjustment: The African Experience
## KIGHOMA MALIMA

It is a special honour for me to be given this opportunity to make a statement regarding the experience of several countries of Sub-Saharan Africa which are undertaking adjustment programmes to this distinguished gathering of scholars and policy advisers. Let me therefore at the outset express my sincere personal thanks and appreciation to Minister Pronk for extending this special invitation to me.

This gathering is indeed crucial and timely since it coincides in some respects with the recent discussion in the International Monetary Fund's Executive Board on the successor programme after a country has exhausted its drawings from the Enhanced Structural Adjustment Facility (ESAF). Tanzania, for example, has been implementing structural adjustment programmes since 1986 and is now in the second year of ESAF II. The successor programme to ESAF therefore assumes a high profile, since it is now clear that, even with the successful completion of ESAF III, we shall not be anywhere near the point where a structural adjustment programme will no longer be needed, as the economy will still be far from self-sustaining. This shows that the period for undertaking structural adjustment programmes has not been as short as was originally expected, and the 'beyond' aspect may be quite distant for many countries of Sub-Saharan Africa.

This raises another important question: What is complete adjustment? Can a situation or scenario be defined as final, and one where further structural adjustment is not required? Is there any country, particularly in the developing world or even in the newly industrialized countries, which has reached that 'stage of maturity' where there is no longer any need for structural adjustment? If so, what are the characteristics of that country? Is the consideration of 'beyond structural adjustment' an invitation to develop programmes which eliminate the words 'structural adjustment' but adopt another name with more or less the same content?

These questions are important to us, because our populations which bear the brunt of adjustment are anxious about whether an end to this process is in sight. We tell them that they must continue to tighten their belts and wait for a better tomorrow. Tomorrow comes and more sacrifices are demanded of them. In fact, for several countries there is a clear message from the sponsors of these programmes that what has been or is being done is not adequate and that more commitment as well as further actions are required if the process is to be completed and tangible benefits realized. This happens even where action programmes are agreed upon between the parties concerned.

As of today, most countries of Sub-Saharan Africa are implementing a structural adjustment programme in one form or another. The exception is probably those few countries where internal conflicts make it difficult for organized economic activity to take place, and even for them, the requirement to undertake specified measures in order to qualify for financial support is almost an obligation. For all the other countries, implementation of a structural adjustment programme is more or less mandatory. This is so because, given the inherent economic difficulties most of them face and the genuine desire for them to solve these problems, external support as well as debt relief will not be forthcoming unless predetermined specific actions are agreed and are also seen to be genuinely undertaken. The only acceptable evidence for this is the active implementation of a structural adjustment programme.

There is no doubt that the results of structural adjustment programmes so far have been generally encouraging, although there is certainly room for improvement. Overall, the hitherto declining or stagnant Gross Domestic Product (GDP) has been reversed. In fact, an average growth of about 3% for adjusting countries in Sub-Saharan Africa has been recorded for the late 1980s and the early 1990s compared with an average of less than 1% before adjustment. Tanzania's average growth rate since 1986 has been over 3.5% per year. Taking note of this, one may ask, since the measure of welfare for the population is not limited to GDP, what has been the performance of other economic and social indicators? Has the increase in GDP been due to structural change as the programme's name suggests or is it due to improved capacity utilization, since implementation of structural adjustment is also a 'licence' for access to international resources?

Looking back at our countries, there is no doubt that, in spite of the efforts and actions taken in the implementation of structural adjustment programmes for well over a decade now in some countries, there appear to be no general and easy prototypes. One would have wished that after so much time and experience among several countries, the way ahead and indeed beyond would have been clearer, more easily understood and probably more readily adaptable, particularly for new-comers. On the contrary, however, experimentation appears be the order of the day. That is why so much expectation and optimism is attached to this seminar which brings together researchers and scholars from all over the world to exchange views on practical research work in this critical area.

Given the breadth of the subject and the comprehensive research already undertaken, I shall limit my remarks to a few highlights which I believe will be representative of the general views in the region on structural adjustment, drawing as much as possible from the experience of Tanzania with which I am more familiar. From a general point of view, however, structural adjustment has become inevitable because:

(i) the economies of these countries have not demonstrated the capacity to transform themselves into modern economies on their own;

(ii) given their basic structures, these economies have not been able to participate effectively as equal partners in the international economy and as such they cannot maximize the benefits from international trade and specialization; and

(iii) these economies have become significantly aid-dependent which at times is due to a combination of the factors given above but is also significantly due to the apparent 'neglect' experienced during the colonial period. No adequate effort was made to develop internally integrated and self-sustaining economies.

The above phenomena are common to many Sub-Saharan countries and there is no question that these problems must be resolved and quickly. Given the anxiety which structural adjustment programmes have aroused and judging by current performance, one is bound to ask: What type of structural adjustment did countries like Japan or even the now rapidly growing South East Asian countries such as China, South Korea, Malaysia, Thailand, etc., have to go through in order to achieve their current status? What is this Asian miracle? Is it not possible for Sub-Saharan Africa?

I want now to return briefly to the observations made by the IMF's Executive Board to which I referred earlier. While discussing the successor facility to the ESAF, the Board noted the progress made by the countries implementing ESAF-supported programmes but also acknowledged the severe problems which still persisted in these countries. These were enumerated as follows:

(i) external viability had not been achieved because of persistent and increasing terms-of-trade losses. The estimated loss was SDR 50 billion since the mid-1980s or 20–25% below the levels prevailing when the ESAF was established;

(ii) during the same period, the stock of debt had increased by about 17% in nominal terms for these countries which had also not benefited from the lower interest rates in the creditor countries;

(iii) fiscal deficits remained excessive and institutional reforms were far from complete, implying that significant concessional financial flows were still required; and

(iv) both the process of adjustment and the lack of it had taken a toll on the poor, necessitating strong safety nets that required increasing donor financing.

If such observations are made by the very institution which is the major sponsor of structural adjustment programmes, one is bound to raise the question of the viability of these programmes and the realism of their design. Are these programmes adequately addressing the problems of developing countries and are the real causes of these problems adequately understood? What, then, is the future of these programmes? These are fundamental questions which I am sure are at the core of your deliberations. The issue here, as I have already stated, is not the necessity of the SAPs, given the unquestionable deterioration of the economies and living conditions in most countries in Sub-Saharan Africa: rather, the question is whether they are a solution to the problems of the region. Let me now briefly address the issue of the design of these programmes.

For countries undertaking structural adjustment programmes, the initial stage is normally the stabilization phase, with the front-loading of macro-economic measures related to exchange-rate adjustment, interest-rate adjustment, the reduction or elimination of budget deficits, trade liberalization, etc. The packaging of these measures has differed from country to country and at times discussion about the phasing of the measures has been fairly protracted.

Given the economic regimes in most countries, these economy-wide measures are important to open up the economy and permit resources to flow freely and efficiently within the country and also between countries. The major problem several countries have faced during this initial phase is the speed and magnitude of the changes that have been proposed. These two aspects, economic as they may sound, have posed serious political problems for many countries and at times have cost several Finance and Planning Ministers their posts. The question is why this has been so. The simple response is that better understanding and some preparation before the measures are taken is obviously necessary. The preparation required is both political and economic, regardless of the economic justification. Structural adjustment has an important political dimension. The issue then arises as to whether there is adequate capacity in these countries to participate effectively in the preparation of these programmes, and whether the programmes can be claimed to be owned by the countries carrying them out.

The other legitimate issue which is often raised relates to the length of the preparation time required for broad involvement, when what is wrong is known and particularly when those designing the programmes feel that more delay only makes the situation worse. There may be no simple answers to these questions. What may be critical is the need to articulate the programme so that it is well understood and is endorsed by at least the leadership of the relevant country and there is no feeling of the programme being imposed. This does not mean that all opposition to the programme will be removed, but such an approach would improve its acceptability.

The experience in implementing these measures has not been particularly smooth, given the pressures from both the Bretton Woods institutions and also from the domestic scene. The problem with the Bretton Woods institutions is that they deal with all countries as though they are homogeneous. The speed of acceptability of a programme very much depends on how it is presented and the background preparation on both sides.

In fact, our own experience while implementing the stabilization measures in Tanzania has not been particularly problem-free. Given the budgetary constraint, the large exchange-rate adjustments have significantly reduced in real terms the allocations for the social services, in particular for health, education and water supply, with a resultant curtailment in the quality and quantity of services for a large segment of the population. The price of a US dollar in shillings, for instance, has gone up from shs. 17 to about 400 between 1986 and 1993, an increase of over 2000%! By the same action, wages and salaries have also suffered large reductions in real terms (the reduction is estimated to be more than 70% over 10 years) with several deleterious consequences. For employees in the public services, in order to survive dishonest and corrupt practices have increased, while efficiency and morale have also suffered. For those in the professional category as well as in institutions of higher learning, the brain-drain has increased, thus threatening future capacity to manage the economy and run the government administration. Given the continuing resource constraint, these problems are bound to take time to solve.

It is obvious that after the initial phase, in order for the stabilization programme to become effective and the resultant macroeconomic framework to be sustainable, adequate institutional reform must take place to complete the structural adjustment. Our experience in Tanzania has shown that this stage is even more complex and demanding. It involves dismantling some institutions and creating others, a process which inevitably generates polarization and confrontation among different interest groups. Here again, success depends on the size and complexity of the changes involved. It also depends significantly on the type of regime in power. The success stories often quoted in Africa appear to follow a special pattern. In this phase also, the packaging and phasing are critical for success.

In Tanzania, for instance, at the moment we have several reforms going on, the most important being in the financial sector, the parastatal sector and the civil service. Apart from the temporary dislocations which are inevitable because of the changing structures of the institutions involved, the financial implications for the Budget are particularly burdensome. A budgetary increase of over shs. 30bn, compared with a total budget of shs. 251bn for 1992/93, is required to pay for the direct costs of the reforms. This is demanded from a budget which is already not providing enough for the education and health services. Further complications are due to the fact that the reforms invariably involve the laying-off of thousands of workers. In fact, in the civil service, about 50,000 out of 330,000 will be laid off over the next two and a half years, beginning with 10,000 during fiscal year 1992/93. Our major concern is what these people will do, when the private sector is still small and quite incapable of creating viable employment opportunities for such large numbers? And there are other social consequences of these actions, which are issues of serious concern.

The next question I want to address is how political pluralism relates to and affects structural adjustment. I have already made reference in passing to the role played by the political regime in enhancing or retarding the pace of the reform process. Many countries in Sub-Saharan Africa are currently facing a wave of political pluralism in which the free expression of economic and political preferences is taking place. I must hasten to add that, for many of the new political parties, the constraint on understanding and articulating economic issues is clearly much greater even than that of the governments in power. Given, therefore, the free articulation of their ideas and the publicity which they have been accorded, there clearly has to be a compromise on the speed with which some of the institutional reforms can effectively take place, particularly in many democratic African countries where 'consensus' is insisted on.

This factor is a relatively new one but is increasing in importance at a time when economic problems also do not seem to be subsiding. I would like to urge scholars to look critically at this aspect and factor it into the complex structural adjustment model. Political pluralism is a reality whose benefits are certainly real, but whose costs may also be reflected in some delay or distortion in implementing programmes considered beneficial to the economy. This is particularly so in a situation where new political parties choose to take the populist route by attacking those programmes and measures which, though necessary for long-term growth and development, are likely to cause hardship and suffering to the general population in the short and medium term.

I would now like briefly to focus on some problems related to the implementation of SAPs which have been raised by others as well but which appear critical for our future survival as viable nations. The major premise of the entire adjustment effort is that the adjusting country should increase its output in a sustainable way, should improve the living standards of its population and should participate effectively in international trade as an equal and viable partner. These premises appear to be compromised by the practices which adjustment programmes impose on countries implementing them. I will mention three of them:

(i) the total trade liberalization advocated in SAPs poses a serious threat to domestic industry, and our experience so far is that some branches of industry may have to close down completely. How, then, can we sustain recovery without a deliberate effort to nurture infant industries so as to alter the structure of domestic production, as was done in many of the now industrialized or newly industrialized countries?

(ii) although the removal of subsidies for budgetary reasons is prudent economic management, it is difficult to comprehend how important economic sectors like industry, agriculture, etc. can survive while paying market interest rates. Nor is it easy to visualize how the transformation of traditional agriculture in Sub-Saharan Africa can be achieved without active government involvement and support;

(iii) we fully share the philosophy of privatization but, taking into account the ownership history of most countries, the speed and coverage normally proposed may not lead to sustainable development, in view of the fact that the indigenous people may be marginalized and left behind because of lack of resources to participate effectively in the programme.

These are not exhaustive criticisms of the current adjustment programmes. They simply help to show that the designs of some of these programmes need to take other factors into account, including measures to ensure sustainable growth and development for the future. In fact, just for the record, the World Bank, 1990 publication called *Adjustment Lending Policies for Sustainable Growth* also reviewed several problems facing these programmes.

Before I conclude, I want to raise an issue which has recently attracted a great deal of attention in our countries, concerning the implementation of structural adjustment programmes. Simply put, it is: Who are the gainers and who are the losers in the adjustment process? Similarly, the question of the short-run, the medium-term and the long-term consequences is also important and should be adequately articulated in order to allay fears and assure all sections of the community that they are bound to gain from adjustment. Given the studies done so far, some of which are contradictory, more work needs to be done in this area.

Tanzania's experience may be of interest in this context. The general feeling is that most measures have only benefited the well-to-do and the business class at the expense of the poor and the peasants, who are not even sure of the prices for their commodities, let alone whether their crops will ever be bought at all. In the cities there are traffic jams on the roads while the public transport system has more or less collapsed. There are more frustrations for the poor in the social programmes. These problems are being picked up by the opposition groups, and make implementation of some measures even more difficult. There is therefore a clear need to address the issue satisfactorily.

What emerges from this discussion is the finding that the poorer the country is, the greater the efforts required for undertaking adjustment and also the more resources are required. Since, however, these resources are not available internally, the more is external support required. Interestingly, however, experience has shown that those countries with better economic conditions attract more resources and the poorer ones get even less. It is therefore extremely urgent to design strategies which ensure that adequate attention is focused where it is most needed.

I want to conclude by noting the following: the state of the economies of most Sub-Saharan African countries justifies the implementation of structural adjustment programmes. Nevertheless, the SAPs designed for these countries need to take into account the economic and political realities of the countries concerned. The contents of the programme should emphasize the need to create sustainable economic structures which must grow and mature in order to benefit these economies in the future.

Finally, structural adjustment in the developing countries cannot succeed if the developed countries continue with their restrictive practices, particularly in trade and resource flows. They too should undertake structural adjustment. The benefits of international interdependence can only be fully realized if all countries strive to maximize trade.

In conclusion, I want once again to thank the Government of the Netherlands and the organizers of this seminar for the facilities provided. I am optimistic that this meeting will be yet another important contribution in shedding light on this topical issue of 'structural adjustment and beyond', which could make all the difference between prosperity and continued poverty and deprivation for the majority of our people.

# PART ONE
# The Underlying Rationale for Structural Adjustment Policies

# 3 Structural Adjustment: Context, Assumptions, Origin and Diversity
## JOHN TOYE

Since its introduction to the practice of development policy at the end of the 1970s, structural adjustment has attracted a vast literature, both official and non-official. The World Bank has produced three internal reviews of its adjustment lending, plus two evaluation studies by its Operations Evaluation Department. The staff of the IMF have written many learned papers of analysis. Research bodies like UNU/WIDER and international organizations like the OECD and UNICEF have mounted elaborate research exercises, based on modelling and country case studies. Official studies have been accompanied by an even greater outpouring of research by a host of independent analysts in universities and NGOs.

It is impossible to list in the references to this paper all that has been written, let alone to mention all these contributions in its text. An up-to-date synthesis of this material is now urgently required. That is not what is provided here. This paper is intended only as an introduction to such a synthesis. As such, it is highly selective, and ventures opinions which will undoubtedly have to be revised and qualified as the work of synthesis proceeds. Synthesis, in any case, will have to proceed at a much less general level. The structural adjustment literature has already developed specialist branches, dealing with underlying theory; the issue of sequencing; evaluation methods; employment; social welfare, and so on. What follows should be viewed as a mere prologue to the larger synthetic task.

## The Context of Structural Adjustment Policies

The world of development co-operation had to assimilate a new phrase from 1980 onwards – 'structural adjustment'. A new task was prescribed for the governments of developing countries which went beyond the normal tasks of economic management. This task was the taking of measures not merely to correct routine resource imbalances of a cyclical kind, but to adjust to structural (i.e. long-term) changes to the terms on which foreign exchange could be acquired and spent. In truth, the phrase 'structural adjustment' was not new. It was an old phrase which had suddenly been given a new meaning. Until 1980, structural adjustment had been a task for the developed countries. It had connoted the state-assisted run-down of their old industries (such as textiles, leather goods and light engineering) which could no longer compete with the new industrial capacity in the developing countries. Since the birth of development economics in the 1940s this kind of structural adjustment had been seen as an essential policy component of the achievement of world economic development (see, for example, Arndt, 1944: 295–7; Staley, 1945: 129–217). The responsibility for industrial readjustment or adaptation was placed on the countries which were already the most economically advanced, as a way of avoiding the damaging protectionist practices which had characterized the Depression era. The new meaning given to an old term in 1980 was significant, not just as an illustration of Humpty Dumpty's claim that 'when I use a word it means just what I choose it to mean', but as a sudden and dramatic reversal of the locus of responsibility for ensuring successful world development, from the shoulders of the economically strong to those of the economically weak.

Both economic and political developments in the 1970s led up to this event. The period between the first oil shock in 1973 and 1980 shows a marked deceleration in the growth of real GDP and real GDP per head both in the industrial and the developing countries. The slackening of growth affected the former more than the latter. Whereas in industrial countries real GDP growth fell back from 4.7% in 1965–73 to 2.8% in 1973–80, and growth of real GDP *per capita* fell from 3.7 to 2.1%, in the developing countries as a whole, the equivalent reductions were from 6.5 to 5.4% and from 3.9 to 3.2% (Mosley *et al.*, 1991: 5–6). In terms of such simple First World-Third World comparisons, the First World appeared to be suffering more from the general worldwide economic slowdown. The commodity power of the Third World oil producers appeared to have succeeded in shifting the balance of advantage towards themselves and away from the industrial countries, within a more generally turbulent economic environment. This perception helped to undermine the post-war consensus that the adjustment burden should rest with the industrial world.

In reality the situation was much more complex than such simple comparisons reveal. In the first place, the Third World was becoming much more economically heterogeneous during the 1970s. Within that category, the oil-exporting developing countries were least affected by slower growth, along with middle-income countries which had built up manufacturing industry that was able to compete in international markets. The 1970s were the decade when the acronyms OPEC and NICs emerged to signify the success stories of particular groups of developing countries. But they were balanced by a much less propitious new acronym – the LLDCs, the least developed of the developing countries, which were largely concentrated in Sub-Saharan Africa (SSA).

In Sub-Saharan Africa, the economic slowdown was much more serious than in the industrial countries. Growth of real GDP fell from 6.4% in 1965–73 to 3.2% in 1973–80. Because the already relatively high rate of population growth in SSA continued to rise further, this translated into a fall in the growth of real GDP per head from 3.6 to 0.3% (*ibid.*). In other words, by the second half of the 1970s, the level of living standards in SSA had already begun to stagnate. If one excluded Nigeria, a large country whose output was swollen by oil exports, the picture would have been bleaker, disclosing absolute retrogression in the rest of SSA. One of the most significant indicators of decline was the virtual stagnation of SSA's merchandise exports between 1973 and 1980, notwithstanding an improvement of 5.4% in the region's terms of trade (Tarp, 1993: 12). It was this statistic, more than any other, which gave rise to the view that internal factors, such as poor economic management, rather than external factors, such as the international trading environment, were responsible for Africa's relatively poor performance. On the one hand, then, the developing countries as a whole seemed to be faring better than the industrial world. On the other, where a serious economic problem was acknowledged, as in Sub-Saharan Africa, the cause was identified as internal policy failure.

This partial conclusion was possible because the growth statistics missed a crucial aspect of the whole economic scenario. The late 1970s growth rates in developing countries were artificially high, in the sense that they were, as it turned out, very vulnerable to shifts in economic conditions which were not correctly anticipated. The second tripling of the price of oil in 1979–80 pulled up the oil exporters' growth of output in 1980, but this was not sustainable in terms of the fundamentals of supply and demand. The oil price fell back to 1973 levels by 1986, but not before it had seriously damaged the dynamism of the non-oil sectors of many of the oil exporters' economies. What is more, the inflationary effects of the two oil price rises in the industrial countries had important political consequences there. They assisted the rise to power of conservatively inclined governments in the UK, the US and West Germany, elected on programmes of economic austerity, designed to squeeze inflation out of their economies, even if that meant permitting previously unacceptable levels of unemployment and depressed demand. Deflationary policies in the industrial world were an important factor which undermined the growth of developing countries' exports in the 1980s.

In addition to lost exports, developing countries' growth collapsed in the 1980s because deflation in the developed countries triggered a severe crisis of indebtedness which had been building up throughout the period 1973–80, largely unnoticed by the commercial banks, the developing country borrowers and the international organizations for economic co-operation. The course of these events is by now well known, but explaining the context of structural adjustment policies requires a brief review of the salient points. In 1979–80, the time when structural adjustment lending was being initiated within the World Bank, the debt crisis was still latent: it was not revealed to the world until August 1982, when Mexico suspended payment on its huge debt and it was realized that fourteen other highly indebted developing countries were in imminent danger of doing likewise. In 1979–80, many developing countries were still adding to their borrowings of recycled petro-dollars, apparently unaware of the danger implicit in the fact that a substantial portion of this debt carried variable interest-rate terms. The big US and UK private banks were still pumping out huge syndicated loans to countries whose economies they rarely bothered to try and understand, as if the fact that they were lending to sovereign governments shielded them from every risk. The international financial institutions which had promoted and praised this form of lending were still sounding no public alarm bells, apparently putting their trust in their own forecasts of consistently strong commodity prices to make manageable the rapid accumulation of commercial debt in the portfolios of developing country governments (Toye, 1992a: 15–20).

The rise in real interest rates from an average of 1.3% in 1973–80 to an average of 5.9% in 1980–86 was the direct result of the economic policies followed by the new conservative governments installed in the major industrial countries after 1979. These policies are not very precisely characterized by the label of 'monetarism', because in practice conflicting interpretations surfaced of the policy imperatives of monetarism. Different variants of the doctrine were implemented and some of these efforts were seriously bungled. Their overall effect, however, was to raise, and then to sustain at historically unparalleled levels (at least since 1945), the real rate of interest. This was enough to disappoint the expectations of all the players in the petro-dollar recycling process. The borrowers had to pay higher nominal rates on all their new debt, and on that part of the existing stock of debt contracted on variable interest-rate terms. The fact that much of the borrowing had been invested in low-productivity schemes meant that there were few surplus resources available to meet this added burden. The bankers realized that, even without any formal government defaults, they were faced with the prospect of being unable to recover their full principal and interest for many years, if at all. The international financial institutions realized that the deflation of the industrial economies invalidated their commodity price forecasts and that failure to supervise the investment practices of borrowing countries made their approval of massive commercial lending foolhardy, to say the least.

This generalized disappointment of expectations, brought to a head by the erratic collection of policies called monetarism and supply-side economics, was already far advanced by 1980, but not yet quite mature. We have now run slightly ahead of our story of the evolution of structural adjustment policies. The post-1982 debt crisis is the context not for the origin of these policies, but for their prolongation and extension. It intensified the stabilization problem for the indebted countries, while at the same time it reinforced in the mind of the IMF and the World Bank the need for policy conditionality in future lending.

The debt crisis had a dramatic and powerful effect on the size and composition of the external financing available to developing countries. By 1980, net flows of private commercial lending to developing countries were more than 30% greater than the $22.8 billion flows of official development assistance (oda). By 1986, when the level of oda had shrunk slightly to $21.7 bn, private commercial lending had collapsed to only 61% of that figure. While oda stagnated in the 1980s (thanks to the reduced aid budgets of the US, the UK and the OPEC countries), the sudden collapse of bank lending in the wake of the Mexican suspension of repayment enforced a savage squeeze on the balance-of-payments deficits of the developing world. In these financial conditions, their deficits at the 1980 level of $70bn were no longer fundable, and by 1986 they had been cut in half. The stagnation of aid, while private flows collapsed, provided the mechanism whereby the burden of structural adjustment could be thrust abruptly from the shoulders of the developed to the shoulders of the developing world.

The effect of the increase in interest rates plus the deterioration through the 1980s of the terms of trade has been calculated for Sub-Saharan Africa by Tarp (1993: 22–3). He finds that the loss of foreign exchange attributable to these two external factors rose from $2.8 bn in 1980 to $13.8 bn by 1987. This translates into a deduction from GDP rising from 1.3 to no less than 9.6% over the first eight years of the adjustment process. Although, unlike Latin America, SSA as a whole continued to receive positive net financial transfers from the rest of the world, by 1987 nine-tenths of these transfers were matched by the loss inflicted by the interest-rate and terms-of-trade shocks. Thus the context in which SSA countries had to undertake adjustment deteriorated very severely, reflecting their structural position as undiversified primary commodity exporters and net debtors to the rest of the world.

## The Assumptions Behind Structural Adjustment

Intellectually, the years from 1973 to 1980 were ones of unusually rapid transition in the field of economic policy-making generally and in development policy in particular. The neo-Keynesian consensus was breaking up quite unexpectedly, challenged from the political Right by the rather simple and implausible doctrines of monetarism and supply-side economics, and from the political Left by no less simple and implausible varieties of neo-Marxism and other radical critiques. No extensive review of these familiar debates will be attempted here. It is enough to note that confidence in the old post-war economic verities (and the social values which underpinned them) was ebbing under the influence of the collapse of fixed exchange rates, volatile energy prices, accelerating inflation and an accompanying increase in social conflicts. The growing intellectual uncertainties in the industrial countries effectively opened the way for a dramatic reappraisal of the economics of development, and consequently of the appropriate economic policies for development.

Structuralism was the established orthodoxy of development theory and policy in the 1960s and 1970s. In the crudest possible terms, structuralism held that, in poor countries, the economies were structurally different from advanced industrial economies, and that therefore a distinct and different set of policies from the neo-Keynesianism practised in the latter was appropriate to bring about development. Opponents of neo-Keynesianism in industrial countries turned aside to try to undermine development economics by tarring it with the neo-Keynesian brush. But this was a misconceived tactic, since the essence of structuralism was to insist on the radical separation between the 'special case' of advanced economic structures (to which neo-Keynesianism applied) and the more general case of poor, disarticulated economies (to which development economics applied). The counter-revolution in development economics did not really begin to capture much intellectual ground until it tackled head-on the structuralist axiom of dualism and this special/general distinction.

It did so by arguing the case for 'monoeconomics', an economics that was universally applicable – a unified set of principles from which policy prescriptions could be drawn and successfully applied in advanced and backward countries alike. In other words, if low interest rates discouraged saving in Germany, they would do so in Ghana; if tariffs reduced welfare in Belgium, they would do so in Bangladesh. This broad assertion was supplemented by critiques of a range of established theoretical constructs in development economics, such as dual-gap analysis, the Lewis theory of growth and the use of input-output tables in planning. These critiques aimed to show how such constructs violated normal economic principles of response to price incentives, while offering empirical proof of rational economic behaviour by the poorest peasants in developing countries. This succeeded in re-establishing a presumption in favour of using 'standard economics' for policy analysis in developing countries, and put structuralist development economists well on the defensive in the early 1980s.

Monoeconomics also helped to undermine the notion that the industrial countries had a special responsibility to carry the burdens of global adjustment. On the one hand, poor countries were assumed to be able to adjust in the same way as rich ones, while on the other hand the division of the world into two distinct types of economy was deprived of its logical justification.

Having made a basic distinction between structuralism and monoeconomics, it is now necessary to add some important qualifications. Monoeconomics was by no means a new doctrine in the early 1980s: it had always had considerable support, especially in North America, which grew as the political mood changed at the end of the 1970s, to the point where it was able to mount its successful challenge to replace structuralism as the dominant paradigm. In addition, this time the challenge differed from its previous encounters with structuralism in that it was combined with important accommodations of its opponents – in practice, if not in its rhetoric. Structuralism had been born, after all, in reaction to the failure of stabilization packages derived from monoeconomics in Chile, Argentina and Uruguay (1956–62) which ignored the effect of the 'bottlenecks' and 'rigidities' that pervaded those countries' agricultural, foreign trade and government sectors. Structuralist policies in turn had failed in Chile and Peru (1965–75) because they focused on long-term structural transformation, while ignoring the imperatives of short-run macroeconomic stabilization (Foxley, 1983). The newly dominant monoeconomics of the 1980s was by no means, as Dudley Seers claimed at the time, simply 'the re-run of an old film' (Seers, 1981: 1). In reality, the original structuralist objection was now addressed.

Although no ground was conceded on the need for short-run stabilization using the traditional instruments of money supply control, fiscal deficit reduction, devaluation and the removal of internal price controls, it was recognized that this orthodox package had to be complemented by medium- and long-term institutional changes. The structural adjustment of the 1980s contains two distinct components – stabilization and structural adjustment in the narrower sense of market liberalization and public sector reform. A schematic representation of the package of policies which typically constitutes 'structural adjustment' is given in Figure 3.1 at the end of this chapter, in an attempt to clarify the two different senses in which the term is currently used (i.e. inclusive and exclusive of stabilization policies). Structural adjustment in the exclusive sense encompasses policies precisely directed to removing the bottlenecks and rigidities which the old-style structuralists identified (rightly in my view) as the reason why orthodox stabilization measures failed in developing countries. The resurgent monoeconomics of the 1980s is, therefore, not simply the old monetarism, but the old monetarism trying to incorporate the insights of the old-structuralists into a new policy consensus. Only in this way is it possible to understand why monoeconomics is the parent of the policies called *structural* adjustment, something which otherwise appears quite paradoxical. Whether this incorporation has succeeded is another matter, to which we turn in a later section of this paper.

The neo-liberal economic agenda is thus characterized by the primacy of macroeconomic stabilization, both in the sense that bringing foreign sector payments into balance is the chief objective to which other structural adjustment policies are auxiliary, and in the chronological sense that these auxiliary policies cannot be implemented successfully before a start is made on stabilization, because private and public sectors alike would then tend to adjust to an unsustainable macro framework. Recall that the great neo-liberal project of the 1970s had been to use shadow prices in project appraisal in order to secure the more rational use of public sector investment resources. In effect, shadow pricing was a method for trying to adjust the public part of the economy, while allowing the macro framework itself to remain out of line with international economic forces. The 1980s neo-liberal concern with 'getting the prices right' has two dimensions, moving to an exchange rate which reflects the relative scarcity of foreign and domestic currency, and then making domestic prices actually correspond to shadow prices, rather than merely using shadow prices for public investment decisions.

Apart from macro stabilization and getting domestic prices 'right', the other main plank of the neo-liberal programme was a major shrinkage in the functions of the state, particularly its withdrawal from the functions of production and finance (other than finance of the government narrowly defined). Indeed, the very industrial investment projects for which the cost/benefit manuals of the 1960s and 1970s were so copiously written were now to be removed altogether from the public sector, on the grounds that the state had become 'over-extended' and unable to cope with its basic functions of provision of infrastructure and social services. The 'over-extension' argument masked a more fundamental change of view about the nature of the state in developing countries, however. The neo-classical cost/benefit manual writers of the 1970s still aligned themselves with the assumption of a benevolent state, i.e. one sincerely attempting to advance economic development and open to instruction as to suitable methods. By the early 1980s they had largely rejected their former position in favour of some variant of the 'new political economy'. This sees the state itself, or state personnel individually, as self-interested actors on a par with self-interested households, firms, trades unions and so on. Space is lacking here to explore the full ramifications of this new political economy, but although it has had a mixed reception it has had strong influence on re-designing the state as part of structural adjustment (see Meier, 1992: Toye, 1991).

The new view of the malevolent state can be interpreted as an attempt by monoeconomists to incorporate insights from another current of 1970s thought, namely neo-Marxism. Most neo-Marxists held to a very negative evaluation of the capability of the state to act in the general interests of society, specifically because of its capture by the dominant social class, the capitalist bourgeoisie – either in a domestic incarnation within developing countries, or located in the metropolitan countries but acting through local compradors. In the new political economy, the role played in neo-Marxist accounts by the capitalist class is attributed to interest groups which lack any particular sociological status and which are formed and dissolved according to the fluctuating self-interest of their individual members. But the thesis remains of a captured state, whose policy decisions are determined, not by autonomous rational calculations of how to advance the public interest, but by a configuration of conflicting interest-group pressures. The state thus uses economic policy to create rents to appease rent-seeking groups, and in so doing it becomes the cause of distorted incentives, wasted resources and accumulating economic failure.

Even without the element of class, this version of the malevolent state constituted a very strong assumption. The state as the source of *all* economic evils was, however, a convenient belief, because it limited the range of bottle-necks and rigidities which had to be removed in the course of structural adjustment to those which had been created by government policies. From this it appeared to follow that, once the correct (neo-liberal) policies were in place, all would be well because *all* bottlenecks and rigidities would have been removed by the process of liberalization and deregulation. Here lay the source of the widespread, but mistaken, optimism about what structural adjustment could achieve. Once the idea took general hold that the state was the single source of economic failure, a panacea seemed to be possible simply by rolling back its boundaries. The influential work of Bates (1981) assisted in promoting the misleading transmutation (Lipton, 1984: 161, n. 12).

Such a substantial reversal of the conventional wisdom of development economics could hardly have gathered the support that it did unless equity-based arguments had been added to those concerning economic efficiency. The resurgent monoeconomics of the 1980s found its distributional appeal by incor-porating a third current of the 1970s – the theory of urban bias. As Jamal (1989: 176) has noted: 'adjustment programs in Africa are . . . based on some notion of "urban bias", which in Africa was almost invariably translated to imply a bias in favour of the urban wage earners'. The rent-seekers whom the malevolent state sought to appease were in the towns – the industrialists (public and private), the urban labour aristocracy and government employees. The economic controls operated by the government were designed to favour these interest groups at the expense of the peasantry, and especially the agricultural commodity exporters who were heavily taxed by state agricultural export monopsonies and an over-valued exchange rate. The policy programme of liberalization would thus result in the erosion of urban bias, as the reduction of rents enjoyed by the urban group permitted the restoration of economic incen-tives in the countryside. Since the urban groups were the better-off and the rural groups the worse-off segments of the income distribution, the removal of urban bias would improve equity of distribution in the economy as a whole. This line of reasoning provided continuity with the established anti-poverty values of development economics, while at the same time subsuming them into the adjust-ment policy package.

Finally, we come to the political assumptions behind the structural adjustment process, and to the role of the international financial institutions themselves. Given the assumption of a malevolent state deliberately creating urban bias, it was clear that the adjustment process would be politically problematic. How could such a state be persuaded to unwind its own creation? After all, as Machiavelli had seen 450 years previously, the reformer 'has for enemies all who have done well under the old order of things, and lukewarm defenders in those who may do well under the new' (1968: 29). The first phase of adjustment must therefore be hazardous as the beneficiaries of urban bias try to protect their rents and the reforming government has to wait anxiously to see whether the intended beneficiaries in the rural sector do really benefit and whether they are able to respond with effective political support. Nor is this a purely mechanical matter of response lags. Expectations play a crucial role: the behaviour of enemies and potential allies alike will depend on their perceptions of the government's resolve to persist with adjustment through the initial political turbulence. The government will be dealing with a very unstable situation, often spoken of in terms of proceeding along a knife-edge.

In the light of this prospect, it is perhaps not entirely surprising that there was considerable support by influential voices within the World Bank for authoritarian governments to be the agents of structural adjustment. 'A courageous, ruthless and perhaps undemocratic government is required to ride roughshod over these newly-created special interest groups', according to Lal (1983: 33), whose views were highly regarded at this time. The Bank itself could not voice such sentiments, given its non-political mandate, but it certainly saw no difficulty in negotiating adjustment finance for authoritarian governments. In doing so, it presumably distinguished between the government and the people of the country and relied on the belief that adjustment would improve both efficiency and equity for the people in the long run. In the short run, finance from the international institutions was seen as essential to bolster a reforming government during the first phase of knife-edge instability. Such finance, if it could be designed to disburse quickly, would permit a rapid improvement in import-strangled economies, by pulling in the spares needed to raise industrial capacity, the inputs needed by agricultural exporters and the consumption goods that would persuade the urban population that structural adjustment policies signified economic recovery.

## The Origins of Structural Adjustment Policies

The origin of structural adjustment policies has to be sought not merely in the deteriorating international economic environment of the 1970s and the revival of monoeconomics (but now incorporating strands of structuralism, neo-Marxism and urban bias theory). It must be sought also in the evolution of policy thinking within the World Bank. Although this was obviously influenced both by the changing world context and by the general intellectual ferment in development policy, these influences had to be absorbed into internal decision-making in the course of addressing specific institutional tasks. The Bank's response to the events of the 1970s was dramatic enough, when the out-going President, Robert McNamara, announced in his 1980 Presidential Address that there had occurred a 'permanent change in the world economy, not . . . some temporary phenomenon which will later automatically reverse itself'. But this *volte-face* had been prepared by specific earlier episodes, in which the Bank encountered problems which it could not resolve adequately with the instruments at its command. It was these that convinced the Bank that it could no longer encourage developing countries to pursue growth regardless of macroeconomic stability, as it had done throughout the 1970s, and that it must now get them to give priority to stabilization and hope that growth could be successfully pursued as well.

If we define structural adjustment lending as programme finance with economy-wide conditionality, the most important specific preparatory experience for what was to emerge fully-fledged in 1979–80 was the Bank's failed liberalization attempt in India in the mid-1960s, when the heavy industry investment of the Third Plan had produced a combined balance-of-payments and food-security crisis. The Bank's response to this twin crisis was to step up quick-disbursing programme aid and to undertake secret negotiations with the Government of India to alter its policies on agriculture, the regime of controls over trade and industry and the value of the rupee. Although the Bank's heavy leverage succeeded up to a point, it created great nationalist resentment in India, produced little improvement in economic performance and the process of Indian liberalization was soon aborted. While subsequently adopting a lower profile in India, the Bank did not altogether relinquish its hopes of combining programme finance with policy conditions, and subsequent attempts in similar vein were in fact made in the 1970s in SSA in Zambia, Kenya and Tanzania, although here the policy conditions were sectoral rather than economy-wide.

But such moves remained *ad hoc*, and the secrecy of each negotiation indicated not only a desire to protect the client government from its own public opinion, but also the Bank's own unwillingness to be seen publicly trading loans for policy reforms, something for which its Executive Board had no stomach at that time, for a variety of reasons. What was it that changed a sporadic and covert practice into a publicly acknowledged policy with lending commitments of $6.5 bn by 1989 and 99 completed operations by 1991? Perhaps the single most important cause was that the Bank's traditional lending mode, the finance of capital projects, was becoming increasingly unsuitable as the vehicle for the transmission of aid funds in the 1970s. The first reason for this was that the disbursement of project funds was very slow. The typical disbursement schedule for a Bank project shows very small disbursements in the first one or two years as the project begins to get under way, then a rapid build-up to a peak of spending in years 4 and 5, followed by a long declining tail, stretching on to 8 or 10 years. This typical profile reflects the difficulties into which most complex projects run, requiring partial re-design in the course of implementation (Lipton and Toye, 1990: 157–161). The yawning payments deficits of the late 1970s in developing countries would not have been greatly assisted by the rapid multiplication of new commitments of project finance. In order to address deficits of the huge size then opening up, much more rapidly disbursing forms of aid would be required.

The second reason was that it was becoming increasingly clear that developing countries did not need more projects. Many had already accepted more projects than they could sustain with the internal resources which they were raising. As a result, particularly in SSA where the pressure to acquire foreign exchange was strongest, the landscape was beginning to be littered with half-built projects long aborted, which would soon deteriorate to the point of collapse, involving a total waste of the resources sunk in them. Such a state of affairs in impoverished countries was little short of scandalous, and in many cases it probably *was* scandalous. Evidently what was needed was a change in the general economic environment which would facilitate the rational utilization of project finance, not more project finance itself. Funds for the completion or rehabilitation of existing projects were the first priority, combined with improved resource mobilization to make them sustainable in the longer run.

The third reason is an extension of this argument. In a country where controls are endemic and domestic prices are distorted and liable to change at administrative whim, it is much harder to design projects which will prove to be economically sustainable throughout their planned lives. The shadow pricing methods of project appraisal referred to earlier may well succeed in eliminating projects of too low Net Present Value (provided that such methods can be institutionalized in countries with weak administrations). But they cannot succeed in ensuring that projects with satisfactory NPVs will be implemented, because supplementary sources of financing may be necessary to keep them solvent, over and above the revenue that they are able to generate through market processes. This problem, which tended to be brushed lightly aside by enthusiasts of the cost/benefit technique, carried the implication that, if its application succeeded, the length of the shelf of viable projects would contract. And, if it was not applied, the situation would be no better than it had been. Unless actual prices approximate to shadow prices, the whole enterprise of development by means of projects becomes attenuated. This logic led the Bank's operational management to embark on a more visible and vigorous attempt to get prices right than they had ventured on before. Previous attempts had been made to do this by the use of policy dialogue, a form of moral suasion that had been leisurely and uncertain in its effects, and the use of performance criteria in the allocation of soft aid funds. In 1979, these tentative approaches were abandoned and the new instrument of structural adjustment lending was unveiled.

In stressing the longer-run factors which prepared the way for structural adjustment lending as an operational instrument for the Bank, we should not lose sight of the crisis of the late 1970s in which that instrument was finally forged. That the external payments situation of developing countries was rapidly deteriorating *before* the second oil shock has already been stated. The need for a 'quick fix' of rapidly disbursing aid was already apparent in early 1979, and internal discussions about large-scale programme lending were taking place at that time. Ironically, the context of that discussion was the problem of how to make the Bank's anti-poverty programme more effective. One proposal was for a large new operation of long-term programme lending to rescue McNamara's failing 'war on poverty'. Programme lending had traditionally been regarded within the Bank as an unsound type of loan, and had been used sparingly because of fear that more extensive resort to it might have unfavourable repercussions on the Bank's star rating in the credit markets. This fear made the proposal unlikely to succeed as it stood. The Bank's operational management decided to make the proposal more internally attractive by coupling expanded programme lending with an ambitious scheme of policy reform conditionality. The original proposal was effectively diverted from the hands of the anti-poverty camp, in a move that combined daring and desperation in about equal measure. In its new form, it still evoked suspicion and dislike from the Executive Board, but nevertheless was presented to the world in April 1979 at the UNCTAD meeting in Manila.

Structural adjustment lending rapidly gained a higher profile in the subsequent rush of events. The second oil price shock made the external payments position of the non-oil developing countries even more difficult, and the quick fix even more urgent. The Berg Report (World Bank, 1981) on Sub-Saharan Africa developed the critique of government internal policy failures dramatically and provided the new policy reform agenda for which policy-conditioned aid was to provide the conduit. Finally, the debt crisis broke in mid-1982, confirming that structural adjustment had a rationale which extended much more widely than SSA.

In the struggle to get structural adjustment lending accepted within the Bank, some very big claims for it were made. The need to defuse internal scepticism seemed to elicit a retreat into grandiose thinking, both about what SALs should be and what SALs could do. Size itself became a virtue, because only size could buy the Bank a seat at the top policy-making table in developing countries. Then the deal had to be seen by all as a big one: if the loan was big, then the list of policy conditions had to be long, to show that the Bank was getting proper value for money. The improvement to be expected in the policy environment was accordingly dramatic. In a one-off operation lasting a few years, structural adjustment would be completed. Then project financing could be resumed, all the previous constraints on its effectiveness being relaxed. In addition – this expectation pre-dating the debt crisis – private investment would be attracted by the reformed economy, banishing the spectre of aid dependence. In return for these benefits, it would be justifiable to downgrade the objective of poverty alleviation while structural adjustment took place. That was something that the Bank could turn back to once the economy had recovered sufficiently to make it affordable. Although more than a decade later these claims can be seen for what they were, outright illusions or gross exaggerations, they generated enough organizational energy to get the structural adjustment enterprise aloft. What had started as an effort to redeem McNamara's lending programmes to aid the poor rapidly became an exercise in inflated expectations which stopped the anti-poverty objective dead in its tracks. Only as the extent of the initial over-ambition was revealed by events in the 1980s did the social objectives of development policy become gradually reinstated on the Bank's agenda.

## Diversity in Design, Implementation and Outcomes

Critics of the practice of structural adjustment in the 1980s often complained that the IMF and the World Bank had only a single policy package, which they forced regardless of its suitability on all their clients for adjustment lending. The two institutions rejected this view, arguing that each package was separately negotiated between the mission team and the government of the developing country, and even that, in some cases, the latter was the prime architect of the design. The truth seems to lie somewhere in between these two extremes. Analyses of the precise content of adjustment loan conditionality show that the country packages, while not by any means identical, do have a family resemblance. No one type of policy condition appeared in *all* the early policy packages of the 1980–86 period, for example. The highest frequency of any one type was 86%, relating to the strengthening of capacity to manage the public investment programme. But appearing in more than 50% of all SAL policy packages were nine other requirements:

(a) to remove import quotas (57%)
(b) to improve export incentives (76%)
(c) to reform the budget or the tax system (70%)

(d)  to improve the financial performance of public enterprises (73%)
(e)  to revise agricultural pricing (73%)
(f)  to revise public investment priorities (59%)
(g)  to revise industrial incentives (68%)
(h)  to increase public enterprise efficiency (57%)
(i)  to improve marketing and other support for agriculture (57%).

These ten familiar types of conditionality were put together with other less frequent types in all sorts of different combinations. While no two prescriptions were identical, the frequency of appearance of the ten created the marked similarity between packages which can be described as a 'family resemblance'.

This limited diversity was produced by various aspects of the loan negotiation process. The basic focus of the Bank's missions was itself limited by a framework of reforming key prices and incentives to bring them more into line with underlying scarcity relations. Despite the Bank's eagerness to publicize instances of local programme design, these were always a minority, and most of them were more or less ventriloquized by the missions, if not actually written by them. The missions themselves were not wholly free agents in the negotiation either. The Bank's country desk officers in Washington and their superiors had to be satisfied with the package. Thus, it was far from unknown for missions to negotiate painfully a package satisfactory to the developing country government, only to have it rejected at headquarters in Washington because it did not look sufficiently orthodox and tough. Finally, the Bank had to operate within a set of parameters agreeable to the IMF. More imaginative or alternative growth-promoting packages often met with the Fund's disapproval on the ground that they conflicted with the strict requirements of macroeconomic stabilization.

Having said all of this, however, the evidence of some diversity is plain enough. How is it to be explained? The original circumstances of the recipient countries were often different. In some, particular sources of economic distortions did not exist and did not have to be addressed. Ghana, for example, had no food subsidies to remove, while Zambia did. When the typical distortions were to be found, they were not always to be found in the same degree, and choices were made about which were the most serious and often these were addressed first. In addition, rather little consideration was given initially to the problems of sequencing, which also made for diversity as some missions tried to follow a carefully planned sequence while others did not. Some opted for a 'big bang' approach, trying to do everything at once, while others took a more gradualist line. The practice of economic reform, particularly in the early years before the lessons of evaluation started to come through, was higgledy-piggledy, under the fierce pressure to do something and get some results as the external environment for policy reform continued relentlessly to worsen during the 1980s.

While the Bank tended to exaggerate the diversity of the design process for economic reform, it minimized the appearance of diversity in evaluating the implementation of reform. Without attributing motives, one may note the fact that the Bank was careful not to give comparative analyses of the implementation record of individual adjusting countries. Instead, its reports concentrated on average levels of implementation for adjusting countries as a group. Since average compliance levels of between 60 and 80% could be calculated on varying assumptions, the overall picture looked quite good, while attention was directed away from the distribution around these levels. In fact, research has shown that the diversity in this respect has been quite large. In the small number of countries where the degree of 'slippage' in the implementation of reform conditions has been measured comparatively, the average of the best performing countries was only 17.6%, while in the worst performing it was over 50.3% (Mosley, 1992: 146, Table 7.4).

The explanation of this variance can be found in a number of different considerations. At the extreme of poor compliance, the problem was almost certainly a lack of commitment by the borrowing government to the whole adjustment exercise. Certainly in the early 1980s the haste to build up the new form of lending led to the approval of operations where the borrower's commitment was comprehensively misjudged. Apart from various Latin American and Caribbean examples, Kenya could be cited as an SSA example of this. Where the slippage figures look slightly less bad, lack of commitment is probably also quite important. A better statistical impression can be created by the phenomenon of countervailing behaviour, whereby the letter of the stated condition is complied with, but offsetting action is taken simultaneously so that the objective of the condition remains frustrated. Also borrowers with a low basic commitment to the reform process did not always suffer the immediate termination of future lending. Partly because of policing difficulties which were inherent in the initial design of the lending instrument, and partly because of more general inhibitions about the results to both lender and borrower of an abrupt cut-off of financial flows, governments with poor compliance records continued to remain inside adjustment programmes. At the same time, however, the Bank came increasingly to realize the importance for successful reform of countries 'owning' their programmes, i.e. actually being convinced that the programmes were the most appropriate way of addressing the economic problems which they faced.

At the middle level of compliance, one finds governments which did have 'ownership' of their programmes in this sense, but which were trying to exercise such ownership with painfully inadequate administrative capacity. It was always a paradox of the implementation of structural adjustment that governments which had been diagnosed as 'over-extended' were faced with the demand for widespread and complex reforms which they themselves were supposed to plan and bring to fruition. Ultimately the withdrawal from economic production was meant to strengthen state capacity by concentrating resources. But regardless of whether this proved true in the long run, in the short run the over-extended state simply had to add to its existing tasks. A borrowing government with both commitment to reform and weak administrative capacity is likely to achieve at best a middling compliance rating. Those conditions which required little administrative skill to perform could be implemented. In this category fall many of the 'pricist' reforms – devaluation, abolition of price controls on goods, tariff reductions, subsidy abolition and similar acts of deregulation of the economy. Much more problematic were reforms with a substantial element of institutional change – better public expenditure programming, tax reform, civil service reform and privatization of public enterprises. Such reforms require extensive pre-planning, widespread retraining programmes and complex inter-departmental co-ordination, which is either beyond the local administration altogether (even with adequate technical assistance) or, at best, can be implemented only much more slowly than was originally envisaged. As always, however, there are exceptions. A minority of adjusting countries – Turkey and Thailand, for example – exhibited both high levels of commitment to the objectives of economic reform and high levels of administrative capacity. Their adjustment programmes were marked by very little culpable slippage in implementation, and they therefore appear at the high-performance extreme of the implementation scale.

Examining the diversity of the outcomes of structural adjustment programmes can only be done properly when due allowance is made for these differences in implementation performance. It is evidently foolish to try to demonstrate these outcomes by comparing 'adjusting' with 'non-adjusting' countries if the so-called 'adjusting' countries are quite disparate in the extent to which they are implementing reform policies. A host of other key factors also have to be controlled for, if the comparison is to be meaningful, including external conditions (including the weather) and the impact of the financial flows accompanying the policy conditionality. The methodological problems involved in isolating the effects of adjustment policies are quite formidable. No single method is uniquely appropriate, and a research strategy based on a number of different imperfect methods may well be the best way to tackle the problem (Toye, 1992). The results of a number of recent studies (including those of the World Bank itself) have tended to focus on the economic outcomes, rather than the broader social concerns which were raised by UNICEF most notably in the mid-1980s (Cornia et al., 1987). The area where the greatest consensus has been achieved concerns the size of the beneficial effects of adjustment policies relative to the size of the external factors which have impacted on developing countries during the period of adjustment. The latter have greatly outweighed the former. This finding seems to lay to rest one of the basic assumptions with which the adjustment exercise began, namely that the economic problems of developing countries were largely (or even entirely) the result of their own flawed policies. Despite the disappointment generated by this conclusion, it does not constitute an argument for abandoning economic reform. Small improvements are, after all, superior to no improvements at all. But it is an argument for diverting the attention of international policy-makers and the resources which they command to other aspects of the development process, where the marginal benefits may be greater.

Within the consensus that the benefits of adjustment policies have been modest, a diversity of views can be found. The clearest benefit is visible in an increased rate of growth of exports, and an accompanying reduction of the deficit on the current account of the balance of payments. Some claim to find clear evidence that this has also contributed to an increase in the overall growth rate of output, while others are more sceptical, suggesting that the better export growth has been fully offset by declines in the growth of domestic consumption and investment. While a decline in the ratio of investment to GDP is a generally agreed outcome, its significance is evaluated differently. Some welcome it as a necessary feature of the adjustment process, on the ground that much pre-adjustment investment was inefficient and produced low returns. Others doubt that only wasteful forms of investment have been squeezed out, and worry about the strength of the investment base for future growth.

Beyond these debates about economic outcomes lies concern about the broader social impact of adjustment policies. If the economic outcomes are hard to identify, tracing through the manifold links from the economic reform package to the welfare of households and small enterprises and making a meaningful aggregation of all the micro-level impacts is even harder (Addison and Demery, 1993: 135). If a pervasive impact of adjustment policies is a reduction in the real wage, it is plausible to argue that those whose sole or main asset is their own labour will be made worse-off unless this is accompanied by an expansion of the demand for labour. But the labour market is still a relatively neglected area for research on the consequences of structural adjustment. Those who own non-labour assets – land and capital – will be likely to benefit from liberalization measures which remove restrictions on their use and rewards. Without a strong up-swing in labour-intensive employment, therefore, a worsening of the inequality of income distribution is likely (Pio, 1992: 240–45). This may well be accompanied by particular problems of falling school enrolment, worsening health conditions and the emergence of nutritional stress in the poorer strata of the population. None of these are inevitable effects, but they do need to be energetically addressed by government policies, especially in the area of public expenditure decision-making and the design of specific social safety-net schemes. Fortunately, the removal of poverty alleviation from the immediate agenda of the international financial organizations in the early 1980s has now been completely reversed, and this issue is at last again getting the attention which it urgently requires.

The diversity of outcomes from the adjustment process needs to be looked at not only in terms of the key economic and social issues, but also in terms of geographical differentiation. Sub-Saharan Africa was the region of the developing world which was already experiencing the greatest economic stress in the 1970s, before the invention of structural adjustment lending. It was also the region whose misfortunes at that time were most confidently attributed to internal policy failures. It is not surprising, therefore, that of the 99 adjustment lending operations completed by 1991, no less than 40 were undertaken in 18 different countries in SSA. Comparing these with the 59 in other regions of the developing world points to some interesting, if depressing, conclusions regarding the special features of SSA's adjustment experience. There is clear evidence of the greater relative weakness of administrative capacity in SSA to implement structural adjustment reforms.

This evidence relates to relative failure with those parts of the reform package which are especially administration-intensive. In comparison with non-SSA adjusting countries, fiscal effort and resource mobilization were weaker, and less success was achieved in lowering inflation rates. Despite the greater emphasis given in SSA packages to public enterprise reform, performance was much poorer, and this in turn implied that the government budget gained less relief from expenditure on subsidies for loss-making enterprises. Since many of these enterprises were in the industrial sector, adjustment in this sector was also relatively poor. This record occurred despite the fact that SSA was by far the largest regional recipient of technical assistance specifically related to structural adjustment (World Bank, 1992).

That SSA should remain the region of greatest concern after a decade of economic reform is not itself a great cause for surprise, given its relative position in the late 1970s and the initial accurate diagnosis of governmental decay. It is, however, a serious testimony to the deep-seated nature of the structural obstacles to good economic performance. The transfer by the developed countries of the burden of adjustment from their own shoulders to those of developing countries is something much easier to wish for than to accomplish in the African context. Half of the SSA countries which have undergone adjustment programmes still carry (partly arising from the adjustment process itself) a volume of debt which does not appear to be sustainable without further concessional aid or debt rescheduling. Especially in SSA, it would seem that monoeconomics' accommodation with structuralism still has some further distance to travel.

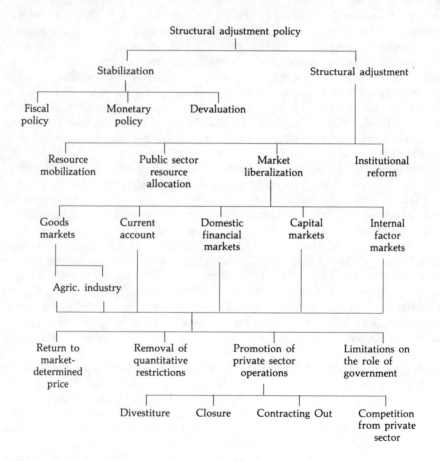

**Figure 3.1.** *A Schematic Representation of Structural Adjustment Policy*

# References

Addison, T. and Demery, L. (1993) 'Labour Markets, Poverty and Adjustment', *Journal of International Development* 5 (2), 135–43.

Arndt, H.W. (1944) *The Economic Lessons of the Nineteen-Thirties*, London: Oxford University Press for the Royal Institute of International Affairs.

Bates, R.H. (1981) *Markets and States in Tropical Africa*, Berkeley, CA: University of California Press.

Cornia, A., Jolly, R. and Stewart, F. (1987) *Adjustment with a Human Face. Protecting the Vulnerable and Promoting Growth*, Oxford: Clarendon Press.

Foxley, A. (1983) *Latin American Experiments in Neoconservative Economics*, Berkeley, CA: University of California Press.

Jamal, V. (1989) 'The Demise of the Labour Aristocracy in Africa: Structural Adjustment in Tanzania' in J.F. Weeks (ed.) *Debt Disaster: Banks, Governments and Multinationals Confront the Crisis*, New York: New York University Press.

Lal, D. (1983) *The Poverty of 'Development Economics'*, London: Institute of Economic Affairs, Hobart Paperback No. 16.

Lipton, M. (1984) 'Urban Bias Revisited', *Journal of Development Studies* 20 (3), April.

Lipton, M. and Toye, J. (1990) *Does Aid Work in India? A Country Study of the Impact of Official Development Assistance*, London: Routledge.

Machiavelli, N. (1968) *The Prince*, London: J.M. Dent, Everyman edition.

Meier, G.M. (ed.) (1992) *Politics and Policy Making in Developing Countries, Perspectives on the New Political Economy*, San Francisco, CA: ICS Press.

Mosley, P. (ed.) (1992) *Development Finance and Policy Reform*, Basingstoke: Macmillan.

Mosley, P., Harrigan, J. and Toye, J. (1991) *Aid and Power: the World Bank and Policy-based Lending*, Vol. 1, London: Routledge.

Pio, A. (1992) 'The Social Dimension of Economic Adjustment Programmes: Economic Feedbacks and Implications for Medium and Long-Term Growth' in Mosley.

Seers, D. (1981) 'Foreword' in S. Griffith-Jones and D. Seers (eds), 'Monetarism and the Third World', *IDS Bulletin*, 13(1) December.

Staley, E. (1945) *World Economic Development*, Second Edition, Montreal: International Labour Office.

Tarp, F. (1993) *Stabilization and Structural Adjustment. Macroeconomic Frameworks for Analysing the Crisis in sub-Saharan Africa*, London: Routledge.

Toye, J. (1991), 'Is there a New Political Economy of Development?' in C. Colclough and J. Manor (eds) *States or Markets? Neo-liberalism and the Development Policy Debate*, Oxford: Clarendon Press.

Toye, J. (1992a) 'Britain, the United States and the World Debt Crisis' in J. Michie (ed.) *The Economic Legacy 1979–1992*, London: Academic Press.

Toye, J. (1992b) 'The Appraisal and Evaluation of Structural Adjustment Lending: Some Questions of Method', mimeo, Institute of Development Studies at the University of Sussex.

World Bank (1981) *Accelerated Development in Sub-Saharan Africa. An Agenda for Action*, Washington DC: World Bank.

World Bank (1992) *World Bank Structural and Sectoral Adjustment Operations. The Second OED Overview*, Report No. 10870. Washington DC: World Bank.

# 4 The Political Economy of Structural Adjustment: An External Perspective

# WILLI WAPENHANS

More than a decade ago development economics as an art appeared to be falling rapidly into disuse (Hirschmann, 1981). This process of rethinking began long before the term structural adjustment became fashionable; it occurred long before the historic events in Eastern Europe and the former Soviet Union caused theoreticians and practitioners alike to turn to what has become commonly known as the economics of transition (Marer and Zecchini, 1991). Much of it has to do with the operational bankruptcy of applied Marxist economics and, at the same time, though somewhat of an apparent contradiction, the renewed interest in the role of institutions – foremost the role of government – in economic development. The historical view, the theory of cultural and technological dependency, and the structuralist approach have received much attention as alternative ways of analysing developmental issues which run counter to the mainstream of economic thought (see, for instance, Furtado, 1987). In more recent times the power of so-called good economics has reasserted itself. The neo-classical paradigm appears vindicated by the performance of East and South-East Asian countries. These cases in particular present skilful use of intervention, usually emphasizing export promotion rather than import compression and often employing specialized institutional arrangements. Indeed, there is now, especially with regard to Sub-Saharan Africa, ever more frequent reference to the importance of good governance and of enabling conditions, calling for an improvement of institutional capacity to implement policy reform including the benign intervention of the state to promote economic expansion (Krugman, 1993).

Economic expansion, of course, has never been a sufficient objective to meet the expectations of the development constituencies. Fair and equitable sharing of the benefits of economic growth has long been a prominent item on the development agenda (Chenery, 1974). More recently the preoccupation with better targeting of poverty-alleviating measures on underprivileged groups and also by gender has been added. At policy level the attack on poverty has acquired a degree of urgency that is clearly manifested today in the call for social safety nets for economies in transition. This perceived need to maintain a social consensus in support of transition is just as legitimate under the often trying circumstances of adjustment. This aspect of the domestic political economy is clearly of concern to external parties which support adjustment.

The interaction between economic activity and the environment has often been seen as a trade-off between preservation and growth as well as between today's welfare and the welfare of future generations. There are those who argue that economic efficiencies, properly measured, are not so incompatible with other goals including ecological values (Harberger, 1987). Decisions based on such measurement can affect public sector resource allocation positively; but administrative intervention to implement such decisions can also cause, at times inadvertently, unproductive rents. The maintenance of inefficient domestic policies under the influence of rent-seeking interest groups has become a major cause of concern. These debates have added further dimensions to public policy-making that can no longer be ignored either in short-term stabilization, in medium-term adjustment, or in long-term development considerations. The perception of waste, fraud and inefficiency has entered the international public consciousness; it thereby affects the political economy of external assistance, including that provided for structural adjustment.

Fiscal constraints and prolonged sluggishness in the global economy have further fuelled adverse tendencies in the international aid climate. Foreign assistance as a tool of export promotion has become less attractive as the ability of recipient economies to provide the changing mix of goods and services needed grew. Replacing the financing of specific goods and services with general-ized balance-of-payments support, on long maturities and concessional terms, has never been a politically attractive alternative. The main thesis of this paper, then, is that considerations of political economy at home and abroad no longer stop at international borders. Their external and internal dimensions reinforce each other in the global village just as much as do the ever increasing financial and economic interdependencies.

When the term was first coined, structural adjustment meant something like a quick fix to adapt to changes in the external economic environment. Once done, the hope was to return to the pursuit of an existing development strategy. That, of course, was always a fallacy. Structural adjustment, like any other policy, is applied in a more or less rapidly evolving situation. The *ex ante* development strategy may well have become obsolete, and adjustment becomes indeed a process of transition.

Robert S. McNamara first used the term in his concluding remarks to the Annual Meeting of the Board of Governors of the World Bank in October 1979 in Belgrade. He was anticipating the dire consequences of a second oil price shock, just about to hit the developing countries. The fragile progress achieved up to then was at stake. Concessional recycling of petro-dollars on a sufficient scale was not likely to be forthcoming, considering the unfavorable responses McNamara's earlier initiatives had received from various quarters (Shapley, 1993: 516ff.). Defensive borrowing on the scale needed was not a sustainable option. Adjustment without external financial assistance was in most cases likely to cause unsustainable social pain. A combination of time and external support was thought necessary to smooth the transition and to facilitate the sharing of the ensuing burdens. In 1979 the World Bank certainly did not set out 'to demolish those structures which we blame for increasing incidence of failures of projects and for the widening gap in economic performance between the Far East and the rest of the developing world' (Mosley et al., 1991: 299). There was no such hidden agenda!

Structural adjustment does not occur in a void. It is part of a more or less complete policy framework and as such becomes an integral element of a policy continuum. In the process of time the concept of structural adjustment has become burdened with a much more ambitious agenda. Expectations associated with structural adjustment today often exceed its inherent potential as a somewhat opportunistic menu of corrective policy measures.

The second thesis of this paper, then, is that structural adjustment, successful as currently measured in only a limited number of cases, may no longer be a sufficient instrument to meet today's challenges, and may never have been an adequate tool to deal with the severe institutional and policy deficiencies besetting many African societies. The combined needs of policy reform, institutional improvement, systemic transition[1] and structural change to deal with poverty in its various manifestations, including gender and ecological considerations, the environment as such, and growth, all without collapse of a sustainable social consensus, simply exceed what can reasonably be expected of this instrument. The business of transition and of sustainable development cannot be accomplished by pure economic rationality alone. What are needed are a theory, a policy, and a process that aim to balance societal goals, clearly and participatorily defined, with the non-exploitative management of resources, and to integrate these to shape politically, socially and economically sustainable structural reform.

## The Case for Structural Adjustment

Internal economic development can be greatly impaired or fundamentally threatened by major external events. The legacy of the 1970s contains telling examples of such shocks: the volatility of exchange rates following the collapse of the Bretton Woods exchange-rate system in 1971; the first oil price shock in 1973/74; the deterioration of terms of trade for developing countries in the mid-1970s; the second oil price shock in 1979/80; and the emergence of the debilitating debt crisis at the beginning of the 1980s. Monetary, fiscal and balance-of-payments deficits, rising inflation, greater rigidity in trade regimes and also in the functioning of domestic markets, were the main consequences for the economies of the world. Many of the causes of these afflictions cannot readily be traced to the developing world. Indeed, very often it was these countries that found themselves at the receiving end.

The consequences of such events for a national economy can be suffered or they can be pro-actively managed. In this sense structural adjustment as a policy instrument retains its relevance. Its ultimate effectiveness in responding to external shocks is likely to be determined far more by the quality of the socio-political framework present in a host country than by any conditionality that may be attached to external support from whatever source. A structural adjustment programme is, under the best of circumstances, a poor substitute for a perceptive, inclusive, and long-term strategy of sustainable development. The absence of a viable strategy has often led to unfortunate attempts to fill the void with an overload of externally imposed conditions.

Structural adjustment programmes and their policy contents should not be expected to cure all or most of the ills besetting developing countries, local and external alike. In Africa viable strategies, based on export-led growth and the liberalization of foreign trade, have few adherents. There is considerable export pessimism.[2] Protection, and especially discriminatory agricultural policies in developed countries, are perceived to make export-led growth strategies unattractive (World Bank, 1989: vii). However, the fact that African traditional exports have lost market share to competing developing countries tends to be ignored and the challenge remains unanswered.

None of the lending criteria in effect in 1979/80 suggested that the World Bank could or should lend for generalized balance-of-payments support. In highly exceptional cases, focused on selected import programmes to increase the capacity utilization of specific industries, loans had been extended based on an exception clause in the Articles of Agreement. The case to be made, then, was one of capacity utilization at the level of the economy at large. The decision to change policy, of course, was properly that of the Board of Executive Directors. Notwithstanding the announcement in Belgrade, neither the management nor the President as Chairman of the Board could change the existing lending policies unilaterally. There ensued nearly two years of struggle between the Board and the management, during which much of today's normative conditionality evolved. It was this adoption of conditionality, with the consent of the borrowing membership, that justified the broadening of the policy exception. Even today it is the exception clause in the Articles of Agreement on which the Bank's support for structural adjustment rests.

During this period of policy dispute something else, exclusively focused on the situation then prevailing in Sub-Saharan Africa, happened, namely the issuance of the so-called Berg Report, which led to the Bank's 1981 Plan of Action for Sub-Saharan Africa (World Bank, 1981). That report projected the neo-liberalist views of a minimalist state and the pre-eminent role of the private sector in Africa's development. Many of its prescriptions eventually found their way into the conditionality of structural adjustment lending in Sub-Saharan Africa, even though that instrument was initially not designed to carry such a demanding freight of policy reform, institution building, and growth. To add further to the complexity, the unfolding of the debt crisis in August 1982[3] focused both Bretton Woods institutions and their policy prescriptions on the external economy. There were many attempts to link the issue of old debt and structural adjustment support.[4] The World Bank, however, evolved a more differentiated approach for the implementation of the Baker/Brady debt strategy. Under that approach, parallel action was both possible and practised, though structural adjustment support was not dependent on debt restructuring. None the less, the application of the debt strategy, on occasion, became a significant source of funding for adjustment programmes.

Indeed, it can be questioned whether structural adjustment is a relevant tool in situations where imbalances are caused by a debilitating coincidence of bad policies, bad government, weak institutions, and adverse external events.[5] There is reason to be equally sceptical about the utility of this instrument in situations of transition from a socialist to a market-based economy. Structural adjustment borrowing as first aid to accelerate recovery following an external economic shock in an otherwise favourable policy environment seems a plausible and justifiable use of creditworthiness.[6] Such borrowing to finance a case of addiction, withdrawal or rehabilitation and, even more challenging, systemic transition in the absence of adequate institutional capacity and without prior reform, including structural reform, would seem ill-advised. Structural adjustment lending in such inhospitable circumstances should most certainly not be justified as a bribe (as suggested by John Williamson in Corbo *et al.*, 1992: 21), lest it destroy the credibility of the instrument and give credence to Holman's concern about collusion (see *Financial Times*, London, 2 March 1993, p. 15).

The World Bank, by its very mandate, has been and continues to be growth-oriented and perforce, because of its preoccupation with investment over a wide range of sectors, structurally based in its policy advice. Its methodological approach, however, has not escaped severe criticism either. This criticism tends to come from neo-classical economists because of the perceived neglect of the importance of relative prices for efficiency and growth. Post-Keynesians argue that the availability of foreign resources does not in itself lead automatically to development. And the Bank's preoccupation with the *ex ante* situation as the basis for the formulation of its conditionality has often been mistaken for lack of equitable treatment. Informed external observers fear that a continuous infusion of highly fungible foreign-exchange funding over extended periods will simply lead to unsustainable levels of consumption. More generally, 'in an unfavorable policy regime, characterized by serious distortions, aid can harm a country by aggravating distortions and imbalances' (Lele and Nabi, 1991: 472). The tension is readily apparent and the instrument reflects the compromise of reconciliation.

This raises the questions of how much of an enabling environment is sufficient to employ structural adjustment policies with reasonable prospects of success; what constitutes a sufficient minimum package of policy reforms; at what speed should it be implemented; and what is the most appropriate sequence? Especially on the latter aspect there remains a fair amount of disagreement in the relevant literature. This disagreement is perhaps more basically a reflection of the demands made on the pre-existence of a sufficient enabling environment than about the shape of the tool itself. Bacha's observation, for instance, that in Eastern Europe structural reform is the prerequisite for stabilization proves the point (Bacha, 1992: 179): adjustment must not be mistaken for structural reform and it certainly cannot substitute for it.

The importance of the political dimension of the domestic policy process and, especially, of policy change tends to be underemphasized in the design of structural adjustment programmes. It is perhaps the single most critical issue, deserving further analysis and better understanding. The political dimension becomes more complex and a more distinct component of the policy process as societies move towards social differentiation and political pluralism. With greater pluralism, policy changes will inevitably become more negotiated, compromising and reflective of social compensation and equity (Lamb and Weaving, 1992: 5). Inherent in such a politically evolving policy process is, of course, the emergence of the process by which a social consensus can be shaped.

Initial country conditions, in terms of both the existing policy process and the economic policy framework, vary drastically from case to case. It follows that programme designs need to be case-specific, though they are rarely based on an analysis of domestic policy processes. There are hardly any two structural adjustment programmes that are alike in economic policy content and programme design. This is to the credit of the designers and has perhaps spared the World Bank the criticism of a textbook approach so often levelled at the IMF. What is commonly missing, however, is an implementation plan based on the realities of the domestic process for policy change.

The *ex ante* diversity also raises the methodological question of the relevance of empirical cross-country comparisons regarding the success of structural adjustment programmes. At least the attempt should be made to corroborate such work by 'with-and-without' case comparisons before drawing conclusions about the efficacy of the tool or its design. Unfortunately, most independent evaluations tend to compare the original design with the ultimate impact, without regard to the level and degree of actual compliance. Partial implementation results from deficient political processes of domestic policy change. These linkages need to be far better understood.

There is thus still tremendous hazard in any generalizations about the design of structural adjustment programmes and about lending in their support. Nor is there agreement on the basis in economic theory or in the area of policy objectives. Most frequent criticism of developing country policy-makers is directed at the apparent neglect of longer-term development objectives and the preoccupation with internal and external macroeconomic equilibrium.[7]

## Adjustment and Growth

The objectives of the management of international economic relations under conditions of open global trade are embodied in the original mandate of the IMF. Its terms of reference are to facilitate the expansion and balanced growth of international trade in order to promote economic prosperity for all member countries. This is to be achieved by maintaining stability in exchange rates, striving to establish currency convertibility, and removing barriers to trade and investment (Nowzad, 1981). Accordingly, the IMF closely monitors balance-of-payments performance and inflation rates in its member countries. Its analytical framework focuses on the short term. It uses a flow-of-funds approach, known as the Polak–Fund Model,[8] to determine a sustainable balance-of-payments position while ensuring price stability. Domestic credit ceilings and changes in the exchange rate are the key policy instruments with which the Fund seeks to achieve the desired targets.[9]

In an open economy internal and external balance is the essential precondition for sustainable growth.[10] Macroeconomic policies are designed to prevent the emergence of imbalance. The contention is that, if and when the force of such a policy is overwhelmed by external shocks, adjustment policies are needed to restore the conditions for growth. The inclinations of national political decision-makers to seek initial recourse to monetary expansion in response to the immediate consequences of such events activate inflationary tendencies. Corrective monetary and exchange-rate action is delayed or prevented by special interest groups. As a result, an overvalued exchange rate emerges. Its defence, in turn, requires administrative intervention with all the ensuing distortions and inefficiencies that entails. Recourse to external balance-of-payments financing can provide temporary relief; it will not cure the affliction unless corrective action is taken to restore balance and international competitiveness. If the situation is allowed to linger before corrective action is taken, the equilibrium may be restored only at a lower level of income.

Consistent with the IMF mandate, in an open system of world trade, the provision of a sustainable policy framework for export expansion has to avoid the anti-export bias otherwise resulting from the indiscriminate protection of import-competing sectors and the artificial appreciation of exchange rates. Complementary export-promotion policies – if indeed intervention is needed – tend to be economically less costly than the economic cost of distortions caused by import-compression policies.[11]

Accordingly, the classical IMF intervention was designed to restore equilibrium as a precondition of growth; any structural adjustment effects were incidental. Its tools and its terms were not meant to support the kind of medium-term structural adjustment called for by the situation following the 1979 oil shock. Nevertheless, the IMF was called upon to shoulder in large measure the initial burden to prevent a global collapse. Especially in Sub-Saharan Africa this led to a rapid rise in debt on terms, especially maturities, that were irreconcilable with the projected economic effects of such structural change. Zambia is a telling case in point.

The IMF approach has been widely criticized as being insufficiently oriented towards the economic development of developing countries. That, of course, was never its primary task. Furthermore, the industrialized countries and other main participants in international trade have consistently supported the Fund as the principal guardian of open trade and global sustainable economic expansion. The international community as represented in such fora as the G-7, G-10, the Interim Committee, or the Development Committee strenuously preserves the policy role in balance-of-payments support and in adjustment financing for the Bretton Woods institutions.[12] It is in this area of tension between the proponents of liberal trade and balanced international growth and of the national economic development of less developed countries that most of the compromises in international political economy manifest themselves.

Even the staunchest critics of the IMF would not dispute the desirability of restoring equilibrium as a precondition for growth. For open economies, stabilization therefore remains the foremost first step in initiating the process of structural adjustment. Curtailing domestic credit will cause the consolidation of public sector budgets as well as private sector investments. In the public sector the ensuing fiscal constraints cause major reductions in public sector investment programmes – usually implemented across the board and without priority-based selectivity. Here economies with a large state share face especially severe rigidities. Investment as the source of future growth is impaired unless financial assistance can be mobilized to sustain a reasonable level of investment.

It is the World Bank's foremost task to find foreign-exchange resources to finance investment projects, with the ultimate objective of attaining a higher growth path for the borrowing member country. Where growth is threatened by external shocks, the Bank attempts to provide resources to help sustain investments at a sufficient level to prevent contraction. To ascertain the aggregate resource needs of a country the World Bank uses the so-called two-gap model

(Chenery and Stout, 1966). This model extends the Harrod–Domar framework by linking domestic savings, capital-output ratios and the availability of foreign exchange to growth. New investments need, of course, to respond to the changes in priorities caused by the very process of adjustment. In turn, these investments require their own policy or regulatory reform in the meso- or micro-economic sphere.

When, in the early 1980s, the Bank began to engage in 'structural adjustment' support, the approaches of the two institutions collided. The IMF's preoccupation with stabilization as a precondition of growth appeared to put the brake on economic development, while the simultaneous infusion of balance-of-payments financing by the Bank seemed to countervail adjustment and essentially fund unsustainable deficits. At the operational level this clash manifested itself around the following critical issues:

– what is a sufficient rate of investment to sustain a minimum level of growth?
– what is an acceptable level of inflation to help smooth the process of adjustment?
– what is the level of external finance that can be mobilized to satisfy the needs of either framework?

While there was concern about the political management of structural adjustment these debates hardly ever included the process of domestic policy change explicity. The notion of 'adjustment with a human face' emerged much later and carried the connotation of financial relief from abroad rather than of social equity at home.

Accordingly, reconciliation of the different views failed most frequently over disagreement on the acceptable rate of inflation and the likely availability of external support. Programmes were soon perceived to be underfunded. As the 1980s witnessed increased collaboration between the World Bank and the IMF in their conditional lending for structural adjustment, their respective approaches began to be integrated. A more consistent framework emerged, linking policies and the availability of foreign resources to targets for growth, inflation and the balance of payments. Today, growth-oriented adjustment programmes attempt to merge the Fund's monetary model of the balance of payments with the Bank's two-gap approach.

Aid levels at that time had already begun to stagnate in real terms. Notwithstanding heroic efforts in the context of Consultative Group Meetings and other devices to co-ordinate and promote aid flows, additional external support for such programmes was hardly ever forthcoming.[13] And, without relief in the form of additional external finance available to the designers of adjustment programmes, they had little choice but to introduce, consistent with the discipline of the integrated model, further stringencies and such conditions as carried early prospects of relief from the binding foreign-exchange constraint. This also led to the early and prominent focus in the conditionality on fiscal deficit reductions, trade regimes, export promotion, especially of non-traditional exports, and incentives to promote the repatriation of flight capital.[14]

Today's rationale for World Bank financial support of structural adjustment programmes is more comprehensively defined as 'to finance unsustainable deficits (current account and/or fiscal) with accompanying policies and actions which are intended to shift the economy to a new, sustainable and poverty-reducing growth path' (World Bank, 1992a). Conditions derived from this objective most typically include measures to improve:

- investment efficiency and the business environment;
- factor markets, especially financial sector and wage policies;
- resource management in the public sector; and
- social policy reform.

To avoid conflicting policy advice, and in particular to reconcile short-term macroeconomic perspectives with longer-term structural objectives, close consultations between the Bretton Woods institutions in the design of such programmes is today enforced by the managements and closely observed by their boards. The approach to consultation has been formalized in the case of the poorest countries eligible for concessional assistance and Extended Fund Facilities. In these instances a tripartite Policy Framework Paper, prepared jointly by the recipient government, the IMF, and the World Bank, defines the critical reform variables and provides guidance on how and where to make the trade-offs with social impact, poverty reduction, and environmental protection. Such papers, while considered by the Executive Directors of both Bretton Woods institutions, do not constitute contracts; they are advisory in nature and serve as a guideline to the independent framing and articulation of conditionality by either institution. Formal cross-conditionality is thus avoided.

The design of programmes, no matter how proficient, does not guarantee their effective implementation. Difficulties with programme implementation have been experienced over a wide area of conditionality. Most important has been the lack of commitment to reform on the part of the government, which is intensely interested in obtaining external finance but also in minimizing the politically difficult and risky process of reform. Overestimation of institutional capacity to carry out reforms has been another frequent occurrence leading to gradualism and loss of synergy. The absence of analysis of the domestic policy process undoubtedly contributes to the failure to recognize such shortcomings. Furthermore, in the wake of the increasing emphasis placed on private sector development, a certain decline in public sector institutional capacity appears to have emerged. A gradual reduction in the role of the state took place when the real need was for a profound change in its role from that of manager of commercial affairs to that of policy-maker and implementer.

Implementation of conditionality invariably leads to redistribution of income, wealth, and opportunity. It follows that, increasingly, organized resistance on the part of adversely affected interest groups must be anticipated. In this respect too, more frequent recourse to careful analysis of the political economy may be called for, the better to prepare for effective implementation. While there is some evidence to suggest that structural adjustment tends to hurt the privileged more than the poor, this assertion needs careful analysis in each case. Relatively little is known about how to accomplish these tasks of societal transformation in the face of strong and traditionally entrenched interest groups, while protecting vulnerable human beings and fragile ecosystems.

Addressing poverty is, of course, the most basic and persistent task of development. It requires a comprehensive approach, centrally embodied in long-term development strategy. However, some aspects of poverty are directly relevant to the consequences of adjustment and therefore pertinent to the design of such programmes. And while the *ex ante* conditions may have been regressive, this surely cannot be accepted as a reason for not addressing the issue in the analysis, design and implementation of structural adjustment programmes.

Adjustment measures typically include reduction in public spending and constraining domestic credit, both of them designed to bring domestic absorption into line with available resources, plus exchange-rate action to increase the price of foreign exchange. These measures will impact on the poor almost instantly. How poor households are affected, however, depends largely on the impact on prices of the goods, assets and services they supply or procure. Determining the net impact will require careful and country-specific analysis since starting positions vary greatly. In Sub-Saharan Africa rural producers are likely to benefit from the positive impact of currency depreciation on the agricultural sector; consumers, however, who are mainly urban, politically volatile and organized, tend to lose from rising food prices.

In societies where lower-income groups find significant employment in the production of tradeables, such a conditionality focus is consistent with international interest in the maintenance of a social consensus. Adjustment postponed is unlikely to benefit lower-income groups; pursuance of unsustainable policies will encourage rent-seeking behaviour; and expansionary public spending is likely to favour better-off groups.[15] Even if, for the poor as a group, the benefits of adjustment outweigh the costs, one cannot exclude the possibility of some negative and potentially stark short-term impact of certain adjustment measures on some part of the disadvantaged. Where such consequences threaten a decline in basic social services and consumption, highly targeted protection of the most vulnerable would seem to be indicated (see also Salop, 1992). This is a primary responsibility of the government undertaking the adjustment programme. Such interventions to mitigate the adverse effects of structural change on the poor should not become a permanent brake on the economy and its growth (see Olson, 1982). In recognition of the at times excruciating circumstances of the policy-imposed fiscal constraints, international assistance has been forthcoming in support of measures designed to alleviate the social costs of adjustment.[16]

More recently, in order to lessen the risk that the process of transition in Central and Eastern Europe will be derailed by adverse political and social reactions to the major short-term dislocations caused by its initiation, the World Bank is building social safety nets into its structural adjustment programmes with the CEE countries. These programmes tend to focus on retraining, the development of labour markets, the design of insurance-based unemployment compensation schemes, and support for the establishment of small-scale enterprises, they are thus much more akin to structural reform measures. Wherever possible, they ought to precede the process of stabilization and adjustment. Other means employed in other parts of the world, notably in Sub-Saharan Africa and Latin America, include targeted food and nutrition programmes, social funds (see Jorgensen *et al.*, 1992), Social Action Programmes and the like. Sustaining a social consensus in support of adjustment through the judicious protection of the most vulnerable has become an increasingly crucial concern of the international constituencies, much reinforced by recent experience in Central and Eastern

Europe. It should be stressed that these are recent innovations, grafted on to an instrument designed for a different purpose, the effectiveness of which cannot yet be assessed.

Structural adjustment measures affect the performance of investments, existing as well as new. The impact on relative prices of exchange-rate action, monetary policy, and efforts at trade liberalization, will change the allocation of resources. It is to be hoped that such reallocations will be concentrated on higher-yielding activities with the prospect of an earlier resumption of sustainable growth. If successful, such adjustment will also restore the environment for increased direct foreign investment. Such renewal, as appears to be emerging now in many parts of Latin America, can only accelerate recovery and growth. That is, after all, what structural adjustment was initially intended to achieve.

## The Business of Sustainable Development

As the preceding discussion has shown, the agenda for adjustment has been greatly expanded. Poverty, natural resources management, institution-building, governance and, most recently, political pluralism, have either been or are about to be added to the menu. These demands reflect urgent and legitimate concerns. They are the critical challenges of socially, politically and economically sustainable development. As such, they far exceed the operational potential of the concept of structural adjustment.

The central issue emerging for the development agenda of the next decade is the interface of economic expansion and environmental concerns. There is growing evidence that acute poverty and environmental degradation are closely linked – and, while not solely, mostly so in poor countries. In Sub-Saharan Africa in particular, agricultural stagnation, rapid population growth and environmental degradation have been common occurrences.

Poverty is on the rise. Its incidence may have declined slightly in developing countries, but the absolute number of poor has increased from 1 billion in 1985 to 1.1 bn in 1990 (World Bank, 1992b). The world population continues to grow at 1.7% p.a. or by some 93 million human beings every year – that is, by more than the equivalent of the entire population of Mexico. More than 95% of this increase is concentrated in developing countries and as much as one half of this in rural areas. Again, Sub-Saharan Africa is the main source of continued high population growth rates, followed closely by the countries of the Middle East. To take just one figure: total fertility rates – measured as births per woman – have remained unchanged in Sub-Saharan Africa for the last 25 years at 6.5. This level is higher than anywhere else in the world, including those countries with otherwise comparable levels of income, life expectancy and female education.

In his most recent book Paul Kennedy resurrects the Malthusian spectre though with much qualification as to the offsetting effects of technological advance. He paints a picture of the crowding-in of more and more people into megacities in the developing world, while the biotechnological progress to feed them occurs in high-income countries (Kennedy, 1993). Friction in agricultural trade between industrial countries, with the only too well known tragic consequences for the agricultural trade of developing countries, is the likely result. Poor countries such as those in Sub-Saharan Africa are threatened with becoming ever more marginalized in an expanding global economy from the mainspring of growth and wealth. Defensive policy reactions such as protectionism and ill-advised administrative intervention are bound to deepen already existing and highly debilitating inefficiencies. The threat to sustainable economic growth is obvious.

The regime of administratively fixed prices and state-controlled resource allocation in socialist economies has proved to be a deadly brew, causing an abhorrently wasteful use of precious natural resources – energy, raw materials, land and water. Socialist regimes have not only been economically highly inefficient, they have also left a catastrophic heritage of pollution and degradation.[17] In the traditional rural societies of developing countries the privatization of village commons has also had disastrous distributional consequences. The threat of disenfranchizing entire classes of people through mindless public policy remains very real. But the picture is by no means clear: there is also evidence to suggest that the public ownership of such resources as forest lands has not been a more benign mechanism for resource allocation.

Rising population, predatory government, injudicious use of technological progress, unreflective public policy, and rent-reserving privilege promote destitution and impoverishment (Dasgupta and Göran-Mäler, 1991). This, in turn, continuously depresses the rewards to labour and leads to a perverse form of export subvention for labour-intensive primary commodity exports. Ill-advised international intervention in the form of support for the stabilization of such primary commodity production further reduces the elasticities of supply; it probably has as much to do with the depression of the terms of trade for these countries as do the swings in the markets for these products. In sum, these effects of domestic public policy combine to deepen poverty and to encourage the wasteful use of natural resources on a global scale.

Some or all of these conditions tend to be present almost as the very manifestation of underdevelopment. Indeed, economic development which does not contain or eliminate these predatory practices may simply mean the continuing condonation of the hijacking of its benefits – or the exploitation of natural wealth – by a privileged few. Today, in the age of instant world communications, this will no longer pass unnoticed. Public opinion is easily mobilized to oppose such practices and their repeated exposure has done much to discredit the otherwise noble mission of external assistance.

Modern advanced societies have developed political processes that keep such tendencies at bay. In socialist as well as in the traditional societies of developing countries such political checks and balances are either absent, rudimentary, or largely ineffective. In consequence, a tremendous amount of unproductive rent-creation and rent-receiving (Krueger, 1974; 291–303; Bhagwati, 1982) proliferates around the centres of power (Thomas et al., 1991, Part III). The socio-political process of transition involves the reduction of such rent-seeking to improve resource allocation but also – and perhaps even more importantly – to make otherwise painful processes of adjustment politically sustainable. The public constituencies of the providers of external resources – whether from capital markets or in the form of concessional aid – tend to exhibit low levels of tolerance regarding excessive rents within their own societies.[18] While restrained by the etiquette of international conduct, they also tend to take a dim view of such abuses in developing countries.

Such donor concerns are increasingly expressed by proxy – and the Bretton Woods institutions appear perhaps the most favoured for this purpose. The demise of global ideological competition has lifted the camouflaging fog of global confrontation, and these debilitating conditions lie exposed, open to much more intense scrutiny.

External support – or the withholding of it – is likely to be increasingly conditioned by societies' success or failure in bringing about a socio-political transition that creates an enabling environment for improved resource allocation and for socially, economically and environmentally sustainable development. The recent events surrounding the postponement of the World Bank-led Consultative Group Meeting for Kenya, and the attendant interruption of external financial support, are a telling harbinger of what lies ahead. Flawed domestic policies are no longer acceptable internationally if they are perceived to be inconsistent with a broad international consensus on social, environmental,[19] and economic goals.

Institutions like the World Bank are increasingly held to account for the behaviour of their borrowing members. A recent example is Michael Holman's article in the London *Financial Times* of 2 March 1993. In it he chastises the World Bank for the confidentiality of its reports and characterizes the relationship of Bank and borrower in Sub-Saharan Africa as 'profoundly unhealthy, protective, secretive or defensive – sometimes all three'. The Bank is expected 'to better see the link between corruption, mismanagement and the failure of structural adjustment programs'. He ends with a crescendo of accusation: 'When information about grave mismanagement is withheld, confidentiality is overlaid with complicity'. This is a serious attack. The credibility of both the host country and the sponsor have come under fire. It is the more astonishing in view of the fact that until fairly recently the focus of attack was the Bank's perceived lack of empathy in the design of adjustment programmes. Its most damaging aspect, of course, is the insinuation of collusion with the 'wrong' parties in the host country.

The World Bank cannot and must not leave unanswered such charges which have no basis whatever in policy. However, the importance of this incident for the thesis advanced here is the evidence it provides that considerations of political economy no longer stop at international borders. Today, such international institutions as the IMF and the World Bank are the magnifying glasses used for their scrutiny and for attempts at resolution.

## Beyond Structural Adjustment

Structural adjustment, with all its limitations, will remain a useful tool to be deployed in situations where external shocks require corrective measures to restore the affected economy to a sustainable growth path. Lending in its support meets the interest of the international aid constituencies if it:

(i) restores conditions for sustainable, i.e. environmentally benign, growth;
(ii) rekindles sufficient growth to prevent contraction;

(iii) improves domestic resource mobilization and allocation to contain the extra demands for external official financial support; and

(iv) sustains a social consensus through the provision of adequate and targeted safeguards for the adversely affected poor.

Even this limited set of economic, political and institutional objectives illustrates the inherent presence of qualitative variables which exceed the formalistic requirements of economic modelling. Hard as it may be to accept, both economic and political processes are essential to the achievement of a society's goals. Reform engenders winners and losers. A better understanding of both the political process of domestic policy change and the social implications of economic decisions would certainly improve the prospects for successful implementation. Just as the models of stabilization and of growth are in need of integration, there now emerges the need to integrate economic and political analysis (see Hettich and Winer, 1993). This improvement is urgently needed and it is gratifying to note that operational research is under way to shape the necessary analytical tools.

In an increasingly interdependent world the boundaries between internal and external economics, between internal and external politics, and between politics and economics become ever more blurred. The surrender of national sovereignty to gain greater economic efficiency, begun in Europe with the successful experiment of the European Payments Union shortly after World War II, is a political process that has not yet exhausted its potential.

Structural adjustment, and international support for it, which can be seen to foster interdependence and which carries the prospect of securing greater economic efficiency in a regional or global context, should cause aid constituencies to react positively. Such support will be reinforced by evidence that adjustment protects the poor and the environment. The political compulsion to sustain external support for balance-of-payments financing in the absence of such evidence has disappeared with the demise of the Cold War. Today, there can be little doubt that performance in the effective use of external assistance will be the critical determinant of the volume and the direction of aid flows in the years to come.

Support for structural adjustment will be much more difficult to sustain if its beneficial results are slow in coming. Crisis management in perpetuity is likely to prove an insufficient argument in its favour. Political management of the process of adjustment will be at a premium. It is in this sense that the creation of political institutions, the process of democratization, the emphasis on participatory approaches, the preoccupation with good governance will be central to the policy dialogue of tomorrow as is its focus on good economic policy and practice today (Wapenhans, 1989: 189). These issues constitute an even more sensitive set of topics and it remains to be seen whether the existing multilateral institutions will continue to serve as efficient proxies for securing the essential compromise.

The reconstruction and development tasks facing the international community at the end of the twentieth century are far more diversified, complex and persistent than those experienced at the time of the creation of the Bretton Woods institutions. Nothing less than a new intellectual foundation is needed to integrate the emerging demands for growth based on participatory policy processes and the need for reliable and integral institutional mechanisms, with the urgency of sustainable resource management. The role of the state needs to be redefined for societies in transition. In today's world, the relationship between nations is far more extensively determined by trade and commerce across international borders than ever before. The concept of structural adjustment and lending in its support should not be expected to suffice in the face of these historical challenges.

## Notes

1. The negative balance-of-payments impact of systemic transition has been explicitly recognized by the IMF in the case of the former Soviet Union and the former CMEA members, as shown by the action of the Executive Board on 23 April 1993 in setting up the Systemic Transition Facility (STF). The questions immediately arising in response to the action are (i) whether the IMF terms are congruent with the needs of economies in transition, and (ii) why the eligibility has been defined in terms reminiscent of the Cold War. For further information on the STF, see IMF, *World Economic Outlook*, 1993, p. 68.
2. In this context the evidence provided by the performance of Mauritius, Morocco, Tunisia and Turkey in successfully developing non-traditional exports is frequently ignored.
3. Initiated by Mexico's unilateral declaration of a moratorium on international debt service.
4. See, for instance, *Die internationale Verschuldung der Entwicklungsländer im Konfliktfeld von Schuldner-Gläubiger-Interessen und multilateraler Auflagenpolitik*, Materialien und Kleine Schriften No. 116, Institut für Entwicklungsforschung und Entwicklungspolitik, Ruhr University, Bochum, 1988. The two contributions to this paper were specifically addressed in the debate surrounding the Annual General Meetings of the Bretton Woods institutions in Berlin in 1988.
5. See, for instance, Balassa (1989), especially in his discussion of the relative success of OOC vs IOC in his Essay 2: 'Policy Responses to Exogenous Shocks in Developing Countries'.
6. For a distinction between 'solvency' and 'creditworthiness' see van Wijnbergen *et al.*, 1992.
7. See, for instance, UN/ECA (1989), which tellingly conveys the limits of structural adjustment programmes and their application under severe conditions of structural rigidities, insufficient sensitivity of unsophisticated economic systems to respond to economic policy signals, and lack of political management to constrain rent-seeking by powerful interest groups. In such circumstances structural adjustment is bound to be a totally insufficient tool to substitute for the much more basic reforms called for. The question that arises, however, is whether such basic reforms justify the use of precious creditworthiness (or, for that matter, concessional assistance).
8. For a critique of the model see Taylor (1987).
9. For a discussion of the desirability of a zero rate of inflation see Dornbusch (1991).
10. Trade policy was high on the agenda of reform in the developing world in the 1980s. The gains from integration into the global economy were known to be substantial. Yet trade barriers proliferated, impeding integration and retarding growth. For a pertinent discussion of the issues, see Thomas and Nash (1991).
11. A thoughtful analysis of what to avoid is contained in the thorough review of the successful case of Korean adjustment in Corbo and Suh (1992).
12. The major exception was the creation of large stabilization funds in conjunction with IMF stand-by programmes to support the Big-bang approach to the initiation of the transformation in Eastern Europe. However, even in this case the G-10 left no doubt that it regarded this practice as highly exceptional and did not endorse its extension to the transition of the successors to the former Soviet Union.
13. It should be noted that debt relief was used as an additional source of external financing, for example in the case of the IMF/Bank-sponsored adjustment programme for Egypt of 1991.
14. As Fischer (1987: 173) pointed out: 'The likelihood that the economy will achieve targets derived using models is, of course, slight. Policy mistakes or other shocks will produce deviations of outcomes from target levels. But the models enforce discipline on the analysis of adjustment, ensure the consistency of policy measures, and provide a framework in which the prospects of meeting balance of payments and growth targets can be coherently discussed.'
15. For a more detailed analysis of the evidence supporting these conclusions see World Bank (1990) and (1992c) especially Chapters 2 and 6.

16. For instance at the Consultative Group Meeting for Egypt, 8–9 July 1991, the donors confirmed their strong support, including co-financing, for the creation of a social safety net and the Social Fund Project for Egypt; see Chairman's Report, 13 November 1991, restricted World Bank document.
17. See for instance Radetzki (1993) who demonstrates from the example of the Baltic Sea the devastating effect of the environmental neglect of socialist regimes on their neighbours.
18. This is not to suggest that rent-seeking behaviour does not exist in so-called stable democracies. In such societies rent-seeking increasingly takes recourse to the law as an instrument for the protection of rents while direct transfers diminish in importance. This may be a consequence of such devices being less exposed to scrutiny and public attack. The effective application of a consistent competition policy thus remains a priority task even in advanced and mature democratic societies. See Dichmann (1992).
19. An equally telling example in the environmental sphere is the dispute surrounding the development of the Narmada Valley in India; see the report of the Bradford Morse Commission on the Damadore Valley Project.

# References

Bacha, Edmer L. (1992) in Corbo et al.
Balassa, Bela (1989) New Directions in the World Economy, Basingstoke: Macmillan.
Bhagwati, J. N. (1982) 'Directly Unproductive, Profit-Seeking, DUP Activities', Journal of Political Economy 90 (October), 988–1002.
Chenery, Hollis (1974) Redistribution with Growth. Oxford: Oxford University Press.
Chenery, Hollis and Stout, A. M. (1966) 'Foreign Assistance and Economic Development', American Economic Review 56 (September).
Corbo, V. and Suh, Snag-Mok (eds) (1992) Structural Adjustment in a Newly Industrialized Country: The Korean Experience, Baltimore, MD and London: Johns Hopkins University Press.
Corbo, V., Fischer, Stanley and Webb, Steven B. (eds) (1992) Adjustment Lending Revisited: Policies to Restore Growth, A World Bank Symposium, Washington DC: World Bank.
Dasgupta, Partha and Göran-Mäler, Karl (1991) 'The Environment and Emerging Development Issues' in Proceedings of Annual Conference on Development Economics 1990, Washington DC: World Bank.
Dichmann, W. (1992) 'Rent Seeking als Resultat der Unvollständigkeit von Verträgen', List Forum für Wirtschafts- und Finanzpolitik 18 (4) Baden-Baden: Nomos Verlag.
Dornbusch, R. (1991) 'Policies to Move from Stabilization to Growth' in Proceedings of Annual Conference on Development Economics 1990, Washington DC: World Bank.
Fischer, S. (1987) 'Economic Growth and Economic Policy' in V. Corbo, M. Goldstein and M. Khan (eds) Growth-oriented Adjustment Programs, Washington DC: World Bank.
Furtado, Celso (1987) 'Underdevelopment: To Conform or To Reform' in Gerald M. Meier (ed.) Pioneers in Development, Oxford; Oxford University Press.
Harberger, Arnold C. (1987) 'Reflections in Social Project Evaluation' in Gerald M. Meier (ed.) Pioneers in Development, Oxford: Oxford University Press.
Hettich, W. and Winer, S. L. (1993) 'Economic Efficiency, Political Institutions and Policy Analysis', Kyklos 46, Basel: Helbig & Lichtenhahn.
Hirschmann, Albert O. (1981) 'The Rise and Decline of Development Economics' in Essays in Trespassing, New York: Cambridge University Press.
Jorgensen, S., Grosh, M. and Schachter, M. (eds) (1992) Bolivia's Answer to Poverty, Economic Crisis and Adjustment, Washington DC: World Bank.
Kennedy, Paul (1993) Preparing for the 21st Century, New York: Random House.
Krueger, A. O. (1974) 'The Political Economy of Rent-Seeking Society', American Economic Review 64, 291–303.
Krugman, Paul (1993) 'Toward a Counterrevolution in Development Theory' in Proceedings of Annual Conference on Development Economics 1992, Washington DC: World Bank.
Lamb, G. and Weaving, R. (eds (1992) Managing Policy Reform in the Real World, EDI Seminar Series, Washington DC: World Bank.
Lele, Uma and Nabi, Jjaz (eds) (1991) Transitions in Development: The Role of Aid and Commercial Flows, San Francisco, CA: International Center for Economic Growth.
Marer, Paul and Zecchini, Salvatore (eds) (1991) The Transition to a Market Economy, Vol. I. The Broad Issues, Paris: OECD.

Mosley, P., Harrigan, J. and Toye, J. (1991) *Aid and Power: The World Bank and Policy-Based Lending*, London: Routledge.

Nowzad, B. (1981) *The IMF and Its Critics*, Essays in International Finance No. 146, Princeton, NJ: Princeton University.

Olson, Mancur (1982) *The Rise and Decline of Nations: Economic Growth, Stagflation and Social Rigidities*, New Haven, CT: Yale University Press.

Radetzki, Marian (1993) 'Economic Growth and Environment', *World Bank Policy Research Bulletin* 4 (1) (January/February).

Salop, Joanne (1992) 'Reducing Poverty: Spreading the Word', *Finance and Development* 29 (4) (December), 2–4.

Shapley, D. (1993) *Promise and Power: The Life and Times of Robert McNamara*, Boston, MA, Toronto and London: Little, Brown & Co.

Taylor, L. (1987) 'IMF Conditionality: Incomplete Theory, Policy Malpractice' in R.J. Myers (ed.) *The Political Morality of the International Monetary Fund*, New Brunswick, NJ: Transaction Books.

Thomas, V. and Nash, J. (1991) *Best Practices in Trade Policy Reform*, Oxford: Oxford University Press.

Thomas, V., Chhibber, Ajay, Dailami, Mansoor and de Melo, Jaime (eds) (1991) *Restructuring Economies in Distress: Policy Reform and the World Bank*, Oxford: Oxford University Press.

UN Economic Commission Commission for Africa (1989) *African Alternative Framework to Structural Adjustment Programmes for Socio-Economic Recovery and Transformation*, E/ECA/CM. 15/6/Rev. 3, Addis Ababa: ECA.

Wapenhans, W. (1989) 'Gegenseitigkeit von Gesellschaftsordnung und Wirtschaftssystem' in *Demokratie und Marktwirtschaft – ein Kuppelprodukt?*, Cologne: Informedia Stiftung.

Wijnbergen, S. van, Anand, R., Chhibber, A. and Rocha, R. (1992) *External Debt, Fiscal Policy and Sustainable Growth in Turkey*, Baltimore, MD and London: Johns Hopkins University Press.

World Bank (1981) *Accelerated Development in Sub-Saharan Africa. An Agenda for Action*, Washington DC: World Bank.

World Bank (1989) *Structural Adjustment in Sub-Saharan Africa. Report on as Series of Five Senior Policy Seminars held in Africa*. EDI Policy Seminar Report No. 18, Washington DC: World Bank.

World Bank (1992a) *Third Report on Adjustment Lending: Mobilization of Private and Public Resources for Growth*. Washington DC: World Bank.

World Bank (1990, 1992b) *World Development Report*. New York: Oxford University Press.

World Bank (1992c) *Poverty Reduction Handbook*. Washington DC: World Bank.

# PART TWO
The Macroeconomic Effectiveness of Structural Adjustment Programmes

# 5 The State of Research on the Macroeconomic Effectiveness of Structural Adjustment Programmes in Sub-Saharan Africa

## SIMEON IBI AJAYI

Over the last two decades, and longer in some cases, Sub-Saharan African countries in general have been plagued by poor economic performance. While the level of performance has varied almost along the lines of the characteristic heterogeneity of Africa itself, most countries have been subjected to virtually the same kind of shocks. The economic deterioration which started in the late 1970s reached alarming proportions by the 1980s. The economic decline in Sub-Saharan Africa has been attributed to both external and internal factors. The external factors were the virtual stagnation of world trade in 1981–83, due primarily to recession in the industrialized countries, decline in the commodity terms of trade, rising world interest rates, decline in capital flows and natural and man-made calamities like drought, flood and war. The internal factors were attributed to macroeconomic policy errors such as currency misalignment, inappropriate trade policies, heavy taxation of farmers' output and an overextended public sector and parastatals which led to very high budget deficits and inflation. In addition, there was civil strife and political turbulence in some countries. The World Bank report prepared by Berg (World Bank, 1981) identified the (internal) domestic policy factors as the main cause of the economic deterioration in SSA countries since inappropriate policies over a long period of time led to the decline in agriculture, which is the mainstay of African economies. It has been further argued by Khan and Knight (1985), for example, that inappropriate exchange-rate policies may have compounded the negative effects of the adverse external factors. For most SSA countries, the 1980s was a lost decade.

Many SSA countries, in an attempt to reverse the decline in macroeconomic trends, adopted economic reforms assisted by multilateral institutions – mostly the World Bank and the International Monetary Fund. At the initiation of these programmes, the countries were characterized by low and declining incomes, both in absolute amount and *per capita*, rising external debt, low investment/GDP ratios, low savings/GDP ratios, declining growth in the value of exports, and mounting current account deficits, etc. The adjustment programmes adopted by SSA countries, with the concurrence of the World Bank and the International Monetary Fund, are little differentiated along country lines. Even though each country is treated separately, the general characteristics of the programmes have been the same.

The short- and the medium-run objectives of the adjustment programmes are the elimination of distortions in the economy and the restoration of macroeconomic equilibria. Emphasis in this regard is placed on ensuring the establishment of accurate price and incentive structures, and moves towards greater privatization and export orientation. It is generally believed that deregulation of the economy, with the free interplay of market forces which structural adjustment implies, will bring about the automatic removal of distortions. Put succinctly, 'structural adjustment programmes consist of policies aimed both at stabilizing the macroeconomy and at reforming the structure of incentives in various sectors of the economy and generally emphasize outward trade strategies' (Elbadawi *et al.*, 1992: 17). Conceptually, there is a second side to structural adjustment programmes, in addition to those policies designed to improve international competitiveness, such as changes in the real exchange rate. This can be compared to the conventional pair of scissors analogy in economics – the supply and demand aspects. The demand side of the structural adjustment programme aims at controlling inflationary trends and correcting temporary disequilibrium in the balance of payments through the utilization of expenditure-reducing policies. This is often referred to as the stabilization component of the programme. The supply-side policies, on the other hand, which are aimed at improving the efficiency of resource use and creating more appropriate incentives, emphasize a constellation of factors including the liberalization of trade, deregulation, reform of the public sector, enhancement of agricultural price incentives, the strengthening of institutions and the removal of obstacles to savings and investment. As can be seen, both demand and supply policies can be used to achieve an improvement in international competitiveness.

There are five sets of policy measures (Mosley, 1987) in the World Bank-sponsored structural adjustment lending programmes (SALs): (i) the mobilization of resources (involving fiscal and financial reforms and improved performance of the public sector); (ii) measures to enhance efficiency through the reform or privatization of public sector companies, price reform and the liberalization of imports and encouragement of direct foreign investment; (iii) trade liberalization (removal or reductions of restrictions such as quotas and tariffs and the promotion of exports); (iv) reform involving the introduction of user fees, greater privatization of services and the direction of resources to basic services; (v) strengthening the public sector through reform of the civil service and public companies, and improvement in the institutions which support the public sector. The difference between SALs and the World Bank-sponsored sectoral adjustment lending programmes (SECALs) is that the latter, though with a a similar orientation, are sector-specific and include more detailed measures.

# The Record of SAPs in Africa: The Macroeconomic Effects

In assessing the macroeconomic impacts of structural adjustment programmes in Sub-Saharan Africa, it is necessary to bear in mind that the macroeconomic effects differ from one country to another as a result of the intensity with which the programme is pursued, the relative strength of the economy before embarking on the programme, and other factors which will be explained later. Over the last ten years in some cases, and over the last five in others, many SSA countries have made substantial progress in the adoption, implementation and intensification of policy reforms. Of the 34 countries in SSA which had adjustment programmes in place in the 1980s, 23 started in 1986. Also 70% of the 114 new loans approved by the World Bank during the decade for policy reforms were made in the period 1986–90 (Elbadawi et al., 1992).

There is now a vast body of literature on the macroeconomic impacts of structural adjustment in Sub-Saharan Africa. Some of these studies have been more specific in assessing the impacts of SAPs on health status (Bell and Reich, 1989; Musgrove, 1987; Kanji et al., 1991), on the poor (Husain, 1992a; Cornia et al., 1992), on living conditions, particularly those of children and other vulnerable groups (Cornia et al., 1987). In addition, there are country case studies dealing with many aspects of structural adjustment policies, such as Wagao (1992) for Tanzania, Tinguiri (1992) for Niger and Seshamani (1992) for Zambia – part of the Cornia et al. (1992) study.

Assessments of the macroeconomic impacts of structural adjustment programmes have not only been varied, but in most cases the various studies dealing with the issues have come to conclusions that are mutually contradictory. The differences in conclusions arise not only when different research methodologies are used, but even when the same methodological approach is adopted. Classified along the lines of the institutional origin of the research, the various studies fall broadly into two major groups – the World Bank-IMF type studies carried out by the staff of the two multilateral institutions and independent research carried out by other scholars. In general, studies in the first category have tended until recently to be more supportive of structural adjustment programmes.

A good starting point for an overview of the second category of scholars is Cornia's statement that:

> adjustment has not removed most structural obstacles to sustainable long-term development. While it is likely that microeconomic efficiency has improved, the IMF's and World Bank's insistence on increased exports of traditional primary commodities, rapid import liberalization and drastic cuts in public investment are retarding Africa's recovery and pushing many African countries away from achieving the long-term objective of greater self-sufficiency, an efficient manufacturing sector, diversified export composition and markets and increased export volume. In the African context, the almost exclusive emphasis of structural adjustment on relative prices, privatization, financial and trade liberalization and interest rate increases has generated extremely modest supply responses which are much smaller than those anticipated at the beginning of the decade (Cornia, 1991: 35).

The disappointing aspect of the structural adjustment programme is also expressed by Stewart: 'The stabilisation and adjustment policies advocated by the IMF and the World Bank and widely adopted in Africa have not succeeded in restoring growth in most countries; indeed, they have often been accompanied by continued economic deterioration' (Stewart, 1992: 332).

The macroeconomic variables used for assessment in Jespersen (1992) include current account/GDP, deficit/GDP, investment/GDP, and manufacturing/GDP ratios, inflation, primary school enrolment, and growth in exports. The changes in primary school enrolment allow an assessment of whether adjustment has involved social costs, while the changes in the ratio of manufacturing to GDP allow an assessment of structural changes within the economy. Assessing the stabilization and structural adjustment performance of a number of African countries, Jespersen shows that of the 24 countries which undertook adjustment programmes in the 1980s, only 6 managed to achieve lower inflation rates and lower deficits (relative to GDP) in the current account balance and government budget simultaneously. For 6 countries the macroeconomic imbalances at the end of the 1980s were as severe as before the adjustment programmes started. With a few exceptions, the achievement of stabilization has involved severe losses in the fields of growth, investment and welfare. Only 5 of the 18 countries which stabilized their economies in the 1980s recorded a positive growth in GDP *per capita*. With a few exceptions, the economic situation in most African countries has not improved since the adoption of structural adjustment programmes. Capital accumulation slowed down in 20 of the countries which embarked on structural adjustment. In 1987–88, the unweighted average gross investment/GDP ratio was 30% lower than in 1981–82. Enrolment rates in elementary education declined over the 1980s in 60% of adjusting countries. The share of manufacturing in GDP increased in the period 1982–89 in only 6 of the 24 countries examined. Turning to growth in the export sector, the volume of exports increased in 11 countries (6 of which were at rates above 5%). In the other 13, the volume of exports stagnated or decreased. In conclusion,

> at the end of almost a decade of adjustment efforts, sub-Saharan Africa found itself still faced with the usual problems of overdependence on primary commodities, a stagnant or shrinking industrial base, and sluggish and highly unstable growth in the food sector. . . . In addition, in 75 per cent of the countries undertaking adjustment programmes, capital accumulation and primary enrolment rates were lower than in the early 1980s. (Jespersen, 1992: 15, 18)

Husain assessed adjustment programmes on the basis of intermediate and final results; 'the intermediate results indicate the extent to which the initial policy distortions have been corrected. The final results show the economic outcomes of reforms over a chosen period of time' (Husain, 1992b: 3). Four intermediate indicators were used: the real effective exchange rate, the fiscal deficit as a percentage of GDP, the inflation rate and the real producer prices index, while the 5 final indicators used were the growth rates of GDP, exports, imports, investment and *per capita* consumption. These indicators were chosen to signify the impacts of programmes in the period 1986–90, the reference period being 1980–85, a period of crisis, both financial and economic, in most SSA countries. After explaining the reasons for the exclusion of some countries, the analysis was based on a total of 14 African countries which, though different in terms of population size, natural endowments and structural features, could nevertheless be grouped together: Nigeria, Ghana, Kenya, Tanzania, Zambia, Zimbabwe, Guinea, Madagascar, Burundi, Namibia, Botswana, Mauritius, Malawi and The Gambia. Husain came to the following conclusions:

- The most significant progress had been made in the real effective exchange rate; most countries had made strides in depreciating their currencies.
- Positive impacts had been made in containing inflation. Inflation had declined from 25% in 1985–87 to only 10% in 1989–90. There was no systematic relationship between the change in the real effective exchange rate and inflation. The price level in most countries that devalued their currencies had already adjusted to the much higher parallel exchange rates which did not result in inflationary pressures.

- Significant progress had been made in reducing fiscal deficits. While variations existed between countries, the deficits had declined from 7.3% to 5.6% of GDP during the adjustment period.
- The movement in real producer prices had been favourable to farmers. This was made possible by depreciation of the exchange rate and liberalization of agricultural marketing.

Turning to the indicators of final outcomes, Husain asserted that the GDP growth rate was twice as high as in the early 1980s and even higher than the historical trends of the 1960s and 1970s. Export expansion in volume terms was growing at a rate of 6% per annum. The decline in *per capita* consumption, though arrested, remained stagnant. While imports and investments rose faster than in the early 1980s, they were still lower than the historical averages. The level of domestic savings was very low, thus causing excessive dependence on foreign savings for investment.

Various World Bank studies have been carried out to assess the macro-economic effects of structural adjustment programmes (World Bank, 1988a, b, 1990b, 1991). In order to assess the effects of programmes in SSA, the various countries are divided into three groups: early intensive adjustment lending (EIAL) countries, other adjustment lending (OAL) countries and non-adjustment lending (NAL) countries.[1] The World Bank (1988a) study attempted to assess the impacts of adjustment programmes on such performance indicators as GDP growth, investment, savings, export growth, the real exchange rate, the current account balance, the budget deficit, inflation and external debt. These indicators measured performance in four policy areas: growth, external balance, internal balance and external debt. Two approaches were adopted for evaluating the performance of these indicators. First, a comparison was made between the performance indicators during the three years before the start of the adjustment programme and the first three years of the programme. Second, a comparison was made between the unweighted average values of the indicators for all countries receiving adjustment lending (the AL countries) and the NAL (non-adjusting) countries, three years before and after the implementation of the programme.

The results showed that the performance of adjustment lending countries in SSA was mixed. There was evidence of improvement in two key imbalances – the current account of the balance of payments and the budget deficit. The external debt situation also improved. The longer-term effects, however, were not so favourable. The following three key variables were unfavourable compared with the NAL countries: GDP growth, the invest-ment/GDP ratio and the inflation rate. The poor performance of GDP growth and the investment/GDP ratio 'suggest that the longer-run prospects for rapid growth have not been enhanced through the policy interventions that have been made. The poor inflation performance suggests that the favourable real exchange rate indication may not continue into the future' (World Bank, 1990c: 22). These findings, which relate to all countries and not necessarily only to Sub-Saharan African countries, are similar to those in the studies by the World Bank and UNDP (1989), Balassa (1988), World Bank (1988b), Thomas and Chhibber (1989) and UN/ECA (1989). The World Bank's first report on adjustment lending

(World Bank, 1988a) concluded that the 30 countries receiving adjustment loans before 1985 performed better on average by the end of 1987 than developing countries not receiving such loans. The World Bank's second Report on Adjustment Lending (World Bank, 1990b) focused on the contributions of adjustment lending to sustainable growth and examined, along with the rate of growth of output, the performance of a set of usual intermediate indicators – the savings, investment and export ratios. Its analyses took into account the fact that the performance of an adjusting country is the result of policies that would have been in effect in the absence of the Bank's adjustment lending, the effects of a Bank-supported programme, the world economic situation and other exogenous shocks to the economy such as droughts, earthquakes, floods, etc. In order to isolate the net contributions of a Bank-supported programme, a counterfactual was created by estimating the effects on performance of: the external shocks in the current period (terms of trade, real interest rates and actual external financing); the initial values of performance indicators (GDP growth, and the ratio of savings and investment to GDP); and the economic policies in the pre-programme period as indicated by the real exchange rate, the fiscal deficit to GDP ratio and the annual rate of inflation. Using the same classification as in the previous study, and making appropriate adjustments for non-programme characteristics such as the initial conditions, external shocks and policies before the programme was put in place, the report concluded that, for all country groups, GDP growth slowed substantially in the period 1970–80 and 1981–84 and then recovered in 1985–88 for both groups of adjustment lending countries. The GDP growth rate continued to slow down in the NAL countries. In the EIAL countries the investment to GDP ratio in current prices fell progressively in the 1980s, while for the OAL and NAL countries the investment ratio rose in 1981–84 and fell in 1985–88. For all groups of countries in 1981–84, domestic savings as a share of GDP declined, but recovered somewhat in the period 1985–88. The export to GDP ratio increased by almost 4 percentage points on average between 1970–80 and 1986–88, while the export ratio of NAL countries declined somewhat over the period.

Two recent studies (Elbadawi, 1992a and Elbadawi *et al.*, 1992) provided analyses of the macroeconomic effects of structural adjustment programmes in SSA following the Bank's classification used in the general reports discussed above (see Annex 5.1). In the first study it is asserted that

despite the similarity in terms of external shocks experienced by EIAL and NAL countries of SSA, the economic performance in the last group has been uniformly superior to the first. Also, despite witnessing twice as many negative external shocks compared to OAL countries, the NAL group has performed better especially in terms of domestic inflation and exports (Elbadawi, 1992a, p. 21).

The second study (Elbadawi *et al.*, 1992) investigated the contributions of the World Bank adjustment programme to five indicators of performance: exports/GDP, growth in real GDP, gross domestic investment/GDP, savings/GDP and the inflation rate. The study utilized three methodological approaches: the 'before-and-after' method and the control-group and modified-control-group approaches. The details of these approaches are discussed in the following section. The initial conditions were the period 1970–80, while the adjustment period was defined as 1985–89 and the pre-adjustment period as 1981–84. The

**Table 5.1.** *Macroeconomic Performance by Groups of Countries 1970–89*

| | 1970–80 | 1981–84 | 1985–89 | | 1970–80 | 1981–84 | 1985–89 |
|---|---|---|---|---|---|---|---|
| | Real GDP growth | | | | Investment/GDP ratio | | |
| EIAL | 3.7 | 0.1 | 3.7 | | 24.7 | 18.4 | 16.9 |
| OAL | 3.2 | 3.1 | 3.0 | | 20.5 | 21.5 | 18.7 |
| NAL | 6.0 | 4.5 | 2.3 | | 21.1 | 18.2 | 17.3 |
| | Domestic savings/GDP | | | | Exports/GDP ratio | | |
| EIAL | 16.1 | 9.9 | 11.0 | | 30.2 | 27.7 | 29.6 |
| OAL | 6.4 | 5.9 | 5.3 | | 21.0 | 19.6 | 18.5 |
| NAL | 12.8 | 10.6 | 15.0 | | 30.2 | 32.9 | 30.3 |
| | Inflation | | | | | | |
| EIAL | 14.9 | 21.0 | 15.0 | | | | |
| OAL | 14.8 | 24.5 | 24.6 | | | | |
| NAL | 10.9 | 8.3 | 5.0 | | | | |

*Source*: Elbadawi *et al.*, 1992: 52.

countries were sub-divided as usual into the three major categories: EIAL, OAL and NAL. The country macroeconomic performance is shown in Table 5.1. A comparison of the means of economic performance indicators for EIAL countries between 1981–84 and 1985–89 revealed that there was an improvement in real GDP growth from 0.1% to 3.7%. Similarly, there was improvement in the export/GDP and the savings/GDP ratios – in the case of the former, from 27.7% to 29.6% and in the latter from 9.9% to 11%. Inflation fell from 21% to 15%. Real GDP growth and the investment/GDP and exports/GDP ratios fell in the OAL and NAL countries. The NAL countries experienced a substantial increase in the savings/GDP ratio and a large fall in inflation. These findings are in conformity with another World Bank study using similar methodology (World Bank, 1991).

**Table 5.2.** *Effects of Structural Adjustment Programmes on Changes in Various Indicators: Modified-control-group Estimates for Sub-Saharan Africa, Comparing 1985–89 with 1981–84*

| Change in GDP growth | Change in EXP/GDP[a] | Change in GDI/GDP[b] | Change in GDS/GDP[c] | Change in inflation |
|---|---|---|---|---|
| −0.014 (−0.830) | 0.080 (2.459)[d] | −0.084 (−2.314)[d] | −0.083 (−1.574)[e] | 0.122 (1.244)[e] |

Notes:
[a] Change in exports/GDP ratio
[b] Change in Gross Domestic Investment/GDP ratio
[c] Change in Gross Domestic Savings/GDP ratio
[d] Statistically significant at the 5% level
[e] Statistically significant at the 10% level
t-statistics in parentheses

Source: *ibid.*

In applying the modified-control-group approach, an econometric assessment of the effectiveness of the structural adjustment programme on economic performance was utilized in order to rectify the inherent weaknesses of the before-and-after method (see Table 5.2). Using this approach, it was found that structural adjustment programmes contributed to increasing exports in a significant way – a finding attributed to the rate of implementation of trade-related or exchange-rate policies, which was, on average, higher than in other policy areas. It was also found that adjustment lending had not specifically affected economic growth in a positive way and had contributed to a statistically significant drop in the investment/GDP ratio in the EIAL countries. While this finding is inconsistent with the World Bank's third report on adjustment lending (World Bank, 1992), it is nevertheless consistent with other views within the Bank as expressed by the Bank's chief economist, who asserted that there was much to be desired in terms of restoring growth and social welfare to Sub-Saharan Africa (Summers, 1992). The marginal decline in investment for SSA countries was estimated to be 8.4%. After controlling for other factors, adjustment programmes were estimated to have increased the exports/GDP ratio of the EIAL countries of SSA by about 8%. It was found that adjustment did not significantly affect inflation, however.

# The Methodology of Assessment and Data Issues

As indicated above, three methodological approaches are used nowadays to assess the impacts of structural adjustment programmes on macroeconomic performance. The 'before-and-after' approach is by far the most popular tool of analysis because of its simplicity. In this approach, the performance of selected indicators is compared after the initiation of the adjustment programme with the same set of indicators prior to the initiation of the programme. Specifically, some macroeconomic data such as the growth in GDP, exports, investment/GDP, etc. are compared in the period following the initiation of the programme with these indicators during a base period before adjustment began. The differences in the indicators is then usually attributed to the programme effects. Thus, the 'before-and-after' estimator is simply the mean change in the target variable over some relevant period (Corbo and Rojas, 1992). The significance of the estimator is usually tested by using the standard t-test and/or non-parametric statistical tests.

While the 'before-and-after' approach gives a fairly useful descriptive analysis of what has happened, it fails to answer the question of the effectiveness of programmes. In addition, it assumes 'other things being equal' (Elbadawi et al., 1992). This assumption is not really trivial, since it is not known whether the change in the performance of the macroeconomic indicators can be directly attributed to the programme's implementation or to other exogenous factors unrelated to the programme. Indeed, 'the situation prevailing before the programme is not likely to be good predictor of what would have happened in the absence of a programme, given that non-programme determinants can and do change from period to period' (World Bank, 1990a: 23). The 'before-and-after' approach is incapable of distinguishing between programme and non-programme determinants of macroeconomic outcomes.

The second approach is the 'control-group' approach. In this approach, the average changes in macroeconomic performance variables are compared for programme and non-programme countries and the difference is attributed to the effects of the programmes. Essentially, this methodology utilizes the behaviour of a group of non-programme countries to estimate what would have happened in the programme group in the absence of adjustment programmes. This approach assumes that countries face the same external (global economic) environment and does not take account of specific country characteristics which are likely to affect economic performance. Thus, the results are likely to be biased if the external environments that countries face are different. A good example given in the literature refers to a situation where programme countries experienced temporary negative shocks in the pre-programme period, 'a comparison of changes in aggregate performance between programme and non-programme countries will overstate the true independent effect of the programmes' (World Bank, 1990a: 24). This overstatement of the true real effects of the programmes is known as 'sample selection bias'.

The third approach is the 'modified-control-group' approach (sometimes referred to as the 'modified-control-group' estimator). This approach is used to eliminate the inherent weaknesses in the two other approaches. It therefore takes account of the changing external economic environment of each country and identifies the particular differences between the two types of countries – that is, the programme and non-programme countries. These are then controlled for in the resulting economic performance. In order to address the issue adequately, an estimation is made for the additional contributions of programmes for given initial conditions and exogenous shocks. As pointed out by Elbadawi *et al.* (1992), this requires the endogenization of the decision to participate in adjustment programmes. Thus the 'modified-control-group' methodology allows estimation of the marginal contribution of adjustment programmes in adjusting countries while: (i) explicitly taking account of the potential endogeneity of the decision to participate in an adjustment programme, since the same non-programme factors that influence performance in the pre-programme period are likely to influence the participation decision; (ii) controlling for other factors unrelated to programmes that also affect performance; and (iii) adjusting for the counterfactual policy stance that would have prevailed in the absence of the programme (Elbadawi *et al.*, 1992: 27). This approach was utilized to identify the marginal effects of reform programmes on macroeconomic performance in EIAL countries of SSA relative to the OAL and NAL countries of the region, including low-income countries in each category. The two possible periods compared were 1985–89 and 1981–84.

The three approaches have been used at various times in World Bank-IMF studies to assess if countries that initiated adjustment programmes with the World Bank performed better than they would have done in the absence of such programmes. In general, the time periods were 1970–80, 1981–84 and 1985–89 (or 1986–90) and in most of the studies, data were used in both current and constant prices (Corbo *et al.*, 1992; Elbadawi *et al.*, 1992; Corbo and Rojas, 1992).

Much of the data that have been used by various studies for measuring the macroeconomic impacts of structural adjustment programmes have been drawn from country data, but the preponderant data were drawn from international publications of the World Bank and the International Monetary Fund. The credibility and the degree of reliability which can be placed on the data depend on the accuracy and the timeliness of data coming from the various countries, and the accuracy of estimates made by the multilateral institutions where data are not available at the country level. There have been cases in the various studies where certain countries have had to be omitted from the analyses because of the non-availability of current information/data. It was not possible, for example, in the Jespersen (1992) study to complete information for Equatorial Guinea, Gabon, Gambia, Guinea and São Tomé. It should also be recognized that, among these sets of countries that are grouped together, there are striking variations in terms of both internal factors (such as strife and civil unrest) and the external economic environments which they face. Consequently, there may be possible outliers in each of these groups which may distort some of the conclusions.

It is not possible to overemphasize the need for good-quality data since policy decisions can only be meaningfully made in the light of accurate and consistent data. African data in most cases are characterised by inconsistency and non-availability. There is need therefore to improve on the quality of African data as well as ensuring that the data are up-to-date.

# What Lessons Have We Learnt about Structural Adjustment in SSA?

Many SSA countries adopted World Bank and IMF structural adjustment programmes when there was virtually no other economically viable choice in sight. The initial reluctance of SSA countries to initiate SAPs was not unconnected with the high degree of scepticism about the success of such programmes in countries that had adopted them and the hardship that had followed in their trail because of the long gestation period required for only minor effectiveness. Increasingly, however, and in spite of initial doubts and uncertainty, quite a large number of African countries have embarked on structural adjustment programmes. Analyses of the factors influencing the decision to participate in such programmes point to the importance of the macroeconomic policies, economic performance and political stability prevailing in the periods preceding adjustment. Of particular importance in the decision process were the country's growth performance, the investment/GDP ratio and the foreign debt burden (Elbadawi et al., 1992). In most cases, the political pressures of the creditor nations were the dominant factor.

A number of lessons have been learnt about structural adjustment programmes in SSA, both by the countries which have embarked on them and the institutions that originally believed and still believe in the efficacy of adjustment programmes as the only panacea for Africa's economic malaise. The first lesson, from the perspective of African countries, is that there is no 'quick fix'. In some cases, the situation had deteriorated very badly before the structural adjustment programmes were undertaken. In the process, the programmes have not turned the economy around as quickly as was expected. Indeed, in most cases the economic situation has worsened. The second is that the issue of 'getting prices right' as the dictum of policy effectiveness has not worked in an environment where the infrastructural facilities leave much to be desired, as is the case in many Sub-Saharan African countries. The third lesson relates to the external environment faced by a number of African countries. These environments have, in most cases, been hostile and unconducive to growth and development. The trade environments, for example, have been no more favourable to African countries in the 1980s than they were in the 1970s. Fourthly, the heavy external burden with the debt overhang has done a lot to retard growth in SSA. A number of African countries have become debt-distressed, while the severity of debt has increased in others in recent times. In 1990, debt service on bilateral funds in Sub-Saharan Africa was estimated at US$2.8 billion, while the debt service to the multilateral institutions amounted to US$2.7 bn (Stewart, 1992). Fifthly, adjustment is a painful process. In many African countries adjustment is not only hurting the poor but is also creating a new category of poor people. Finally, putting in place structural adjustment programmes is not enough. From time to time it has been necessary to adopt compensatory policies to mitigate the unintended negative impacts of structural adjustment programmes. This has inevitably created not only a lot of strain on resource allocation and efficiency but has also adversely affected economic performance in many cases.

The noticeably poor macroeconomic performance of SSA countries involved in structural adjustment programmes has been attributed to a host of factors (Elbadawi et al., 1992; Jespersen, 1992; Cornia et al., 1992). The first is the allegation that some African countries have pursued some of the policies in a half-hearted manner, thereby making the full realization of the positive effects of adjustment impossible. It has been found, however, that about 75% of all programmes were fully or substantially implemented in Africa in the 1980s (World Bank, 1988a; 1990a). Given this high rate of compliance, poor compliance cannot be adduced as the main cause of poor macroeconomic performance. It has also been claimed that the uncertainty created by the 'stop-go' policy of implementation constitutes a major impediment to supply response. While some countries have not been consistent in the pursuit of structural adjustment programmes, many countries in SSA have been consistent. Secondly, the external environment has deteriorated badly since the early 1980s. The often quoted example in this area is the decline in the terms of trade, which in essence is the effect of dependence on commodity trade, and the quantitative and non-quantitative restrictions on trade. Commodity terms of trade declined on average between 1980 and 1990; the share of exports from developing countries in general subject to non-tariff barriers rose from 19.5% in 1981 to 20.6% in 1984 (World Bank, 1986).

The third cause of poor macroeconomic performance is inadequate financing. New financing was not forthcoming to compensate for the deterioration in the terms of trade. Fourth, the protracted deadlock in the debt problem meant a growing drain of resources for debt servicing. Fifth, most African countries were dependent on import contraction, the net effect of which was a depressive effect on growth and investment because of the imperfect substitutability between imported intermediate inputs and domestically produced goods (Ndulu, 1991). Sixth, the failure of the SAP is attributed to the wrong premise on which it is based, namely the assumption of fully competitive markets and well-developed institutions. It is claimed that markets are imperfect in Africa and financial institutions are poorly developed. Indeed, many SSA countries are characterized by poor infrastructural facilities, low levels of education, etc. It has been further claimed that while currency devaluation is expected to increase the competitiveness of productive sectors, in particular the tradeables, the rigidities inherent in the processes of production, distribution and consumption make any expected rapid switching of resources into the tradeable sector difficult, if not impossible, in some cases. If anything, raising the cost of imported productive inputs rapidly, as happens when there is a massive devaluation of the currency, erodes the competitiveness of domestic enterprises and intensifies inflationary pressures.

Seventh, the market interest-rate structure which has developed in some African countries has not only failed to elicit the intended savings behaviour but has also stifled business investment initiatives, since the margin between profit and investment costs has been eroded. Eighth, the ambitiousness of adjustment programmes and the exaggerated improvements in economic performance expected may be the cause of disappointment. Ninth, structural adjustment programmes generate negative effects which have to be combated from time to time. Policy instruments and resources for dealing with these negative effects are often limited in Sub-Saharan Africa. The limitations of policy instruments, and financial resources in particular, affect the effectiveness of programmes. Lastly, poor economic performance can be attributed to the poor design and implementation of structural adjustment programmes. Since these programmes in general are not country-specific, they fail to take cognizance of the particular characteristics of different African economies which are in most cases highly relevant to success.

## Summary and Conclusions

Over the past decade, the economic fortunes of Sub-Saharan African countries have declined, compared with the situation in the 1960s in most countries and in the 1970s in some others, despite the initiation and implementation of structural adjustment programmes in the 1980s. The results of the different empirical analyses conflict in some ways with the IMF-World Bank-type studies which were, until recently, more supportive of structural adjustment programmes. Nevertheless, a number of results with regard to the macroeconomic impacts of the programmes stand out. The fact that the marginal contributions of adjustment programmes have not had a significant positive effect on overall growth in SSA and have had a disheartening effect on investment is not only worrying but also casts doubt on the emergence of light at the end of the seemingly long tunnel through which a lot of African countries are passing. Given what we do know, there is a convincing need to judge the success of structural adjustment programmes from two intertwined perspectives. It is necessary to examine the extent to which the programmes have succeeded in eliminating the components of Sub-Saharan African crises. Specifically, has adjustment succeeded in controlling inflation, eliminating distortions in the economy, fostering investment and growth and diversifying the export basket? And have the goals of adjustment programmes been achieved without costs?

The ideal situation is one in which structural adjustment programmes are accompanied by 'non-negative' changes in a number of macroeconomic indicators such as output, investment, etc. The growing literature on 'adjustment with a human face', 'growth-oriented adjustment' and 'the social dimension of adjustment' point to the fact that this is not the case. Judged from the second perspective, adjustment programmes are assessed in terms of their ability to remove distortions and bottlenecks, such as the limited industrial base, the distorted trade structures, the low level of human resource development, etc. which are responsible for the economic malaise afflicting African countries. The removal of such distortions is likely to result in more balanced growth and enable the achievement of long-term development goals. Seen from these two perspectives, a set of questions logically arise (Cornia *et al.*, 1992):

- Has the dependence on food imports been reduced or totally eliminated?
- Has the export base been diversified and has there been a significant movement from commodity-based to other forms of production?
- How has the quality of life been improved as a result of adjustment?
- Has the resource base of African countries improved?

While it would be illogical to assume that the initiation/implementation of structural adjustment programmes in SSA countries has worsened the economic situation, it is appropriate to claim that their implementation has failed to bring about statistically significant positive impacts on macroeconomic variables in many countries. Indeed, Stewart (1992: 332) has pointed out that

> in many respects the policies are pushing African economies away from a desirable long-term structure especially because they are dampening local capabilities, reorienting economies towards heavy specialisation in export agriculture (or other primary products) and not permitting a build-up of dynamic comparative advantage in non-traditional agriculture and industry.

Thus, the policy conclusions based on what we do know about the macroeconomic impacts of structural adjustment programmes at the aggregative level in SSA are very important.

The issue of economic performance in SSA has to be seen in its multidimensional aspects, taking due cognizance of the international dimensions in particular. The return to the path of economic growth may be difficult for a number of African countries within the context of huge external indebtedness and a high debt-service ratio, which is consuming a significant proportion of resources. Even though debt forgiveness has been the subject of discussion at many international fora, there is need for more concrete action with regard to African countries if the issues of the growth and development of SSA countries are indeed to become realizable. Effective action in this area will release a lot of investible resources needed for growth to a sizeable number of African countries.

While free market forces no doubt have inherent advantages, the important roles of government as an engine of growth in many African countries cannot be ignored. Thus, investments in infrastructures, human capital and technology are crucial for African prosperity. It is necessary to ensure that investments in education and health, the effects of which are not noticeable in the short run, are not tampered with during the course of structural adjustment programmes. Some SSA countries, as part of the belt-tightening in the adjustment process, have reduced investments in these areas, thus courting disaster in the not too distant future. In addition, government should still play the role of umpire through the provision of the necessary enabling environment for the private sector.

Not only are there differences between African countries, Africa itself is different in significant ways from other developing regions. There is need therefore to give prominence to these differences in the design, structure and implementation of structural adjustment programmes if success, perceived as substantial improvement in economic performance, is to be achieved in any meaningful way.

It is important to point out that the various aggregative studies covering the macroeconomic impacts of structural adjustment programmes in SSA are very important as they give a broad view of the economic situation and economic performance. There is a need, however, to continue to study the macroeconomic impacts of structural adjustment programmes on a country-by-country basis and also to study the impacts of adjustment on different sectors and groups within each economy. Further research efforts should be devoted to these areas. In addition, it is necessary to focus on the positive long-run impacts of structural adjustment programmes and how to achieve them in SSA countries.

## Note

1. EIAL countries received two or more SALs or three or more adjustment loans (SALs or SECALs) before 1986; OAL countries started a programme after 1985 or received fewer than two SALs or fewer than three adjustment loans before 1986; and NAL countries did not participate in adjustment in the period 1980–88 (Elbadawi et al., 1992).

## References

Ajayi, S. Ibi (1991a) *The Macroeconomic Approach to External Debt: The Case of Nigeria*, African Economic Research Consortium Research Paper No. 8. Nairobi: Initiative Publishers.

Ajayi, S. Ibi (1991b) 'Reflections on the Linkages Between Macroeconomic Variables and the Health Sector', Paper prepared for ICO. Geneva: WHO.

Ajayi, S. Ibi (1992) *An Economic Analysis of Capital Flight From Nigeria*, Policy Research Working Paper No. 993. Washington DC: World Bank.

Balassa, B. (1988) *Quantitative Appraisal of Adjustment Lending*, Policy Research Working Paper No. 79, Washington DC: World Bank.

Bell, D. E. and Reich, M. R. (eds) (1989) *Health, Nutrition and Economic Crises: Approaches to Policy in the Third World*, Cambridge, MA: Harvard University Press.

Corbo, V., Fischer, S. and Webb, S. B. (eds) (1992) *Adjustment Lending Revisited: Policies to Restore Growth*, A World Bank Symposium. Washington DC: World Bank.

Corbo, V. and Rojas, P. (1992) 'World Bank-Supported Adjustment Programmes: Country Performance and Effectiveness' in Corbo et al.

Cornia, G. A. (1991) *Is Adjustment Conducive to Long-Term Development? The Case of Africa in the 1980s*, Innocenti Occasional Papers Economic Policy Series, No. 21. Florence: Spedale degli Innocenti.

Cornia, G. A., Jolly, R. and Stewart, F. (eds) (1987) *Adjustment with a Human Face*, Vol. 1. Oxford: Clarendon Press.

Cornia, G. A., van der Hoeven, R. and Mkandawire, T. (eds) (1992) *Africa's Recovery in the 1990s: From Stagnation and Adjustment to Human Development*, A UNICEF Study. London: Macmillan.

Elbadawi, I. (1991) 'Economic Performance and Effectiveness of World Bank-Supported Adjustment Programmes in sub-Saharan Africa', unpublished paper. Washington DC: World Bank.

Elbadawi, I. (1992a) *World Bank Adjustment Lending and Economic Performance in Sub-Saharan Africa*, Policy Research Working Paper No. 1001. Washington DC: World Bank.

Elbadawi, I. (1992b) *Real Overvaluation, Terms of Trade Shocks and the Cost to Agriculture in sub-Saharan Africa*, Policy Research Working Paper No. 859. Washington DC: World Bank.

Elbadawi, I., Ghura, D. and Uwujaren, G. (1992) *World Bank Adjustment Lending and Economic Performance in Sub-Saharan Africa in the 1980s*, Policy Research Working Paper No. 1000. Washington DC: World Bank.

Husain, I. (1992a) 'Adjustment and the Impact on the Poor: The Case of Africa', Paper presented at EDI/ADB Seminar on Adjustment and Poverty held in Abidjan, 9–12 March. Washington DC: World Bank.

Husain, I. (1992b) 'Structural Adjustment in sub-Saharan Africa: The Record, Lessons and Prospects', Keynote address at the Seminar on 'Structural Adjustment in Low-Income Countries', organized by the Food Studies Group, Queen Elizabeth House, Oxford, 22–24 March. Washington DC: World Bank.

Jespersen, E. (1992) 'External Shocks, Adjustment Policies and Economic and Social Performance' in Cornia *et al.*

Kanji, M., Kanji, N. and Manji, F. (1991) 'From Development to Sustained Crisis: Structural Adjustment, Equity and Health', *Social Science and Medicine* 33(9), 985–93.

Khan, M.S. (1990) 'Exchange Rate Policies of Developing Countries with External Shocks', *The Pakistan Development Review*, 25 (3), 403–421.

Khan, M.S. and Knight, M.D. (1985) *Fund-Supported Adjustment Programmes and Economic Growth*, IMF Occasional Paper No. 41. Washington DC: International Monetary Fund.

Mosley, P. (1987) *Conditionality as Bargaining Process: Structural Adjustment Lending, 1980–86*, Princeton, NJ: Princeton Papers in International Finance.

Musgrove, P. (1987) 'The Economic Crisis and Its Impact on Health and Health Care in Latin America and the Caribbean', *International Journal of Health Services*, 17 (3).

Ndulu, B.J. (1991) 'Growth and Adjustment in sub-Saharan Africa' in A. Chhibber and S. Fischer (eds) *Economic Reform in sub-Saharan Africa, A Symposium*. Washington DC: World Bank.

Seshamani, V. (1992) 'The Economic Policies of Zambia in the 1980s: Towards Structural Transformation with a Human Focus?' in Cornia *et al.*

Stewart, F. (1992) 'Short-Term Policies for Long-Term Development' in Cornia *et al.*

Summers, L. (1992) 'The Challenges of Development: Some Lessons of History for sub-Saharan Africa', *Finance and Development* 29 (3).

Thomas, V. and Chhibber, A. (eds) (1989) *Adjustment Lending: How It Has Worked, How It Can Be Improved*. Washington DC: World Bank.

Tinguiri, K.L. (1992) 'Stabilisation without Structural Adjustment: The case of Niger, 1982–89' in Cornia *et al.*

UN Economic Commission for Africa (1989) *African Alternative Framework to Structural Adjustment Programmes for Socio-economic Recovery and Transformation*. E/ECA/CM, 15/6/Rev. 3. Addis Ababa: ECA.

Wagao, J.H. (1992) 'Adjustment Policies in Tanzania, 1981–89: The Impact of Growth, Structure and Human Welfare' in Cornia *et al.*

World Bank (1981) *Accelerated Development in Sub-Saharan Africa: An Agenda for Action* Washington DC: World Bank.

World Bank (1986) *World Development Report*. New York: Oxford University Press for the World Bank.

World Bank (1988a) *Adjustment Lending: An Evaluation of Ten Years of Experience*, Policy and Research Series No. 1. Washington DC: World Bank.

World Bank (1988b) *The Challenges of Hunger in Africa: A Call for Action*. Washington DC: World Bank.

World Bank (1990a) *Adjustment Lending Policies for Sustainable Growth*, Policy and Research Series No. 14. Washington DC: World Bank.

World Bank (1990b) *Report on Adjustment Lending II: Policies for the Recovery of Growth*, Washington DC: World Bank.

World Bank (1990c) *Making Adjustment Work for the Poor: A Framework for Policy Reform in Africa*. Washington DC: World Bank.

World Bank (1992) *Adjustment Lending and Mobilization of Private and Public Resources for Growth*, Policy and Research Series No. 22. Washington DC: World Bank.

World Bank/UNDP (1989) *Africa's Adjustment and Growth*. Washington DC: World Bank/UNDP.

**Annex 5.1.** *World Bank Country Classification, 1992*

1. EIAL (Early Intensive-Adjustment-Lending Countries)

| | |
|---|---|
| Ghana | Kenya |
| Madagascar | Malawi |
| Nigeria | Senegal |
| Tanzania | Togo |
| Zambia | Mauritius |
| Mauritania | Côte d'Ivoire |

2. OAL (Other Adjustment-Lending Countries)

| | |
|---|---|
| Burundi | Burkina Faso |
| Central African Republic | Congo |
| Guinea | Guinea Bissau |
| Mali | Niger |
| Sierra Leone | Somalia |
| Sudan | Zaire |
| Zimbabwe | |

3. NAL (Non-Adjustment-Lending Countries)

| | |
|---|---|
| Benin | Botswana |
| Cameroon | Ethiopia |
| Liberia | Rwanda |

Source: Elbadawi *et al.*, 1992: 89.

# 6 Decomposing the Effects of Structural Adjustment: The Case of Sub-Saharan Africa

## PAUL MOSLEY

## Background

Originally launched as an innovative and reliable technique for closing resource gaps in developing countries while at the same time boosting their growth rates,[1] 'structural adjustment' is now increasingly coming to be seen as a policy experiment which does not necessarily achieve either objective, and which imposes unforeseen social costs into the bargain. Whereas the World Bank, as the instigator of many of the hundred or so structural adjustment programmes which have been launched in the Third World since 1980, has been able to demonstrate that countries which, on its own definition, 'have adjusted' have done better than countries which 'have not adjusted', it has also conceded (World Bank 1988, 1990a, 1992) that there has been very substantial variance around mean performance in both categories[2] and that poor countries, particularly in Africa, have so far derived far less benefit from adjustment programmes than middle-income countries. Many adjustment programmes have simply not worked in these poorer countries. It would appear urgent to know why this is the case, and what can be done to improve matters.

This paper approaches the problem in the following manner. The next section reviews the existing World Bank assessments of the effectiveness of adjustment in relation to the rest of the literature and argues that the phrase 'adjustment', as used by the Bank, embraces too wide a range of experiences to have meaning as an independent variable; the question therefore is which adjustment instrument or which coherent combinations of adjustment instruments work in which environment. Three potential analytical approaches to this question show some promise: comparison of the experience of countries with similar initial conditions and policy configurations; regression analysis; and model-based simulation within individual countries. The following two sections report on the first two approaches and the next on the third. The final section draws out some policy implications.

## Existing Results: A Critical Review

### (i) Growth, trade and investment

The World Bank has conducted three reviews of the structural adjustment process, which were published in 1988, 1990 and 1992. Although differing in emphasis – but with a notably more intensive focus on poverty in the second of these reports and on private investment in the third – these studies shared a common methodological approach, which was to compare the performance of 'adjustment lending countries' with that of 'non-adjustment lending' countries. The results of these studies are summarised in Table 6.1.

Although overall the performance of the 'adjustment lending' countries was better on all the indicators selected (except investment) than that of 'non-adjusting' countries, within the low-income and Sub-Saharan groups the growth and export performance of 'non-adjustment lending' countries was superior to that of the countries which received adjustment loans.

The apparently unsatisfactory adjustment performance of Sub-Saharan Africa has been taken up in more detail in two papers by a World Bank staff member, Ibrahim Elbadawi, the first of which reports that:

> despite the similarity in terms of the external shocks experienced by early intensive adjustment lending and non-adjustment lending countries of Sub-Saharan Africa, the economic performance in the last group has been uniformally (sic) superior to the first (1992: 13)

and the second that, in the Sub-Saharan region,

> World Bank adjustment lending has not significantly affected economic growth and has contributed to a statistically significant drop in the investment ratio. (Elbadawi et al., 1992: 5)

All of this is, of course, disturbing; but what it signifies for the design of an effective adjustment policy is far from clear, as there seem to be fundamental problems with the Bank's methodology of comparing 'adjusting' with 'non-adjusting' countries. In the first place, there were enormous variations (for details, see Annex 6.1) in the packages *prescribed*: some centred on trade liberalization, some on agricultural price reform, some on public enterprise reform, some on all of these. In the second place, there was for political reasons tremendous diversity in the *implementation* of the conditions prescribed among those countries which did accept adjustment loans. Some, such as Mauritius, implemented nearly all the policy conditions set by the Bank; others, such as Kenya and Malawi, implemented about half; others, such as Sierra Leone, Sudan and Zaire, implemented almost none.[3] In the third place, a great deal of adjustment, as shown in Table 6.2, was carried out by 'non-adjusting' countries: if one takes the group of countries characterized by the Bank as 'not accepting adjustment loans', it is clear that, in the course of the 1980s, they carried out very substantial modifications to their real exchange rate, public sector deficit, interest rates and real agricultural prices.

Given these facts, it is not clear that the policies followed by the 'adjustment lending' group had enough in common to warrant their being grouped together for analytical purposes or even that the intensity of the 'structural adjustment effort' which they carried out was greater than that carried out by the 'non-adjustment lending' group. If we are to understand the apparently weak leverage of the structural adjustment policies on African economies, a new approach is clearly needed.

*(ii) Income distribution and poverty*

Similar observations apply when the focus is switched from the output to the social effects of adjustment. There is some discussion of these in the World Bank's second report on adjustment (World Bank, 1990a) and more particularly

**Table 6.1.** *World Bank Assessments of Impact of Structural Adjustment*

| Study | Country Group | Real growth rate of GDP | | | Investment/GDP | | Exports/GDP | | | Growth of real per capita private consumption | | Nutrition (%) |
|---|---|---|---|---|---|---|---|---|---|---|---|---|
| | | 1982–7 | 1985–8 | 1986–90 | 1985–8 | 1986–90 | 1982–7 | 1985–8 | 1986–90 | 1985–8 | 1986–90 | 1980–86 |
| World Bank 1988 | Intensive adjustment lending | 4.7 | | | | | 8.5 | | | | | |
| | Non-adjustment lending | 4.8 | | | | | 7.1 | | | | | |
| World Bank 1990 | *Intensive adjustment lending* | | | | | | | | | | | |
| | All countries | | 4.2 | | 18.6 | | | 28.1 | | 1.4 | | 5.7 |
| | Low-income | | 3.9 | | 16.6 | | | 29.6 | | 1.0 | | –5.3 |
| | *Non-adjustment lending* | | | | | | | | | | | |
| | All countries | | 2.7 | | 20.0 | | | 24.6 | | –0.7 | | 5.4 |
| | Low-income | | 2.7 | | 15.5 | | | 15.5 | | 0.2 | | –5.5 |
| World Bank 1992 | *Intensive adjustment lending* | | | | | | | | | | | |
| | All countries | | | 4.2 | | 17.9 | | | 28.4 | | 1.6 | |
| | Sub-Saharan Africa | | | 3.5 | | 16.3 | | | 28.0 | | – | |
| | *Non-adjustment lending* | | | | | | | | | | | |
| | All countries | | | 2.4 | | 18.4 | | | 28.4 | | 0.6 | |
| | Sub-Saharan Africa | | | 3.9 | | 15.6 | | | 31.7 | | – | |

Source: World Bank (1988), Table 3.2; (1990a), Table 2.6; (1992), Table A1, p. 27.

Table 6.2. *Sub-Saharan Africa: Non-Adjustment Lending Countries: Median Levels for Specific Policy Variables, 1983–85 and 1986–90*

|  | Real effective exchange rate | Annual rate of inflation | Black market foreign exchange premiums |
|---|---|---|---|
| 1983–85 | 122.6 | 8.9 | 40.0 |
| 1986–90 | 110.1 | 6.2 | 25.4 |

Source: World Bank (1992), Table A5, p. 28.

in its 'framework paper' *Making Adjustment Work for the Poor* (World Bank 1990c), but both of these stop well short of comparing poverty in Africa 'with and without adjustment', let alone splitting adjustment into its component parts. The data problems are extremely severe (to give but one example, no African country has a time series even of the headcount index of the number of people in poverty for the 1980s), and an entire chapter of the latter publication is devoted to the data requirements of the 'macro-meso-micro analysis' which the Bank would ideally like to see.

In face of these difficulties, the road now forks. Down one fork lies the approach of using the existing data, and applying to them the less than ideal methodology of before-versus-after comparison. Travellers down the other branch of the road may use the more sophisticated methodology of with-versus-without comparison, but given the data problems previously discussed, pay the price of having to impose arbitrary values of coefficients – even the very response elasticities which their analysis purports to estimate.

There are now many examples of the first type of analysis for individual countries, but the writers who have sought to make comparisons across countries are Stewart, 1992, Sahn, 1992, and Sahn and Sarris, 1991. Both present time-series through the 1980s of various components of the welfare of low-income groups, including government social spending and (in Stewart, 1992) the utilization of women's time. The evidence is ambiguous. In the five African countries sampled by Sahn 'there is no unequivocal pattern of increase or decline in the real welfare of the rural poor' (Sahn and Sarris, 1991: 279) but, as Stewart notes, 'there is evidence of rising malnutrition in quite a few countries in Sub-Saharan Africa, and in some elsewhere'. A major question, however, is how far the structural adjustment process as such has added to or subtracted from the welfare of the rural poor, and this issue before-versus-after approaches cannot by their very nature resolve. In his second paper, Sahn is willing to commit himself to the proposition that

> a commitment to major policy reform, particularly exchange rate reforms and market liberalisation, has strongly positive distributional implications and is essential to protecting the welfare of the poor in the face of an economic crisis. . . . There is little evidence that these countries which were quick off the mark in making reforms jeopardised the welfare of the poor: quite the contrary. (Sahn 1992: 34 and 36).

This conclusion does not emerge, however, from his painstaking time-series evidence on the welfare of African rural smallholders (Sahn and Sarris, 1991): rather, it emerges from an *a priori* argument, many of the linkages in which have yet to be tested. These include:

(i) the effect of a 'structural adjustment' programme will be to raise the relative price of tradeables, and lower the relative price of non-tradeables;

(ii) hence the gainers from adjustment programmes will be producers of tradeables and consumers of non-tradeables;

(iii) many of the rural poor will be in the first of these categories (if not the second also), and will therefore gain on balance from adjustment;

(iv) most existing subsidies, including food subsidies, do not effectively target the poor, hence their removal will not cause a deterioration in the average living standards of the poor.[4]

Table 6.3 below shows that all of these propositions may be either true or false depending on the country and, crucially, the nature of the adjustment programme under consideration. In one of the sections of his paper where the detail of individual countries' adjustment programmes is considered, Sahn most valuably illustrates this point, but at the cost of undermining the argument quoted above.

> Our results indicated that adjustment policies did not have any appreciable impact on incomes of rural smallholders. The reasons for this are instructive. In Côte d'Ivoire, adjustment was followed by a decline in real incomes because it is a CFA country where devaluation was precluded and where relative price changes were minimal. In Madagascar, the absence of any large increase in incomes is attributable to the fact that prices for Madagascar's export crops (vanilla, cloves and coffee) did not rise as a consequence of adjustment. In the case of Ghana, the model indicates that the incomes of the rural poor did not benefit from the early successes of adjustment, [partly because] agricultural incomes are heavily weighted in the form of non-tradables, the relative prices of which are expected to fall as a result of expenditure switching policies. And in Malawi, rural incomes did not increase because administered prices in agriculture contributed to a continued high level of taxation. (Sahn, 1992: 12a)

These useful examples demonstrate that, whatever the distributional merits of the idealized 'World Bank model' of structural adjustment might be, those merits were not always realized in the programmes actually implemented. The nature of the individual adjustment programme matters for poverty, just as we have already argued that it matters for growth. It is the merit of the OECD to have explored the alternative fork in the road and to have sponsored the only serious comparative test of the effects of alternative adjustment packages currently available (most conveniently summarized in Bourguignon, de Melo and Morrisson, 1991). The approach chosen is to simulate alternative adjustment packages with the same net deflationary effect (i.e. a balance-of-payments improvement of $ X million) and to compare their social consequences; the general finding is that exchange-rate devaluation and cuts in public service real wages have a relatively small social cost in relation to the alternatives examined. The sample of countries analysed in this way by the OECD project contains only one from Sub-Saharan Africa (Côte d'Ivoire) and all of the analyses are carried out on a CGE model, some of whose assumptions, as discussed in a later section, are bizarre. Nonetheless, in analysing the effects of adjustment on growth and distribution simultaneously, and even more in presenting structural adjustment as a range of technologies some of which will be helpful and some harmful to both objectives, the OECD study breaks important new ground.

The next step is to build on these insights by asking what alternative approaches are available for answering the fundamental question which is posed: what are the effects, for both growth and equity, of varying the mix of policy

**Table 6.3.** *Likely Effects of Different Structural Adjustment Measures and 'Catalysts' on Components of Aggregate Supply and Demand*

| | Structural adjustment measures | | | | | 'Catalysts' | |
|---|---|---|---|---|---|---|---|
| | Real exchange rate | Tariff reduction | Reduction in government credit and subsidies to agriculture | Removal of interest rate controls | Increase in public utility prices | Reductions in development expenditure | Increase in policy stability |
| *(i) Relationships governing real output* | | | | | | | |
| (a) Private aggregate supply | +[a] | ? | −[b] | + | + | ? | + |
| (b) Aggregate supply of public goods | .. | .. | − | + | − | | : |
| (c) Aggregate demand | +[a] | ? | − | − | − | − | : |
| (d) Shape of aggregate supply/transaction costs | .. | | −[c] | + | ? | − | + |
| Overall effect on real output | + | ? | − | ? | ? | − | + |
| *(ii) Relationships governing the welfare of particular occupational groups* | | | | | | | |
| (a) Capitalist farmers | +[a] | | − | ?[d] | −[e] | − | + |
| (b) Industrialists | +[a] | | : | ?[d] | −[e] | − | + |
| (c) Urban wage workers | − | + | : | ?[d] | − | − | : |
| (d) Subsistence farmers | .. | .. | − | : | : | : | : |
| Overall effect on welfare of poor groups (c) and (d) | ? | ? | − | ? | − | − | + |

*Symbols:* +, expected positive effect; −, expected negative effect; ?, both positive and negative effects, hence overall effect could cut either way; .., expected neutral effect.

*Notes*
a) If elasticity conditions are satisfied, real devaluation will raise exports and real incomes of exporters, and lower imports and real incomes of importers.
b) For an estimate of the responsiveness of agricultural yields to the level of credit and fertilizer prices in three African countries, see Mosley (1993).
c) For discussion of the effect of infrastructure on transactions costs in agriculture, see de Janvry et al. (1991), and de Janvry and Sadoulet (1992).
d) Positive for savers, negative for borrowers (but to some extent positive if access to credit is improved).
e) Short-term effect. There is a long-term positive effect if public services are made more sustainable.

instruments within the structural adjustment package? The rest of this paper is directed to this question.

## Partial Decomposition: the Tabular Approach

In seeking to understand the effects of structural adjustment, it is useful to start from a statement of its objectives. In the words of the man who introduced policy-based lending into the World Bank and presided over the first eight years of the experiment:

> the objective for the developing countries must be to introduce policy changes to permit a reduction in the current account deficit over the next several years while minimising the penalties to growth in the long run, hence allowing continued progress towards the achievement of their development objectives . . . structural adjustment lending is intended to assist governments to adopt necessary, though often politically difficult, policy and institutional reforms designed to improve the efficiency of resource use. (Stern, 1983: 88–9)

However, as is well known in principle, no ready-made handbook for 'improving the efficiency of resource use' in developing countries exists, and nobody would dare to write one. Whereas under certain restrictive assumptions (perfect knowledge, absence of uncertainty, decreasing returns to scale, no externalities, optimal income distribution) a regime of free competition offers greater economic welfare than any other (Graaff, 1957: 162), these assumptions are not in practice satisfied in developing countries, and even if they were, there is no guarantee, as the theory of the Second Best demonstrates, that a *partial* liberalization of a highly monopolized economy would necessarily increase economic welfare at all (Lipsey and Lancaster, 1957). The recommendations attached to structural adjustment programmes, in other words, lack any serious theoretical basis, and should be seen essentially as an improvization. In some cases, where the restrictive assumptions of welfare economics are satisfied, market liberalization will 'improve the efficiency of resource use'; in other cases, where a crucial market is missing or other conditions are not satisfied, the opposite will be the case. It may be that in Sub-Saharan Africa the degree of endogenous market imperfection, *not* caused by policy, is greater than elsewhere, and hence that policies of pure market liberalization will cause more movements away from the production possibility curve than elsewhere. In particular, access to the capital market on the part of the poor is certainly less,[5] and in the presence of imperfect capital markets, various countervailing state interventions, from infant-industry tariff protection to fertilizer subsidies for small farmers to the creation of 'quasi-formal' credit institutions for micro enterprises, may, if correctly designed, not only not distort but actually serve as preconditions to an efficient allocation of resources.[6]

The general argument can usefully be clarified by the use of the aggregate supply and demand framework of elementary macroeconomics, as portrayed in Figure 6.1.

Starting from a position of balance-of-payments disequilibrium such as, say, $X_1$ in Figure 6.1, a country may 'minimise the penalties to growth in the long run' if it is able to 'improve the efficiency of resource use' and thus move the aggregate supply curve to the south-east, so that a new equilibrium is achieved

Price level

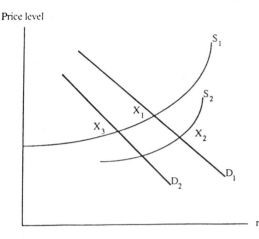

Figure 6.1.
*Structural adjustment:
Intended and unintended effects*

real output

with *higher* output and a more competitive price level, at $X_2$, rather than with lower output and a lower price level (at $X_3$) as under the conventional IMF strategy of deflating aggregate demand.

Such is the classical argument for structural adjustment policies; we may call this the *price incentive effect*. However, both *a priori* reasoning and the experience discussed in the previous section suggest that these policies may have effects of other types.

Policies of structural adjustment may cause the supply curve for certain services which in developing countries assume the nature of public goods (e.g. agricultural research, credit for low-income groups, minor feeder roads, electrification, health) to shift inwards, even though the supply curve for private goods is at the same time being shifted outwards. Worse, where public goods are in joint supply with private goods, this fact may limit the possibilities of increasing private aggregate supply (e.g. farmers' desire to expand marketed maize production in response to a higher on-farm price may be frustrated because 'structural adjustment' policies at the same time restrict their entitlement of credit and fertilizer). We call this the *public goods supply effect*. To the extent that structural adjustment is interpreted as market liberalization, this effect is likely to be negative: a north-westward movement of the aggregate supply curve.

Structural adjustment policies, if they alter aggregate consumption or investment at all, move the *aggregate demand* as well as the aggregate supply curve. The move may be in either direction, and may arise either from a change in aggregate income or from a redistribution between income groups.

Finally, structural adjustment policies can alter not only the position of the aggregate supply curve but also its slope by changing the level of *transactions costs* associated with particular lines of business. This can happen through many channels from the absolutely literal (as when tax rates on particular lines of business are altered in a structural adjustment programme) to the metaphorical (as when repeated changes of policy associated with a programme of this type and political response to it create uncertainty about the rate of return on inward investment which can be interpreted as a 'tax' on such investment, see Rodrik, 1990; 1991).

The response of African economies to structural adjustment, as the World Bank emphasizes, has been disappointing, but it has been very diverse, in a way that averaging the performance of 'adjusting countries' does not reveal. It would seem, at the least, a hypothesis worth exploring that these variations around the mean, both in growth and in the welfare of the poor, can be explained by differences in the way the policies actually implemented contributed to factors (i) to (iv) above. This will require us to jettison the Bank's approach of dividing Africa into 'adjusting' and 'non-adjusting' countries and to decompose such adjustment as took place, whether or not it was backed by Bank lending, into its component parts.

Table 6.3 presents our best *ex ante* guess concerning the effects of a randomly chosen set of particular structural adjustment measures, first of all on the different components of aggregate supply and demand as discussed above, and secondly on the real incomes of particular income groups. In some cases this guess is based on a substantial volume of empirical research, as detailed in the footnotes to the table; in some cases purely on *a priori* reasoning. It is, however, likely, if the *ex ante* expectations set out in Table 6.3 are anything like accurate, that the response of both real output and income distribution to different types of structural adjustment measures will, as argued in the previous section, be in no sense homogeneous. In particular, we expect the following:

(i) On balance, the net effect on real output of real exchange-rate depreciation will be positive. If the Marshall-Lerner conditions are satisfied, the balance of trade (hence aggregate demand) will improve, and the economy's external competitiveness (hence aggregate supply at a given internal price level) will increase.

(ii) On balance, the net effect on real output of reductions in government development expenditure will be negative. Cuts in real development expenditure reduce aggregate demand and the aggregate supply of public goods directly; they also reduce the quality of the infrastructure, and hence raise the transactions costs of private agents – and the slope of the aggregate supply curve, as argued by de Janvry and Sadoulet (1992). The effect on the position of the aggregate supply curve is more ambiguous, as an early expectation of structural adjustment programmes was that cuts in public investment would encourage increases in private investment through a reversal of the 'crowding-out' mechanism. However, there is little evidence of such a mechanism working in practice, in Africa at any rate (Table 6.1 above; Taylor, 1988: 51–7; Mosley *et al.*, 1991: Chap. 6). In general, therefore, it would seem at least a valid working hypothesis that the overall effect of cuts in government development expenditure on real output is a negative one.

(iii) The effects of an increase in the stability of macroeconomic policy are expected to be positive specifically for private investment and more generally for real output as a whole. Uncertainty concerning the future direction of macroeconomic policy, according to the argument of Rodrik (1990; 1991), discourages private investors by preventing them from making reliable calculations of future profitability if they commit money to a particular project or sector. Because they are discouraged, overall investment stays low, and the transactions costs of the private sector are *pro tanto* increased.

(iv) As a special case of (ii), the net effect of reductions in government credit and subsidies to agricultural inputs is expected to be negative. Cuts in such expenditures reduce the supply of public goods directly; they reduce real agricultural incomes and hence aggregate demand directly; they reduce adoption of modern inputs (Mosley, 1993) and hence agricultural yields and the overall agricultural supply curve. Any benefit from such cuts must come, as in case (ii), from a re-emergence of private sector credit to 'replace' the putative cuts in public sector provision, and more generally from whole-economy effects working through a reduction in the budget deficit. In the absence of any evidence of such effects, we hypothesize that the overall effect of such measures, and structural adjustment programmes centred around them, will be negative. We see policy stability and growth in public investment as *catalysts* which, while not themselves part of the structural adjustment arsenal, are crucial in determining the effectiveness of structural adjustment measures.

(v) Although the taxonomy of income groups presented in Table 6.3 is a crude one, it appears that, of the types of structural adjustment package listed, that which is likely to produce the least damaging effects on lower-income groups (urban wage-workers and subsistence farmers) is real exchange-rate depreciation. This parallels the findings of the OECD team led by Bourguignon, de Melo and Morrisson (1991) for a sample of developing countries including Ecuador, Morocco, Malaysia and Indonesia, who also argue for cuts in public service wages as a 'relatively humane' mode of adjustment.

Let us examine whether these hypotheses are confirmed by data from Sub-Saharan Africa in the late 1980s. The simplest way of doing this (let us call it Method I) is to group African countries by their initial policy stance, and to examine whether this or the 'complementary policy variables' discussed above appeared to influence economic performance. This is done in Table 6.4, drawn from a previous paper (Mosley and Weeks, 1993) which suggests that:

(i) both adjustment packages which focused on trade liberalization and agricultural price reform and those which focused on the agricultural sector appeared to have their effectiveness (in relation to economic and social indicators) greatly enhanced in the presence of the 'catalysts' of real exchange-rate depreciation and a steady growth in public investment;

(ii) 'adjusting countries', in which these catalysts were not present, performed significantly worse than 'non-adjusting countries' in which the catalysts were present.

This approach already begins to demonstrate that the decomposition of structural adjustment packages by type may yield useful insights; but it is not, of course, able to measure the individual effectiveness of particular structural adjustment instruments.

**Table 6.4.** *Sub-Saharan Africa: Economic and Social Performance in Relation to Policy Stance 1980-90*

| Initial Policy Stance | Nature of Complementary Policy | Indicators of economic performance: | | | Per capita food production 1990 (1980 = 100) | Social Indicators: | |
|---|---|---|---|---|---|---|---|
| | | Growth of GDP | Growth of investment 1980-90 | Growth of exports 1980-90 | | Annual rate of change of under-5 mortality (%) | Annual change of share of health and education in GDP (%) |
| I. Trade liberalization (above or in combination with other liberalization measures) | Real exchange rate depreciating 1980-90 | 3.8 | 3.5 | 4.2 | 96 | −1.9 | −0.2 |
| | Real exchange rate appreciating 1980-90 | 1.6* | −3.6** | −1.3** | 90* | −1.5 | −0.5 |
| II. Liberalization focused on agriculture sector | Real public capital expenditure increasing 1980-90 | 4.3 | 10.3 | 10.1 | 96 | −2.1 | +0.9 |
| | Real public capital expenditure declining 1980-90 | 2.2* | −4.2** | 0.2** | 90** | −1.6** | −2.3* |
| III. 'Adjusting countries' (on World Bank criteria) | Real exchange rate increasing, public capital expenditure declining | 1.6 | −6.3 | 0.6 | 94 | −1.8 | −9.6 |
| 'Non-adjusting countries' | Real exchange rate declining, public capital expenditure increasing | 7.1** | −0.2** | 8.4** | 84* | −2.7 | +1.2** |

Notes: *Difference between sample means significant at .05 level of probability.
   **Difference between sample means significant at .01 level of probability.

Sources: Mosley and Weeks (1993), Tables 7 and 8.

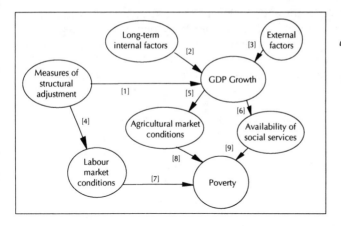

Figure 6.2.
*Growth, poverty*
*and structural adjustment:*
*A simple model*
*of the linkages*

# Partial Decomposition: Regression-based Approach

In order to do this, a highly simplified model of the relationship between growth, poverty and structural adjustment has been constructed. This is as set out in Figure 6.2.

In linkage [1] on the diagram, measures of structural adjustment determine GDP through the various pathways depicted in Figure 6.1. GDP is also influenced by a number of other factors to which the 'new growth theory' has recently drawn our attention: among internal factors we may list investment, quality of the labour supply and population growth, and among external factors, terms of trade and the growth of world demand.[7] These groups of factors make up linkages [2] and [3] on Figure 6.2. If we bring them together to create an estimating equation for GDP we end up with a function of the type

$Y$ = constant + ($a_1$ . . . $a_4$) ['new growth theory' variables] +
($a_5$ . . . .$a_9$) [structural adjustment policy implementation
indicators] +
($a_{10}$ . . . $a_{12}$) [indicators of international economic
environment].                                                    [1]

The results of estimating such an equation for Sub-Saharan Africa in the years 1980–91 are as set out in Table 6.5. The results appear to confirm the *a priori* impression emerging from Table 6.3 that competitive real exchange rates and increases in government development spending are significantly correlated with GDP growth rates, even when the orthodox variables in the macro production function – capital and skilled labour – are taken into account. These components of structural adjustment, then, appear on balance to have a positive effect on growth rates. The coefficients on these variables, however, are in all cases insignificant. By contrast, lower levels of nominal tariffs of agricultural credit and subsidy, again contrary to the ideology of structural adjustment but in accordance with the *a priori* argument summarized in Table 6.3, have a negative and significant influence on growth rates.

There is an obvious multicollinearity problem arising from the presence of both the aggregate share of investment and the level of real government expenditure in the same equation, but if this problem is tackled by removing the aggregate investment variable, the level of real public development expenditure retains its positive influence. There are, of course, potential interactions between the five 'structural adjustment instruments' examined in Table 6.4. The *combination* of trade liberalization and exchange-rate depreciation, or financial decontrol and increases in agricultural prices, has been argued on theoretical grounds to be more effective than either of these policies in isolation (Collier and Gunning, 1992; Smith and Spooner, 1990, respectively). To test these propositions effectively will require a simulation approach, as used in the following section, but Table 6.5 does indicate that the regression coefficients on tariff levels and agricultural input subsidies (the two apparently 'ineffective' policy instruments) remain positive even in those countries where complementary policies were apparently favourable – i.e. the 'adjusting' countries. The foreign finance coefficient is insignificant, but the export growth has a significant independent impact on growth rates.

We now wish to examine the influence of different structural adjustment instruments on measures of poverty. In Africa, however, measurements of the distribution of personal incomes, or even of the headcount of persons in absolute poverty, do not exist on a year-by-year basis, if they are available at all.[8] We therefore have to take a 'second-best' approach, which will be based on the premise that most poverty in developing countries is found amongst those who either work for wages or grow subsistence crops, and use real wages and grain yields as indicators of poverty levels. The most significant gap in this approach is the omission of the 'urban informal sector', on which, however, statistics are very poor. Referring back to Figure 6.2, we reason that poverty levels are determined – through linkages (7) to (9) on the diagram – by labour market conditions and agricultural market conditions (both of which are influenced by the 'structural adjustment' instruments and independently by the rate of GDP growth) and by the availability of a social safety net to counterbalance a decline in income below the poverty line. This yields an estimating equation of the type:

$$\text{Poverty indicator} = \text{constant} + a_1 \, [\text{growth of GDP}] +$$
$$a_2 \ldots a_6 \, [\text{structural adjustment indicators}] +$$
$$a_7 \, [\text{index of policy instability}] +$$
$$a_8 \, [\text{foreign resource inflows}] +$$
$$a_9 \, [\text{index of social welfare provision}]. \qquad [2]$$

To this equation is added an additional independent variable specific to the poverty indicator under discussion: growth of agricultural GDP in the case of the real wage equation, and agricultural prices in the case of the grain yield equation. The results of estimating equation [2] are set out in Table 6.6. In general, the correlation coefficients are lower but, as in the case of GDP growth, the real exchange rate and government development spending, together with policy stability, are correlated with positive movements in the two poverty indicators, whereas cuts in agricultural subsidies and credit, once again, are associated with negative movements in agricultural yields. In a broad sense, these results confirm

**Table 6.5.** *Sub-Saharan Africa 1980–91: Results of Regression Analysis Linking GDP Growth, New Growth Theory Variables and Various 'Structural Adjustment Indicators'*

Dependent variable: Growth rate of GDP (% annual change)

| Data set | Number of observations | Constant | 'New growth theory variables' | | | Regression coefficients on independent variables — Indicators of 'structural adjustment' | | | | | 'External disturbances' | | r̄² | D.W. |
|---|---|---|---|---|---|---|---|---|---|---|---|---|---|---|
| | | | 1970 per capita income | Growth of literacy | Share of investment in GDP | (1) Real effective exchange rate | (2) Average tariff level | (3) Agricultural credit and input subsidies | (4) Real interest rate | (5) Real govt. development spending | Aid inflows as % GDP | Growth of exports as % GDP | | |
| *OLS estimation* | | | | | | | | | | | | | | |
| All SSA counties 1980–91 | 37 | 1.90 (1.68) | −0.20 0.12 | −0.006 (1.31) | 0.06** (4.30) | −0.007 (0.82) | 0.14** (3.53) | 0.007* (2.46) | −0.10* (2.59) | 0.012 (0.33) | 0.0059 (0.16) | 0.28** (5.50) | 0.69 | 2.0830 |
| Pooled data | 37 | 0.07 (0.56) | 0.002 (0.99) | 0.004 (0.77) | | −0.01 (0.87) | 0.14** (2.60) | 0.007* (1.78) | | 0.005 (0.11) | −0.05 (1.22) | 0.24** (3.82) | 0.43 | 1.9698 |
| 'Adjusting countries'[a] (n=21) | 21 | 2.7 (0.96) | −0.001 (0.17) | 0.002 (0.02) | 0.02 (0.37) | −0.01 (0.64) | 0.19** (2.64) | 0.001* (1.68) | 0.046 (0.58) | 0.004 (0.54) | 0.04 (0.96) | 0.17** (1.83) | 0.42 | 2.2748 |
| 'Non-adjusting countries'[a] (n=16) | 16 | 1.39 (1.25) | 0.001 (0.38) | −0.036 (0.64) | 0.41** (3.60) | −0.007 (0.54) | 0.25** (5.03) | 0.003 (1.26) | −0.012* (2.89) | 0.0013 (0.41) | 0.002 (0.02) | 0.31** (5.73) | 0.89 | 1.7335 |

83

**Table 6.5. (cont.)**

| Data set | Number of observations | Constant | 'New growth theory variables' | | | Regression coefficients on independent variables | | | | | 'External disturbances' | | $\bar{r}^2$ | D.W. |
|---|---|---|---|---|---|---|---|---|---|---|---|---|---|---|
| | | | | | | Indicators of 'structural adjustment' | | | | | | | | |
| | | | 1970 per capita income | Growth of literacy | Share of investment in GDP | (1) Real effective exchange rate | (2) Average tariff level | (3) Agricultural credit and input subsidies | (4) Real interest rate | (5) Real govt. development spending | Aid inflows as % GDP | Growth of exports as % GDP | | |
| For Comparison: 101 Less-developed countries 1970–89 (Levine and Renelt 1991) | 101 | −0.85 (0.98) | −0.35** (2.50) | 3.17* (2.46) | 17.5** (6.35) | | | | | | | | 0.46 | n.a. |

Notes: a) 'Adjusting' countries are those which have received World Bank policy-based loans to 1990, including Burundi, Cameroon, Ghana, Senegal, Malawi, Kenya, Zambia, Mauritius, Burkina Faso, Côte d'Ivoire, Gambia, Sierra Leone, Tanzania, Mali, Nigeria, Madagascar, Mauritania, Uganda, Mozambique. 'Non-adjusting countries' are those countries in Africa for which data are available, including Botswana, Ethiopia, Liberia, Somalia, Zimbabwe, Rwanda, Sudan, Zaire, Swaziland, Niger, Lesotho.

*Significant at the 5% level.

**Significant at the 1% level.

Sources: Real Growth of *per capita* GDP, Current *per capita* GDP: World Bank, *World Tables* – various issues.
Rate of secondary school enrolment: United Nations Children's Fund (UNICEF), *The State of the World's Children*, various issues.
Share of investment in GDP: World Bank, *World Development Report*, various issues.
Overseas aid inflows: OECD Development Assistance Committee, *Geographical Distribution of Financial Flows to Developing Countries*, various issues.
Indicators of 'structural adjustment':
1. Real effective exchange rate (1980 = 100) from IMF, *International Financial Statistics*, January 1993 and preceding issues. (A rise in the real exchange rate connotes a *decline* in competitiveness).
2. Average nominal tariff level (1990) from United Nations, *Handbook of International Trade Statistics*, and World Bank SAL/SECAL appraisals.
3. Agricultural credit and input subsidies per hectare (1988) from Lele (1989) and national statistical publications.
4. Level of real interest rates (1990), from United Nations, *International Financial Statistics*, January 1993, and preceding issues.
5. Real government capital spending (growth 1980–90) from IMF, *Government Financial Statistics Handbook*, 1992 and preceding issues.

**Table 6.6** *Sub-Saharan Africa 1980-91: Results of Regression Analysis Linking Social Indicators and Various Indicators of 'Structural Adjustment'*
Dependent variable: as indicated in left-hand column

| Dependent Variable | Data Set | Number of observations | Regression coefficients on independent variables: | | | | Indicators of 'structural adjustment' | | | | | | | $r^2$ | D.W. |
|---|---|---|---|---|---|---|---|---|---|---|---|---|---|---|---|
| | | | Constant | GDP growth rate | Real agricultural output | Index of grain prices | (1) Real effective exchange rate | (2) Average tariff level | (3) Agricultural credit and input subsidies | (4) Real Interest rate | (5) Real govt. development spending | Policy instability Index | Aid inflows as % GDP | | |
| Real agricultural wages (Index 1980=100) | All SSA countries for which data are available | 209 | 82.4** (3.79) | 0.14** (1.94) | −0.29** (3.31) | | −0.77** (4.64) | 0.016 (0.61) | 0.13 (1.79) | 0.04 (1.53) | 0.22* (2.01) | 0.01 (1.31) | 0.04 (0.86) | 0.63 | 1.6916 |
| Grain yields (tons/ha) | All SSA countries for which data are available | 308 | 1.09** (2.66) | 0.21 (0.93) | | 0.63* (1.87) | 0.24* (1.75) | 0.17 (0.13) | 0.24** (3.36) | −0.31 (0.45) | 0.18 (0.97) | 0.14 (0.66) | 0.03 (1.31) | 0.49 | 1.5607 |

Sources: As for Table 6.4, except real wages which are from United Nations, *Yearbook of Labour Statistics*, various issues, and grain yields, which are from FAO, *Production Yearbook*, various issues.
Key to structural adjustment indicators:
1. Real effective exchange rate (1980 = 100).
2. Average nominal tariff level.
3. Value of agricultural credit and input subsidies per hectare (1988).
4. Level of real interest rates.
5. Real government capital spending (in constant 1980 dollars).

Sources for these indicators are given in Table 6.5.
*Significant at 5%.
**Significant at 1%.

the findings of Mosley and Weeks (1993), who suggest that those adjustment policies which favour growth most, also reduce poverty most.

These results, then, give tentative support to a view of the structural adjustment process in which the instruments of structural adjustment are seen, not as inseparable components of a simple mechanism which pushes the aggregate supply curve outwards, but rather as separate interventions with distinctive, and in some cases counter-productive, effects on aggregate supply and demand. How well warranted each of these interventions is in a particular country will vary from case to case, but the preliminary econometric analysis of Tables 6.5 and 6.6 suggests that tariff reduction and reduction in agricultural input subsidies are the structural adjustment measures which appear to have *negative* effectiveness in the African environment. This is not surprising, since the theoretical welfare economics case for these two policy reforms, above all in an African context, is particularly weak.[9] They also suggest a view of the adjustment process in which the *price-based* policy instruments listed in Tables 6.5 and 6.6 can work only if other variables which we describe as 'catalysts' are also present: the ones which we examine in this paper are policy stability and growth in development expenditure, which the processes of stabilization and structural adjustment can very easily undermine rather than reinforce.[10] It may be that the absence of these catalysts in many African countries is a major reason for the common inability of structural adjustment processes to work well in Sub-Saharan Africa.

## Partial Decomposition: A Simulation-based Approach

Although regression-based techniques based on pooled data can take us further than the methods employed so far to discriminate between the effects of different structural adjustment instruments, they have the limitation of telling us little about the mechanism by which output and poverty respond to particular instruments and of being unable to measure the influence of structural adjustment instruments on the economy's flexibility. For that purpose, a model is needed, and in recent years much work has been done in developing countries, as discussed in an earlier section, with computable general equilibrium (CGE) models designed above all to illustrate the social consequences of deploying alternative policy instruments. Much of this work is summarized in Bourguignon, de Melo and Morrisson (1991); it has the merits of incorporating micro behavioural assumptions into a macro model and also of examining policy effects on growth and poverty at the same time. However, it has the disadvantage of being based on *a priori* assumptions rather than on actual data. For example, little of the work so far done with CGE models has been carried out on Sub-Saharan Africa, but the 'African archetype' presented by Bourguignon, de Melo and Suwa (1991) makes the following assumptions *(bracketed figures are page numbers)*.

there is no bond market [343];
firms have no access to the international capital market [343];
there is elasticity of agricultural supply = 0.5 [344];
there was full employment equilibrium before adjustment [345].

All of these assumptions are to the present writer's certain knowledge inaccurate in respect of the three African economies for which he has data (Kenya, Malawi, Zimbabwe);[11] moreover, Bourguignon *et al.* go on to argue: (p. 345) that:

> We do not model directly [the] supply-augmenting effect which structural adjustment policies were intended to have because of the lack of reliable information on the extent of resource idleness caused by inappropriate incentives. Rather we assume that in the no-shock (e.g. prior to structural adjustment) scenario economies would have had sufficient access to external funding to have normal capacity use.

This is tantamount to assuming out of existence the very problems of inefficient utilization of labour, capital, and other factors of production which structural adjustment policies were intended to tackle.[12] All of this suggests that in order to obtain a grip on the effects of adjustment policies it may be worth trying an alternative approach more directly based on the available data. This section outlines a model based on such an approach and the results obtained with it so far. The hope is that it can be used, as none of the CGE models has been so far, for actual policy analysis within developing countries.

The model which we propose uses as its point of departure a prototype prepared for the 1990 World Bank report on *Growth Through Poverty Reduction in Malawi* to illustrate the effects of alternative adjustment policies on different income groups in an African context. It also has something in common with the econometric model of Sahn and Sarris (1991).[13] However, it contains a number of new features specific to the latter model, namely:

(i) an explicit treatment of the urban informal sector, which is assumed to be a great deal more labour-intensive than the 'estate agriculture' and 'industry' modern sectors;
(ii) modelling of both the formal and informal financial markets;
(iii) a direct linkage from policy variables, including input prices and the availability of credit under (ii), to productivity in food crops.

A flow diagram of the model is set out as Figure 6.3. There are six sectors: government; capitalist agriculture; large smallholders; small smallholders (less than 0.5 ha., hence unable to produce the food they require from their holdings); urban wage-workers; and the 'urban informal sector'. Production functions (the inputs into which are in part policy-determined) in conjunction with output prices determine sectoral GNP levels; these, in conjunction with labour supply conditions, determine the shares of particular income groups; consumption functions applied to these determine local demand, which in conjunction with export demand determines the level of imports and hence the balance of payments. There are separate sub-models for the labour market, the formal and informal capital market, and the balance of payments. The model is relatively complex, with 45 equations and unknowns, but is the simplest which we believe can capture the available range of policy instruments, the relevant market imperfections and the segmentation into different income groups which is required for analysis of poverty impact.

At this stage of the research, the model has not been estimated econometrically, and for purposes of simulation plausible levels of the relevant coefficients have been imposed in respect of the Malawian economy (for which the

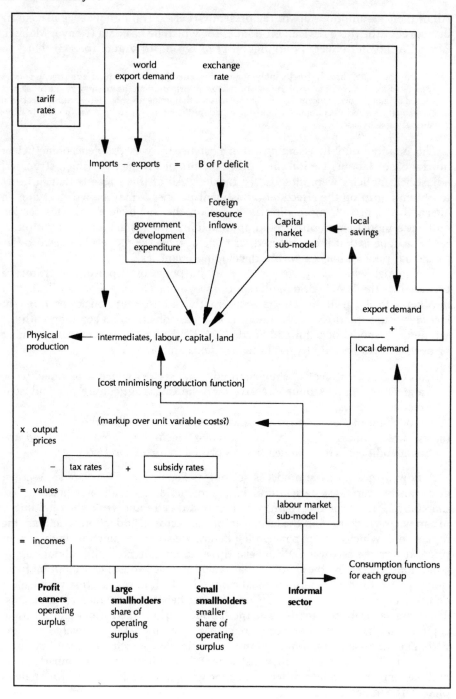

Note: Government policy variables are in boxes

**Figure 6.3.** *Malawi model: Flow chart of current working version*

model was originally designed). The forecasts of the impact of alternative policies which were obtained with the help of the model, and which are presented in Table 6.7, therefore suffer from precisely the fault which we have criticised with CGEs. This fault will be corrected in subsequent phases of the research. What has been done at this stage is to imagine two different levels of foreign resource inflow for the three years 1993–96 (i.e. a continuation of the current level and an increase of $50m., or about 25% for each of the next three years) and within each of those assumptions the implications of varying the rate of fertilizer subsidy (currently a highly controversial policy instrument in Malawi), the rate of external tariff and the level of real public investment have been explored. The illustrative results of Table 6.7 suggest that, contrary to World Bank conventional wisdom, but consistent with the results of Table 6.5, increases in fertilizer subsidy have a powerful positive effect on the incomes of smallholders, particularly – it must be admitted – the larger and less poor small-holders whose purchases of fertilizer are greater. There are positive spillover effects into the urban informal sector. As in our tabular and regression analysis (Tables 6.4–6.6) the influence of real public investment is strongly positive for both GNP and the welfare of low-income groups; the effect of liberalizing import tariffs is close to neutral, except, as might be expected, in relation to imports. To repeat, these results have been obtained with imposed rather than econometrically estimated coefficients, and the range of instruments which has been examined is smaller than in the analysis of Table 6.5. But the fit between the results obtained by the two approaches, so far as they go, is encouraging.

# Conclusions

We have argued here that it is misleading to treat the amalgam of policy changes commonly referred to as 'structural adjustment' as a unity. Empirically, there are major intra-group differences both in *ex ante* intention and in *ex post* implementation; theoretically, there is no reason to suppose that all or any of the policy changes in a structural adjustment package will necessarily, as its founders intended, improve the net efficiency of resource allocation and push the production frontier outwards. Particularly in Sub-Saharan Africa where so many of the requirements for a competitive equilibrium are lacking, we believe that any worthwhile evaluation of the structural adjustment experience must decompose that experience into its component parts.

Our analysis suggests three ways in which this can in principle be done: (i) tabular comparison of countries with similar 'policy clusters', (ii) regression analysis in the spirit of 'policy-augmented new growth theory', and (iii) simulations on an econometric model. Given the fragility of the data base, it is appropriate to try out and compare the results from each of these methods to insure (as far as possible) against the intrinsic defects of each of them and to obtain an idea of which of them are robust. The preliminary results of this exercise are depicted in Table 6.8. They suggest:

(i) that tariff reduction and reductions in credit and agricultural input subsidies are policy instruments which, although routinely recommended by donors

**Table 6.7.** *Simulation with Imposed Coefficients: Effects of Alternative Policy Packages – Malawi 1993-96*

| | (1) Base run value (1991) | Effect of Policy Packages: (mean % deviation from base run over a 3-year period) | | | |
| --- | --- | --- | --- | --- | --- |
| | | (i) if foreign resource inflows remain at present level in real terms | | (ii) if foreign resource inflows increase by $50m p.a. at 1993 prices | |
| | | (2) Eliminate fertilizer subsidy | (3) Halve nominal tariff rates | (4) Increase fertilizer subsidy to 30% | (5) Increase real public investment by $30m p.a. |
| *Production (million Kwacha)* | | | | | |
| Estate agriculture | 450 | −1.4 | +0.4 | +1.5 | +0.6 |
| Smallholder agriculture | 1,375 | −8.6 | −0.1 | +3.4 | +1.2 |
| Industry and services | 1,200 | −0.3 | −0.3 | +0.9 | +2.2 |
| Informal sector | 470 | −0.5 | 0.0 | +1.0 | +0.9 |
| Production of government services | 960 | −2.5[a] | −1.0[a] | +6.5[a] | +7.4 |
| Total GDP | 4,450 | −0.6 | +0.2 | +1.3 | +1.3 |
| Imports | 1,685 | +1.4 | +5.6 | +4.2 | +5.8 |
| Exports | 960 | −0.9 | +1.4 | +2.2 | +3.1 |
| Investment (private) | 390 | −0.7 | +0.2 | +1.5 | +4.6 |
| Consumer price index (1980 = 100) | 407.4 | +1.1 | −0.8 | +2.1 | +3.2 |
| *Real annual household income (Kwacha per capita)* | | | | | |
| Large smallholder | 395 | −7.3 | −1.4 | +10.4 | +7.9 |
| Small smallholders (0.5 ha) and estate employees | 192 | −5.4 | +0.6 | +4.7 | +5.3 |
| Urban informal sectors | 645 | −3.2 | −0.1 | +2.8 | +6.8 |
| Urban wage earners | 1,105 | −2.4 | +2.1 | +3.7 | +4.1 |

Note: a) Imposed by exogenous assumption from 'outside' the model.
Sources: (Base run values): Malawi, *Monthly Statistical Bulletin*; some extrapolations from World Bank, 1990b.

**Table 6.8.** *Sub-Saharan Africa: Evaluation of Structural Adjustment Instruments: Comparison of Results from Different Analytical Methods*

| Analytical Method | Impact of specific 'structural adjustment instruments': | | | | | |
| --- | --- | --- | --- | --- | --- | --- |
| | Structural adjustment instruments proper: | | | 'Catalysts' | | |
| | Reduction in nominal tariff rate | Reduction in agricultural subsidies and credit | Increase in real interest rates | Reduction in real exchange rate | Reduction in real public investment | Increase in policy instability |
| I Tabular comparison between 'policy clusters' | .. | .. | .. | (+) | — | — |
| II Regression analysis | — | — | (—) | (+) | (—) | .. |
| III Simulations with econometric model | — | — | — | + | — | .. |

Symbols: +, positive impact; —, negative impact; .., impact not measured.

Notes: a) Impact on real GDP only is considered in this table.
b) Brackets ( ) around an arithmetic sign denote that the impact of the policy instrument indicated on real GDP was statistically insignificant (at the .01 level of probability) with the analytical method chosen.

Sources: Same as Tables 6.4, 6.5 and 6.7.

in policy dialogue, may have negative effectiveness in the African context. This is not surprising, since the theoretical welfare economics case for these two policy reforms, above all in an African context where capital markets are imperfect, is particularly weak.

(ii) that the price-based policy instruments typically recommended in structural adjustment programmes can work only if other variables which we describe as 'catalysts' are also present: the ones we have examined are a competitive real exchange rate, policy stability and a rising tendency to government development spending.

What is crucial is that the policies of stabilization and structural adjustment which the World Bank and IMF advocate can, if unthinkingly applied, undermine these 'catalysts'. It may be that if future structural adjustment programmes in Africa are to be effective, they will need to take note of the interrelationship between these catalysts and the levers of 'structural adjustment proper', rather than examining the latter in isolation.

## Notes

1. Early World Bank Structural Adjustment loan documents foresaw that during a loan period averaging five years the balance-of-payments deficit would be reduced to an average of zero and two percentage points (on average) added to the annual growth rate of GNP (Mosley et al., 1991, Table 4.6).
2. See, for example, World Bank (1992), Table 7a, which shows that low-income and Sub-Saharan 'early intensive adjustment lending' countries achieved GDP increases of 1.2% and 1.6% respectively, as between 1976–80 and 1986–90, by comparison with 2.7% for the adjustment lending group as a whole.
3. For detailed evidence on the level of implementation of Bank programmes and a discussion of its determinants, see Mosley et al., 1991, Vol. 1, chap. 5 and Vol. 2 passim.
4. The first three propositions are contained in World Bank, 1990a and the fourth is in Sahn, 1992: 13–15.
5. Proportion of small farmers (<5 hectares) with access to formal-sector loans:

| | | | |
|---|---|---|---|
| Kenya | 22% | India | 38% |
| Malawi | 13% | Pakistan | 43% |
| Zimbabwe | 16% | Sri Lanka | 45% |

Source: Mosley (1993) Table 10. For an illustrative discussion of the implications of imperfect access to capital markets, see Stigler (1967).
6. It is also worth noting that such economic rationality as was incorporated into the original design of structural adjustment programmes was often swept away for political reasons at the implementation stage. In a comparative study of 9 countries, we were unable to find any correlation between the degree of *ex ante* distortion observable in the markets of developing countries and the degree of corrective action undertaken to remove such distortions (Mosley et al., 1991, Table 4.4).
7. The papers by Fischer (1991) and Easterly (1992), among others, combine policy variables and 'long period factors of productions' in regression equations with growth as the dependent variable. But the policy variables are macro-indicators such as the budget deficit and inflation rate rather than measures of 'structural adjustment'; in addition, measures of the 'external environment' are ignored.
8. For a through analysis of the availability of data for the assessment of adjustment-with-poverty-reduction packages in Sub-Saharan Africa, see World Bank (1990c) Chap. 6.
9. Tariff protection for 'infant' industries on a temporary basis can be justified on the grounds that it is necessary, in the presence of uncertainty and an imperfect capital market, to enable such industries to survive during the period in which they are moving down their cost curve and becoming internationally competitive. Subsidy for 'green revolution' inputs can be justified as

the only possible means of enabling small impoverished farmers to buy such inputs in the presence of an imperfect capital market. It is likely therefore that the removal of such strategic state interventions will be harmful for real output.

10. Stabilization frequently requires cuts in public expenditure, which for political reasons often fall on the development budget. These cuts in public capital spending – whether or not transmitted onward to the private sector – will weaken infrastructure and support services for producers and therefore reduce the economy's elasticity of supply. If the cuts are subsequently reversed under political pressure, and then perhaps reversed again under renewed financial pressure, the government's reputation for maintaining a stable policy stance will suffer.

11. Kenya and Zimbabwe have a stock exchange and bond market, with a number of firms including locally owned ones borrowing on the international markets. Estimates of the overall price elasticity of agricultural supply (which is lower than the price elasticity for individual crops) in the countries mentioned, range from 0.7 to 1.2. Underemployment of both labour (on a seasonal basis) and capital (see Ndulu, 1991) was widespread both before and during the structural adjustment process and, indeed, is a symptom of precisely the distortions which structural adjustment policies were intended to cure.

12. For a more extensive critique of the use of CGE models in developing countries, see Stern, 1989: 647–8.

13. Sahn and Sarris, however, note that they have stopped short of the type of modelling that is required to explain how policy has influenced the observed price trends, and hence cannot attribute the evolution of smallholder real incomes to adjustment programmes or any other specific factors (1991: 282).

## References

Bourguignon, F., de Melo, J. and Morrisson, C. (1991) 'Poverty and Income Distribution During Adjustment: Issues and Evidence from the OECD Project', World Development 19 (11), 1485–1509.

Bourguignon, F., de Melo, J. and Suwa, A. (1991) 'Distributional Effects of Adjustment Policies', World Bank Economic Review 5, 339–66.

Collier, P. and Gunning, J. W. (1992) 'Aid and Exchange Rate Adjustment in African Trade Liberalisations', Economic Journal 102, 925–39.

Easterly, W. (1992) 'Endogenous Growth in Developing Countries with Government-induced Distortions', in V. Corbo, S. Fischer and S. Webb (eds) Adjustment Lending Revisited: Policies to Restore Growth, A World Bank Symposium, Washington DC: World Bank.

Elbadawi, Ibrahim (1992) World Bank Adjustment Lending and Economic Performance in sub-Saharan Africa, Policy Research Working Paper No. 1001, Washington D.C.: World Bank, Country Economics Department.

Elbadawi, I., Ghura, D. and Uwujaren, G. (1992) World Bank Adjustment Lending and Economic Performance in sub-Saharan Africa in the 1980s, Policy Research Working Paper No. 1000, Washington D.C.: World Bank, Country Economics Department.

Fischer, S. (1991) Growth, Macroeconomics and Development, Cambridge, MA: MIT, Department of Economics Working Paper 580.

Graaff, J. de V. (1957) Theoretical Welfare Economics, Cambridge: Cambridge University Press.

de Janvry, A., Fafchamps, M. and Sadoulet, E. (1991) 'Peasant Household Behaviour with Missing Markets: Some Paradoxes Explained', Economic Journal 101, 1400–17.

de Janvry, A. and Sadoulet, E. (1992) 'Structural Adjustment under Transactions Costs', Paper presented to European Association of Agricultural Economists Meeting, Stuttgart.

Lele, U. (1989) Agricultural Growth, Domestic Policies, the External Environment and Assistance to Africa: Lessons of a Quarter Century, Washington DC: MADIA Discussion Paper No. 1.

Levine, R. and Renelt, D. (1991) Cross-Country Studies of Growth and Policy: Methodological, Conceptual and Statistical Problems, World Bank Working Paper No. 608, Washington DC: World Bank.

Lipsey, R. G. and Lancaster, K. (1957) 'The General Theory of the Second Best', Review of Economic Studies 16.

Mosley, P. (1993) 'Policy and Capital Market Constraints to the African Green Revolution', unpublished paper, University of Reading, to be published by UNICEF.

Mosley, P., Harrigan, J. and Toye, J. (1991) Aid and Power: The World Bank and Policy-based Lending, 2 Vols, London: Routledge.

Mosley, P. and Weeks, J. (1993) 'Has Recovery Begun?: "Africa's Adjustment in the 1980s" Revisited', World Development 21(9), 1583–1606.

Ndulu, B.J. (1991) 'Growth and Adjustment in sub-Saharan Africa' in A. Chhibber and S. Fischer (eds) *Economic Reform in sub-Saharan Africa, A Symposium*, Washington DC: World Bank.

Rodrik, D. (1990) 'How Should Structural Adjustment Programmes Be Designed?', *World Development* 18 (7), 933–47.

Rodrik, D. (1991) 'Policy Uncertainty and Private Investment in Developing Countries', *Journal of Development Economics* 36 (6), 229–42.

Sahn, D. (1992) 'The Impact of Macroeconomic Adjustment on Income, Health and Nutrition', Paper presented to Conference on Adjustment and Development in Sub-Saharan Africa, Florence, November.

Sahn, D. and Sarris, A. (1991) 'Structural Adjustment and the Welfare of Rural Smallholders: a Comparative Analysis from Sub-Saharan Africa', *World Bank Economic Review* 5 (2), 259–89.

Smith, L. and Spooner, N. (1990) 'Sequencing of Structural Adjustment Policy Instruments in the Agricultural Sector', unpublished paper, University of Glasgow.

Stern, E. (1983) 'World Bank Financing of Structural Adjustment' in J. Williamson (ed.) *IMF Conditionality*, Washington DC: Institute for International Economics.

Stern, N. (1989), 'The Economics of Development: a Survey', *Economic Journal*, Vol. 99 (September), pp. 597–685.

Stewart, F. (1992) 'The Many Faces of Adjustment' in P. Mosley (ed.) *Development Finance and Policy Reform*. Basingstoke, Macmillan.

Stigler, G. (1967) 'Imperfections in the Capital Market', *Journal of Political Economy* 75, 287–92.

Taylor, L. (1988) *Varieties of Stabilization Experience: Towards Sensible Macroeconomics in the Third World*. Oxford: Clarendon Press.

World Bank (1988) *Report on Adjustment Lending*, Document R88–199, Washington DC: World Bank, Country Economics Department.

World Bank (1990a) *Report on Adjustment Lending II: Policies for the Recovery of Growth*, Washington DC: World Bank, Country Economics Department.

World Bank (1990b) *Malawi: Growth through Poverty Reduction*, Report 8140-MAI, Washington DC: World Bank, Southern Africa Department.

World Bank (1990c) *Making Adjustment Work for the Poor*, Washington DC. World Bank.

World Bank (1992) *Adjustment Lending and Mobilisation of Public and Private Resources for Growth*, Policy and Research Series No. 22, Washington DC: World Bank, Country Economics Department.

**Annex 6.1.** *World Bank Adjustment Programmes in Sub-Saharan African Countries, 1981–91*

| Country | Exchange rate | Public Expend. | External trade | Agriculture | Public Enterpr. | Taxation | Financial Sector |
|---|---|---|---|---|---|---|---|
| 1. Benin | (CFA Zone) | Civil service reduction | Eliminate quotas | Remove fertilizer subsidies | Rationalize public enterprises | None | None |
| 2. Burkina Faso | (CFA Zone) | None | None | Reduce fertilizer subsidies | None | None | Extend credit to agricultural cooperatives |
| 3. Burundi[a] | Devaluation with IMF approval | Reduce deficit | Eliminate most import licences | Raise export prices; liberalize agric, marketing; remove fertilizer subsidies | Close non-viable enterprises | None | Deregulate interest rates; auction of treasury bills to financial institutions |
| 4. Cameroon[b] | (CFA Zone) | None | Eliminate export taxes | Privatize fertilizer distribution; establish agric. extension service | Prepare performance contracts | Introduce VAT | Restructure state-owned banks |
| 5. Côte d'Ivoire | (CFA Zone) | Reduce deficit; reduce education budget | Replace quotas by surcharges; eliminate export taxes (other than cocoa & coffee) | Reduce coffee & cocoa producer prices; introduce quality premiums on these | Higher electricity & water prices | None | None |
| 6. Gambia | None | Reduce civil service | None | Eliminate subsidies to groundnut marketing | None | None | Reduce Central Bank net credit to government and parastatals |
| 7. Ghana | Foreign exchange auction | Civil service reform; increase user charges for health & education | Replace quotas by tariffs; duty drawbacks for exporters | Cocoa producer price increases; reduce fertilizer subsidies | Cocoa board privatization; state enterprise rationalization | Unify corporate tax rates | Allow banks to set own interest rates |

**Annex 6.1.** *(cont.)*

| Country | Exchange rate | Public Expend. | External trade | Agriculture | Public Enterpr. | Taxation | Financial Sector |
|---|---|---|---|---|---|---|---|
| 8. Kenya | Devaluation with IMF approval | User charges for health, education, & other public services | Remove import bans; rationalize tariff schedules | New pricing for fertilizers; reduce role of maize marketing board | None | None | 'Market-determined' interest rates, to raise rates |
| 9. Madagascar[c] | Devaluation with IMF approval | None | Reduce import bans; eliminate export taxes; reduce tariffs | Reduce import subsidies on foods | Liquidate 14 public enterprises | None | None |
| 10. Malawi[d] | None | Ceiling on growth of recurrent expenditure; reduction of deficit; | Introduce 10% tax on tobacco & tea exports; reduce import & export licensing | Raise producer prices for cotton, tobacco; eliminate fertilizer subsidies | Enterprise reform | Expand excise tax base & move to ad valorem system | Deregulate interest rates on deposits |
| 11. Mali | (CFA Zone) | None | None | Eliminate export tax on cotton & coarse grains | Liquidate 5 public enterprises | None | None |
| 12. Mauritania[e] | None | None | None | None | Privatize, liquidate, reduce role of certain public enterprises; increase electricity & petrol prices | None | Restructure state-owned banks |
| 13. Mauritius | Devaluation with IMF approval | None | Replace quotas with tariffs | None | None | Introduce sales tax | None |
| 14. Mozambique[f] | Devaluation, additional adjustments agreed with IMF | Reduce deficit | Convert tariffs to ad valorem basis, establish duty drawback scheme for exporters | None | Industrial pricing to reflect exchange-rate movements | None | Raise interest rates |

| | | | | | | | |
|---|---|---|---|---|---|---|---|
| 15. Niger | (CFA Zone) | None | None | Reduce agric. input subsidies | Liquidate enterprises; remove price controls | None | None |
| 16. Nigeria | None | None | Remove import bans & import surcharges (some exceptions) | Reduce fertilizer subsidies | None | None | None |
| 17. Senegal[g] | (CFA Zone) | None | Increase customs duties; eliminate quotas; eliminate export taxes (except for groundnuts & phosphates) | Increase groundnut producer prices; privatize rice marketing | Reduce subsidy to public enterprises | Reform corporate & personal income taxes | Raise interest rates |
| 18. Sierra Leone | Float exchange rate (1985) | Reduce wage expenditures | Tariff reduction; eliminate quotas | Remove fertilizer subsidies; raise producer prices; privatize rice marketing | None | None | None |
| 19. Tanzania | Devaluation; prioritize foreign exchange allocations | None | Eliminate export taxes on sisal, coffee, tobacco; reduce tariffs; implement duty drawbacks for exporters | Eliminate restrictions on internal grain markets; reduce fertilizer subsidies | None | None | Raise interest rates |

**Annex 6.1.** (*cont.*)

| Country | Exchange rate | Public Expend. | External trade | Agriculture | Public Enterpr. | Taxation | Financial Sector |
|---------|---------------|----------------|----------------|-------------|-----------------|----------|------------------|
| 20. Togo | (CFA Zone) | None | Eliminate most quotas | Increase producer prices of coffee, cotton, tobacco | Close a number of enterprises; establish plan for full privatization | None | Raise interest rates |
| 21. Uganda | Devalue, then float | None | None | Increase producer prices of coffee, cotton, tea tobacco | Sell 5 parastatals | None | Raise interest rates |
| 22. Zaire | None | Reduce civil service wage expenditure | Reduce tariffs; eliminate taxes on non-traditional exports | None | Improve efficiency of certain parastatals | None | None |
| 23. Zambia | Devaluation with IMF approval | None | Levy tariff on all intermediate goods; reduce tariff levels | None | None | None | Decontrol interest rates |

Source: World Bank Adjustment Loan Conditionality Index.

The following footnotes give conditionalities not falling into the seven categories:

a Develop a poverty alleviation programme.
b Implement strategies to increase role of women in development.
c Carry out environmental impact study for titanium plant.
d Strengthen capacity to monitor and analyse impact of adjustment programme on the poor; undertake an integrated household survey on poverty issues.
e Define target groups to receive food distribution, based on Social Dimensions of Adjustment survey.
f Improve safety net for providing goods to the poor.
g Formulate population policy.

# PART THREE
The Social Consequences
and Political Dimensions
of Adjustment

# 7 The Uncertain Distributional Impact of Structural Adjustment in Sub-Saharan Africa
## JEAN–PAUL AZAM

Although the issue of the social impact of structural adjustment has attracted a lot of attention since the mid-1980s (Cornia *et al.*, 1987; Azam *et al.*, 1989; World Bank, 1990), there is still very little evidence to show whether any general rule can be determined about winners and losers in the adjustment process. One can distinguish two main domains where adjustment policies lead to a social impact, namely the distribution of real income by the market mechanism and the provision of public goods by the state (Azam *et al.*, 1989). In the present paper, the analysis is restricted to the former. Moreover, we further restrict our field of investigation by reducing the issue to that of the impact of macroeconomic policy reforms on the welfare of the poor.

The distributional outcome of policy reforms seems to depend to a large extent on the nature of the problems facing each individual country, on the type of policies adopted, which may sometimes involve quite heterodox elements, and on the different external shocks to which the economy is subjected during the course of the adjustment programme. This general uncertainty about the social impact of adjustment programmes is not only due to the limitations of the empirical analyses of the issue which have been completed so far, but is intrinsically rooted in the concept of structural adjustment. The uncertainty can be predicted from the simplest theoretical analysis, within the Salter-Swan framework (Kanbur, 1991). This is illustrated very briefly in the following section, where the distributional impact of inflation and of public sector retrenchment is discussed as well.

In addition to this theoretical ambiguity, the empirical analysis of the issue is complicated because national accounts are usually of little use in tracking national income and its distribution between even the most globally defined aggregates during a period of structural adjustment. This is again due both to conceptual reasons and to practical problems. In particular, the abrupt changes in the productive structure of the economies undergoing structural adjustment usually lead to a large and increasing underrecording of GDP, as the informal sector develops both absolutely and relatively to the formal sector. As a result of this probable change in the ratio of recorded to unrecorded economic activity, considerable uncertainty occurs in using the national accounts to track the changes in income *per capita* in a given country, let alone in trying to compare the changes affecting different countries. In addition, structural adjustment is fundamentally about changing relative prices, so that there is a basic index number problem in determining the change in national income. This is illustrated in a later section.

It was therefore considered necessary to collect specially designed information in order to evaluate the social impact of structural adjustment. This has been attempted through a large number of household surveys, in Africa and elsewhere, most notably under the aegis of the World Bank. Unfortunately, it takes time to extract the relevant information from the existing surveys, so that there are in fact very few examples of definite results emerging from this type of exercise. The Côte d'Ivoire Living Standard Survey is one such example (Grootaert, 1993). This survey was run for four consecutive years (1985–88), and some of its results have recently been published. We comment on them later on, as well as on some less systematic information. But here again some measurement issues could be raised, in particular about poverty when changes in explicit or implicit food subsidies, and more generally in the relative price of food and non-food goods, occur. This is not presented here.

Hence, there is no firm knowledge about the social impact of structural adjustment. The theory leads to ambiguous results, the national account data are of no reliable help, and the survey data have not yet been made widely available. Moreover, in addition to the evaluation issue, i.e. the question of knowing whether any economic change is good or bad for some classes of the population, there is a conceptual issue in determining whether any given event occurring in the wake of the adoption of an adjustment programme is due to the programme or would have happened anyway, with possibly worse consequences, without it. This is the issue of counterfactuals, which is central to the proper definition of the impact of economic policy reforms, after controlling for other events.

But this global uncertainty about the social impact of structural adjustment only concerns the direct effects. We are asking whether such and such a policy change, whose main goal has nothing to do with income distribution, will affect different groups in the population, and there is generally no firm conclusion available. This turns out to be of limited practical interest. As it is generally agreed that some form of structural adjustment cannot be avoided when countries find themselves in a difficult position with a severe macroeconomic imbalance, the interesting question is whether structural adjustment needs to conflict with the policies aimed at poverty alleviation. This is the issue briefly addressed in the penultimate section of this chapter. It is a vast question, which can only be touched on here. But there are some political economy arguments which can be (provocatively) advanced to support the view that structural adjustment, as we commonly understand it, is the only option open for making poverty alleviation possible despite adverse economic conditions.

## The Theoretical Ambiguity of the Distributional Impact of Adjustment

Some of the basic elements of a structural adjustment programme can be analysed within the framework of the standard Salter-Swan model (see e.g. World Bank, 1990). Within this framework, one can analyse the distributional consequences of policy reform by looking at its impact on the purchasing power of the wage rate. In most countries, the welfare of the poor is bound to depend positively on this variable, as labour is their main productive asset. It is known, however, that labour remuneration rarely takes the form of a wage payment in the strict sense (Sen, 1975). This is particularly true in rural Africa, where some form of sharecropping is the rule. Nevertheless, it would be very surprising if the price of labour were able to remain completely unrelated to its marginal productivity. The following analysis can therefore be regarded as a reasonable approximation.

First of all, as structural adjustment aims at encouraging some supply-side policies for improving the balance of trade, it is very common to regard a depreciation of the real exchange rate as the central point of such a reform programme. This does not need to be effected by a nominal devaluation, and would not in fact follow mechanically from a nominal devaluation if inflation swamped its impact (Devarajan and de Melo, 1987; Guillaumont-Jeanneney, 1985). Aggregate demand management plays a crucial part in determining the real impact of a nominal devaluation. It is in fact the main element of any policy aiming at depreciating the real exchange rate. As this policy move aims to increase the level of output in the sector producing tradeables, while simultaneously reducing the output level of non-tradeables, it can be quite straightforwardly shown that the impact on the real wage rate *must necessarily* be ambiguous: the real wage in terms of tradeables must go down, in order to induce the firms in this sector to hire more labour and produce more, while it must go up in terms of non-tradeables, in order to induce the firms in this sector to free the required amount of labour and reduce production there. Hence the impact on the consumption wage, which is relevant for evaluating the welfare effect on workers, will in fact depend on the shares of tradeables and non-tradeables in the representative consumption basket, and on the share of the tradeables sector in total employment.

A depreciation of the real exchange rate is good for the purchasing power of the wage rate, and hence for the welfare of the poorest agents in the economy, if (i) the share of tradeables in their total consumption is small, because the real depreciation increases the price of tradeables relative to that of non-tradeables, and if (ii) the share of the tradeables sector in total employment is large. This follows from the fact that a real depreciation has a positive impact on the demand for labour by the tradeable sector, and a negative impact on the demand for labour by the non-tradeable sector. The larger the former, relative to the size of the labour market, the more likely is a positive impact on the consumption wage following a real depreciation. Kanbur (1987, 1991) has further analysed the issue of the impact of structural adjustment on poverty and income distribution, along the lines sketched above. But he uses a more disaggregated model, bringing out even more causes for the ambiguity of the results.

Moreover, the distributional impact might depend on whether the real depreciation is obtained from a nominal depreciation or by other means (Azam et al., 1989; Guillaumont and Guillaumont-Jeanneney, 1992). The main difference between the two cases has to do with the impact of the rise in the price level which is triggered by the exchange-rate realignment. The devaluation entails an increase in the general price level, which results in a fall in real cash balances, provided the nominal money supply is kept under control. The inflation tax will affect the agents who hold money balances, and will be evaded by two types of agents. First, many rich people have access to indexed financial assets, or even more generally to assets denominated in foreign currency. The devaluation will not affect them. Second, many rural people hold their assets in kind, in granaries or livestock. These agents will similarly escape the inflation tax. Therefore, the devaluation-induced inflation will normally mainly affect the urban poor, and the poorest rural workers who do not own any land or real assets (Azam et al., 1989).

From a macroeconomic point of view, the cut in real balances implied by the devaluation should mainly affect private consumption via the real cash balance effect, and private investment inasmuch as the interest rate rises. If capital is perfectly mobile, as in the famous Mundell-Flemming model, the latter effect will not occur. Moreover, a credit squeeze may follow, with possibly some adverse impact on employment, entailed by the cut in the real value of working capital (Taylor, 1983).

Contrariwise, when devaluation is not used, real depreciation must be brought about by a cut in public spending. Generally it is politically easier to cut public investment than public consumption. Although some cuts in the public sector wage bill are likely, it is the fall in public investment which will usually bear the brunt of the fall in demand. The case of Côte d'Ivoire offers a vivid illustration of this case (Azam, 1993a). It will normally entail a contraction of the construction sector, with some second-round effects on wage income and poverty. This might be partly offset by the increase in working capital resulting from the cut in public sector borrowing, with a resulting increase in labour demand by the private sector. But the main difference from the devaluation case is that the real depreciation must be disinflationary or even deflationary in the no-devaluation case, whereas it must be inflationary in the opposite case. The impact on private consumption will therefore be different. Ceteris paribus, the real depreciation brought about without devaluation should leave the level of private consumption at a higher level than in the devaluation case, and thus result in a smaller increase in poverty.

In the long run, the impact of the real depreciation also depends on whether it has been brought about by devaluation or deflation. In the latter case, we have seen that a cut in public investment is very likely to occur. Its impact on private investment will be crucial for determining the long-run impact of the policy reform. Conventional wisdom, such as could be found in most macroeconomics textbooks in the 1970s, would welcome the cut in public investment, and would predict that this cut would crowd in private investment, as the supply of credit to the private sector is to some extent freed by the cut in government borrowing. Unfortunately for this argument, and despite all the uncertainty surrounding the empirical analyses of investment in developing countries, it now seems that the evidence leans in favour of the cuts in public investment having a negative impact on private investment (Greene and Villanueva, 1991; Bleaney and Greenaway, 1993). There is some complementarity between public and private investment, which is entailed by infrastructure, human capital, and other positive externalities brought about by public investment, and it seems to dominate the indirect impact through the availability of finance that a cut in public investment would imply. Hence, the choice between devaluation and deflation as a means of promoting real depreciation entails a trade-off between poverty now and poverty later, leaving some scope for smoothing the incidence of poverty over time.

Thirdly, structural adjustment usually implies some restructuring of public sector firms, often leading to job losses and some real wage cuts in this sector. However, the employees so affected, and thus their often large families, do not generally belong to the poorest segments of society. One therefore needs to emphasize the indirect impact of these retrenchments on the demand and supply of labour in the private sector in order to assess their impact on poverty. A lot depends on the assumption that one is prepared to make regarding the links between public sector wages and private sector ones. A common assumption in policy debates is that the level of public sector wages plays a leading role in the labour market. In this case, a cut in the wages and salaries of employees in the public sector is a direct way to trigger a fall in the wages and salaries of the private sector, and hence to enhance competitiveness.

In developing countries, such an assumption sounds plausible only for skilled labour in the formal sector. It is not convincing for unskilled labour, where it is the level of public employment which seems to matter, more than the level of public sector wages (Lindauer, 1991): the higher the level of public employment, the higher the wage rate in the private sector, *ceteris paribus*. The reason for this view is that the marginal wage rate is determined by supply and demand in the informal segment of the market, as no worker in developing countries can afford to remain unemployed. What public sector employment does in this framework is to reduce the residual supply of labour to the private sector, with a resulting upward pressure on the wage rate.

Hence, according to this view, labour retrenchment in the public sector will depress the wage rate, by increasing the supply of labour to the private sector. But one may find some offsetting forces at work. For example, in many countries the government has reduced its demand for skilled labour, for example by discontinuing the habit of systematically providing a job in the public sector to any graduate of the education system, or has provided some incentives for skilled labour to quit the public sector, by reducing wage differentials, offering attractive severance pay, etc. (Lindauer *et al.*, 1988). Then, as the skill intensity of employment in the private sector increases, so does the marginal productivity of unskilled labour. As a result, the wage rate for unskilled labour may increase, *ceteris paribus*.

Thus we have found many reasons why it is impossible to predict the impact of structural adjustment on poverty and the distribution of income from a purely theoretical point of view. There are many arguments going in opposite directions, resulting in an intrinsically ambiguous distributional impact. But this theoretical ambiguity cannot easily be lifted by empirical analyses. There are some daunting measurement problems, which prevent these issues being amenable to a satisfactory analysis using the type of data usually collected in developing countries. There is thus a need for some specially collected data, which is costly for developing countries.

## Some Measurement Problems

The policy shocks entailed by structural adjustment result in changes in relative prices and in the sectoral composition of output which make national accounts

Non-Tradeables

Figure 7.1.
*The ambiguity of
the change in GDP*

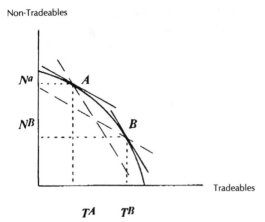

rather unreliable as a tool for tracking changes in income. This results both from
a basic index number problem, and from a practical problem. The former problem is illustrated in Figure 7.1, which again uses the standard Salter-Swan
model. The output of tradeables is measured along the horizontal axis, and the
output of non-tradeables along the vertical axis. Given the real exchange rate
$r^A$, the equilibrium point is A, where the slope of the tangent to the production
possibility frontier is equal to $r^A$. Similarly, B is the equilibrium point cor-
responding to the real exchange rate $r^B$. As $r^B > r^A$, one can regard the move
from point A to point B as resulting from a real depreciation. The output level
of tradeables has gone up, from $T^A$ to $T^B$, and the output level of non-
tradeables has gone down, from $N^A$ to $N^B$.

Whatever the chosen numeraire, it is obvious that the move from A to B will
be measured as a fall in GDP, if it is measured using the relative price $r^A$, and
as an increase in GDP if it is measured using $r^B$ as the relative price. To check
this point, draw through B a line with slope $r^A$, and through A, a line with
slope $r^B$. As B is located above the line through A with slope $r^B$, GDP is higher
in B than in A, at this relative price. Notice that this result is true whether we
measure the change in GDP in terms of tradeables or non-tradeables, or any combination of the two, provided it is measured at constant relative prices. On the
other hand, the line through B with slope $r^A$ lies below A. Therefore, whatever
the chosen numeraire, GDP has grown from A to B, when valued at the new
relative prices, and it had declined, when valued at the old relative prices. In
other words, given the level of technology and the supply of production factors,
the success of structural adjustment is shown by a *fall in output*, if the latter is
measured at the pre-adjustment relative prices, and by an increase in output, if
it is measured at the post-adjustment relative prices. Of course, such comparisons
will be a little more complicated in the real world, because of events which may
occur independently at the same time as the adjustment policies, such as changes
in factor productivity or the increase in the supply of production factors implied
by past investment and demographic growth.

This simple result has some important consequences for the measurement
of growth between two dates before and after the adoption of a structural
adjustment policy. To the extent that the latter entails a real depreciation, as it

should in general, and assuming (hopefully) that the new relative prices are less distorted than the old ones, then GDP at constant (pre-adjustment) prices will underestimate the actual growth in output, and may even point to a fall in output, even if there is real growth. Azam *et al.* (1988) have illustrated the size of the measurement problem involved by this type of change in relative prices, by computing GDP growth for a large number of countries over the period 1970–81, partially rebasing the data by taking in turn the relative prices for every year as constant prices, using a GDP decomposition in 12 sectors. The average growth rate for the same country, computed from the different series so produced, can vary quite widely for countries which have experienced wide swings in relative prices over the period of study. For example, the average growth rate of Nigeria over the period 1970–81 is 0.93%, when computed using the 1972 relative prices, and it is 8.09% at the 1973 relative prices. In this case, it is the change in the relative price of oil which makes the difference. But any massive change in relative prices, of the type brought about by real devaluation in some countries in the 1980s, could have an impact on the series of the same order of magnitude. It is thus difficult to diagnose correctly the change of real GDP over a given period of time, when relative prices exhibit such violent swings.

A related issue concerns the measurement of the output of the so-called informal sector. In times of structural adjustment, when some of the most protected industries in the formal sector are more or less gradually dismantled, and when a lot of rents are dissipated by the removal of various distortions, an important share of the productive resources has to be transferred from the formal to the informal sector. Many workers retrenched from the public sector have to find some activity in the informal sector, and many small firms must go informal in order to obtain the flexibility required for undergoing the necessary changes.

In this case GDP as usually measured in developing countries will probably get completely out of line with the actual output growth. The reason for this is that in the real world national accounts have only a very distant knowledge of what is going on in the informal sector. Very often, especially in Africa, the figure for the GDP of the informal sector is more an artefact of the Ministry of Planning than an actual observation. One generally has an old survey of this sector, dating back to the early 1970s or the late 1960s, giving some relative order of magnitude for the formal and informal sectors. This figure is then updated year after year, using some simple formula based on the observed growth of the formal sector and of the population. Roughly speaking, it is therefore fair to say that the share of the informal sector in GDP is mainly a function of the formula used, rather than of any type of actual events. Thus, when an abrupt process of sectoral recomposition occurs, of the type entailed by the usual programmes of structural adjustment, there are very few chances that the behaviour of the informal sector will be tracked with any accuracy.

One can in fact conjecture that GDP will be systematically underestimated, as there is some substitution between the two sectors on the production side, while the national accounts impose some form of complementarity. It follows that GDP, or GDP *per capita*, will under these circumstances be a very poor indicator of the actual change in income of the population. In other words, the income data from the national accounts are bound to become less accurate, the more information is required on actual income changes. There is thus a need for using some different sources of information for assessing the distributional impact of policy reform.

## Some Lessons from Household Surveys

There are very few data sets available allowing one to analyse over any interesting period of time the economic changes undergone by households in Sub-Saharan Africa in times of structural adjustment. The most interesting data set available is for Côte d'Ivoire, where a Living Standard Measurement Survey (LSMS) was performed during four consecutive years (1985–88). The panel of households was made up of 1,600 households, with half of them being renewed each year. We do not therefore have cohorts of households which can be followed year after year over the whole period, but many of the households surveyed can be followed for two consecutive years.

Côte d'Ivoire experienced a fairly changing macroeconomic situation over this period of time (Azam, 1993a). After a public investment boom in the late 1970s, in the wake of the coffee and cocoa booms of the mid-1970s, the country undertook its first programme of structural adjustment, which was regarded as a success by the World Bank up to 1986 (ibid.) After this date, the terms of trade deteriorated dramatically reaching a historical trough in the 1990s. The government initially reacted to this massive negative shock by suspending its external debt service and speculating on a return to normal of the prices of its export crops. It maintained producer prices at a high level, which turned out to be unsustainable for budgetary reasons, which was quite evident ex post, and refused to sell the cocoa crop on the world market. This move was aimed at speculating (quite appropriately) on the behaviour of the French Government, which eventually bought most of the crop at an unknown price, generally thought to be above the market price (ibid.). Eventually, the country undertook a new adjustment programme, with a difficult start, in 1989–90. This second programme is not generally regarded as a success, and the year 1991 was especially difficult for Côte d'Ivoire from a financial point of view. The World Bank temporarily suspended the disbursement of its loans, because of some payment arrears in July 1991.

In other words, for the purpose in hand, the results of the LSMS allow for some interesting analyses, as they cover two years at the end of the successful 1981–86 adjustment programme, and two years during which the government postponed adjustment, in the hope of better days to come.

These data have been analysed by Grootaert (1993), and they show that the abandonment of the adjustment effort in 1987 and 1988 occurred at the same time as a serious deterioration in the poverty situation. This exercise does not allow one to draw strong causal interpretations, so that it would be wrong to conclude that the suspension of the adjustment effort was the cause of the increase in poverty incidence. Nevertheless, it does suggest that the structural adjustment programme cannot be regarded as a direct cause of the deepening of poverty which took place during the non-adjustment years. Before that, the incidence of poverty remained steady, and the incidence of extreme poverty fell. Moreover, it is interesting to note that poverty increased in 1987–88 even among export-crop farmers, while the government was making great efforts to protect them from the collapse of the world price of their products (coffee and cocoa). It supported the producer prices by an implicit subsidy paid by the *Caisse de Stabilisation* (Azam, 1993a), and tried to support the world price unilaterally by refusing to sell the crop in 1988. These two actions were disastrous for the country's financial position, and they failed to save the farmers from a deterioration in their situation. According to the survey data, the quantities sold by the farmers fell, despite the price support given by the state. This was probably due to the lack of liquidity of the traders, to whom the *Caisse de Stabilisation* was increasingly in debt.

Interestingly enough, Grootaert (1993) offers a breakdown of the change in poverty into a part due to growth or the lack of it, and a part due to a change in distribution. The results show beyond doubt that it was the lack of growth which was responsible for the deepening of poverty, while the changes in distribution played a somewhat equalizing role. In this case therefore macroeconomic policy can be regarded as the main ingredient of a policy aimed at poverty alleviation. Nevertheless, it seems that the deterioration of poverty did not fall neutrally on all groups in the economy, as the employees in the urban informal sector and the planters in the West Forest zone were hit most adversely.

Hence, the only piece of hard evidence that we have on the distributional impact of structural adjustment fails to support the view that adjustment necessarily worsens the poverty situation. It suggests on the contrary that it is the lack of adjustment which may entail some very detrimental effects in this respect. Nevertheless, this finding is not completely satisfactory, as one should in fact be able to compare the poverty situation in 1981, at the start of the adjustment process, with that of 1986, in order to assess the full impact of the successful adjustment programme.

Sahn and Sarris (1991) attempt such a comparison, using some simulation techniques, focusing on rural smallholders who were undoubtably the poorest people in Côte d'Ivoire at the start of the adjustment period. Their results show a very slight deterioration in their real income *per capita* during the first adjustment period, from 100 in 1981 to 97.8 in the forest zone in 1986, and to 96.3 in the savannah zone. A sharp deterioration occurred afterwards, as in Grootaert's data, with income *per capita* falling to 87.0 in 1987 in the forest zone, and to 86.6 in the savannah zone. However, some counterfactuals would be necessary for analysing whether the deterioration would have been worse or not if the government had reacted more rapidly, and had adjusted immediately to the shock. Such an exercise falls outside the scope of the present paper.

No other data sets exist in Sub-Saharan Africa for analysing with such detailed information the impact of structural adjustment on the poor. But some partial information exists in some countries, which can be used to compensate for some of the gaps left by the national accounts data. For example, in the case of Niger, which started its structural adjustment programme in 1983, one can use two establishment surveys of the informal sector, which took place in 1982 and 1987

(Azam *et al.*, 1993). Although these data have not been collected for this purpose, and their comparability is far from perfect, they suggest some tentative conclusions regarding the evolution of poverty during the adjustment phase. The most striking feature is the increase in the level of activity in the informal sector. According to these data, the number of enterprises has gone up during this period as well as the number of employees per firm and the wage. This suggests that the level of urban poverty has gone down, provided one is prepared to assume that the employees in the informal sector are the poorest people in town, as is found in other surveys, including the Côte d'Ivoire LSMS discussed above.

This is an interesting example of the way in which a programme of structural adjustment can unleach the dynamism of the informal sector, resulting in a true liberalization of production, with positive effects on employment and income generation. Of course, this raises fundamental issues for public finance, as the informal sector is not well covered by the tax net. Hence, there may be a basic conflict in times of structural adjustment between the objective of restructuring the production sectors, with the increased flexibility entailed by the informalization of production, and the objective of a quick return to macroeconomic equilibrium. As the private sector picks up, there is a risk of the collapse of fiscal revenues, as in Niger, which may jeopardize the budget balance. This practical opposition raises the broader issue of the political economy of structural adjustment and poverty alleviation.

## Political Economy of Structural Adjustment and Poverty Alleviation

The need for structural adjustment felt at the beginning of the 1980s could be blamed on particular groups in society. It is true in many Sub-Saharan African countries that the public expenditure spree which took place in the wake of the commodities boom of the mid-1970s laid the ground for the stabilization *cum* structural adjustment episodes of the 1980s. But this public spending spree cannot be regarded as sociologically neutral. The study of the reaction of various types of economic agents to these shocks is quite revealing (Bevan *et al.*, 1993). Private agents consistently tend to save their windfall gains, when the state allows them to get hold of these gains (which it can confiscate in some cases), whereas a more diverse type of response occurs when the government inherits the income from a boom. In this case, the government control over public expenditures often disappears, with the bureaucracy capturing the loot. Bevan *et al.* (1993) present a large set of examples of such a loss of control over expenditures on the part of the government. Exceptions occur sometimes when the President is in a strong position.

The political economy of the bureaucratic state in developing countries is in its infancy. But Findlay (1991) has provided an interesting theoretical framework into which analysis of the behaviour of the bureaucracies of developing countries can be fitted quite convincingly. The bureaucratic state is then perceived as trying to maximize the budget which it can spend. It is to be distinguished from the predatory state, which maximizes the surplus of public revenues over public expenditures, in order to seize it for private consumption.

In many cases, one can regard the political economy stake of stabilization and structural adjustment as the return of the political power from the hands of the bureaucracy to the civil society. The bureaucracy has often obtained its power from the windfall money accruing to the state during commodity booms, when the loss of government control has given *de facto* discretion over public expenditure to the bureaucrats. Public enterprises and other parastatals mushroomed during the external shocks of the 1970s, with some amplification due to foreign credit. These bodies provide very convenient opportunities for spending public money for the benefit of certain privileged groups. Overmanning, excessive luxurious investment with generous payments on the side, etc. are the hallmark of this period in many developing countries. In the franc zone countries, the public enterprises are in addition the most convenient means for circumventing the institutional controls on government expenditures which are entailed by the 20% rule. This rule limits to 20% of the fiscal revenues of the preceding year the deficit that any government of a member state can finance from its local banking sector (Guillaumont and Guillaumont, 1984). But the deficits incurred by the public enterprises are not covered by this rule, and can be financed by the banking system with almost no government control.

The adjustment packages offered by the IMF and the World Bank launch their attack directly at the root of the problem, by offering to reduce public expenditure, restructure or privatize public enterprises, reduce the control of the state over the economy, etc. Most of these measures threaten the basis of the bureaucratic way of life. But these institutions are called in by some states, when they are cornered by mounting deficits and foreign indebtedness. In other cases, they appear to fit in with the plans of the President for regaining power over the bureaucracy. This was the case in Côte d'Ivoire, where a zealous President Houphouët-Boigny started to restructure public enterprises as early as 1980, before having reached any agreement with the Bretton Woods institutions.

Hence, structural adjustment programmes have a definite political economy content, by shaking the foundations of bureaucratic power. They impose some countervailing power to confront the bureaucracy, which can be used for pushing economic policy in directions which are not directly in the interests of the ruling bureaucracy. In this case, some poverty-conscious restructuring of public expenditures can occur, if the external institutions choose to go in this direction. The periods in which adjustment programmes are negotiated or implemented thus offer some unique opportunities for influencing the choice of policies that support the interests of politically weak groups, such as the poor are in most countries and especially in non-democratic ones. This mainly concerns the composition of public spending rather than the impacts on prices and incomes of structural adjustment, analysed above. A new twist is given to this question by the process of democratization which has recently started in many Sub-Saharan African countries. It raises several issues, such as whether or not the poor are going to obtain better political influence in a democratic system, and whether democratization may entail some economic costs which run counter to the aims of structural adjustment (Azam, 1993b). It is possible, on the other hand, that the bureaucrats and other urban white-collar workers end up getting even more influence through the ballot box than they had in the past.

These observations raise the issue of the appropriate role of international agencies in determining the social impact of structural adjustment. In most countries undergoing such policy reforms, it is quite evident that there is really no choice: not adjusting is not an option. In the recent past, after 1986, most developing countries found themselves in a situation where their terms of trade had experienced one of the worst deteriorations in history, where interest rates and debt-service obligations had reached unprecedented heights, and where the net flow of bank credit had dried up. The options therefore were either to adjust with no external help, while keeping full control over the measures to be adopted, or to try to find some external support, at the cost of some loss in policy discretion, as conditionality was then a well understood concept.

The second option offers two advantages over the first, with respect to the social impact of adjustment. First, by providing some financing for external imbalance, foreign intervention (which recently means, as a prerequisite, signing an agreement with the IMF) allows for a softer and more gradual stabilization. Instead of immediately bringing down aggregate demand to the level of supply, the use of foreign savings helps to carry out the adjustment more gradually, with a smaller demand contraction inflicted upfront. Therefore, if it is so decided, consumption *per capita* of the poor may fall less compared with the case where adjustment has to be carried out with no external support. Secondly, in the absence of any external intervention, the ruling groups are bound to try and manage the stabilization effort in such a way that their own interests are affected least, whereas external agencies (and bilateral donors) can, if they wish, to some degree defend the interests of the politically weak groups, including the poor. Thus, the main potential support of the poor in times of structural adjustment may come from external agencies.

## Conclusion

In this paper, we have tried to undermine a lot of received ideas about the social consequences of adjustment. For many people, this expression refers to the changes affecting the welfare of the poor in times of structural adjustment. It has often been taken as a postulate that the policy reforms undertaken in the 1980s by most governments of Sub-Saharan Africa, usually with some support from external agencies, had dismal consequences. It has been argued here that this generalization is far from warranted.

The theory of structural adjustment, which can be based on the simplest Salter-Swan framework, shows that there are no theoretically compelling reasons why this type of policy reform should especially harm the poor. Even when taking a richer view of the different aspects of this type of programme than this simple model, one still gets the impression that the ambiguity of the impact becomes more convincing, rather than being lifted by the increased complexity of the framework used.

Moreover, this theoretical ambiguity cannot be simply lifted or sidestepped by looking at the most easily available data for developing countries, namely national accounts. In times of structural adjustment, relative prices undergo wide changes, and this poses a fundamental index-number problem for correctly measuring the changes in income *per capita*. This problem is compounded by the lack of usable information on the level of activity in the informal sector that prevails in most of Sub-Saharan Africa. There is a strong presumption that GDP is increasingly underestimated when the informal sector increases its share of GDP, as is certainly the case in times of structural adjustment.

Hence, it seems that the whole issue of the social impact of structural adjustment is bound to remain fundamentally unresolved in the future, from both a theoretical as well as an empirical point of view. Nevertheless, this does not mean that the relationship between structural adjustment and poverty should be neglected. On the contrary, it suggests that the issue should be analysed case by case. Moreover, there are some good arguments to suggest that the external interventions allowed by the adjustment needs of the various governments open up an interesting avenue for compensating for the general lack of political influence that the poor have in developing countries. It is up to the international agencies (and the bilateral donors) involved in the conception and implementation of policy reforms to make adjustment work for the poor.

## References

Azam, J-P. (1993a) *La faisabilité politique de l'ajustement en Côte d'Ivoire (1981–1990)*, Paris: OECD Development Centre.

Azam, J-P. (1993b): 'Democracy and Development: A Theoretical Framework', *Public Choice*,

Azam, J-P., Chambas, G., Guillaumont, P. and Guillaumont, S. (1989) *The Impact of Macroeconomic Policies on the Rural Poor*, UNDP Policy Discussion Paper. New York: United Nations Publications.

Azam, J-P., Guillaumont, P. and Guillaumont, S. (1988) *Methodological Problems in Cross-Country Analyses of Economic Growth*, PPR Working Papers, Working Paper Series 22, Washington DC: World Bank.

Azam, J-P., Bonjean, C., Chambas, G. and Mathonnat, J. (1993) *Le Niger: la pauvreté en période d'ajustement*, Paris: L'Harmattan.

Bevan, D., Collier, P. and Gunning, J.W. (1993) 'Trade Shocks in Developing Countries. Consequences and Policy Responses', *European Economic Review* 37, 557–65.

Bleaney, M. and Greenaway, D. (1993) 'Adjustment to External Imbalance and Investment Slumps in Developing Countries', *European Economic Review* 37, 577–85.

Cornia, G.A., Jolly, R. and Stewart, F. (eds) (1987) *Adjustment with a Human Face – Protecting the Vulnerable and Promoting Growth*. Oxford: Clarendon Press.

Devarajan, S. and de Melo, J. (1987) 'Adjustment with a Fixed Exchange Rate: Cameroon, Côte d'Ivoire and Senegal', *World Bank Economic Review* 1, 447–87.

Findlay, R. (1991) 'The New Political Economy: Its Explanatory Power for LDCs', in G.M. Meier (ed.) *Politics and Policy Making in Developing Countries*. San Francisco, CA: ICS Press.

Greene, J. and Villanueva, D. (1991) 'Private Investment in Developing Countries', *IMF Staff Papers* 38, 33–8.

Grootaert, C. (1993) *The Evolution of Welfare and Poverty Under Structural Change and Economic Recession in Côte d'Ivoire, 1985–88*, Working Paper No. 1078. Washington DC: World Bank.

Guillaumont, P. and Guillaumont, S. (1984) *Zone Franc et développement africain*, Paris: Economica.

Guillaumont, P. and Guillaumont-Jeanneney, S. (1992): 'Les conséquences sociales de l'ajustement en Afrique selon la politique de change', *Politique africaine*, 101–22.

Guillaumont-Jeanneney, S. (1985) 'Foreign Exchange Policy and Economic Performance: A Study of Senegal, Madagascar, and Guinea', in T. Rose (ed.) *Crisis and Recovery in Sub-Saharan Africa*, OECD, Development Centre Seminar. Paris: OECD.

Kanbur, S.M.R. (1987) 'Structural Adjustment, Macroeconomic Adjustment, and Poverty: A Methodology for Analysis', *World Development* 15 (12), 1515–26.

Kanbur, S.M.R. (1991) 'The Theory of Structural Adjustment and Trade Policy', in J.H. Frimpong-

Ansah, S. M. R. Kanbur, and P. Svedberg (eds) *Trade and Development in Sub-Saharan Africa*, Manchester: Manchester University Press.

Lindauer, D. L. (1991) 'Government Pay and Employment Policy: A Parallel Market in Labor', in M. Roemer and C. Jones (eds) *Markets in Developing Countries, Parallel, Fragmented, and Black*, San Francisco, CA: ICS Press.

Lindauer, D.L., Meesook, O. A. and Suebsaeng, P. (1988) 'Government Wage Policy in Africa: Some Findings and Policy Issues', *World Bank Research Observer* 3, 1–25.

Sahn, D. E. and Sarris, A. (1991) 'Structural Adjustment and the Welfare of Rural Smallholders: A Comparative Analysis from Sub-Saharan Africa', *World Bank Economic Review* 5 (2), 259–89.

Sen, A. K. (1975) *Employment, Technology and Development*. Oxford: Clarendon Press.

Taylor, L. (1983) *Structuralist Macroeconomics*. New York: Basic Books.

World Bank (1990) *Making Adjustment Work for the Poor*. Washington DC: World Bank.

# 8 Structural Adjustment and Poverty Alleviation: Some Issues on the Use of Social Safety Nets and Targeted Public Expenditures
## VENKATESH SESHAMANI

Conspicuous poverty and poor living standards are generally associated with countries with low or negative rates of economic growth. By inference, then, poverty alleviation and the enhancement of living standards require reasonable levels of sustained economic growth as an important prerequisite. Structural adjustment programmes (SAPs) are aimed at stimulating economic growth in the stagnant and crisis-ridden countries of Sub-Saharan Africa. By the end of the 1980s, more than two-thirds of the SSA countries had adopted SAPs. Only in some of these countries that have doggedly persisted with the SAPs has economic growth been achieved in a significant way. The relatively larger number of SAP failures vis-à-vis the fewer success stories has raised a debate regarding the appropriateness of orthodox SAPs to achieve economic growth. We shall not go into this debate here. Our own view is that the failures in several cases have been due not so much to the lack of soundness of the programmes themselves as to a lack of sincerity, commitment and discipline at the implementation level.

The noteworthy point, however, is that even in the few cases where SAPs have proved to be successful in stimulating growth, poverty alleviation has not been achieved. In Ghana, for instance, since the introduction of the SAP, the economy has achieved consecutive growth of 6% on average for several years since 1984. Even in *per capita* terms, real GDP growth averaged 2.4% in 1984–89. However, 'the welfare and living conditions of the poor and vulnerable groups continue to decay' (Kusi, 1991: 203). Varying estimates of poverty in Ghana have been provided by different authors. In terms of the percentage of the population living below two-thirds of the mean *per capita* annual household expenditure, the estimates vary from 36% (Boateng et al., 1992) to 41% (Baffoe, 1992). Similarly, Uganda has been enjoying 5% growth with monthly inflation rates since late 1992 of only 0.3%. But Ugandans are worse-off than they were 20 years ago. According to a recent World Bank study, even if the economy grows at 5% a year, the standard of living will not improve until well into the twenty-first century. The essence of such country experiences therefore is that, while economic growth is indeed a necessary condition, it is far from being a sufficient condition for addressing poverty.

Zimbabwe constitutes another example. This country initiated an adjustment programme in 1990, after a decade of attempting independent adjustment without the assistance of the Bretton Woods institutions. A recent investigation (ILO, 1993) established:

(1) Adverse effects on the poor of the adjustment package which included (i) a fall in employment, (ii) severe cuts in health and education expenditure of at least 20% in recurrent expenditure, 1990–92, (iii) worsening priority ratios (i.e. a sharper fall in preventive health and in primary and secondary education than for the sector as a whole), (iv) a fall of 10% in the availability of nurses per person and a worsening pupil-teacher ratio, (v) rising charges for health and education, (vi) cuts and eventual elimination of maize subsidies;
(2) Worsening condition of the poor as evidenced by (i) a household survey (urban) showing a rise in the number of people below the poverty line from 23% to 43%, with a decline in income of over 50% for the bottom quartile, (ii) a fall in the use of health care facilities, and rising BBA (births before arrival) and deaths among BBA, and (iii) rising drop-out rates and absenteeism from school and a fall in O-level candidates. (Reported by F. Stewart at the seminar)

It is in this perspective that the need for direct poverty alleviation programmes (PAPs) such as the Social Dimensions of Adjustment (SDA), Social Action Programmes (SAPROGs) and Social Safety Nets (SSNs) and transfers has been recognized. The purpose of this paper is to look at the scope of SSNs to mitigate the adverse impacts of SAPs on the poor and vulnerable groups and to indicate ways of improving their efficacy both in terms of their short-term objectives and long-term impacts.

## SAPs and PAPs

It is interesting that PAPs are often created as a follow-up to SAPs which themselves produce the consequences which PAPs are expected to mitigate. The pertinent question then is: Why institute SAPs which produce such negative effects and then seek resources (which are hard to come by) for PAPs in order to offset these negative effects? Perhaps it is an indication of the complexity of the economic development process that we do not as yet know of any viable alternative path by which self-sustaining economic growth can be revived in chronically stagnant economies without having to face highly adverse consequences in the short run.

The first phase of every SAP is stabilization. And stabilization requires stringent monetary and fiscal measures that are bound to bring about heavy compression of demand as an immediate result. Growth, on the other hand, implies increases in the supply of output and employment aimed to be brought about initially through improvements in the use of idle capacities (plants, machinery, manpower) and subsequently through the enhancement of capacities (new plants, new technologies, employment generation). Thus, while stabilization is short-term, growth is long-term. In the interim, one has to put up with the impact of stabilization.

The issue, therefore, is not in respect of the *existence* of a trade-off between the short-term costs and the long-term benefits but in respect of the *extent* of the trade-off that could be politically and socially acceptable (avoiding placing the 'last straw' on the backs of the poor) and economically feasible (in terms of the resources required to ensure that the last straw does not fall on the backs of the poor). SAPs, in other words, call for sacrifices and increased suffering in the short run. The promise they hold is of an improved life in the long run. But in the long run, most, if not all, are dead. For the poor, this could mean unmitigated suffering until they die in the short run itself. PAPs are aimed at mitigating this suffering in order to enable the poor to survive the short-run hardships and live to enjoy a better day in the medium to longer term.

The rationale of PAPs is much broader, however, than the aim of mitigating the adverse consequences of SAPs. Over the years, PAPs have come into sharper focus since the advent of SAPs because of the immediate hardships that SAPs have been known to produce. One tends to gloss over the fact that poverty did not originate with SAPs. SAPs intensify the plight of the chronic poor and, to some extent, push people who are just above or on the margin of subsistence below the poverty line, thereby creating the 'new poor'. But poverty was present in a substantial way in the SSA countries long before the advent of SAPs and poverty would have continued to grow in these countries even if SAPs had not been adopted. Green (1991) points to three factors that have caused poverty in SSA and that have nothing to do with SAPs:

(i) continuing absolute poverty, enhanced in some cases by expanding populations overloading and degrading pastural land and pushing into areas of poor soils (and pastures) and/or risky rainfall.
(ii) economic stagnation, decline and/or disintegration which have hit the once vulnerable, now absolutely poor.
(iii) wars and droughts which create refugees, internally displaced and severely affected people.

The alleviation of poverty, therefore, requires at least three approaches:

(a) Policies for stimulating and sustaining growth. SAPs do provide such policy packages.
(b) An effective social service delivery system. Neglect of the social sectors in many SSA countries over the years has reduced these sectors to a state of near shambles. And this has led to a significant decline in the performance of these countries on many social indicators. Indeed, after nearly three decades, the performance of several countries has remained at independence or pre-independence levels.
(c) Promotion of PAPs (to mitigate the adverse short-run consequences of SAPs).

## The Logic of SSNs and Transfers

Growth-oriented policies aim to redress poverty through financial empowerment of the poor by providing them with increasing opportunities to participate in the productive process. But as the *World Development Report 1990* on poverty states, there are certain categories of the poor whom it may take a very long time to fully participate (such as those in remote regions) or they may never be able to do so (the old or disabled). There are also others who may benefit from the policies but nevertheless remain acutely vulnerable to adverse events. These people also need to be assured of some form of income insurance to help tide them over such events.

Government interventions to support poor and vulnerable groups could be in the form of a universalistic transfer programme or of targeted transfers. Although many countries in Africa and elsewhere have implemented universalistic transfers, especially in the form of general food subsidies (e.g. Egypt, Zambia), in principle such transfers are not very appealing on two well-known grounds:

(i) they are very costly and create a big burden on the public budget, (e.g. 10–17% in Egypt between the mid-1970s and 1984);

(ii) they usually involve significant leakages of benefits to those who do not need them. In Egypt, for example, an urban household and a rural household in the richest quartile received £E18.1 and £E15.2 respectively compared with an urban household and a rural household in the poorest quartile who received only £E15.4 and £E11.9 respectively.

In the case of Egypt, the food subsidy programme, despite being costly, is assessed as having succeeded in reaching the poor. But this is not always the case. A general food subsidy can benefit the poor only if they can be assured of access to food at the subsidized price and not at the high parallel market prices. In most Sub-Saharan African countries this has not been so, and hence the food subsidies have not been effective in reducing food insecurity for the poor.

All this provides an automatic case for targeted transfers. But targeted transfers have their own problems.

Firstly, they can minimize costs and eliminate leakages only if the targeting is perfect. But this is virtually impossible since one can never accurately define poverty and identify all the poor households in a country.

Secondly, even if this was done, it would create a strong disincentive for work. For every additional unit of income a person receiving a transfer earns, his transfer would be reduced by the same amount. This is tantamount to a 100% marginal income tax (see World Bank, 1988: 3).

Thirdly, the more precise the targeting, the greater the administrative costs of doing so. In the words of Beasley and Kanbur (1988), 'in principle it requires the means testing of hundreds of thousands, if not millions, of households every year'. Consequently, targeted subsidies tend to be introduced in practice more with a view to reducing the huge expenditures which generalized subsidies entail than with a view to reaching all deserving beneficiaries. For instance, in Zambia a coupon system for maize meal was introduced in 1989 in lieu of the general subsidy and this reduced expenditures from a possible ZK1.2 billion to less than ZK400 m. However, the coupons were targeted on urban households below a certain annual income level. The system thus left out people not resident in the urban areas and those resident in the urban areas but working in the informal sector. This obviously excluded a large majority of the poor households. Hence, as Richard Pearce (1990) observed: 'the manner of issuing coupons appears to have been designed with a view to minimizing expenditures rather than ensuring food security'.

Fourthly, better targeting on the poor is possible if the government knows where the poor live. But where poverty is widespread and pervasive, it may be easier to identify who the non-poor are and where they live. For example, according to preliminary estimates made by the World Bank (1993a), by 1991, the percentages of rural and urban households in Zambia below the 1980 poverty line were 86.5% and 91.5% respectively. And using a 1980 reference food basket, by 1991 54.2% of urban households and 42.7% of rural households were unable to afford this basket. In such a situation where fewer people are not vulnerable and do not need assistance and given that money available for PAPs is limited at any point in time, the government will have the onerous task of identifying those who are most direly in need – the ultra-poor – on whom the expenditures should be targeted with priority.

Thus, given the drawbacks of universalistic programmes and the costs and difficulties of identifying target groups, the *via media* seems to be to build Social Safety Nets for self-targeted groups. It is in this context that public employment schemes and food-for-work programmes have sprung up in several countries in SSA. In Botswana, Cape Verde and Kenya strategies based in part on the provision of employment are deemed to have saved many thousands of lives over the past decade. These programmes are particularly effective as drought relief. In Botswana, a variety of food interventions was complemented by a Labour-Based Relief Programme (LBRP) which provided the rural poor in drought-stricken areas with opportunities for earning cash income on village-improvement projects. The LBRP provided employment for between 60,000 and 90,000 persons each year during the drought period (1983–87).

Despite the merits of such SSNs, they also have limitations. Not all the weak and the vulnerable can be caught in the self-targeted SSNs. Many, for instance, cannot avail themselves of food-for-work programmes because chronic malnutrition puts them in need of food *before* work. There are also individuals in the community who, as Green puts it, are simply not empowerable. Such vulnerable groups have to be identified and assisted through transfers. All the same, if complemented by growth-stimulating macroeconomic policies and an efficacious social service delivery system, SSNs and targeted transfers can go a noticeable way to alleviating the sufferings of the poor, especially during periods of SAPs. There are, however, a number of issues that will have to be addressed in order to maximize the benefits from expenditures on SSNs and transfers. Experiences in several countries with targeted programmes have revealed several weaknesses and difficulties at the level of formulation and implementation of these programmes.

## Targeted Programmes: Some Important Issues

*Recognizing the importance of PAPs*
In the first place, to the extent that poverty exists in SSA independent of SAPs, PAPs should be accorded importance in their own right. In this regard, they should form integral components of the overall programmes of stabilization, restructuring, growth and human development. In most cases, PAPs are accorded only an honourable mention in the well-known PFPs (Economic and Financial Policy Framework Papers) drafted by national governments in collaboration with the IMF and the World Bank. Very little is reflected in the operational schedule of adjustment and structural measures. Zambia's current PFP 1992–94, for instance, contains a 5-page summary statement of the measures proposed to be implemented, with asterisks denoting the areas for priority action. Programmes on health, nutrition and education which have the most direct relevance to the poor appear right at the end and none of them are marked with

asterisks. A sample of asterisked areas contains the following: the exchange rate moving to a market-determined rate; reducing arrears to the IMF; eliminating arrears to other multilateral creditors; clearing recent arrears to the Paris Club; eliminating transport subsidies on maize meal and subsidies on maize meal and fertilizer; limiting government borrowing from the banking system; raising interest rates if warranted by inflation; maintaining petroleum products and electricity rates at economic levels. While all these are undoubtedly important and necessary measures, they are nevertheless measures that are bound to cause hardships to the population, especially the poor. The only asterisked measure relating to the poor calls for an improved targeting of current expenditure (NB: not increased expenditure) towards priority sectors and vulnerable groups. The criticism that PAPs are nothing more than appendages to SAPs appears legitimate. As Green (1991: 20) pithily describes them, PAPs appear as 'baubles hung on the christmas tree of macroeconomic policy'. An alternative analogy would be to describe the macroeconomic policy package of SAPs as a big dry tasteless cake topped with a thin icing of PAP as an afterthought. SAPs and PAPs should be well integrated into a single development programme that looks like a marzipanned fruit cake which will be palatable enough even without any icing!

*SAP-PAP lags*

That PAPs are developed as an afterthought is evident from the fact that in several countries they have been introduced long after the introduction of SAPs. In Ghana, the first phase of the SAP covered the period 1983–86, and the second phase the period 1986–88. It was only in 1988 that the government, conscious that the sustainability of the SAP could be endangered by inadequate attention to its social dimensions, introduced PAMSCAD (Programme of Action to Mitigate the Social Costs of Adjustment). But Kusi remarks, not surprisingly, that

> the failure to integrate initially the human dimension of the adjustment into the programme's core strategy has also exacerbated the incidence of poverty which PAMSCAD cannot redress. (Kusi, 1991: 205)

In Zimbabwe, which finally accepted an IMF-type SAP in 1990 after a protracted period of adjustment without the Fund, the SDA package has been very late in implementation. By December 1992, only one sector (payment of school fees for the destitute) was addressed under the umbrella of the SDA. Thompson (1993) states: 'The SDA fund remains US$4 million, a paltry amount in the midst of the worst drought of the century.'

In Zambia, where the new government elected in October 1991 began a rapid enforcement of SAP policies in January 1992, commitment to a PAP still remains by and large at the rhetorical level. The point that needs to be understood by policy-makers is that the more PAPs lag behind SAPs, the greater will be the social dimensions unleashed and hence the greater will be the resources required to mitigate them. Conversely, integrating PAPs with SAPs right at the beginning will entail social dimensions of much lesser magnitude and hence fewer resources at any given time to tackle them.

*Initial conditions and pace of policy reforms*
The debate regarding gradualism versus speedy policy reform is not a useful one in our view. Policy-makers in every country will have to decide for themselves what is the appropriate pace of change. In this regard, they need, like medical practitioners, to be well-versed in the art of titration (to borrow the phrase from a noted Indian journalist) and to know the right dosage of medicine that should be administered. While too little will prove ineffective, too much can kill. One should neither be so overcautious as to adopt small ineffective doses of policy change nor be so overenthusiastic as to adopt large overdoses. Highly gradualistic changes can produce little effect in an economy that is severely distorted and unbalanced. Too fast a pace, on the other hand, can create very serious social dimensions with which neither the government nor the populace can cope.

Two factors need to be considered in determining the appropriate pace of reform. One is the initial economic and social conditions at the time of implementation of the SAP. Let us give an illustration here. The World Bank's Country Economic Memorandum on Zambia states that the removal of the urban maize coupon system (despite the limitations pointed out earlier) in late 1991, 'no matter how justified in economic and budgetary terms, was a major factor in increasing the risk of undernutrition for all but the wealthiest urban households, at least in the near term' (World Bank, 1992). By the beginning of 1992, well over 60% of households had become unable to afford a subsistence basket of food in which maize meal constituted the predominant item. By that time, the country was also in the midst of a serious drought. And yet the government eliminated all food subsidies by June 1992, when the IMF-World Bank agenda itself had set the target date at mid-1993. In our view, this is clearly an example of overdosage.

The second factor to note in many SSA countries is that, while it is administratively easy for a government to introduce liberalizing policy changes at a fairly rapid pace, it is far more difficult for it to administer PAPs at a pace that is in step with the policy changes. Consequently, over time as the implementation of PAPs lags behind the enforcement of SAP policies, the PAPs may fail to assist in the coping strategies of the poor in the face of the immediately immiserizing policy changes. This not only enlarges the social dimensions of the SAP which may call for larger resources for 'PAMSCADs', it also contributes to the building up of a dormant volcano of social discontent which could erupt at any time without warning. The pace of reform should therefore be linked to the capacity to administer PAPs whose objective, among others, is indeed to contain such social eruptions.

*Prioritized expenditure*
If alleviation of poverty is a fundamental goal of economic development policy, then public expenditures ought to reflect poverty awareness. Gyimah-Brempong (1989), on the basis of his analysis of defence spending and social expenditures in 20 African countries, shows that there has been an increase in defence spending since independence in the 1960s and that, while changes in the defence budget share have a negative effect on the budget share of social services, the reverse is not true. A recent World Bank paper (1993a) on Zambia states (p. 5):

A comparison of military expenditures with expenditures on social and public services for the period 1985–1990 also reveals that the government on average spent at least 100 percent more on the military than on education and 200 percent more than on transport, power and energy.

In the 1993 budget, defence has been allocated ZK18 bn while allocations to health and education are ZK17.48 bn and ZK13.44 bn. In both the 1992 and 1993 budgets, Social Action Programmes have been allocated ZK1 bn. The inadequacy and unfairness of such an allocation has been brought out in the following rhetorical question posed recently by the Church (1993):

> Is there justice in having millions of vulnerable or poor citizens sharing one billion Kwacha while less than one hundred and fifty citizens in the leadership enjoy billions of Kwacha in soft car loans, salaries and tax-free allowances?

What is more, even the meagre allocation assigned to PAPs does not get spent. Of the ZK1 bn that was allocated, only 25% was actually spent, and of this, only a small fraction reached the targeted groups. Again, although the total budget for PAMSCAD in Ghana for a period of two years was about $85 m, monitoring and *ex post* evaluation of projects showed that actual expenditures might have been slower and much smaller than originally anticipated (Quarcoo, 1990: 20). We have also already indicated that SDA in Zimbabwe was allocated a very meagre amount. All these illustrate that in SSA there is scope for poverty-conscious restructuring of public expenditures. There is also need to ensure prompt disbursement of funds to the implementing agencies and their timely expenditure.

### Non-paternalistic treatment of the poor

While the poor need assistance, they should not be treated merely as beneficiaries. But this often happens in many countries owing to the paternalistic and top-down approach underlying SSNs and other welfare programmes. Administrators of these programmes need to have empathy for the poor and a deep understanding of their problems. For this, it is necessary to involve the target populations right from the planning stage through to the implementation, monitoring and evaluation of the targeted programmes. The top-down approach must be reversed and there must be active involvement of community-level organizations such as the Church and local NGOs, several of whom have considerable community-level contacts and experience in designing programmes for the poor. Recent experience in Botswana underscores the importance of such a bottom-up approach. Despite the presence of reasonably effective local government institutions, the New Agricultural Policy (1991) and programmes such as FAP and ALDEP, because of very little public input, have resulted in their not being recognized by the target groups (see Thompson, 1993).

### Need to overcome regulatory problems

Even when monies are provided for targeted programmes, they do not easily reach the target groups. Rules and regulations constitute a major slip between cup and lip. In Zimbabwe, three different sectors (waiver of school fees, waiver of health care fees and compensation for rising maize meal prices) have three different criteria for a household to gain eligibility for the programmes. In addition, requirements for the separate drought relief programme differ from the other three. As a result, few have signed up for the various programmes because the vulnerable have not been able to meet the requirements of multiple legal certificates such as those for birth, marriage, etc. The brief experience of administering public Welfare Assistance Schemes in Zambia also suggests an unimaginative adherence to regulations on the part of the implementing authorities. Physically handicapped people including the blind had to be certified by a doctor before getting assistance under the scheme. At times, such persons had to travel 200 kilometres for this purpose. Those in charge of targeted programmes will do well to remember that, like justice, assistance delayed is assistance denied.

*Logistical and manpower support*
Many targeted programmes have been stymied by logistical and manpower constraints. Essential drugs do not reach rural health centres because of lack of transport. Welfare schemes become confined to the neighbourhoods of district headquarters administering such schemes because of the absence of feeder roads or canals leading to the remote areas and/or lack of motorcycles, bicycles and boats.

Manpower shortages exist both in terms of number and quality. The Social Sector Planning Unit in Zambia's National Commission for Development Planning which is supposed to handle all the social sectors has only two members of staff. Such dearth of manpower constrains a nation's capacity to administer PAPs. In 1992, ZK500m allocated for public employment schemes was unused and returned to the Treasury owing to administrative constraints.

Lack of personnel training, commitment and integrity is perhaps one of the biggest hurdles in the implementation of PAPs. According to a recent statement by the former Zambian Minister of Community Development and Social Welfare, the biggest problem in administering the targeted programmes has been 'to find human beings who can be entrusted with public funds and who can ensure that the resources reach the people for whom they are intended' (Maka, 1993: 5). There are proven instances of funds being misappropriated by the administrative committee members and civil servants who considered themselves also as 'needy' persons.

Ultimately, all these logistical and manpower constraints are the result of meagre allocations to PAPs, and hence to a great extent can be overcome by improved finance for these programmes.

*Programme evaluation*
There is need for a constant in-depth evaluation of PAPs to know their genuine merits and demerits. There is a danger that a programme may otherwise be judged by some standard criteria and be deemed a success when a closer look might yield a different picture. In Zambia, the Project Urban Self Help (PUSH), for instance, is regarded as a successful case of a SSN. Designed by the World Food Programme and administered since 1990, PUSH involves community participation in a number of projects such as creating drainage ditches, building latrines and roads and helping in garbage disposal. Participants are required to work for four hours a day and are given food as payment. In 1992, PUSH received a big fillip with a total of 20 NGOs and agencies getting involved in

40 projects and giving employment to 3,000 Lusaka-based families. What is more, 95% of the participants were women, one of the most vulnerable groups in any SSA country. PUSH was, therefore, judged a success in terms of employment creation, infrastructure consolidation and support of women. A closer look at the achievements reveals, however, that, in the first place, the very high percentage of women employed was because men were not interested in food for work as they preferred cash for work. More importantly, it has tended to make women more disadvantaged than before in certain respects. It increases women's workloads, since they have to spend four hours on 'food for work' *in addition to* their already heavy workload in terms of agricultural, domestic and child-caring functions. Also, the payment in kind limits their ability to cater for other needs such as health, education and transport.

## Moral dilemma

Where the task of development is huge and the resources required for this task are acutely scarce, economic principles dictate that these scarce resources should be used in a manner that will contribute the maximum to the development process. And yet there may be need, purely from a human perspective, to spend on certain SSNs that have a high opportunity cost in terms of development. The rapid spread of the HIV/AIDS phenomenon in many SSA countries presents such a dilemma. As Green (1992) points out, the starkest moral dilemma is posed by orphans who are HIV positive. None of them will live five years and most well under two. Hence none of them can directly contribute to productivity enhancement and the economic growth of their countries. Yet providing them with institutional or household-based care in the most afflicted SSA countries such as Zambia, Malawi, Uganda and Zaire could cost several times as much as a universal access primary health services system.

> To anyone who understands the realities and is not an enthusiastic proponent of euthanasia, the choices are not merely stark but agonising. Pretending there is no dilemma and muddling along is also a choice and not necessarily the best available one. (Green, 1992: 34)

## Targeted Programmes for long-term development

Targeted Programmes are essentially conceived as short-term palliatives for those hurt by SAPs. Longer-term development and eventual poverty elimination depend basically on the other two approaches set out earlier in this paper, namely in sustained economic growth and an effective social service delivery system. Yet, there are certain SSN programmes which incorporate elements that are interlinked with the other approaches. Sustained economic growth requires the building up of human capital whose stocks have dwindled to very little in most SSA countries. This has been the result of lower resources *per capita* brought about by high population growth rates and inadequate investments in health and education leading to high mortality rates among infants, children and adults. The high infant and child mortality rates in turn perpetuate a high total fertility rate, thereby ensuring a high population growth rate.

Given the above vicious interactions among variables that contribute to poverty, some SSNs can be used to weaken these interactions alongside cushioning the vulnerable groups. For example, among the targeted households, all those couples of reproductive age who have fewer than the national average number of children and who are prepared to undergo permanent sterilization could be rewarded with a substantial cash payment. It would, of course, be costly in the short run but would be beneficial in the longer run and could be tried on an experimental basis in selected sites.

Again, while food need not be directly subsidized, government could subsidize the nutritional fortification of the staple food. For example, a small addition of soya flour to the coarser variety of maize meal consumed exclusively by the poor could significantly improve their nutritional status.

A related method is supplementary feeding programmes which in several instances have been known to be cost-effective and also very effective in reducing malnutrition. The Iringa Nutrition programme in Tanzania is an outstanding example. Assisted by the existence of village organizational structures and a well-developed rural health care infrastructure, the programme between 1984 and 1988 reduced severe malnutrition by 72% and moderate malnutrition by 32%. If such feeding programmes are targeted on all primary school children and female secondary school children, they can, despite some leakages, achieve several other objectives besides nutritional enhancement – increased enrolment rates, better scholastic performance, an increase in the number of female children in secondary schools, and reduction in illiteracy rates. In particular, a high negative correlation exists between infant and child mortality rates and the total fertility rate on the one hand and the educational level of mothers on the other. The increased secondary school enrolment of potential mothers can, therefore, contribute to the development of human capital.

## Conclusion

SSNs and targeted expenditures are very important for protecting the poor during structural adjustment. Their effectiveness will depend on the extent to which some of the issues raised in the previous section are addressed. They are, however, only part of a broader strategy necessary for poverty alleviation. Sustained economic growth requires the development of human capital and hence policies must be put in place that will deal with those factors that determine human capital development – factors such as food security; level and quality of education, especially female education; primary health care; and productivity and income-generating capacity.

References

Baffoe, J. K. (1992) 'Income Distribution and Poverty Profile in Ghana, 1987–1988', *African Development Review* 4 (1), 1–28.
Beasley, T. J. and Kanbur, R. (1988) 'Food Subsidies and Poverty Alleviation', *Economic Journal* 98, 701–19.
Boateng, E. O., Ewusi, K. Kanbur, R. and McKay, A. (1992) 'A Poverty Profile for Ghana', *Journal of African Economies* 1 (1), 25–58.
Church, the (1993) 'Role of the Church in Protecting the Less Privileged', Paper at a Workshop on Ways of Protecting Vulnerable Groups from the Short-Term Impact of the Economic Structural Adjustment Programme and Alleviation of Poverty, Lusaka, 21–22 April.

Green, R. H. (1992) 'Toward Livelihoods, Services and Infrastructure', Paper at a Conference on the Eradication of Poverty in Africa, Ota, Nigeria, 27–29 July.

Green, R. H. (1991) 'Reduction of Absolute Poverty: A Priority Structural Adjustment', Paper at SAIFC/SAPHD Workshop on Structural Adjustment in SSA, Falmer, Brighton, 18–19 January.

Gyimah-Brempong, K. (1989) 'Is the Trade-off Between Defense Spending and Social Welfare an Illusion? – Some Evidence from Tropical Africa', *Eastern Africa Economic Review* 5 (2), 74–91.

ILO (1993) 'Structural Change and Adjustment in Zimbabwe', Occasional Paper No. 16, Geneva: ILO Inter-departmental Project on Structural Adjustment.

Kusi, N. K. (1991): 'Ghana: Can the Adjustment Reforms be Sustained?' *Africa Development* 16 (3/4).

Maka, G. (1993) 'The Government Role and Policy of Protecting Vulnerable Groups', Paper at a Workshop on Ways of Protecting Vulnerable Groups from the Short-Term Impact of the Economic Structural Adjustment Programme and Alleviation of Poverty, Lusaka, 21–22 April.

Pearce, R. (1990) *Food Consumption and Adjustment in Zambia*, Working Paper No. 2, Oxford: Food Studies Group, International Development Centre, Queen Elizabeth House, Oxford University.

Quarcoo, P. K (1990) 'Structural Adjustment Programmes in Sub-Saharan Africa; Evolution of Approaches', *African Development Review* 2 (2), 1–26.

Thompson, C. B. (1993) *Drought Management Strategies in Southern Africa: From Relief to Rehabilitation and Reduction of Vulnerability*, Windhoek, Namibia and Nairobi: UNICEF.

Van der Hoeven, R. C. (1993): 'Can Safety Nets and Compensatory Programmes Be Used for Poverty Alleviation?,' in R. Van der Hoeven and R. Anker (eds): *Poverty Monitoring: An International Concern*, Basingstoke: Macmillan.

World Bank (1988) 'Targeted Programs for the Poor During Structural Adjustment', A summary of a symposium on Poverty and Adjustment, April. Washington DC: World Bank.

World Bank (1990) *World Development Report, 1990: Poverty*, Oxford: Oxford University Press.

World Bank (1992) *Zambia: Economic and Financial Policy Framework, 1992–94*, Washington DC: World Bank.

World Bank (1993a) 'Zambia: Prospects for Sustainable and Equitable Growth', (Green Cover). Washington DC: World Bank.

World Bank (1993b) 'Zambia: Fight Against Inflation: The Way Forward', Paper at National Conference on Inflation, Lusaka.

# 9 The Political Conditions of Adjustment in Africa 1980–90

# CHRISTIAN MORRISSON
# JEAN-DOMINIQUE LAFAY and
# SEBASTIEN DESSUS

Many developing countries embarked on rigorous stabilization programmes in the 1980s to reduce the gap between supply and demand and consequently exterior deficits which had become unbearable. These measures were often accompanied by structural adjustment programmes intended to increase the economy's production capacity in the medium term. These policies were undertaken either independently or under pressure from international organizations.

The technical aspects of adjustment, understood to mean both stabilization measures and structural reforms, as well as its effects on income distribution and poverty, have been the subject of much research. The OECD Development Centre contributed notably by publishing eight works on the theme 'Adjustment and Equity'. Conversely, the political consequences of adjustment in developing countries have rarely been studied systematically. In fact, the economics of development in general, and not just adjustment analyses, tend to underestimate the political factor.

As a general rule, economists have always been reluctant to cross the line established long ago between economics and political science. Nevertheless, since the 1970s, analysis of public choice (see Mueller, 1989) and political economic theory have made a significant contribution to progress in research in developed countries. In the case of developing countries, however, the movement came much later and was considerably less systematic. This analytical delay is paradoxical when one considers that it is in developing countries, rather than in developed countries, that the disturbances caused by stabilization or adjustment measures can create tens or hundreds of victims. To a large extent, the first studies were done under the pressure of events that took place.

The authors who began to look into the problems of the interaction between economics and politics in developing countries came from a diversity of backgrounds: development economists interested in studying social groups, public choice economists trying to extend their analyses to the case of developing countries, macroeconomists working on the causes of the chronic deficits and indebtedness in the Third World, political scientists concerned with the study of interactions between economics and politics and the consequences of institutional differences.

In view of the serious malfunctioning of the public sector which was disclosed by the external shocks of the 1970s–1980s in many developing countries, several researchers proposed that these phenomena should be explained by transposing certain analyses in public choice theory. The idea was to show that the basic cause of the difficulties encountered was the predominance of 'political rationale' over 'economic rationale' in government choices (Bates, 1988; Nelson, 1990). According to them, traditional economic theory, which takes no account of this aspect of the problem, includes a major error of specification. For this reason, the policies it inspired often proved to be not only difficult to implement but also seriously inadequate.

Clearly, problems of the public deficit, indebtedness and, in several developing countries, hyperinflation are due in large part to political reasons, as is the weak reaction of the governments confronted with them. Macroeconomists' studies on these subjects largely confirm this (Berg and Sachs, 1988, Sachs 1989; Alesina and Tabellini, 1990; Alesina and Drazen, 1990).

From the theoretical standpoint, transposing economic analyses of political behaviour posed a specific problem: these analyses in general dealt only with democracies in industrialized countries, whereas a large number of developing countries had an autocratic or semi-autocratic regime. The study of this form of government was thus the subject of major theoretical and empirical developments (Bloch, 1986; Tullock, 1987; Paldam, 1987; Anderson, 1988; Wintrobe, 1989). At the same time, several authors decided to explore the effects of institutional differences on the choice of economic policies, considered either in the development context or in an adjustment context (Weede, 1983; Berg-Schlosser, 1985; Haggard et al., 1990). Notably this made it possible to renew the old debate on the relationship and compatibility between democracy and development, by giving it a much more solid theoretical and empirical foundation (Pourgerami, 1992).

The malfunctioning of the state associated with the political logic of decisions was particularly clear in the case of public enterprises,[1] justifying broad programmes of shut-downs and privatization (Bouin and Michalet, 1991). Further to the work of Anne Krueger, the study of problems of corruption and seeking unearned income was also stimulated by use of the analytical instruments of public choice theory (Lafay and Lecaillon, 1993).

The previous analyses, devoted to the operation of the state 'as it is', rather than 'as it should be', led to a position in favour of less public intervention (Lal, 1987) or of reforms to make the state more apt to fulfil its functions (de Janvry et al., 1990). In any case, the need to 'rethink the state', to use the revealing title of Chapter 7 of the 1991 World Bank World Development Report, seems a priority to a growing number of development specialists.

Adjustment plans, given the unpopular measures that they entail, are exemplary cases of the close interaction between economics and politics: at times they cause violent reactions on the part of social groups, to the point of threatening the very survival of the existing authorities (Sidell, 1987). As shown in the detailed analysis propounded by Lafay and Lecaillon (1993), we now have a sufficiently large number of studies, albeit disparate, on the form that this reaction may take, the way the media can influence it and how the process of protest and socio-political violence are triggered.

Since the vast majority of adjustment plans were the subject of agreements negotiated with the IMF, the 'bureaucratic' logic of the behaviour of international organizations should normally interact with the political-economic logic of the governments applying for loans. Attempts to transpose economic theory on national bureaucracy to administrative international organizations, although they are subject to discussion, have cast an interesting light on the question (Vaubel and Willet, 1991).

The studies we have just mentioned have shown the considerable inter-dependence of economic, political and bureaucratic factors and its decisiveness in the definition and implementation of adjustment plans. The problem now is to set up global political-economic models for developing countries which can formally represent and quantify that interdependence, analogous to those which exist for the large industrialized countries (Borooah and Schneider, 1991). Frey and Eichenberger (1992), in a ground-breaking study, recently developed the theoretical bases for these models. The research presented in this text shows that this type of model can also be used for empirical estimates and that the values obtained for the various coefficients provide a new path for exploring the conse-quences of different measures associated with adjustment programmes by simulation.

As we show, reducing subsidies for food products, increasing taxes on con-sumer goods, privatizing semi-public companies and severely reducing customs protection affect the incomes or threaten the employment of groups which are well organized and/or capable of desperate reactions, given their already low standard of living. These measures can lead to strikes, demonstrations, or even riots or attempts at *coups d'état*. In turn, these disorders incite governments to change their policy: many adjustment programmes have been postponed or heavily modified for this reason. It is therefore impossible to consider an adjust-ment programme exclusively from the technical standpoint. The entire chain of interactions between the economy and politics must be considered, and only a global political-economic model is able to do this.

Here we shall show how a model of this kind, specifically devised for develop-ing countries and adapted to the analysis of adjustment problems, can be developed and estimated using economic and political data collected for 23 African countries over the 1980–90 period. The principles of this model and the main results obtained are presented in the next section. This model-creation exercise has led to several simulations which are interesting for policy-makers; these simulations are reproduced and commented on in the following section. In the final section, several important lessons are drawn, from the standpoint of political feasibility, about the preparation of stabilization and structural adjust-ment programmes.

## The Political-economic Model and its Results

Our knowledge of political-economic interactions in industrialized countries has grown greatly over the past twenty-five years thanks to the studies of political reactions to economic indicators, popularity functions, and political-economic models. Conversely, there are very few studies on developing countries, although there are many indications that the interactions between politics and the economy are decisive there also.

In Africa notably, the deterioration of the economic situation during the 1980s went hand in hand with increased political violence and the exacerbation of internal conflicts. In all regions, not just in Africa, violent reactions to certain stabilization measures were observed, whether they were independent adjustment programmes or were applied in the framework of an agreement with the IMF. Because of these reactions, many media, political parties, pressure groups (for example, trade unions, churches, NGOs) have regularly reproached the IMF for causing or increasing political instability, by imposing stabilization measures which were unbearable for the population, most notably for the poor, in countries forced to borrow from it because of a financial crisis. True, the grounds for this criticism can be challenged, as Sidell (1987) did by showing that the relationship between the IMF interventions and the incidents was not always empirically demonstrated, in fact far from it. But the impact in the media of this kind of scientific work is negligible as compared with that of the criticism of political parties and pressure groups. As a result, the IMF often stands accused in discussions on adjustment programmes.

In order to understand the relations between economic and political variables, we have developed a political-economic model inspired by the models made for industrialized countries and the pioneer study of Frey and Eichenberger (1992) on developing countries. It gives a simple representation of the essential relations between policies and events, both political and economic, during the adjustment period, and takes into account the role of the IMF and external aid.

### (a) The political-economic model

Setting aside outside influences three groups of agents are distinguished: economic agents (the 'economy'), social groups and the government (one individual can, of course, belong to several groups simultaneously).

The 'economy' is considered as a set of simple structures, in keeping with standard macroeconomic theory, where the agents show a limited capacity of anticipation. This part of the model presents only two original factors:

- it takes into account the direct economic consequences of the behaviour of certain social-political groups. Strikes, demonstrations, attempts at *coups d'état*, because of the turmoil and fear they engender, can cause a fall in the growth rate, capital flight, and curtailment of outside aid and investments;
- particular attention is given to the impact of economic policy measures. This choice reflects the attempt to centre the analysis on the effects of adjustment decisions.

Individuals who make up the various social groups will try to promote their own interests in several ways: by more or less covert negotiations, by favourable or unfavourable votes, by threats, by peaceful protestation, by riots or even general insurrection. Many developing countries have autocratic or quasi-autocratic regimes: elections either do not occur or are organized under conditions quite different from what Western democracies consider necessary for free and fair elections. Consequently, pressure on the government is exercised by competing forms of activity. This gives social groups a central role in the political process.

Certain groups are in a better position than others to negotiate their support of those in power:

- urban groups, whose organizational costs are lower, will try to obtain favourable decisions by using strikes, demonstrations or riots. Rural groups, on the contrary, will have more difficulty in acting effectively and will seek refuge in a subsistence economy or will content themselves with offering passive support to guerrilla movements;
- in key sectors such as transportation (which ensures the arrival of vital supplies to the cities) or mining (when it represents an important source of foreign exchange) or in branches where the trade unions are strong, wage-earners have strong bargaining power. Conversely, the influence of other groups, such as people active in the informal sector or primary school teachers, is often very limited;
- civil servants have the option of applying adjustment policies more or less zealously. Tax and customs agents, who collect state revenues, or employees of vital semi-public sectors like electricity or railway transport, have a particularly determinant role. Finally, the support given by the armed forces (army and police) in the case of disturbances is decisive for the very survival of the government.

In certain cases, the influence of a group results less from its particular position than from its numbers. For this reason, populations which *a priori* are politically less decisive, like poor or low-income urban populations, can constitute a threat to the government if, for example, a sharp rise in the cost of food products leads them to desperate action. Given the level of aggregation retained for the model and the information available, we cannot trace the means of action of these groups in detail. It is assumed that this action can be summed up by strikes, more or less violent demonstrations and attempts at *coups d'état*.

In the perspective of positive, non-normative public economics, the government is an agent among others, whose decision-taking logic has to be explained. The way it uses the various economic and political instruments at its disposal has to be described, given its objective function and the constraints of the environment. We have assumed that the government's objective is to remain in power. It has two means to attain this objective: increasing the support of the population through popular economic measures or repression. But for several reasons, repression is a source of counterproductivity for the government. Consequently, it uses repression only if it is forced to do so (if the probability of remaining in power falls below a minimum threshold). In the case of adjustment, the conditionality imposed by the IMF obliges the government to reduce expenditures in favour of certain groups; consequently support for the government decreases and disturbances may break out, and this can lead to repression. Sandwiched between the financial constraints imposed by the negotiations with the IMF and the risk of disturbance, a government often accepts unpopular measures, hoping to then negotiate modifications or to delay their application until a time when a new flow of aid, induced by the agreement with the IMF, will enable it to counterbalance these unpopular measures.

Figure 9.1 summarizes the relations between the four categories of agents concerned in adjustment: the government, social groups, the external world and the economy.

The government can take economic or political measures:

- the former concern either the economy as a whole (recurrent and capital expenditures, monetary policy, exchange-rate policy), or certain areas (subsidies, additional wages or specific tax measures); these measures are popular or unpopular as they improve or worsen the short-term situation of the population or of certain groups. Initially, in order to simplify the analysis, we have considered the economic measures as a whole, whether they concern the entire population or certain groups;
- political measures, like economic measures, can be popular (liberalization) or unpopular (repression). Arrow 4 in Figure 9.1 shows the effects on the political situation of political or economic measures affecting certain groups. Reciprocally, arrow 2 corresponds to the effect of this political situation on government policies; demonstrations or riots will occasion repressive measures. But overall economic measures also act on the political situation; they influence the economic situation (arrow 3) and the population reacts to it (arrow 9). The government, moreover, must take the economic situation into account. The most obvious case is when balance-of-payments problems force it to take unpopular economic measures like reducing recurrent or capital expenditures or subsidies. The political situation can also directly influence the economic situation (arrow 10): for example, long strikes have a direct effect on the rate of growth of GDP.

Introducing outside agents adds several relations to this scheme. By definition, conditionality means that the IMF has a direct influence on the government's economic policies (arrow 5). Outside agents react to the country's economic situation and particularly to the financial crisis (arrow 6); they can also react to the political situation, for example by reducing aid if they condemn severe repression (arrow 7). They thus modify the economic indicators directly (in particular the indicators of aid and debt) by intervening financially (arrow 10).

Among the set of relations represented in Figure 9.1 three blocks of relations can be distinguished:

- The first explains how economic indicators and political events depend on the measures taken by the government and the decisions of donors or the IMF. For example, unpopular economic measures like eliminating subsidies on foodstuffs create strong discontent in the urban population, thus causing demonstrations. A measure such as reducing the growth rate of the money supply decreases the rate of inflation. External loans increase the rate of indebtedness but can stimulate the growth of GDP.
- The second block shows how the government reacts to political events and economic indicators with political and economic measures. It corresponds to political-economic reaction functions. Thus a government reacts to demonstrations by repression, or it reacts to a high deficit in the balance of payments and the IMF's conditions for a loan by taking unpopular measures;
- Finally, the third block concerns the IMF and aid. IMF decisions could have

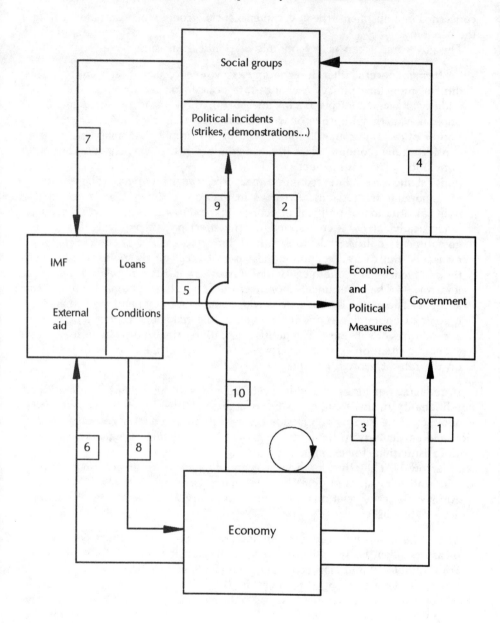

Block 1: Influences of economic and political measures taken by the government and external agents (IMF and other donors). Arrows 3, 4, 10 and indirectly 8 and 9.

Block 2: Functions of economic and political reactions to economic and political events. Arrows 1, 2 and 5.

Block 3: Functions explaining external aid given the economic and political conditions. Arrows 6 and 7.

**Figure 9.1.** *Politico-economic relations*

been explained (see Vaubel and Willet, 1991; Lafay and Lecaillon, 1993 for their attempts), but we preferred to consider the number of IMF interventions as an exogenous variable. This choice is justified by the fact that a given unfavourable economic situation does not necessarily entail an intervention by the IMF. African history in the 1980s shows that, depending on the case, a government may choose to adjust on its own or with the aid of the IMF. On the other hand, aid is an endogenous variable. The amount of aid (as a percentage of GDP) is linked to the internal economic situation (rate of growth of GDP, external deficit) and to the IMF interventions which, as we know, play a very important role, since an agreement with the IMF often conditions the award of new loans or donations from donor countries.

We can see from Figure 9.1 that these three blocks correspond to three sets of relations or arrows respectively:

- block 1: arrows 3, 4, 10 and by an indirect effect 8 and 9.
- block 2: arrows 1, 2 and 5.
- block 3: arrows 6 and 7.

Moreover, the loop referring to economic indicators recalls the relationships between these various indicators. For example, the balance of payments depends on the rate of indebtedness.

We can view the interactions described by Figure 9.1 dynamically and trace a political-economic cycle specific to adjustment. Given a serious deficit in the balance of payments, a government must take unpopular stabilization measures (arrow 1). If it wants to borrow from the IMF, the Fund will require this kind of measure (arrow 5). In general, the measures correspond to:

- reducing operating and investment expenditures;
- increasing indirect taxes and/or reducing subsidies;
- enacting a more restrictive monetary policy;
- decreasing wages and possibly the number of civil servants;
- devaluing (unless the countries are in the franc zone).

Because they are unpopular, these measures lead to strikes and demonstrations directly (arrow 4) or indirectly (arrows 5 and 9). These disturbances lead to repressive measures (arrow 2). But, in many African countries, repression is not constant. After a few months, the government takes political liberalization measures (arrow 4): prisoners are set free, prohibited publications are authorized, universities are re-opened. This type of process is typical of most of the countries studied, which are autocratic rather than democratic but not totalitarian. When external aid gives the government renewed room to manoeuvre, it takes popular economic measures (arrows 3 and 4): it liberalizes monetary policy, increases public expenditures, reinstates certain subsidies. Unfortunately, if the macro-economic imbalances have not been sufficiently reduced in the interim, this return to a lax policy may bring the situation back to where it started – with a serious external deficit. In this sense, the IMF can justify the terms of conditionality since these terms bind the government to a durable stabilization policy and prevent a cyclical process which would condemn the economy to stagnation.

*(b) The data*
To test the validity of the political-economic model, we drew up a data base for 23 African countries for the period 1980–90 characterized by the large number of adjustment programmes in these countries. As the model contains many dynamic interactions, it seemed essential to constitute a panel with a significant temporal factor. On the one hand, empirical studies on the transversal data cannot reveal this type of interaction (for example, a check has been made as to whether certain unpopular economic measures led to strikes or demonstrations using a sample of countries under consideration in a given year). On the other hand, the chronological series available on a single country are not long enough. Most economic indicators exist on an annual basis only. The only satisfactory solution therefore consisted of using a pool of chronological series.

The list of 23 countries retained shows their geographical diversity (countries of North Africa, Sub-Saharan Africa), their political diversity (whatever the type of regime or ideology), their linguistic and monetary diversity (10 of the 23 belong to the franc zone): Algeria, Burkina Faso, Cameroon, Central African Republic, Congo, Côte d'Ivoire, Egypt, Gabon, Ghana, Kenya, Madagascar, Mali, Mauritania, Morocco, Niger, Nigeria, Rwanda, Senegal, Sierra Leone, Tanzania, Togo, Tunisia and Zambia. Most of the African countries not on the list were not considered either because they underwent civil wars in the 1980s, or because the necessary information was not available for the entire period.

In principle, the number of observations is 23 × 11 for each variable, but since we used lagged variables a year is lost, so that we have in fact only 230 observations per variable.

For the economic variables (growth rate of GDP, rate of inflation, exchange rate, rate of indebtedness, imports or exports/GDP, balance of payments/GDP, etc.) we referred to the World Bank's *World Tables*, 1992 and *World Debt Tables*, 1991–92. The statistics on the amount of public aid for development are from the OECD. Finally the number of interventions by the IMF per year was taken from the magazine *Marchés Tropicaux*, which gives one or two pages of information every week on each country. This same source was used to collect information on the political situation (strikes, demonstrations, successful or attempted *coups d'état*) and on political measures (repression or liberalization) and economic measures (recurrent expenditures, capital expenditures, subsidies, wages of civil servants, indirect taxes).

We calculated seven indicators using these data: unpopular economic measures; popular economic measures; strikes; demonstrations; attempts at *coups d'état*; repressive measures; and political liberalization measures. In most cases, we used a scale of four values (nil, weak, intermediary, high) to give a code to each measure or event. For example, it is clear that a decrease in subsidies which leads to a 5% or a 50% rise in the price of foodstuffs must be considered weak in the first case and high in the second. By and large, the intermediary value is determined by elimination: the intensity of a measure seems neither weak nor high. In a few cases, only binary values were used; for example, a university is, or is not, closed. We took into account the immediate impact of each measure on the government's popularity. Thus the decision to privatize a semi-public company is considered as an unpopular measure, given its effect on employment, even if it may subsequently increase GDP growth. For economic measures and often for political measures, a measure concerning the same elements may be coded positively or negatively. For example, a reduction of 5% in real wages of civil servants will be coded −1 as an unpopular economic measure, whereas a rise of 5% will have a code of +1 for a popular economic measure.

Each measure was thus coded with values, +1, +2, +3 or −1, −2, −3. For two variables, strikes and demonstrations, we retained the maximum value reached in the year. For other values, positive and negative variables were cumulated separately. Then in a second stage the margin of variation was reduced to 0–3 using the following table of correspondence.

| Value of the indicator | Amount |
| --- | --- |
| 0 | 0 |
| 1 | 1 |
| 2 | 2 and 3 |
| 3 | 4 and more. |

There is a disadvantage to this coding procedure: the results depend on the choice made by the person coding the measure or the event. This disadvantage is tempered by the fact that only one person is involved in the coding, so that if there is a bias, it is constant. On the other hand, when governments take decisions rapidly, they only have approximate information, much less specific and reliable than that established later by historians. We can consider that the approximate nature of our indicators of disturbance corresponds to that of the information available to the government.

*(c) The results*
Without going into the technical difficulties that had to be solved, given that certain explicative variables are endogenous and that several variables are qualitative, and without getting into a discussion on the coefficients and their level of significance, we shall simply present the essential results of this econometric analysis.

– Block 1. This block includes six equations explaining the economic indicators and two equations for the political indicators. The equations on the economic indicators confirm relations already known with regard to growth, inflation, foreign trade and indebtedness. We simply note that the stabilization or lax policies (unpopular or popular economic measures) have an entirely significant effect on the growth rate of GDP *per capita* in the same order of magnitude in absolute value, which demonstrates the symmetrical nature of the two policies. The results show that measures to reduce or increase overall demand have the expected effect. We also note the mechanical effect of strikes: by temporarily stopping certain activities, they decrease the growth rate.

Two other equations concern demonstrations and strikes. The political risks of a stabilization programme appear undeniable: the unpopular economic measures significantly explain strikes and demonstrations. But inflation is an equally important and significant factor of disorder. The destabilizing role of inflation is understood if the unpopular economic measures are broken down into three categories:

(i) reduction in recurrent and/or capital expenditures;
(ii) reduction in real wages and/or employment (in the public or semi-public sector)
(iii) rise in indirect taxes on consumer goods (including petroleum products) or reduction in subsidies given to these goods.

The measures in category (i) have no effect on demonstrations or strikes. Those in category (ii) explain the strikes and have an effect, but are less significant for demonstrations. Finally, the measures in category (iii) explain demonstrations very well. This result proves that the measures with an impact on prices, or increased inflation, are precisely the ones which lead to demonstrations. These therefore represent a more or less violent reaction to rises in prices, whatever their origin.

Thus the first reason for demonstrations is a sharp drop in the purchasing power of poor or fairly poor urban populations. This is an inevitable reaction, because the drop in purchasing power can be much greater than that in developed countries, since it affects populations whose purchasing power is already much lower, and finally because the political institutions do not allow for a vote in the near future to change the government. In one sense, these are the reactions of poverty or even desperation. The process is different with regard to strikes: the same factors trigger them, but with a lag. Wage-earners react to the drop in real wages after a certain time. These differences in behaviour are explained by different standards of living. Wage-earners who go on strike are part of the modern sector and for the most part belong to middle-income classes. It is not surprising that under the circumstances their behaviour is close to that observed in developed countries. Conversely, a sharp rise in the price of prime necessity food products causes riots, the demonstrators being principally from the poor or very poor classes.

If these disturbances depend directly on the level of prices, the economic climate also plays a role, a moderating role when it is favourable. So higher growth in purchasing power or an increase in external aid in t-1 will decrease disturbances. Here, aid acts as a factor of social peace because it lightens the budgetary constraint and gives the government more means to satisfy demands.

– Block 2. This block contains six equations, four of which explain the economic measures and two the political measures. In addition to monetary and exchange-rate policies, in the two other equations we have considered unpopular and popular economic measures. As was predictable, stabilization programmes are associated with deteriorating indebtedness and intervention by the IMF. Conversely, the more a country was aided in the previous year, the more it can postpone adjustment. A return to lax policies with popular economic measures follows political liberalization measures and higher growth the previous year. In addition, the government is more prone to lax policies if there are strikes. It is significant here that the authorities are repressive with regard to demonstrations, but may give way to strikes because their demands do not bring the regime into question.

The two equations concerning repression and political liberalization give interesting indicators on government choices in Africa. The attempts at *coups d'état* and demonstrations lead almost automatically to repressive measures. In the case of *coup d'état* attempts, the government's violent reaction to ensure its survival is not surprising: these kinds of incidents, on the rare occasions they have taken place in industrialized democratic countries, have caused relatively comparable reactions. Conversely, a major difference can be observed in government reactions with regard to demonstrations. The poor functioning of electoral mechanisms in the countries studied means that governments cannot solve crises by recourse to a calm vote. Any conflict may become a challenge to the institutions of the regime (and not of a particular government within these institutions, as in the democracies of industrialized countries). In a certain sense, practically any serious demonstration carries a potential threat to the regime and incites the authorities to rapid, severe repression. From this standpoint, the status of strikes, which do not appear as an empirically significant determinant of repression, is very different. Everything occurs as if the government considers that this type of social disorder, dealing mainly with material demands, does not threaten political stability. This result can have major consequences with regard to the type of conditions to be stipulated in adjustment plans. If the government must choose between two unpopular measures with similar economic effects, it will prefer the one which may lead to strikes rather than the one that may cause demonstrations.

The equation concerning political liberalization is also very simple: a government liberalizes after a period of repression, unless the repression results from a *coup d'état*. This decision to liberalize after repressive measures is explained by the political context. Repression entails growing costs as it continues in time, due to the reactions of developed countries which may suspend aid or boycott the products and services of the country and also due to internal consequences (increased dependence of the government on the police and the army). In view of these costs, the government prefers to liberalize. This confirms that most of the regimes are autocratic but not dictatorial.

– Block 3. This contains only one equation concerning aid. Aid meets the needs of the country: it decreases if the balance of payments improves or if growth has been faster, and it increases if indebtedness worsened the previous year. The intervention of the IMF also plays a very significant role, which confirms the multiplier effect of 'loans' from the IMF. But the high coefficient of the aid/GDP variable in t-1 shows the inertia of aid policies. There are therefore strong trends that the IMF can only modulate, by curtailing aid; for example, if it cannot reach an agreement with a country in difficulty.

## Political Lessons from Simulations

With a model which simultaneously integrates the economic and the political behaviour of governments and populations, simulations can illuminate government choices by showing all of the consequences of their decisions.

These simulations were performed using a reference simulation which corresponds to a stationary, long-term equilibrium (where the results of the model are identical from one period to the next). It should be noted that this reference simulation does not correspond to an equilibrium situation in the usual economic sense. This simulation reflects the average values of the different variables;

consequently there is an external deficit,[2] the currency is devalued, unpopular economic measures are taken in the same proportion every year. When performing simulations, we introduce shocks to an economy which is already moving downhill at the same pace every year.

There are two versions of the model in equilibrium given the specification of the rates of exchange, one for the franc zone, the other for countries outside the franc zone. As the model is in a stationary situation, various types of shocks are introduced to answer various questions. The comparison with the values obtained and the values for the reference situation makes it possible to analyse dynamically the effects of each initial shock. Because of the importance of their influence, we have retained four questions as examples:

(a) What are the consequences of an intervention by the IMF?
(b) What are the effects of an increase in aid?
(c) What are the effects of a restrictive monetary policy which is often advised by the IMF?
(d) What would be the consequence of a devaluation of the CFA franc?

(a) First, the most controversial question: is the IMF responsible for disorders in an adjustment period? We shall assume that, due to macroeconomic imbalances, notably a very large external deficit which it is impossible to finance by a loan, a stabilization programme has to be applied in any case. This hypothesis excludes the other option of the financial crisis: a drastic rationing of imports. This option can only be envisaged for dictatorships with a strong repressive capacity which can impose a major drop in the standard of living (consequent on the drop in imports) without fear of the reactions on the part of the population or of other countries (since they do not expect significant aid).

The simulation thus consists of comparing the consequences of two policies: stabilizing with the intervention of the IMF or stabilizing without it. This choice is not purely theoretical or of only academic interest. During the 1980s, several African governments opened a heated public debate on the question: should stabilization be undertaken independently or in collaboration with the IMF? As a general rule, public opinion, including that of the opposition to the government, seemed hostile to the second option.

In order to compare these two cases, countries in the franc zone need to be distinguished from the others: IMF intervention has an effect on exchange-rate policy outside the franc zone, but not within it. First, let us consider the countries outside the franc zone (Figure 9.2a). The overall economic consequences of an IMF intervention in these countries seem favourable, whereas the overall political consequences are rather unfavourable. By taking the same stabilization measures in the first year, the IMF intervention precludes a drop in the standard of living: after six years GDP *per capita* is 1 point higher than the reference value, whereas it is 1 point lower if the country stabilizes on its own. The balance of payments evolves more favourably since, after 10 years, a drop in the deficit of 2.7 points is achieved as compared with 0.8. These performances are associated with faster growth of exports (due to larger devaluations) and external aid which in part depends on relations with the IMF. But this intervention by the IMF leads to more strikes and demonstrations in the second year, and consequently more repression. As from the third year, the political consequences are less clear-cut:

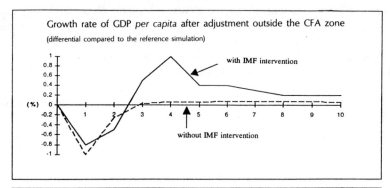

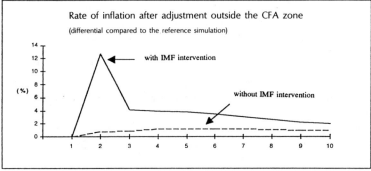

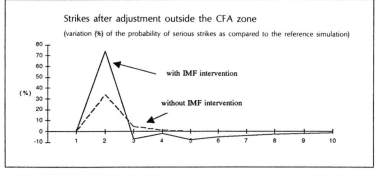

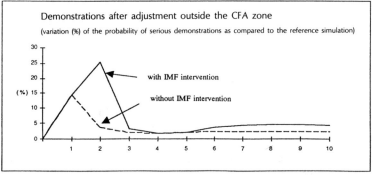

**Figure 9.2a.** *Adjustment with or without IMF intervention (non-franc zone)*

because of the IMF intervention, there are fewer strikes, given the higher growth rate of GDP *per capita*, but slightly more demonstrations (the difference is small) because of higher inflation. The IMF intervention is in part responsible in that it means a higher devaluation in the second year.

In the case of the franc zone (Figure 9.2b), the consequences of an IMF intervention are favourable from both the economic and the political standpoints: social disturbances are less serious, there is less repression, more growth, and a clearer improvement in the balance of payments. The intervention of the IMF is not associated with a high rate of devaluation, and subsequently of inflation, as in the other countries. As the acceleration of inflation has been avoided, there is less disorder, particularly since other factors contribute to social stability: more aid and, as from the second year, more growth. We note, however, that these countries do not benefit like the others from a high growth rate of exports as a result of the devaluation recommended by the IMF.

In conclusion, it is clear that countries in the franc zone have an interest in adjusting in collaboration with the IMF for both political and economic reasons. For the other countries, the economic advantage, which is sizeable, entails a political cost: a more difficult second year, due to higher rates of devaluation and inflation. But in the third year, the political advantages and disadvantages of the collaboration balance out.

These relatively favourable results of an IMF intervention are due to the aid policy of the developed countries. The agreement with the IMF presents economic and political advantages, in particular because it is associated with an increase in aid. On the other hand, the IMF intervention means a more severe adjustment of the exchange rate which has immediate political disadvantages but longer-term economic advantages.

(b) As aid to Africa is at the heart of many debates because the political, economic and social trends in the region are a cause for concern to donor countries, we have estimated the consequences of a high increase in this variable (+50%) in one year (Figure 9.3). In fact, this effort will have an influence on the other years, given the very high value of the aid coefficient in t-1 (0.8) in the aid equation. Only after 8 years is the increase lower than 10% of the reference value for the countries outside the franc zone. As they receive relatively less aid, the consequences in absolute value of this effort of the donor countries are smaller. Nevertheless, they are significant. The government takes fewer stabilization measures for two reasons: a direct effect (these measures have a negative correlation to aid in t-1) and an indirect effect (aid stimulates economic growth on which these measures also depend). Given that fewer unpopular measures are taken, there is less disorder and repression and consequently fewer liberalization measures (this is a virtuous political-economic circle). As there are fewer demonstrations and strikes, the exchange rate rises as from the third year, which slows down inflation and reinforces social stability since the disturbances are due to inflation. The political effects are thus beneficial overall; these effects die out only at the end of the period (years 9 and 10) when the aid falls to its reference level.

The gains seem even clearer for the franc zone. Unlike the other countries, the exchange rate does not vary here and therefore the rate of inflation is not affected. But the gains in terms of growth are greater. The cumulative effects of

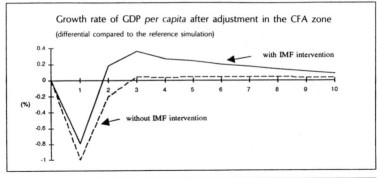

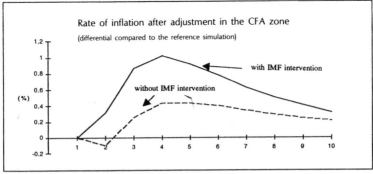

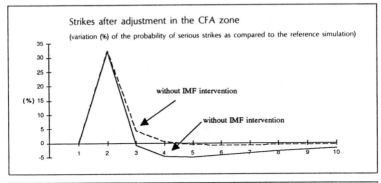

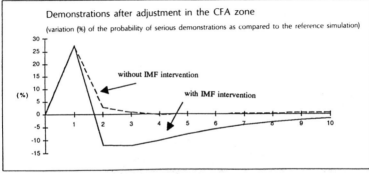

**Figure 9.2b.** *Adjustment with or without IMF intervention (franc zone)*

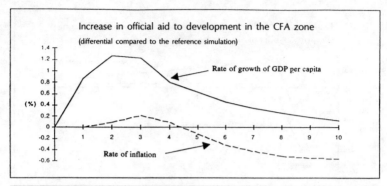

Increase in official aid to development in the CFA zone
(differential compared to the reference simulation)

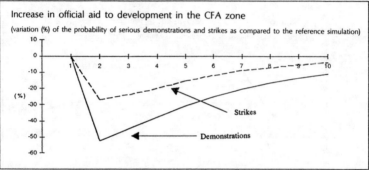

Increase in official aid to development in the CFA zone
(variation (%) of the probability of serious demonstrations and strikes as compared to the reference simulation)

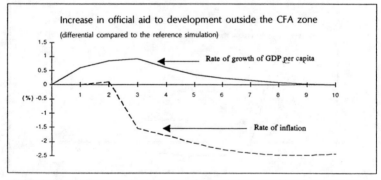

Increase in official aid to development outside the CFA zone
(differential compared to the reference simulation)

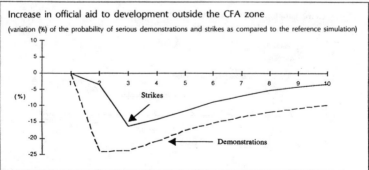

Increase in official aid to development outside the CFA zone
(variation (%) of the probability of serious demonstrations and strikes as compared to the reference simulation)

**Figure 9.3.** *The effects of an increase in aid*

more aid and more rapid growth than in the other countries explain a stronger reduction in stabilization measures, strikes and particularly demonstrations, with the usual consequences on repression and political liberalization. Thus aid in the franc zone countries has a determinant influence, it seems, on political stability. It must be stressed that this influence remains important even 6 or 7 years later when aid approaches the reference value. Conversely, any major curtailment of aid will have dangerous consequences for the stability of these countries.

(c) A restrictive monetary policy has very different effects depending on whether it refers to the franc zone or countries outside the franc zone, because the exchange rate is set in the one case, whereas it depends on the rate of inflation (or more precisely the differential of inflation with the OECD countries) in the second. Moreover, a drop of 50% in the growth rate of the money supply corresponds to different absolute variations since this rate is much lower in the franc zone countries.

In these countries (Figure 9.4), we observe the 'pure' effect of a monetarist policy, meaning by this its direct consequences on inflation only, without considering its indirect effects on the exchange rate. On the one hand, the rate of inflation drops sharply, which explains an important decline in demonstrations and consequently less repression. But the incidence on strikes is much smaller and, already in the third year, on the contrary, we can observe a rise, due to the negative impact of a restrictive monetary policy on economic growth. Wage-earners react to this less favourable evolution of their standard of living by triggering more strikes. These results show that a government which has decided to fight inflation can benefit from popular support, or at least political stability, at the cost of a slower growth rate and, for this reason, more determined opposition on the part of wage-earners, which must be compensated by the support of other groups in the city or rural areas.

In the countries outside the franc zone, monetary policy has an important impact on the exchange rate: it leads to a strong revaluation of the national currency. Because of this indirect effect, the drop in the rate of inflation is much higher than in countries belonging to the franc zone. This rise in the exchange rate slows down exports and contributes to the deterioration in the balance of payments. This set of phenomena explains a higher cost in terms of growth of GDP *per capita* than in the franc zone.

As stabilization measures are associated with devaluation, the government will take fewer because of this rise in the exchange rate. There are subsequently many fewer strikes and demonstrations and therefore less repression and fewer measures of political and economic liberalization. This optimistic picture must be qualified, however. As from the third year, the trend for strikes reverses: they grow from year to year given the drop in GDP *per capita* which is relatively high as compared with that in the franc zone countries.

(d) With regard to exchange rates, everyone knows that the first question which comes up in Africa is that of the devaluation of the CFA franc. The IMF and the World Bank have advised several African countries to adopt this measure. The problem was the subject of discussions, at times very tense, between these institutions and the countries which, with the support of France, reject any idea of devaluation. But the arguments expressed for or against the devaluation of the CFA franc are by and large economic, whereas

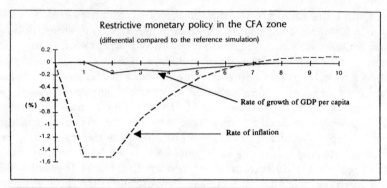

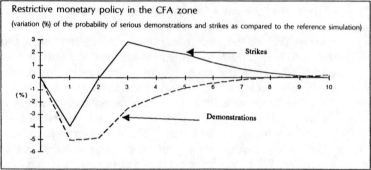

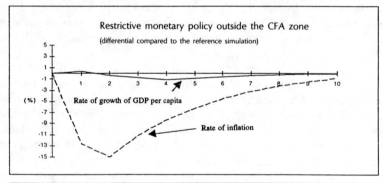

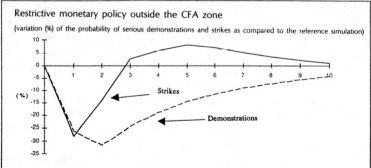

**Figure 9.4.** *The effects of a restrictive monetary policy*

the problem also obviously has a major political aspect. In this case, it is helpful to have a political-economic model the better to assess the possible effects of a devaluation.

Simulating a 50% devaluation without compensatory measures shows how misleading a purely economic analysis can be (Figure 9.5). True, we obtain a strong increase in exports, a clear improvement in the balance of payments and higher growth overall (the loss recorded in the first year is more than compensated by gains in subsequent years). But several governments could lose power under the pressure of riots if we believe in the disastrous rise in the demonstrations indicator, which is mainly due to the acceleration in inflation caused by the devaluation. This simulation (devaluation + severe stabilization programme) shows the considerable political risks of an operation justified by its positive economic effects. It can be argued that, already in the second year, the political consequences are no longer unfavourable: strikes fall off in proportion to the rise in demonstrations. But this argument is not admissible for a government concerned about its probability of survival; recovering a certain amount of political stability in the second year serves no purpose if it has lost power in the first year as a result of riots. It is true that this simulation shows orders of magnitude only, but the resistance of certain African Heads of State to the devaluation of the CFA franc, however sound the economic arguments may be, seems to have a real basis in political reasons. Unless exchange rates are adjusted at the right time, they are confronted with an insoluble political problem, like governments which allow subsidies on basic agricultural products to rise to a point which means that abruptly suppressing them would threaten the survival of the government.

Because of the political cost of devaluing the CFA franc, we have calculated the effects of a considerable increase in aid (+50%) in order to avoid too much disorder (Figure 9.5). If aid is increased in this way during the devaluation year, and subsequently in a decreasing proportion in the following years to reach the reference level after about ten years, strikes will increase greatly during the first year due to the rise in prices caused by the devaluation, but by the second year there will be fewer because of the high growth rate. This rise results from the climate created by a boom in exports caused by the devaluation and the additional aid. As demonstrations depend on the amount of aid in the previous year, a spectacular drop in demonstrations is recorded as from the second year (in 1 on the graph). The fact that there are many fewer political liberalization measures must not be considered negative: this is the simple consequence of a strong reduction in repression. Thus, as from the second year, the political consequences are very favourable, and the government has not run any risk of demonstrations due to the devaluation in the first year.[3] The economy reaches a significantly higher rate of growth *per capita*, a better balance of payments, and a strong reduction in indebtedness. As there are also fewer disturbances and less repression, except for the year of the devaluation, this is a success from all standpoints.

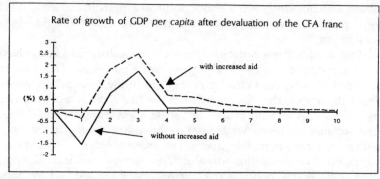

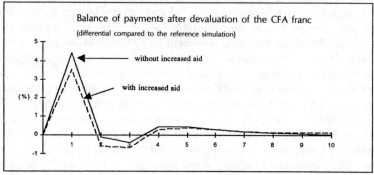

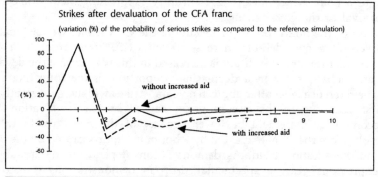

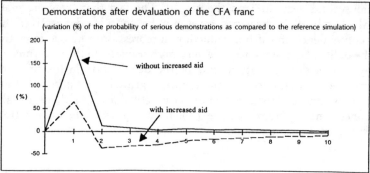

**Figure 9.5.** *The consequences of a devaluation of the CFA franc*

# Conclusion

These simulations show the advantage for all officials, be they African governments or aid agencies, of using an analysis which integrates the political and
economic factors. This is the only way to get a realistic assessment of the consequences of stabilization policies or any other decision, such as on aid policy. It
is clear that a coherent method of integrating economics and politics will provide
a better guide for choices than the usual dichotomous approach where either an
economic measure is taken without considering the political effects, or is rejected
in the name of arbitrary political arguments.

## Notes

1. Whereas the debate on the effectiveness of companies leads to much less certain conclusions in
   the case of developed countries.
2. The co-existence of a high stable foreign deficit and a constant rate of indebtedness may seem
   surprising. This can be explained by two phenomena: the rate of indebtedness is not equal to the
   accumulation of foreign deficits owing to the cancellations of debts; furthermore, the foreign
   deficit before official transfers is covered by aid for the most part.
3. As in principle a devaluation should be accompanied by a tight monetary policy, we simulated
   the same devaluation assuming that the amount of money in circulation does not change with
   regard to the reference simulation. In this case, the advantage of the devaluation in terms of GDP
   growth *per capita* is somewhat smaller (less than 2% instead of 2.5% for period 3). But we obtain
   a drop in the probability of demonstrations already in period 1 which accelerates in the following
   period, rather than a rise in this probability during the first period. A devaluation accompanied
   by a tight monetary policy and a rise in aid is thus compatible with an overall drop in the risk
   of demonstrations.

## References

Alesina, A. and Drazen, A. (1990) *Why are Stabilizations Delayed?*, London, Ontario: University
of Western Ontario: Papers in Political Economy 1 (August).

Alesina, A. and Tabellini, G. (1990) 'A Positive Theory of Fiscal Deficits and Government Debt in
a Democracy'. *The Review of Economic Studies* (June).

Anderson, C. (1988) 'Public Finance in Autocratic Process: An Empirical Note', *Public Choice* 57.

Bates, R. H. (ed.) (1988) *Toward a Political Economy of Development: A Rational Choice Perspective.* Berkeley, CA: University of California Press.

Berg, A. and Sachs, J. D. (1988) *The Debt Crisis: Structural Explanations of Country Performance*,
National Bureau of Economic Research Working Paper No. 2607, Cambridge, MA: NBER.

Berg-Schlosser, D. (1985) 'African Political Systems: Typology and Performance', *Comparative
Political Studies* 17.

Bloch, P. C. (1986) 'The Politico-Economic Behavior of Authoritarian Governments', *Public Choice*
51, 117–28.

Borooah, V. and Schneider, F. (eds) (1991) 'Politico-Economic Modelling', *European Journal of
Political Economy*, Special Issue, 7 (4), 435–638.

Bouin O. and Michalet, C. (1991) *Le rééquilibrage entre secteurs public et privé: l'expérience des
pays en développement.* Paris: OECD Development Centre.

Frey, B. S. and Eichenberger, R. (1992) *The Political Economy of Stabilization Programmes in
Developing Countries*, Technical Paper No. 59. Paris: OECD Development Centre.

Haggard, S., Kaufman, R., Shariff, K. and Webb, S. (1990) *Political Inflation and Stabilization in
Middle-Income Countries.* Washington DC: World Bank.

de Janvry, A., Fergeix, D. and Sadoulet, E. (1990) 'Economic, Welfare, and Political Consequences
of Stabilization Policies: An Analysis for Ecuador and Latin America', University of California
at Berkeley, CA. (mimeo).

Lafay, J. D. and Lecaillon, J. (1993) *The Political Dimension of Economic Adjustment*. Paris: OECD Development Centre.

Lal, D. (1987) 'The Political Economy of Economic Liberalization', *World Bank Economic Review* 1 (2), 273–99.

Mueller, D. C. (1989) *Public Choice II*. Cambridge: Cambridge University Press.

Nelson J. (ed.) (1990) *Economic Crisis and Policy Choice*. Princeton, NJ: Princeton University Press.

Paldam, M. (1987) 'Inflation and Political Instability in Eight Latin American Countries 1946–83', *Public Choice* 52 (2), 143–68.

Pourgerami, A. (1992) 'Authoritarian Versus Nonauthoritarian Approaches to Economic Development: Update and Additional Evidence', *Public Choice* 74 (3), 365–78.

Sachs, J. D. (ed.) (1989) *Developing Country Debt and the World Economy*. Chicago, IL: Chicago University Press.

Sidell, D. R. (1987) *The IMF and Third World Political Instability. Is There a Connection?*, London: Macmillan.

Tullock, G. (1987) *Autocracy*. Dordrecht: Martinus Nijhof.

Vaubel, R. and Willet, T. D. (eds) (1991) *The Political Economy of International Organizations: A Public Choice Approach*. Boulder, CO: Westview Press.

Weede, E. (1983) 'The Impact of Democracy on Economic Growth: Some Evidence from Cross-National Analysis', *Kyklos* 36 (1), 21–39.

Wintrobe, R. (1989) *The Tinpot and the Totalitarian: A Simple Economic Theory of Dictatorship*. London, Ontario: University of Western Ontario: Papers in Political Economy 4 (August).

# PART FOUR
# Structural Adjustment and Long-term Development Perspectives

# 10 Structural Adjustment and the Long-Term Development of Sub-Saharan Africa

## ISHRAT HUSAIN

The determinants of economic growth and development are complex, varied and not fully understood. There is no single model of economic development that has universal validity or which could be applied either to explain or to predict the course of development of every developing country or even groups of countries. But the experience during the past thirty years of more than 100 developing countries does provide some broad lessons.

Empirical studies that have examined determinants of economic development over an extended period of time have concluded that human capital and public investment coupled with outward-oriented trade policies exert a positive and significant influence on economic growth. Better policies are typically associated with faster growth. So is political and social stability. Using this empirical knowledge and the unique characteristics of Sub-Saharan African countries, the 1989 Long-Term Perspective Study on Sub-Saharan Africa (World Bank, 1989a) has set out an agenda for long-term development that is a reflection of a broad consensus among Africans, donors, and the development community at large.

The agenda calls for African economies to grow by at least 4–5% a year. This requires an enabling environment of incentives and infrastructure services to foster efficient production and private initiative. It also requires enhanced capacities on the part of people and institutions. The growth strategy must be both sustainable and equitable – sustainable in an environmental sense because sound environmental policies are required in order to protect the productive capacity of Africa's natural resources, and equitable because long-term political stability is impossible without equity. Equitable means, in particular, that measures are taken to reduce poverty, especially by improving the access of the poor to productive assets. The question this paper addresses is: How does structural adjustment fit into this long-term development agenda for SSA?

## What Does 'Adjustment' Mean And How Should We Measure Its Impact?

Adjustment involves abandoning certain notions of development that have not worked in the past and adopting a different approach. The underlying objective of structural adjustment in Sub-Saharan Africa is to restore the conditions for growth and to improve the basis for long-term social and economic development. The attainment of this objective involves reshaping and redirecting policies and institutions and eliminating severe macroeconomic imbalances and microeconomic distortions that pervade the economy. Economic development can only proceed once these changes have taken place. Adjustment, of course, is a continuous process that requires sound economic policies and management, otherwise imbalances and distortions will once again surface and institutional decay will set in. During the late 1970s and early 1980s, African countries allowed imbalances and distortions to accumulate and reach a crisis stage. Today, prompt responses and corrective measures along the way can prevent the recurrence of crisis. When countries are no longer forced to react to crises, they can better focus their attention on fundamental long-term development challenges: building human and institutional capacities, protecting the environment, slowing population growth and assimilating new technology.

What, exactly, does structural adjustment mean? The popular connotation is that adjustment means restraint in demand as typified by IMF programmes. But, in fact, the IMF and the World Bank use different categories of measures: one reduces overall demand and the other stimulates supply. The term stabilization is normally used for reducing demand and structural adjustment for stimulating supply. Stabilization measures mainly focus on financial disequilibria (i.e. the fiscal and external accounts and the rate of inflation). Structural adjustment policies seek to restructure production capacities in order to increase efficiency and help restore growth. While stabilization is concerned with the short term, structural adjustment extends over the medium to long term. Certain measures have stabilizing and structural effects at the same time; devaluation, for example, both reduces overall demand and restructures the productive sectors.

Notwithstanding the distinction made between stabilization and adjustment, the two sets of policies follow a common logic. The imbalances in an economy that lead to financial crisis are partly due to the inadequacy of domestic supply with respect to demand. Once equilibrium is established by the stabilization programme the best way to prevent imbalances from recurring is to remove structural impediments and microeconomic distortions that may impede the increase in productive capacities. The inadequate supply is partly due to the inappropriate structure of the economy reflected in, for example, an inefficient and loss-making public sector, overprotected industries and agricultural systems that discourage production.

In brief, structural adjustment programmes and policies are essentially intended to improve the incentive structure, the trade regime, the allocation of resources and efficiency in the use of resources to stimulate growth-enhancing impulses in the economy. A reorientation of public expenditures and investment towards human capital and infrastructure, an expansion of exports and efficient import substitutes, efficient trade policies, and liberalization of prices and deregulation of controls to allow producers to increase output of goods and services are the essential characteristics of structural adjustment programmes. Although the initial conditions, resource endowments, and specific country circumstances necessitate variation in the design of these policies and programmes, the basic objective – to restore growth, consumption and employment – remains unchanged.

A misunderstanding about the concept, content and intensity of adjustment efforts is responsible for many erroneous conclusions that are drawn about the impact of adjustment. A number of considerations must be kept in mind in looking at the adjustment experience in SSA:

- First, a clear understanding of the initial conditions of the countries undergoing adjustment is absolutely critical. The protracted economic and financial crisis that preceded adjustment has made it particularly difficult to achieve a quick turn-around and improvement. In Tanzania, for example, the real cash incomes of smallholders fell almost continuously throughout the 1970s and early 1980s, as receipts from official crop sales failed to keep pace with inflation, and rural-urban terms of trade turned against the farmer (Ellis, 1982). Had the government not taken corrective measures, economic and social conditions in Tanzania would be much worse than they are today.

- Second, reform measures must be correctly identified for what they are and are not. If, in the first phase of reform, the emphasis was on restructuring the budget and shifting the balance in the current account through expenditure reductions, it would be incorrect to call this a structural reform. These are stabilization measures and their impact is very different from that of structural reforms. Several African countries have called their stabilization efforts structural adjustment programmes. The wrong labelling of adjustment, inaccurate grouping of adjusting countries, and incorrect choice of periods and duration of adjustment have been the single source of confusion in this debate.

- Third, it is important to know whether the reforms were implemented both in the spirit and the letter. A number of countries have started adjustment programmes and even borrowed from the international financial institutions, but under political pressure have made reversals and slippages during the course of their implementation. This stop-go approach has to be distinguished from a sustained implementation of planned reforms, since reversals of policies benefit some segments of the population at the expense of others.

- Fourth, exogenous shocks which were not anticipated or built into adjustment programmes have a significant impact on their success. If world prices of key commodity exports decline appreciably, or rainfall is lower than expected, it would be unfair to attribute poor economic and social performance to the adjustment programme alone.

- Finally, in a number of adjusting countries the external funding promised by donors or the debt relief projected under the programme have not materialized. This has had a negative effect on imports and consequently on the growth of output, exports and the level of public spending. This factor should be fully taken into account when judging the success or otherwise of the adjustment programme or its social consequences. The quantity of external resources is not the only important factor here; equally important are the timing, the rate of actual disbursements and the tied or untied nature of the assistance.

## History of Adjustment in Sub-Saharan Africa

Before examining the impact of adjustment, it is important to understand the background to the current crisis. How did structural imbalances originate and what has been the history of the response?

The two oil price shocks of the 1970s gave rise to huge macroeconomic imbalances in SSA countries. However, these were effectively kept in check by controls of various kinds such as import licensing, foreign-exchange allocation, investment permits, domestic price controls and regulations. External borrowing, facilitated by excess liquidity in the commercial banking system and negative real interest rates, helped most African countries maintain consumption levels. Then commodity prices started declining, real interest rates began rising and the burden of debt service became unbearable. Economic and social indicators for the period 1980–85 bear out the intensity of the resulting crisis.

Most SSA countries experienced large current account deficits and huge public sector deficits, with high and rising inflation rates. Thus, the first order of business was to stabilize the economy and many countries adopted various stabilization programmes in the first half of the 1980s with the assistance of the International Monetary Fund.

It was soon realized that, while the IMF packages were necessary, they were by no means sufficient to restore growth and set African economies on the path to long-term sustainable development. Structural weaknesses in African economies – poor infrastructure, underdeveloped markets, weak human resource bases and institutions – required a different kind of effort. Stabilization, by its very nature, was a short-term remedy intended to bring macroeconomic imbalances in line with the production capacity of the country. The tools used were mainly expenditure reduction, tax increases and import compression. Unless an approach was adopted to *expand* productive capacity, the poor countries of Africa would be forced to maintain levels of aggregate demand that would not be sufficient for growth and development.

Structural adjustment programmes were conceived as a set of policies and instruments (devaluing the exchange rate, liberalizing imports, freeing agricultural pricing and marketing, improving the quality of public investment, reducing unnecessary regulations and restrictions on the private sector) that would act on the supply side of the economy. As these were entirely new tools – both for donors as well as for recipients – the learning curve has been shallow. There was initially a resistance to these reforms. Politically influential and vocal groups were unwilling to give up the rents they were collecting from the existing system. But as the crisis deepened so did the commitment by African countries. Many countries began structural reform programmes which resulted in improvements, and the demonstration effect led to a widening of the group of reforming countries.

The results of adjustment have been modest, in so far as economic decline has been reversed. (For evaluation of structural adjustment programmes see Husain, 1993; Elbadawi *et al.*, 1992; World Bank, 1988a, b, 1990, 1992a, b; World Bank/UNDP, 1989.) There has been improvement in the policy environment in the intensively adjusting countries through reduction in macro imbalances, shifting incentives to favour the tradeable sectors and reducing government interventions in the markets. Where African countries have diligently and assiduously pursued the path of adjustment, their performance in terms of key macroeconomic indicators has been more than satisfactory. Countries that have succeeded in establishing a stable macro framework and improving relative prices for

**Table 10.1.** *Sub-Saharan Africa: Economic Performance by Groups of Countries 1975–91*

| | (Annual average % change) | | | | |
|---|---|---|---|---|---|
| | 1975–80 | 1981–85 | | 1986–91 | |
| | | Unweighted | Weighted | Unweighted | Weighted |
| **A. GDP growth rate** | | | | | |
| Countries with social unrest | 2.9 | 1.4 | 1.9 | 2.1 | 2.7 |
| CFA countries | 4.4 | 3.1 | 1.1 | 1.1 | −0.2 |
| Small economies | 5.0 | 4.6 | 4.1 | 2.9 | 3.8 |
| Adjusters | 1.9 | 1.5 | −0.2 | 4.0 | 4.5 |
| **B. Growth in agriculture** | | | | | |
| Countries with social unrest | 4.2 | 0.8 | 0.8 | 1.7 | 1.4 |
| CFA countries | 2.7 | 2.5 | −0.7 | 3.5 | 2.7 |
| Small economies | – | 0.9 | 1.0 | 2.7 | 3.1 |
| Adjusters | 0.6 | 1.1 | 0.9 | 2.8 | 3.6 |
| **C. Growth in exports** | | | | | |
| Countries with social unrest | 0.5 | −0.2 | 4.3 | 3.2 | −2.2 |
| CFA countries | 7.2 | 1.5 | 5.7 | 1.3 | 0.3 |
| Small economies | NA | 4.7 | 10.6 | 5.2 | 5.2 |
| Adjusters | 2.0 | −1.6 | −2.5 | 4.6 | 5.1 |

Source: World Bank, Africa Region. Internal data, 1993.

the export sector, and especially for agriculture, while keeping inflation under control, are enjoying the biggest pay-offs from the reforms.

Countries receiving aid under the Special Programme of Assistance (SPA) for low-income, debt-distressed African countries performed better than the region as a whole. Furthermore, in a core group of 15 countries which have implemented policy reforms successfully over time, economic outcomes have been impressive compared with the first half of the 1980s, and the turn-around in growth is strong (see Table 10.1). All key performance indicators for this group of countries have been better than those for the region as a whole. GDP grew on average by 4% annually. The efficiency of this core group of countries, as measured by export growth and the degree of capacity utilization, improved significantly in relation to other countries in the region. Exports grew at a rate of 5% per annum (or nearly twice the rate for the region) and the incremental capital-output ratio declined more rapidly. Countries in this group have also improved their fiscal stance by increasing revenues. Financial imbalances, both internal and external, were thus reduced drastically, which in turn reduced inflationary pressure.

The overall growth performance of the adjusting countries in SSA has been affected by the declining growth in the franc zone countries. In the CFA countries, the inability to devalue the currency meant that adjustment and real depreciation could be achieved only through domestic policies aimed at reducing demand. While the inflation record of this group of countries has been spectacular, both by African and developing country standards, it has been paid for by declining growth rates, depressed levels of economic activity and increasing poverty and unemployment.

Agriculture, the sector in which most Africans make their living, has been a particular success. The most important way adjustment has affected agriculture is by reducing the level of taxation through macro policy changes and marketing reforms to achieve a relative shift in price incentives in favour of agriculture. But this improvement can be sustained in the long term only if infrastructural deficiencies, technological changes and institutional weaknesses are given equal importance. It is found that countries adjusting price and marketing policy in favour of agriculture also invest more in agricultural services and rural infrastructure. Kenya, Nigeria and Burkina Faso have become countries with relatively good agriculture policies, and have the best agricultural extension services. African countries which have shown significant improvement in agriculture in the past five years are Benin, Burkina Faso, Tanzania, Nigeria, Ghana, Guinea Bissau and, until very recently, Kenya.

There is always a problem of how much observed performance can be ascribed to particular policies, where so many things are all happening at once; where exogenous forces are strong, where time lags are important, and data sources are not completely reliable. This is even more so in the case of the food and agriculture sector where weather conditions are a dominant factor. But if we construct a picture using direct production data and indirect observations of price movements, trade, and food aid, and average them out for good and bad years, a fairly consistent story emerges. With the obvious exception of those countries which have been devastated by civil war, drought and other ecological disasters, reforms have generally succeeded in arresting the long decline in *per capita* agricultural output, reversed the internal terms of trade to one more favourable to agriculture and reduced the enormous deficits in food availability. The agriculture sector now receives more serious domestic policy attention and thus better producer incentives, improved rural infrastructure, greater rural credit, more sustained interest in the role of women and increased recognition of the crucial importance of farming systems to environmental sustainability.

The story of agriculture's success can be illustrated by the example of Nigeria. The upsurge in oil revenues and the resulting urban bias had led to a neglect of agriculture, adverse rural terms of trade and sizeable migration from rural areas. Consequently, food production suffered and Nigeria became a large net food importer. In the first half of the 1980s, the food import bill averaged $2 billion to $2.5 bn annually. Since 1986, the restoration of producer incentives has interacted positively with investment made previously in rural infrastructure and agriculture services to generate the turn-around and produce a high aggregate supply response. There has been reverse migration to rural areas, educated people have taken to farming, and rural terms of trade have appreciated significantly. According to the FAO, *per capita* food production rose by 25% between 1986 and 1991 despite a 3% annual increase in population. Food imports currently average about $300-$400 million a year – one-sixth of the level of the early 1980s. Maize output has almost doubled in the last five years compared to the previous five-year average. And the success story is not limited to food crops. Contrary to popular perception, there has been an increase in cash crop output too. The export crop production index has also increased by about 42%. Production of cotton, cocoa, rubber, palm oil and groundnuts has reached peak levels and the domestic textile industry is utilizing cotton produced locally instead of relying on imports. It is not obvious that such a large turn-around could have been possible if the rural infrastructure, extension and research, and the supply of inputs had not been put in place in the earlier pre-adjustment period.

Why has so much importance been attached to agriculture and why do we express satisfaction at the progress achieved under adjustment programmes in recent years in Africa? Is it that we want to keep Africa trapped at the low-level equilibrium of primary commodity producers? Agriculture can play a major part in moving SSA countries to a higher, more sustainable growth path for several reasons. First, it accounts for a large share of economic activity and the rate at which agriculture grows will have a large impact on the overall rate of growth. Sustainable industrial growth in most developing countries has been facilitated by increased purchasing power and demand on the part of the rural sector, enlarging the domestic market for industrial products. Second, agriculture accounts for the largest share of the labour force and most of the poor depend on agricultural incomes. Thus, agricultural growth plays a big role in poverty alleviation. Third, agriculture can play a major role in conserving or depleting natural resources and thus in ensuring sustainable growth. Fourth, agriculture has been and will probably continue to be the biggest generator of foreign exchange in most SSA countries. Foreign exchange saved by substituting domestic food production for imports can provide the basis for capital equipment and intermediate inputs to expand industrial production. Fifth, growth in the food sector reduces imports, helps maintain wage rates at low levels and contributes to competitiveness. The link between agricultural growth and efficient industrialization is quite direct.

Despite satisfactory performance on the part of intensive adjusters, and particularly successful results in agriculture and food production, it must be conceded that the overall results of adjustment achieved so far have been modest relative to original expectations. Adjustment has not yet succeeded in raising the rate of growth to the levels needed to make major inroads into poverty. Region-wide economic recovery is still fragile, although there is a great deal of variation in outcomes. Currency depreciation and inflationary pressures have not been subdued in several countries, due to expansionary fiscal and monetary policies. Many countries still rely exclusively on external grants and concessional financing to close their fiscal gaps. Per capita consumption remains stagnant and private investment has not yet revived. Unemployment rates, particularly in urban areas, are still high and poverty is on the rise. Where there is civil strife, adjustment has, of course, not worked.

There are several reasons for SSA's sluggish response to adjustment:

- First, historically, SSA's growth has never been spectacular and has been the weakest among developing countries. Even at its peak, i.e. between 1965 and 1973, growth in GDP was not more than 5% per annum (see Table 10.2). Poor endowments and political and social instability limit the potential in SSA. To

Table 10.2. *GDP and Per Capita Income Growth in SSA 1965–92*

|  | 1965–73 | 1974–80 | 1981–85 | 1986–90 | 1991 | 1992 |
|---|---|---|---|---|---|---|
| GDP growth | 4.7 | 3.2 | 1.2 | 2.5 | 1.7 | 2.7 |
| *Per capita* income | 2.0 | 0.3 | −1.8 | −0.1 | −1.4 | −0.4 |

Source: *ibid*.

expect better results than this immediately after almost two decades of decline and stagnation is not realistic.

- Second, a number of countries have not fully committed themselves to reform and have adopted a stop-go stance. This half-hearted and haphazard implementation of reform, without having arrived at a broad internal consensus and under the 'coercion' or 'incentive' of financial support from the international financial institutions and the donor community, was not likely to create any positive durable effects. Adjustment programmes should be owned by the adopting government and not perceived as imposed by outsiders. Adjustment programmes usually involve up-front costs to many groups in society and the benefits usually take time to emerge. This complicates the tasks of many governments in securing a domestic constituency. But to be effective, reforms must be followed through and sustained despite the short-term transitional costs they impose upon some vocal segments of society. Reversing or switching gear in mid-stream also reduces the credibility of subsequent adjustment efforts. The lack of credibility and continuity in government policies has been more harmful than if adjustment policies had not been put in place in the first instance, as uncertainty among economic agents and investors paralysed the initiation of fresh economic activity.

- Third, the original premise that these programmes would enable economies to revive growth and consumption in five to seven years was over-optimistic. The intensity of the distortions and of the demands made on the response capacity of African economies was underestimated. The limitations of the government's capacities to implement policies, the resistance by politically influential groups to these changes and the sequencing and phasing of reforms were not fully taken into account. Policy convergence among the major donors on support for structural adjustment also took longer than expected.

- Finally, the adjustment response has been constrained by other external factors such as losses from declining terms of trade, deepening debt, recession in the OECD countries and, more recently, by the tumultuous process of political transition which has diverted the attention of policy-makers from economic management, leading in some instances to a virtual breakdown of normal economic activity.

More broadly, however, it must be recognized that the expectations from adjustment have been unrealistic. While adjustment policies can correct the distortions which are so pervasive in African economies, reconfigure the incentive structure and reverse economic decline, they are not a substitute for other actions that must become an integral part of a broadly gauged reform effort. The choice in accelerating sustained long-term development is not between adjustment or some alternative, but whether adjustment will be accompanied by additional actions such as:

- investment in infrastructure
- build-up of human capital
- establishment of an enabling environment for private initiative, such as: a credible commitment by government to a clear reform programme, reduction in incentives and opportunities for rent-seeking and corruption, and creating space for the private sector (privatization, deregulation, etc.)

These types of measures take time to implement and are not quick to show results. Private investors will have to be convinced that the new economic environment is there to stay, that changes in government will not reverse the policies put in place, and that fairness and the rule of law rather than arbitrariness and discretion will drive the conduct of business. In Africa, it will take some time before these conditions are established.

## Adjustment and Poverty Reduction[1]

There has been a continuous evolution in thinking on adjustment which has led to some improvement in the quality and design of reform programmes. In the initial phase of the reforms the social dimensions of adjustment were not given the attention they deserve. It was thought that adjustment policies would not create any major social disruptions. This proved to be wishful thinking as there were clearly winners and losers in the radical alteration of the structure of economic incentives. In the second phase of adjustment, the social dimension was explicitly taken into account through extraordinary means such as Social Action Programmes or other targeted measures. While this was a major step forward, it fell short of the need to integrate concerns about poverty alleviation with those of restoring growth in the design of adjustment programmes themselves. Analysis of the short-term costs of restructuring the economies and their distributional impact should provide a basis for designing compensatory programmes.

There are many complementarities between poverty reduction and adjustment policies. Private sector development, for example, promotes growth and income-earning opportunities for the poor. Trade policy that promotes labour-intensive and agriculture-based exports and substitutes imports with domestic raw materials will disproportionately favour the domestic producers of those goods – mainly the poor. Efforts to reduce loss-making in public enterprises and improve their financial efficiency will free state revenues for priority expenditures in education, health and nutrition.

Empirical evidence clearly shows that growth that makes greater use of the factors of production owned by the poor – principally land and labour – can have a significant effect on poverty. But if the pattern of growth is highly capital-intensive and import-intensive, as was the case with the African countries, higher growth will not have much impact on poverty. Therefore, the choice of instruments for promoting growth and ensuring free mobility of factors, particularly labour, is an important consideration in the design of adjustment programmes. Ineffective capital markets inhibit employment growth and institutional or regulatory barriers constrain the poor's access to labour and product markets. Attempts to reform the financial sector and remove these barriers are certainly going to help the poor.

Because the majority of Africans – and the majority of Africa's poor – live in rural areas and are self-employed small landholders, adjustment programmes that focus on broad-based growth in agriculture offer the most immediate opportunity for alleviating poverty and promoting economic growth. Agricultural growth, and the resulting increase in the purchasing power of rural Africans, is the engine of growth for manufacturing and services – activities which must expand if Africans are to enjoy a much wider range of economic choices than is now conceivable. Earlier strategies neglected agriculture, a sector in which Africa has a clear comparative advantage. Agriculture currently provides 33% of Africa's GDP, 40% of its exports and 70% of its labour force. Even when full account is taken of the environmental limits to land exploitation, the scope for expanding production through increased productivity is great. Rising agricultural and rural incomes through a doubling of the agriculture growth rate form the mainstay of adjustment programmes.

How can growth in agriculture be accelerated? As shown in an earlier section, both price and non-price factors affect agricultural development in Africa equally. By correcting overvalued exchange rates, eliminating marketing monopolies, removing consumer food subsidies and reducing taxation of agriculture and bringing in remunerative producer prices, structural adjustment programmes have altered the incentive structure in favour of exports and import substitutes, particularly domestic food production. Devaluation increases the domestic currency returns of exportables and importables. Real devaluation alone cannot provide positive incentives and stimulate the supply response unless it is complemented by market liberalization, which allows the market-determined or border prices to be transmitted to producers, ensures the free flow of goods and reduces state taxes and the monopoly rents enjoyed by state marketing boards. The evidence from producer prices before and after adjustment in SSA indicates that, in most adjusting countries, taxation of agriculture has decreased and the proportion of world prices paid to African agricultural producers has increased significantly.

It is important to stress that the notion that emphasis on export crops diverts food production and therefore undermines food security at the national and household level is not substantiated by empirical evidence. A number of studies have shown complementarity at the aggregate level between increased food production and export crops. In Burkina Faso, Ghana, Guinea, Mali and Nigeria, *per capita* food production is much higher today than it was in the pre-adjustment period, while the volume of agricultural exports has also risen.

Prior to adjustment, biases against agriculture were extreme in the form of direct taxes and the effects of overvalued exchange rates and industrial protection. Well-intentioned efforts to provide farmers with services through public sector input supply and marketing institutions commonly went to waste because the institutions concerned were hopelessly inefficient. When low growth turned into full-scale crisis in the early 1980s, many governments responded by increasing the rationing of foreign exchange and domestic goods. This slowed down growth and hurt the poor. In Tanzania, for example, the bulk of what little foreign exchange was available was allocated to extraordinarily inefficient industries, while most basic consumer goods became unavailable in rural areas.

The aim of policy reform in Africa has been to redress these past biases. Depreciating real exchange rates and liberalizing external and internal trade both raise the prices of tradeable agricultural goods. Cocoa farmers in Ghana and Nigeria experienced a doubling or more of the purchasing power of their crops because of exchange-rate depreciation and rises in the share of the final price they received. Rural dwellers in Tanzania discovered that they could again have access to consumer goods, and they responded by increasing agricultural supply. A severe lack of data makes a firm assessment impossible, but the combination of a recovery in growth and the removal of some of the worst anti-rural biases helped many of the poor.

However, experience to date also shows the difficulties entailed in tackling Africa's agricultural problems. In some countries, failure to implement policies that build up the competitiveness of exports has contributed to a squeeze on tradeables that has hurt agricultural producers. In other countries, producer prices for exports have stagnated or fallen despite price reforms, reflecting trends in international commodity prices. In others, economy-wide reforms need to be complemented by a far-reaching reform of marketing. While successes in Ghana and Nigeria were partly due to marketing reforms, in Tanzania delays in implementing marketing reforms for some export crops caused delays in passing on benefits to producers. In Malawi, until recently, restrictions were placed on the production of profitable export crops by small farmers. These restrictions have since been removed and an increasing number of smallholders are being given licences to take their products directly to the auction floor.

In the food crop sector, the liberalization of prices and marketing has contributed to an increase in food production. *Per capita* food production held steady in the latter half of the 1980s after a fall in the first half. This has helped to limit food imports in many countries; overall, cereal imports in the late 1980s were 8% lower than at the beginning of the decade and food aid has been halved to 2.5 million tons from 4.8 million tons. Food prices show no overall trend in real terms, but increased domestic food production may have contributed to income gains by net producers. Stable food prices help those among the poor who are net purchasers of food.

The first round of reforms has clearly brought benefits to some of the poor, but deeper policy reform will be required in the 1990s to achieve the growth that is a prerequisite for bringing about a major turn-around in poverty. However, it is clear that adjustment is not enough to bring about significant changes that will benefit the rural poor. Investing in rural roads, developing research and extension services, and developing private services are equally important for broad-based rural development. This will take time and different kinds of government action.

It is equally clear that higher growth by itself, even of the type that increases the incomes of the poor through reallocation of resources and increased returns on the assets they hold, is not sustainable unless human capital formation, upgrading of skills and access to social services – in other words, social development – are placed on an equal footing with income augmentation processes.

As the UNDP's *Human Development Report* 1992 has shown, human development is not anti-growth but is concerned with the development of human capabilities and with using them productively. The former requires investment in people, the latter that people contribute to GNP growth and employment. Both sides of the equation are essential. Recent empirical work strongly confirms that development in human resources is an excellent investment in terms of its contribution to sustainable economic growth. There is a strong positive association, for example, between school enrolment and the average rates of growth. An educated population is the key to long-term growth. A country may grow for limited periods on the basis of mining its natural resources or by large infusions of foreign aid – but to sustain growth there is no substitute for educated people. Education raises the output of farmers, as educated farmers absorb new information quickly and are willing to innovate. Educated women have healthier and fewer children. Women's education also has environmental benefits because it reduces the fertility rate, discourages forest clearing by ensuring that women have better work options, and improves women's ability to manage natural resources. Similar findings show up in health, education, nutrition and family planning. Indeed, improvement in any one of these areas tends to raise economic returns in the others.

Of course, investing in social development does not guarantee growth all by itself. The poor cannot benefit from more education and better health if they are not able to use their human assets to increase their incomes. The fast-growing countries of East Asia have not only invested heavily in social programmes but have also avoided macroeconomic distortions that discourage the use of labour. The countries that have the poorest growth performance are those that have neglected both investment in social development and pursuit of sound macroeconomic policies. Thus, there is close complementarity between economic policies and social development which are mutually reinforcing. Education, health and nutrition have suffered more in countries undergoing periods of economic crisis and severe budgetary pressures.

Evidence from a sample of SSA countries shows that real expenditures on education and health have increased by 17% and 10% respectively over the 1980s. However, real expenditures in *per capita* terms stagnated as governments could not keep up with rapid population growth. While there is no major reallocation from the social sector, this does not mean that spending levels are adequate, that the intra-sectoral composition of these expenditures is optimal or that the wage-non-wage balance is satisfactory. More attention needs to be paid mainly by the countries themselves but also by the donors supporting adjustment programmes to ensure that social expenditures are protected and allocations towards primary education, basic health services, population planning, etc. are increased within the overall sector allocations.

Despite the crisis and cuts in social expenditures, the social indicators of Sub-Saharan Africa have continued to improve as can be seen in Table 10.3. The period 1986–91, i.e. the adjustment period in most African countries, does not show a reversal of this trend. It is remarkable that this improvement cuts across all groups of countries. Even the countries suffering civil wars and social unrest have seen an increase in life expectancy and a decline in infant mortality. Nineteen countries have reduced their infant mortality rates to below 100 in 1991 compared to only seven a decade ago.

Table 10.3. *Sub-Saharan Africa: Social Indicators 1973-85-91*

|  | 1973 | 1985 | 1991 |
|---|---|---|---|
| Life expectancy at birth | 45.1 | 49.3 | 50.8 |
| Infant mortality rate | 137 | 118 | 107 |
| Adult literacy rate |  |  |  |
| Male | 37 | 56 | 62 |
| Female | 11 | 33 | 39 |
| Female primary enrolment | 38 | 43 | 45 |
| Calorie intake per capita | – | – | 2117 |

Source: *ibid.*

There is no doubt that, in the long run, the poor will gain from a vibrant economy, though their opportunities to participate in this process need to be expanded, and the pattern of growth needs to maximize the use of factors commonly owned by the poor. But it is also illustrative to see what happens without adjustment and restoration of growth. One such case for which two time period data are available is Côte d'Ivoire. Between 1981 and 1986, the country was engaged in an adjustment effort. These programmes had a positive effect on the internal and external balances and, helped by a favourable trend in world prices for coffee and cocoa as well as good harvests, the country experienced positive economic growth until 1985–86. A subsequent decline in the terms of trade and a rapid rise in the real effective exchange rate led to a decline in economic growth in 1987–88.

The effects of these macroeconomic changes on household welfare and poverty have been dramatic (Grootaert, 1993). During 1985–86, the incidence of extreme poverty was reduced by over one third and welfare levels for the poor actually increased in 1986 relative to 1985. In contrast, in 1987, the incidence of both poverty and extreme poverty rose and this trend accelerated sharply in 1988. In that year alone, the incidence of poverty rose by 32% and the incidence of extreme poverty by 55%. The data show that this cost of non-adjustment was not limited to decreases in the level of household expenditure *per capita*, but included lower fulfilment of basic needs as well.

In the short run, the impact of adjustment policies depends on whether the poor are net producers of tradeable goods, since these policies tend to raise relative prices, wages and employment for this group. At the same time, many of the policies that benefit Africa's rural poor are in the short run understandably detrimental to its minority urban population.

*Overall, the poor in Sub-Saharan Africa have largely gained from the adjustment experience or, where there have been hardships, they have in general not suffered disproportionately.*

It would be a mistake to expect that the agenda for poverty alleviation in SSA will be implemented simply by removing economic distortions or undertaking structural reforms. The constraints of rapid population growth, fragile agro-ecological systems and poor administrative capacity will still remain after policy and institutional changes under structural adjustment have been implemented. Creating an efficient economic system which generates and further improves the economic opportunities for the poor is inevitably a slow process. The strategies are still weak at defining measures that will, in addition to faster growth and increased social expenditures, benefit the poor more directly, decisively, and disproportionately than other segments of the population. The threats from the established vocal and articulate groups in African countries of hijacking the benefits accruing to the poor remain serious. Weak administrative capacity and the elitist hold on the political system do not make the task of designing and implementing special measures of assistance to the poor any easier. Rapid economic growth that provides the solid basis for reduction of poverty is not expected soon. Political instability and ethnic divisiveness are not going to disappear. Under these difficulties and uncertainties, progress in poverty reduction will be limited even if economic and structural reforms remain in place.

## Structural Adjustment and the Environment

The interaction between broad-based economic reforms, such as those concerning the exchange rate, export taxes, commodity prices and the incentives governing resource use and consumption, is complex, cross-cutting and not yet fully understood, particularly in the way it affects individual household or firms' choices. The structure of incentives for resource use is affected both by price-related and by institutional factors. Unfortunately, many efforts to trace the impact of price, tax or subsidy policy reforms on the environment, have not explicitly considered the interplay of economic and institutional factors governing resource use and conservation. The direction of changes in resource use will depend to a large extent on the nature of intervening institutional factors. Thus, there is no simple relationship between price-related policy reforms and the environment. As most instances of resource over-exploitation and environmental degradation are due to long-standing policy and institutional distortions, adjustment reforms that attempt to reduce such exploitation should generally be beneficial. But it is also true that economic reform programmes have not usually considered the potential environmental impact of these price reforms in a careful or consistent manner. Opportunities have undoubtedly been missed for combining poverty-oriented or efficiency-oriented reforms with the complementary goal of protecting the environment. But the recent awareness and sensitization with regard to environmental issues seem now to permeate the thinking of those entrusted with the design of adjustment policies and programmes.

Limited empirical work has highlighted the fact that poverty is one of the greatest threats to the sustainability of the physical environment in Sub-Saharan Africa. Half the poor in Africa live in the region's most ecologically vulnerable areas. They over-exploit their marginal lands for fuelwood and for subsistence and cash-crop production, further endangering the physical environment. For them, there is no choice between economic growth and environmental protection. Growth is not an option – it is an imperative. Lack of economic development gives rise, among other things, to inadequate sanitation and water supply and to indoor air pollution from biomass burning. Many types of land degradation have poverty as their root cause. Accelerating equitable growth along with improved access to resources and technologies will make a difference to the environment.

Some environmental problems will decline as income increases. This is because increasing income provides the resources for public services such as sanitation and rural electricity to substitute for fuelwood. When individuals no longer have to worry about day-to-day survival, they can devote resources to profitable investments in conservation. These positive synergies between economic growth and environmental quality must not be underestimated. Some problems initially worsen but then improve as incomes rise. Most forms of air and water pollution fit into this category, as do some types of deforestation and encroachment on natural habitat. There is nothing automatic about this improvement; it occurs only when countries deliberately introduce policies to ensure that additional resources are devoted to dealing with environmental problems. On the other hand, some indicators of environmental stress worsen and fail to improve as incomes increase. Municipal wastes and emissions of carbon and nitrogen oxides are examples.

Two broad sets of policies are needed to tackle the underlying causes of environmental damage. Both are necessary; neither will be sufficient on its own:

- Policies that seek to harness the positive links between development and the environment by correcting or preventing policy failures, improving access to resources and technology, and promoting equitable income growth.
- Policies targeted at specific environmental problems: regulations and incentives that are required to force the recognition of environmental values in decision-making.

Many environmental problems are exacerbated by the growth of economic activity. Industrial and energy-related pollution, deforestation caused by commercial logging, extensive agriculture and overuse of water are the result of economic expansion that fails to take account of the value of the environment. Under these circumstances, the recognition of environmental scarcity has to be built into decision-making.

Aside from price-related changes, institutional factors also affect the incentives for resource management. Rapid population growth and agricultural stagnation contribute to environmental damage. Over the next four decades SSA's population is expected to rise from 500 million to 1.5 billion. Traditional land and resource management systems will be unable to adapt fast enough to prevent overuse, and governments may be unable to keep up with the infrastructural and human needs of the growing population.

Shifting cultivation with limited capital and little technological change cannot cope with the pace of population growth. Thus, low agricultural productivity, caused mainly by poor incentives and poor provision of services, has delayed the demographic transition and encouraged land degradation and deforestation, which in turn have lowered productivity.

Fortunately, many policies that are adopted under structural adjustment programmes for improving efficiency, are also good for the environment. For example, higher agricultural productivity and a better educated labour force will speed the demographic transition and encourage more sustainable use of land. Policies that encourage efficiency lead to less waste, less consumption of raw materials, and more technological innovation.

Some government policies are downright harmful to the environment. Notable here are distorted prices in general and subsidized input prices in particular.

Subsidies for energy, for example, cost developing country governments more than \$230 billion a year – more than four times the total world volume of official development assistance. The removal of all energy subsidies would not only produce large gains in efficiency and in fiscal balances, but would sharply reduce local pollution and cut worldwide carbon emissions from energy use by 10%. Logging fees in a sample of five African countries ranged from 1 to 33% of the costs of replanting. Pesticide subsidies ranged from 19 to 83% of costs.

Distorted incentives are particularly evident in the behaviour of state-owned enterprises. This is important because many sectors in which state enterprises are prominent – power generation, cement, steel, and mining – are heavy polluters; the 'commanding heights' are also the 'polluting heights'. Thus the environment can benefit if the managers of state enterprises are made more accountable and are exposed to the same competition as the private sector.

There are not many detailed empirical studies of the relationship between adjustment and environment. One study by Barrett (1990) found that, although higher output prices may lead to soil depletion, the aggregate production impact of price policy changes in many low-income countries in Sub-Saharan Africa is slight. He concluded that if sufficient incentives are provided to build up soil fertility, farmers may be more receptive to conservation and may sacrifice current profits for bigger harvests in the future. Two other country studies have tested this relationship, one for Ghana and the other for Côte d'Ivoire. The Ghana study (Pimentel et al., 1991) was critical of adjustment programmes. But the criticism that structural adjustment in Ghana has promoted deforestation through devaluation does not take into account the historical volumes of log extraction and exports. Simply comparing the values of exports before and after adjustment does not help in isolating the effects of higher unit export prices in nominal terms. Deforestation in Ghana was more affected by the pre-adjustment crisis when farmers converted fresh land for food production.

A second study by the World Wildlife Fund (Reed, 1992), assessing the adjustment experience in Côte d'Ivoire, concluded that the net impact of adjustment on the environment remained ambiguous. The lack of a consistent and secure land tenure system had contributed more to deforestation than the effects of government pricing policies.

The gap in knowledge about the links between economy-wide policies and the incentives governing natural resource use is quite wide. But in areas where some empirical basis has been established, environmental considerations should be increasingly reflected in the design of reform programmes. Potentially more far-reaching is the process under way for countries to develop national environmental action plans. This process, if successfully followed up with concrete programmes, will provide a strategic focus for a country to address its most critical environmental problems in the context of overall macroeconomic policies and microeconomic incentives. The trade-offs and complementarities will become obvious and hard choices will have to be made.

# The Role of the World Bank in African Long-Term Development

The World Bank's approach to adjustment is guided by the institution's overriding objective: the alleviation of poverty and the improvement of people's living standards. This is the standard by which the Bank should be judged.

Over time, adjustment lending has become more poverty-focused. Firstly, many adjustment loans have given more attention to safety nets and to restructuring public spending. The most common safety nets have been nutrition programmes, labour-intensive public works, and targeted food subsidies. The restructuring of public expenditure has taken the form of maintaining or increasing the share of expenditures on social services, particularly basic social services. In some cases, the focus has also been on improving the composition of social expenditures. In Ghana, for example, in the context of the structural adjustment credits, the government has been restructuring recurrent expenditures in favour of non-salary expenditures. In The Gambia, budget allocations for recurrent expenditures have been increased. Secondly, some loans are based on an overall assessment of how the reforms will affect the poor both in the transition and in the long term. In financial year 1992, three operations supported the gathering of poverty data and the monitoring of the impact of adjustment on the poor. Thirdly, an increasing number of adjustment loans include conditions for the release of tranches relating to the country's efforts to reduce poverty. The share of loans that include social sector conditionality increased from less than 5% of all adjustment loans in FY1984–86 to almost 30% during FY1990–92. In FY1992, 11 of the 13 Structural Adjustment Loans and 3 of the 5 Sectoral Adjustment Loans contained tranche release conditions dependent on poverty reduction measures. Most of these conditions have related to increasing or maintaining public expenditures on social services (Burundi, Côte d'Ivoire, Sierra Leone, Uganda, Malawi, Mozambique, Zambia). Other conditions have included a programme report on land distribution and the transfer of land rights to smallholders and private enterprises (Mozambique). In Sierra Leone and Zimbabwe, tranche release was conditional on the implementation of actions aimed at reducing poverty.

Social funds and social action programmes were originally established to protect those adversely affected by adjustment, but they can also operate as wholesale financing mechanisms that target the poor. They are often able to play a role in increasing political support for reform and in mobilizing external resources. The Bank has supported 19 of these interventions in 17 countries, including 11 in Sub-Saharan Africa. Usually these programmes channel resources to small, demand-driven sub-projects proposed by a local group (usually a NGO) or a local government agency. Typically, the programmes involve local governments, private sector groups, and NGOs in the design and implementation of these projects.

The reviews of public expenditure undertaken by the Bank staff in collaboration with African governments focus on intersectoral and intrasectoral trade-offs and contribute to the restructuring of public expenditures. They examine the equity, effectiveness and efficiency of the planned expenditures in the context of the macroeconomic framework and the poverty alleviation strategy. Possible imbalances between capital and recurrent spending, analysis of social safety net programmes for cost-effectiveness and coverage of target groups, and the impact on the conditions of the poor are issues that enter the policy dialogue between the Bank staff and governments.

The Bank's adjustment loans have not taken considerations of environmental sustainability explicitly into account in the past. But a 1989 study of adjustment lending operations found that there was no conclusive evidence that policy changes associated with adjustment lending were necessarily related to environmental degradation (World Bank, 1989b). Contrary to the above criticism, it concluded that adjustment programmes appeared, on balance, to have a positive effect on the environment. Using a partial equilibrium approach, it demonstrated that there were many potential complementarities between major adjustment policies and environmental goals – primarily through measures designed to improve efficiency and reduce wasteful use of resources. For example, changes in producer prices for agricultural output or adjustments in agricultural export taxes may have important consequences for soil productivity and erosion. Tree crops are usually associated with relatively low rates of soil erosion. Thus higher prices for tree crops would appear to have a beneficial environmental effect.

The reasons for the neglect of environmental considerations in adjustment operations are manifold, but the most crucial was a lack of understanding of the mechanisms through which adjustment affects the environment. The heightening of awareness of environmental issues and the building of in-house capacity to assess the impact of these issues are slowly and gradually enhancing the Bank's understanding. But the progress will remain limited until the analytical and empirical foundations of this assessment are strengthened. A host of questions remain unanswered and the framework for evaluating the trade-offs between efficiency-generating policies and environmentally sustainable policies is still fragmentary. Investment in research on these issues – both within the Bank and outside – will have a high pay-off.

A serious misconception exists that the World Bank is assisting African countries through structural adjustment lending only. Adjustment lending accounts, on average, for only 30% of the Bank's total lending to Sub-Saharan Africa (although in 1993 it will be only around 22%), while 70% goes to investment and sectoral lending. In FY1991–92, more than 60% of total lending was allocated for investment in smallholder agriculture, human resource development and infrastructure. In the coming years, the Bank expects an even stronger thrust in the field of the environment and in combined population-agriculture-environment-related projects.

For its investment projects, procedures have been set up to categorize projects and assess their environmental impact up-front. To encourage African countries to incorporate environmental considerations regularly into their economic planning process and budgeting, the Bank has assisted 11 countries to complete National Environmental Action Plans (NEAPs) and to mobilize donor funding for their implementation. It is currently involved in helping develop plans in 22 more countries and is prepared to assist others when they begin the process.

In forestry lending, the policy of the Bank in Africa is not to finance any forestry project unless it is demonstrated to be environmentally sustainable. The

Bank has also pledged unequivocally not to finance commercial logging in primary tropical moist forests.

## Influence of External Factors

The challenges of alleviating poverty, protecting the environment and enabling Africans to enjoy a much wider range of economic and social choices than is now conceivable cannot be addressed without recognizing the decisive influence of external factors in Africa's development.

Africa depends on primary commodities such as oil, minerals and agricultural products for its export earnings. The decline in terms of trade has caused serious erosion in export earnings for the region. For the period 1985–90, when a large number of African countries undertook adjustment, the deterioration in the barter terms of trade of 9 major export commodities resulted in a 40% decline in average export revenues (compared to the 1977–79 average), despite a 75% increase in export volume. A similar trend was observed for agricultural exports as a whole.

To compensate for the terms-of-trade losses, donors may have to consider swift and automatic mechanisms of compensatory concessional flows to adjusting countries. This will avoid the derailing of economic reforms and ensure that the adjustment effort is sustained. The existing mechanisms have not proved to be particularly agile in responding to these contingencies.

Africa's external debt has tripled since 1980 and exceeds its total GNP. Debt service actually paid was equivalent to 20–25% of total exports of goods and services. An equal amount is not paid and accumulates each year in the form of arrears to creditors and eventually accretion to the debt stock. Africa cannot escape its present economic crisis without significantly reducing its debt burden. Several important initiatives have been taken in recent years to provide debt relief, but the actual impact has been limited.

An almost universal consensus exists today that, although most African countries are not servicing their debt fully, the uncertainty and opportunity costs of managing and negotiating protracted debt reschedulings far exceed any cash flow relief that may become available. It is time that some bold and decisive action is taken to relieve the adjusting countries of this lingering burden and redirect their attention and energies from crisis management to long-term development issues.

There have been some positive signs of the international community's support for Africa. Official development assistance flows to Sub-Saharan Africa have risen in the last five years and the Special Programme of Assistance (SPA) for Africa ensures that the efforts of low-income, debt-distressed countries in pursuing structural adjustment are not constrained by a lack of adequate funding. The SPA epitomizes the World Bank's leadership and catalytic role in development assistance. The Programme supports a multi-donor strategy to tackle debt and adjustment – combining additional concessional resources that go to the low-income, debt-distressed countries that are undertaking adjustment. Without the financial assurance that the SPA provides, Africa might still be in the tentative position of five or six years ago, when governments were unwilling or unable to implement reforms for fear that the support necessary to succeed would not materialize.

The SPA mechanism has worked satisfactorily and countries which remain on track in their reform programmes are assured full funding of these programmes through quick-disbursing balance-of-payments support by multilateral and bilateral donors. However, there are serious concerns about the sustainability of these flows. While the momentum of aid generated in the recent past will need to be maintained during the 1990s to facilitate resumption of economic growth, it is not clear that the amounts required will be forthcoming. A number of factors give rise to this concern. First, there are some major new entrants to the list of IDA-eligible countries. Secondly, the major donor countries are facing serious budgetary problems of their own. Thirdly, the domestic support for foreign aid, in an environment of high unemployment and slow economic growth in OECD countries, may be eroding. Finally, new kinds of conditionalities under consideration by a number of donor countries that will take into account political liberalization, democratization and human rights, may further slow the pace of donor fund disbursements.

It would be most unfortunate if, at a time when most African countries are in the midst of implementing difficult economic changes and taking steps to improve the flexibility and efficiency of their economic structure, vital and much needed external support were either to slow down or be reduced. Political liberalization will have a positive and beneficial impact on economic performance and governance in the long run, but the short-run costs of dislocation and disruption in economic reforms should not be underestimated. Given the limited administrative and managerial capacity of most African countries, the diversion of attention from economic to political reforms can further exacerbate these costs.

The expectations about a quick turn-around in Africa's economic performance, and the growing frustration that the results of donor efforts and assistance are hard to discern, need to be tempered by a sense of realism. The adverse external economic environment, the simultaneous pursuit of political and economic reforms, the impact of harsh natural and man-made disasters such as drought and civil war, and the relatively weak human and institutional capacity, should be factored in before expectations are formed. Abandoning Africa at this juncture would only validate the self-fulfilling prophecy of Afro-pessimists. Working hard, steadily and collaboratively with African countries that are seriously embarked on the path of structural adjustment, can eventually produce enduring rewards.

## Summing Up

This paper has shown that structural adjustment programmes and policies, if correctly conceived and properly implemented, are the foundation upon which the superstructure of sustainable long-term development for most African countries can be built. The complementarities between adjustment, poverty reduction and environmental protection are much stronger than is generally believed.

But adjustment policies alone are not sufficient. Additional actions such as investment in infrastructure and human capital, and the establishment of an enabling environment for private initiative, such as a credible commitment on the part of government, reduction in incentives and opportunities for rent-seeking and corruption, improved public administration and creating space for the private sector, are equally needed. It was a mistake in the first place to expect that by pursuing adjustment alone Africa would accelerate its growth. What adjustment promises to do is to correct the distortions, reconfigure the incentive structure and reverse the decline. In this respect, adjustment has succeeded. But this is not good enough. The problem is that, although economic decline has been reversed, rapid growth in incomes, employment and consumption still remains an elusive goal. Supply response remains muted. Private sector investment is still constrained. Good governance and strong institutional capacity have yet to take hold. The long-term development agenda is well defined and broadly agreed and includes both adjustment policies and other additional actions that need to be taken. The challenge for African leaders and the international community is not to re-invent the wheel but to fully implement this agenda. The expectations about Africa's development should also be tempered with realism. This is a long-haul partnership which does not promise quick or spectacular results and is ridden with setbacks and disappointments along the way. Even after successfully implementing most of the broad elements of this agenda, *per capita* incomes in SSA will grow at best by only 1–2% and the incidence of poverty will still rise both in absolute and relative terms. Dependence on foreign assistance will continue unabated. There should be no illusions. The choice is either to work hard and steadily and ensure that at least these modest gains are realized or to abandon this continent of over 500 million people to live in misery and impoverishment and allow many more Somalias to surface.

## Note

1. This section is drawn from Husain, 1992.

## References

Barrett, S. (1990) *Macroeconomic Policy Reforms and Third World Soil Conservation*, London: London Business School.

Elbadawi, I., Ghura, D. and Uwujaren, W. (1992) *World Bank Adjustment Lending and Economic Performance in Sub-Saharan Africa in the 1980s*, Policy Research Working Paper No. 1000, Washington DC: World Bank.

Ellis, F. (1982) 'Agricultural Price Policy in Tanzania', *World Development* 10 (4), 263–83.

Grootaert, C. (1993) *The Evolution of Welfare and Poverty under Structural Change and Economic Recession in Côte d'Ivoire, 1985–88*, PRE Working Paper No. 1078, Washington DC: World Bank.

Husain, Ishrat (1992) 'Adjustment and the Impact on the Poor: The Case of Africa', Paper presented at the EDI/ADB Seminar at Abidjan, 9–12 March.

Husain, Ishrat (1993) 'Structural Adjustment in Sub-Saharan Africa: A Preliminary Evaluation', Paper presented at EDI/NY Office of the World Bank Seminar, New York, 18 May.

Pimentel, D., Floyd, B., Tell, W. and Bourn, J. (1991) 'Deforestation, Biomass Depletion and Land Degradation Linkages to Policy Reform in Sub-Saharan Africa' in J. Lassoie and S. Kyle (eds), Cornell Natural Resources Research and Extension Series No. 3, Ithaca, NY: Cornell University.

Reed, D. (1992) *Structural Adjustment and the Environment*, Boulder, CO: Westview Press.

UNDP (1992) *Human Development Report 1992*, New York: UNDP.

World Bank (1988a) *Adjustment Lending: An Evaluation of Ten Years of Experience*, Policy and Research Series No. 1, Washington DC: World Bank.

World Bank (1988b) *Report on Adjustment Lending*, Washington DC: World Bank.

World Bank (1989a) *Sub-Saharan Africa: From Crisis to Sustainable Growth, a Long-Term Perspective Study*, Washington DC: World Bank.

World Bank (1989b) *World Bank Support for the Environment: A Progress Report*, Washington DC: World Bank Development Committee.

World Bank (1990) *Adjusting Lending Policies for Sustainable Growth*, Washington DC: World Bank.

World Bank (1992a) *Structural and Sectoral Adjustment Operations, The Second OED Review*, Washington DC: World Bank.

World Bank (1992b) *Adjustment Lending and Mobilization of Private and Public Resources for Growth*, Policy and Research Series No. 22, Washington DC: World Bank.

World Bank/UNDP (1989) *Africa's Adjustment and Growth*, Washington DC: World Bank/UNDP.

# PART FIVE
Discussion and
Conclusions

# 11 Discussion and Conclusions
## ROLPH VAN DER HOEVEN and FRED VAN DER KRAAIJ

## The Context and Goals of Structural Adjustment Programmes

During the discussion following the papers by Toye (Chapter 3), Wapenhans (Chapter 4) and Husain (Chapter 10), but also on other occasions, most participants agreed with one of the major observations made by commentator Harrigan, who explicitly mentioned that *a shift can be noted in the focus of stabilization and adjustment programmes.*

Initially these programmes were narrowly concerned with restoring internal and external balances as quickly as possible. They then began to pay increasing attention to economic growth, and more recently also to social (equity), and political issues. Moreover, structural adjustment programmes no longer tend to ignore environmental concerns. According to Husain, the complementarities between adjustment, poverty reduction and environmental protection are much stronger than is generally believed. However, several participants argued that the experience of adjustment in various Sub-Saharan African countries failed to lead to the conclusion that adjustment policies had brought higher economic growth and improved social policies – despite their broader objectives of growth and social protection.

Both Toye's and Wapenhans' papers indicated that *recent* adjustment policies have more of a tendency to touch upon internal political issues such as democracy, accountability on the part of political leaders, etc. Inclusion of these political issues was explained not only as part of a moral stance by the donor community but also as the outcome of a political economy model emphasizing changes in the national institutional environment that would be more conducive to adjustment. Several speakers noted that the position of the World Bank among others had shifted as compared with the past when autocratic regimes were apparently to be preferred, or at least not to be rejected, in order to launch an adjustment programme quickly and to keep it manageable. On the one hand, this change in position from accepting autocratic management of the economy to rejecting it could be explained by *the change in focus* of the adjustment policies themselves from the short-term concerns of stabilizing economies to longer-term attention to equitable and sustainable growth. A macroeconomically oriented programme with a short time horizon could be forced through autocratically, but a programme with a much longer time horizon needed a broad social consensus and would certainly fail if it were to be implemented by autocratic means alone. On the other hand, the shift could also be considered a logical consequence of the fact that in adjusting countries the economic reform programmes are increasingly accompanied by *political reforms* whereby autocratic rulers are being replaced by (to a varying degree) democratically elected governments.

The position of bilateral and multilateral donors was mentioned by various participants. Wapenhans clearly stated that he did not want an institution like the World Bank to take on the role of arbiter of the correct application of democratic rules. However, in the views of some other participants, an international agency is to be preferred to a loosely associated set of multiple actors (such as the various bilateral donors) who have at times widely converging motivations and different interests in fulfilling such a role. Yet it was also argued that the primacy of one organization setting the agenda for policy reform could go awry. A specific situation was quoted where the bilateral donors had managed to co-ordinate pressures on the leaders of the country to release political prisoners and to allow some degree of democracy, only to be frustrated by a large volume of lending by the international financial institutions, which effectively nullified the leverage which the donors had developed as a community. Jan Pronk stressed the fact that bilateral donors need the international financial institutions which in the recent past have generally shown themselves able to listen to criticism. He pleaded for a constructive but critical attitude towards the Bretton Woods organizations to whom he made an appeal to continue their open attitude. In a different context, Azam called on international agencies and bilateral donors alike to act as advocates for the politically less influential and less vociferous poor in adjusting countries and to make adjustment work for the poor.

The question of political reform is closely related to the question of institutional reform, an issue which both Wapenhans and Toye raised. Wapenhans speaks in this respect about structural reform. 'Governance' has become common parlance among many multilateral donors. Here again there was no great divergence of views among the participants. The need for structural reform or institutional change, and even the necessity of financial aid in order to allow for structural reform, were widely acknowledged. However, the question which divided some participants was whether adjustment policies, and the conditionality attached to them, were the best vehicles for structural changes. Commentator Wuyts stressed that donors, bilateral as well as multilateral, have their own agendas and often do not act in an altruistic manner. Others also saw difficulties with this. One participant argued that donors have for years supported institutions which were often responsible for the crisis; the very role which donors could play in changing or replacing these institutions was therefore doubtful. Others argued that the obsession with democracy on the part of foreign donors was out of all proportion.

It was recalled that a number of countries during recent years had made strong moves towards democracy, not as the result of interference by outside donors but largely generated by social forces acting within the country. The challenge for donors is to support such democratic movements by providing support for the groups which have brought these internal changes about. This could be achieved by improving conditions for employment, by the provision of essential needs such as health, education, etc. and by allowing governments to function properly through the provision of recurrent budgetary support, if necessary.

Several participants expressed concern about foreign aid and the effect it appears to have on increased domestic rent-seeking practices. Even the more 'altruistic' aid in the form of (untied) balance-of-payments support may lead, in the absence of a proper institutional framework and because of its directly convertible nature, to increased rent-seeking.

## Macroeconomic Perspectives and Methodology

Ajayi (Chapter 5) and Mosley (Chapter 6) provided an overview and interpretation of the various adjustment policies that have been applied in Sub-Saharan Africa, mainly from a macroeconomic perspective. Mosley evaluated the effect of the policies through the 'before-and-after' method and the 'modified-control-group' approach, followed by a decomposition analysis using regression analysis and by using a general equilibrium model. Ajayi discussed in great detail the different experiences with the 'before-and-after' and the 'modified-control-group' approaches.

Ajayi emphasized the need to assess the programmes from two angles. First, have the adjustment policies succeeded in eliminating the components of the crisis in Sub-Saharan African countries by such means as controlling inflation, eliminating distortions in the economy, promoting faster investment and diversifying the export basket? Secondly, has this been achieved without cost? While he portrayed a bleak picture of Sub-Saharan Africa's economic achievements under adjustment, he concluded that in many African countries structural adjustment programmes are not only hurting the poor but are also creating a new category of poor people. Commentator Wangwe agreed with the main thrust of Ajayi's paper, i.e. his rejection of the before-and-after and the control-group approaches.

One of Mosley's major conclusions was that the analysis of adjustment experiences ought to be decomposed to be meaningful. By doing this and carefully checking against the results obtained through the various approaches, he argued that certain essential components of adjustment policies, such as reductions in tariffs and in credit, frequently have negative effects on growth. Furthermore, price-based policies, another essential part of adjustment programmes, appear to work only when supported by other catalyst policies such as policy stability and increased spending on development and social services. In the past, adjustment policies often undermined the growth or development of these catalysts rather than supporting them. In this context he also noted the absence of a sound theoretical basis of structural adjustment programmes, a point that Toye had already raised in his paper.

Azam (Chapter 7) wondered whether it was indeed possible to measure progress under adjustment. Progress is often measured by GDP growth; GDP, however, is a composite measure combining production of tradeables and non-tradeables. However, since the very outcome of the adjustment process is to change the (internal) terms of trade or relative prices between tradeables and non-tradeables, measurement of GDP could be influenced by the price set used. He effectively demonstrated this, using Nigeria as an example.

Throughout the seminar, there was considerable consensus on the difficulty of interpreting the adjustment experiences and of attributing failure or success rates to these programmes. Some participants even argued that such detailed *ex post* analyses were not very useful and that simple case studies of whether poverty increased or not during the period of adjustment should be used instead. It was also argued that the decomposition of the various policy instruments of the adjustment package should take into account a typology of different groups of countries, since countries cannot be treated similarly in the way the various catalysts work. However, according to commentator Yao there is no such thing as a distinct African economic reality – different from that of other regions. This view was shared by some, e.g. Wapenhans, but according to others (notably Ajayi, Mosley, Toye) the African problem is quite specific. These differences should be acknowledged if adjustment programmes are to be successful.

Commentator Elson raised the question as to the extent to which experience of unpaid labour and informal sector activities had been reflected in any of the macroeconomic analyses. According to her, there are three important aspects of the economics of unpaid labour in Sub-Saharan Africa: (i) work in own account subsistence agriculture, (ii) unpaid labour in family enterprises, producing for the market, and (iii) unpaid labour in human resource production. All three aspects have a gender dimension and are hardly taken into account in macroeconomic analysis. This view was supported by many participants. The point was also raised by Azam in his paper, where he questioned the use of GDP figures which often neglected the informal sector. He even went so far as to state that GDPs can be assumed to be systematically underestimated.

A similar concern about statistics was expressed by commentator van Arkadie. He took a similarly extreme position, indicating that macroeconomic cross-country comparisons based on official figures have become virtually meaningless. A casual observation was often preferable to intensive number-crunching. Despite the data problems, van Arkadie subscribed to the general conclusion that structural adjustment policies have not yet been very successful in Sub-Saharan Africa, although some traditionally poor performers were apparently doing better now than in the past.

Ajayi, van Arkadie and Mosley cautioned against looking for quick successes and a speedy revival of the economy. Adjustment programmes, in effect, ought to change the underlying forces of uncontrolled capitalist development and should lead to the creation of different institutions to guide such a development process. This is much more a long-term process whose effects cannot be evaluated quickly.

Various participants emphasized the important roles of households and of parallel markets, where various kinds of adjustment were to be noted. There was disagreement, however, about whether increased activities in these spheres could be classified as desirable adjustment patterns or whether they should be explained merely as coping mechanisms which households and informal sectors undertook mainly to deal with the negative effects of the various stabilization measures.

Many participants raised the issue of the appropriate role of the state in the adjustment process. Among others, Ajayi made a plea for recognizing the important role of government in investing in infrastructure, human capital and technology. Seshamani (Chapter 8) and others argued in favour of targeted public expenditure and publicly financed social security safety nets to cushion the negative effects which structural adjustment programmes (may) have on the poor and vulnerable groups in society. Other participants pointed to the programmes' neglect of the obstacles to a proper functioning of the market. A broad consensus emerged supporting the view that adjustment policies should aim not only at letting markets work and at creating an enabling environment for private initiative, but also at letting governments work.

In looking at the positive or negative role of the state (often a dividing point between the structuralist and the neo-classical economists), participants stressed that deteriorating infrastructures made it impossible for the government to act in a meaningful manner, even if its main task was perceived as only to let markets work. Moreover, while economic growth is indeed a necessary condition for fighting poverty, it is far from being a sufficient condition for addressing poverty, as Seshamani argued (see also below). Hence, the need arises for government interventions to support the poor and vulnerable groups.

## Social Consequences and Political Dimensions of Structural Adjustment

The relations between social progress, poverty and the political situation were treated in the papers by Seshamani (Chapter 8) and Morrisson and his colleagues (Chapter 9), and also partly by Azam in his paper (Chapter 7).

*The social consequences*
Seshamani argued that in many countries undergoing structural adjustment the poor have suffered. He also noted an increasing concern for the poor on the part of international donors who meanwhile have contributed financially to a number of social safety nets (SSNs) and other poverty alleviation programmes (PAPs). However, these programmes, which contain good elements, are often too little and come too late. Moreover, these PAPs as well as the targeted public expenditures, and transfers aiming at the poor, are basically short-term reactions. More emphasis should be put on human capital development by means of existing programmes of education, health services, social security delivery systems and food security.

Commentator Mengistae drew attention to the urgent need for reliable information systems, not only for the SAPs but also for the planning, financing and execution of social safety net programmes. He also argued for welfare targets to be an integral part of regular structural adjustment programmes. Commentator Stewart, like most of the participants, agreed with Seshamani's conclusions. She emphasized the need for a review of the structural adjustment package in order to take concern for the poor explicitly into account. This could be done by changing some of its components, i.e. by allowing for a more gradual approach, by increasing the finance available and by applying meso policies which should compensate within the macro framework for the negative effects of adjustment as measured by various indicators of policy performance based on progress towards protecting the poor. Adjustment programmes and the so-called social action programmes (SAPROGs), which tried to compensate for some of their negative effects, often paid great attention to proper targeting. However, according to Stewart, two errors can be made in targeting: E-errors (leakages to higher-income groups) and F-errors (failing to reach the poor). Social action programmes, by actually being project-oriented and not using generalized price subsidies, often reduced the E-errors but at the same increased the F-errors. In order to reduce the F-errors, which are the important errors, it was argued that the drought relief efforts in Botswana and Zimbabwe, for example, both of which were very effective in reaching the poor, should be evaluated. Crucial elements of these programmes were large, open-ended employment schemes and low wages, and targeting of food and food subsidies by area and by product, not by household. Social safety net programmes should be modelled on these successful programmes, leaving other social issues to 'normal' macro, meso and sectoral policies.

Other participants acknowledged the success of the drought programmes, but indicated that, because of the drought in various African countries, a 'before-and-after' analysis of the social effects of adjustment was faulty. It was also argued that poverty had existed all along and that poverty questions ought to be dealt with independently of adjustment policies. This also reflected some of the conclusions of Azam's paper. He argued that, from a theoretical basis, one could not deduce whether structural adjustment programmes (in his case, narrowly defined as policies to shift the internal terms of trade in favour of tradeables) were affecting the poor positively or negatively, as poor households are both producers and consumers of tradeables and non-tradeables. Furthermore, the way of arriving at a depreciation of the real exchange rate, whether through successive nominal devaluations or through tight budgetary policies, had different effects on households and on growth. Theoretical ambiguity could, in principle, be overcome by means of careful analysis of empirical evidence, but this was not borne out in practice because of problems in measuring GDP and the absence of information on the informal sector. However, based on a case study of Côte d'Ivoire and an analysis of political economy which singled out the state as being neither benevolent nor a predator but still being concerned with maximizing its own power, Azam concluded that structural adjustment policies could help the poor by limiting the power of the state.

Azam's argument was contested by a number of participants but accepted by others. Commentator Mule agreed with Azam that there is no firm knowledge about the social impact of structural adjustment. He concluded that much more research is needed, and this implies an improvement in both the level of statistics and the efficacy of the research methodologies. This research should not only be directed at macroeconomic issues and distributional aspects but should also include the political economy. Like other participants, he also expressed the view that structural adjustment, in the African context, is not a short-term phenomenon.

Others argued that the narrow definition of adjustment used by Azam and the application of a 'standard' Salter-Swan model were inappropriate for the questions asked. Commentator Sarris argued for the use of general equilibrium models which have sufficient flexibility. He also made a strong plea for expanding the analysis from the macro-meso connection to meso-micro relations, looking at the effects of prices on households. Several commentators argued that both for theoretical analysis and for policy-making, it did not make sense to treat the poor as one or two homogeneous groups (urban poor and rural poor), even if poverty had become much more of an urban problem than in the past. Any meaningful analysis should be concerned with the production and consumption patterns of various socioeconomic groups in order to assess questions about the development of poverty.

Several participants also argued that the reduction of the role of the state had also reduced its capacity to undertake social policies. Various participants singled out the negative effects of most policies on women, who often had to combine increased involvement in the education and health programmes of their children with greater production of funds and shrinking households to cope with the problems.

Discussing possible trade-offs in adjustment programmes between growth and poverty alleviation, some participants (among them Toye) argued that this was not the right trade-off to discuss, since the major aim of structural adjustment policies was *not* to maximize growth but to protect the debt portfolio of donors. Another trade-off to be analysed and commented on would therefore be debt payment versus social advancement in Africa.

## The political dimension

Morrisson and his colleagues dealt explicitly in their paper with the political dimension of adjustment, by developing a political-economic model of adjustment and utilizing it in various scenarios. A major conclusion was that optimizing an objective function which consisted only of economic variables was misjudged, since a trade-off exists between changes in economic variables and the behaviour of economic groups and the economic agents. For example, a sudden, steep decline in real wages would result in a reaction from the trade unions, leading to strikes and interruption of the production process, thus frustrating the structural changes needed for adjustment policies to work. Large increases in the price of staple food often led to national riots, which frequently resulted in unwinding some of the earlier proposed policies and making the government less able than before to promote reforms.

Morrisson's conclusions were in general accepted, although quite a few participants had difficulties with the way the model and the database were constructed. Commentator Deme argued that gaining endorsement and finding a social consensus are necessary conditions for the success of SAPs, and in many cases this would warrant the overhaul of existing institutional and administrative structures and a complete review of the state. For this, it is necessary to take account of the power relations between the various interest groups that make up the state (the political elite vs the civil servants, the urban vs the rural population, and the monetary modern economy vs the informal traditional economy) and to design policies which take them into account. In fact, he argued, structural adjustment programmes constitute the perfect interaction between economics and politics in Sub-Saharan Africa. The changing role of the state applies both to economic and to political reforms. Commentator Bugnicourt emphasized that the way ordinary people interpret SAPs (even if this is believed to be false) is as important as the perception of the decision-makers. Ordinary people are more concerned with poverty; SAPs should be built around these concerns. He pleaded emphatically for the poor to be listened to in order to solve their problems, and joined other participants (including Husain) in the view that economic growth alone is not sufficient to combat poverty and does not necessarily imply sound environmental practices.

Several participants noted the malfunctioning of the state in providing social protection and promoting social development. Useful funds for social development were often misappropriated or spent on the wrong people (corruption and nepotism). Hence the need for institutions to prevent this. Others wanted to see more analysis of how political and social systems could cope with external shocks better than in the past, and pleaded for policies which would increase the capacity to respond to such shocks.

# Structural Adjustment and Long-term Policy Perspectives

Most participants agreed that, when they were started in Sub-Saharan Africa in the early 1980s, structural adjustment policies were intended to deal with the continent's external crises as quickly as possible, by bringing about internal and external balances enabling the various countries to return to a more traditional development path in which foreign donors would provide support through project lending and inflows of capital. As Toye indicated, in order to 'sell' the concept of policy-based lending within the World Bank, adjustment policies carried high expectations which were often not justified, given the weak institutional capacities of many Sub-Saharan African countries and the ambiguous theoretical underpinnings of the functioning of their economies.

Husain highlighted in his paper (Chapter 10) the early history of adjustment lending and frankly admitted some of the mistakes made in the past. For policies to be more effective and to contribute to long-term development, he argued firstly that a distinction should be made between stabilization and adjustment policies and that stabilization should precede adjustment. Stabilization policies often result in a contraction of the economy which in most cases cannot be avoided. Secondly, he argued that adjustment policies could not be effectively implemented if they were not complemented by proper investments in infrastructure, by a building up of human capital and by an enabling political environment. More specifically, he stated that adjustment was not enough to bring about significant changes that would benefit the poor. Thirdly, therefore, poverty concerns should be taken into account in designing adjustment policies. The same applies to environmental considerations since many environmental problems are exacerbated by the growth of economic activity. In order to foster long-term development, social action programmes, public expenditure measures, environmental sustainability and appropriate foreign investment and sectoral lending, especially for smallholder agriculture, for human resources and for infrastructure, are all important. Last but not least, he stated that it would be difficult to embark on a long-term development strategy without a sizeable reduction of Africa's debts and new resource inflows in the form of aid and foreign capital. The latter point was also further elaborated by Kasonde, who gave an overview of how Zambia was managing to attract more foreign resources.

Commentator van der Hoeven welcomed the overriding concern for long-term development and argued that most agencies and scholars in Africa, and more recently also in the donor countries, share the same objectives of adjustment policies, namely that they should lead to equitable long-term growth in a situation in which African countries are less vulnerable than they are today. Unlike the situation five years ago, the discussion was no longer about whether adjustment was necessary or not; instead it had gradually become more focused on arguing about which policy instruments were the *proper* instruments.

In this respect, he questioned the separation of stabilization and adjustment policies. Research and evidence had shown that poorly thought-out stabilization policies could cause considerable damage to the later growth potential of a country, a point which Azam (Chapter 7) also raised. Furthermore, it remained worrying that structural adjustment policies had not been able to make Sub-Saharan African countries any less dependent on exports of primary products and had not led them towards a more sustainable development path. He argued that concern for income distribution and basic needs policies as well as for people-oriented development should be put back on the agenda, but, of course, in the present context of processes of globalization and a more interdependent world. The present instruments of adjustment policies should therefore be scrutinized to see whether they support or impede long-term equitable development. Furthermore, in several countries, other instruments should be added to make structural adjustment policies an integral part of a long-term development strategy.

Commentator Okeyo argued that an important question, namely how the masses cope with adjustment, had been missing from most of the discussion. It was up to African countries to come forward with solutions which should not only be of a macroeconomic nature. More attention needed to be given to the interface of adjustment policies and the capabilities of institutions to carry forward the necessary changes as well as to unravel the effect of negative external shocks. This should be built into the various adjustment programmes.

In the discussion, some participants stressed the fact that, in some cases, the current adjustment policies (or the direct outcomes of these policies) still undermined a balanced and equitable long-term strategy. Prime examples discussed were: (i) Sub-Saharan Africa's continued or renewed specialization in primary commodity exports, which leads to greater vulnerability and contributes to the declining terms of trade, (ii) the processes of de-industrialization and (iii) of de-education which many countries are undergoing and which severely undercut the continent's long-term development perspective. However, other participants questioned this view and argued that more attention should be given to the fact that, even in primary commodity exports, Sub-Saharan African countries had lost parts of their market share to better performing countries.

# The Interaction between Structural Adjustment Policies and Research

Most participants considered that the evaluation of past experiences and more theoretical analyses had enriched adjustment policies as compared with the situation in the early 1980s when they were launched. Policy-makers from Africa, Europe and North America argued that research needs to play a more important role in Africa's development and adjustment policies. The interaction between research and policies could be greatly improved in a number of ways. There need to be fora where researchers and policy-makers can meet more frequently. Currently, research in industrialized countries is carried out by bilateral donor and multilateral organizations which provide relatively little feedback to the countries in question, while research in Africa is carried out in (ill-equipped) universities which often house substantial movements in opposition to the government. Thus, there exist large institutional barriers which prevent a dialogue and a maximum use of the research results.

A second impediment to a proper interaction between research and policy relates to the questions relevant for research. Policy-makers often want a quick analysis or even an informed judgement from researchers on certain questions. The institutional barriers mentioned above often prevent the use of research and researchers in this way. Researchers have their own agenda and their own working pace, which discourage policy-makers' interest. This is especially the case in Sub-Saharan African countries with weak government institutions which do not allow for a think-tank or a policy formulation unit which could play a useful intermediary role between policy-makers and researchers.

Several participants also argued that it was difficult to influence adjustment policies on the basis of research findings, since the design and negotiation of the programme were often secret and aimed mainly at obtaining as quickly as possible a sufficient amount of foreign resources to help bolster the external position of the country. The last thing a Minister of Finance in a country in need would want is a delay in the finalization of the Policy Framework Paper and consequently in the allocation of foreign exchange, in order to accommodate research findings. This is, of course, related to the question of the ownership of the programme, which many participants raised. Does the host government really regard itself as the owner of the programme and is it thus in principle willing to improve it with whatever information is available, or does it view the programme as a necessary condition, and possible source of problems, in order to obtain foreign exchange? If the latter view is correct, the government may rightly not be interested in research and in applying research results.

Various suggestions have been made to improve the interaction between research and policy. The Hague seminar was seen as an important step in this direction, but it needs to be followed up by concrete measures to improve existing and to create additional capacity in Africa. Several participants, among them van der Kraaij, suggested the establishment of a regular newsletter which would exchange information on research activities and results. Furthermore, bilateral and multilateral donors should provide the resources for organizing regular research conferences in various African countries, where policies would be discussed openly.

The seminar provided various pointers as to the issues policy-makers and researchers themselves regarded as necessary for further research. In general, although most participants concurred with the statement by Paul Mosley that structural adjustment policies and programmes have a very weak theoretical underpinning, not all agreed that improving the understanding of the theory would be feasible, or indeed appropriate. As Toye had argued, adjustment policies nowadays, contrary to those in the early days, vary considerably among countries and contain specific policy instruments whose content and weight in the overall policy package are different and depend on the specific country situation. Despite this diversity, there remains, however, a number of issues which are germane to the situation in most countries.

As acknowledged by virtually all participants, a first prerequisite for a better understanding is an *improved database* containing both economic and social variables which would describe the economic and social realities. In this context, several participants stressed the importance of *gender-specific* information. Domestic capacity should be developed for this, which would give African policy-makers direct access, rather than huge surveys dominated by foreign researchers. Furthermore, this would add to African capacity-building.

A second area of research related to the *household sector and the informal sector*. Which micro adjustments took place at the household level and did these affect the social fabric in the country and the long-term growth potential? Should the informal sector be seen as a dynamic force or as a coping mechanism? Is special support for these programmes necessary?

A third cluster of issues concerned the different *policy transmissions* and especially the relation between *macroeconomic policies*, to which most adjustment policies belonged, and the functioning of the *microeconomy* which governs the behaviour of individuals and enterprises and also is crucial for stability and growth. How were macroeconomic policies affecting long-term development perspectives? The specific conditions in the countries belonging to the franc zone form an important and interesting component of this question.

A fourth set of issues related to the *structural transformation* which many African countries need to undergo in order to build up a visible industrial export sector. To what extent are the various elements of the structural adjustment package compatible with the necessary protection of industries, without leading to continuous and growing inefficiency?

A sixth set of issues which was frequently raised was that of the *role of the state* in the adjustment process. Here various suggestions were made. Firstly, what are the minimum institutions needed to accomplish successful adjustment and to enable countries to react adequately to foreign shocks and foreign influences? Secondly, what is the role of appropriate fiscal and expenditure policies in this? Thirdly, how important is transparency and accountability ('good governance') for a correct implementation of the programmes? Fourthly, what is the *role of the state and of foreign agencies* in designing adjustment policies; how can the political economy better be taken into account? How important is the internal political situation in bringing about *popular support* for the programme?

A related research area is the role of *external influences and external finance in adjustment policies*. What has been the impact of *technical assistance*? Is foreign aid a catalyst or a deterrent for institutional and structural change in many developing countries? How critical a factor is the *external debt situation*? Furthermore, how can domestic resources be better mobilized and can external resources contribute here?

Answering some of the above questions would also throw light on the *evaluation of adjustment policies* and the consequences for *growth and poverty alleviation*, about which controversy still exists. Some participants argued that research in these areas should not be focused on proving whether adjustment policies were right or wrong, but rather on decomposing the various measures and providing indications as to which kind of policies would yield greater success in equitable and sustainable growth, and under what circumstances. Given (i) the data problem, which is likely to continue for some time, (ii) the absence of a sound theoretical base for structural adjustment policies in Sub-Saharan Africa, and (iii) the methodological problems encountered, there remains a strong argument for *country-specific case studies*.

Such studies can contribute not only to a more rigorous evaluation of the adjustment and other policies undertaken, taking into account the specific programme applied as well as the specific economic, social and political setting of the country, but also to the design of future programmes. If such studies were carried out by, or under the auspices of, local researchers, this could also contribute considerably to the ownership of the programme by the country itself. Most participants therefore strongly endorsed the suggestions made to bilateral and multilateral organizations to continue and augment funding for increasing research capacity in Sub-Saharan African countries on these issues.

# 12 Epilogue*
# JAN PRONK
# and FRED VAN DER KRAAIJ

A series of meetings, conferences, workshops and seminars has been organized by, or under the auspices of, the Directorate-General for International Co-operation of the Netherlands Ministry of Foreign Affairs in the recent past, trying to link political decision-making in respect of specific development issues with research. For policy-makers it is important to listen regularly to researchers in order to make better decisions and to take better stands in the international political dialogue on a number of development questions. Understandably, for researchers it is of equal importance to listen to policy-makers. The seminar 'Structural Adjustment and Beyond' certainly represents a significant meeting in this respect. We think one of our major aims, namely to have a real and fruitful dialogue between researchers and decision-makers has been well served by this seminar.

## Urgent Need for a Dialogue Between Researchers and Policy-makers

It is high time for discussion between researchers and policy-makers on structural adjustment policies in Sub-Saharan Africa. Four reasons emerge for the urgency. First, because we are now entering a new era. We are not only beyond the mere stabilization policies but we are also beyond the first, second and third generations of adjustment programmes. Moreover, it is becoming increasingly clear that we are entering a period which can be characterized by the transformation of societies. To a certain extent this is the same terminology as that used by Wapenhans when distinguishing between structural change on the one hand and structural reform on the other.

The second reason for holding this discussion urgently is that we are not only temporarily but also structurally in an international deadlock, as far as the external environment and policies are concerned: a deadlock in policy-making on trade and on the resolution of the debt problem as well as on international resource flows. The structural character of this threefold deadlock has to be taken into account.

The third reason is that after the major political changes which took place in the international community following the events in Eastern Europe and the former Soviet Union from 1989 onwards, important political changes have been taking place within nations. We refer not only to the fact that there is much more attention and emphasis given to the concepts of good governance and democratization, but also to the simultaneous emergence in many countries of new political generations, post-decolonization as well as post-Cold War. This offers new opportunities for policy-making.

A fourth reason why it is so important to hold such meetings on structural adjustment in Africa is that international attention is becoming increasingly inward-looking and diverted to national or regional themes and issues. This has both political consequences and repercussions in the fields of trade, debt and aid policy-making to which reference has already been made.

This transition to another era has resulted in new insights, experiences and research outcomes. It has also led to new questions and challenges. Therefore, these four reasons have combined to make a new, more intensive dialogue between policy-makers in Africa, policy-makers from donor organizations with a commitment to Africa and researchers a timely affair.

# The Contribution of Research to the Policy Debate on Structural Adjustment

The contribution of research to the policy dialogue between researchers and policy-makers may take different forms. They are all equally important for us in order to understand and to improve the different adjustment processes which have recently been introduced in Sub-Saharan Africa and elsewhere. Thus, research may result in, or contribute to, a better understanding of the phenomena which claim our attention and of their relation to each other (fundamental, strategic research). The seminar has indeed paid some attention to this, and elsewhere in this volume one can read more about the participants' observations, especially those of Toye and Mosley, with respect to the theoretical basis underlying structural adjustment policies.

Yet another type of research may help us to find solutions for the problems we are faced with (applied research), or it may lead to knowledge of the effects and consequences of certain policies in the short, medium and long term (policy-forecasting research). This was central to the papers presented by the seminar's main speakers, the comments of the discussants and the interventions of the other participants. Although with respect to the specific research outcomes and the discussions regarding the underlying assumptions, methodologies and theoretical concepts a number of observations would seem to be warranted, we shall focus here only on a limited number of issues which have not been dealt with in the preceding chapter (Discussion and Conclusions) or have been treated differently.

Logically, certain conditions should be fulfilled in order to establish a good relationship between research and policy-making. Hence, we can ask the question: Under what conditions is research useful for policy-makers? The answer to this question seems to be threefold. Firstly, basic among these conditions is the willingness to listen to each other. Therefore, on the one hand, researchers should be willing to provide easy access to their research results. On the other hand, policy-makers should be willing to make a serious effort to pay attention to those results. Moreover, they should indicate problems to researchers. Secondly, and this follows from the foregoing, research should take place on the basis of relevant choices as far as its themes and subjects are concerned. Though this should not be interpreted as being too restrictive or directive, it implies that researchers should be familiar with the situation of policy-makers and executors, and with the internal and external constraints they face. Thirdly, it is important that the research should not be too abstract, whether with regard to the modelling of the processes or the research methods, or with regard to the assumptions on the basis of which the research is being carried out.

This discussion was intended to be based on research results obtained from a learning process over the years. However, one of the problems resulting from the relative abundance of research results is that one can more or less prove anything. This makes it difficult for policy-makers to take decisions or for diplomats and representatives to adopt a stand. In order to have an impact on policy decisions, it is important that researchers, if they do not agree with each other, should explicitly spell out the specific reasons for their disagreement. These reasons may include the different paradigms which have been implicitly embodied in the research, or the specific assumptions which underlie the research and the models which have been used.

This is important because if researchers do not spell out the specific assumptions on which their research has been based and which determine their policy conclusions, there may be counterproductive consequences in terms of policy-making. In international policy gatherings one is frequently confronted with different research results, and this sometimes creates the impression that researchers are not fully aware that their work is being used in ways different from what they intended, and that at times they are being abused.

It is to be hoped that these open discussions between researchers and policy-makers at different levels will be continued, organized either by a bilateral donor or by the World Bank or the IMF which have shown themselves willing to participate actively in such gatherings.

## What is the Role of Researchers and Research Institutions in Sub-Saharan Africa?

The feedback of research results to the real situation in Sub-Saharan Africa must aim at both the policy and the implementation levels, and presumes an important role for the governments in Sub-Saharan African countries and for the international donor community. Equally important is the role of African researchers and research institutions. Up till now their effective role has been very limited, because of a lack of qualified researchers and because of financial and institutional constraints. This observation applies not only to economic research, but is valid with respect to research in general. Most research in Sub-Saharan Africa is carried out in universities which are either still in the process of establishing themselves or are severely affected by the existing budgetary constraints which reflect the precarious financial position of these countries and the low priority given for various reasons to science and technology policy by their governments.

The already existing problems of 'staff retention' and 'brain drain' have worsened in recent years to reach now alarming proportions, partly because of the often necessary cuts in public expenditures and other measures introduced under economic reform programmes. In his Keynote Address Malima rightly rang the alarm bell. These phenomena seriously undermine ongoing attempts in various sectors aimed at institution-building and form clear indicators of the short-term orientation of actual policies which cannot and should not be ignored. In the Republic of South Africa some 6,000 university-trained professionals from other Sub-Saharan African countries work in universities and secondary schools, a number of them directly or indirectly engaged in research. More than 4,000 well-trained Africans teach in secondary schools in France; they form only a small fraction of the estimated 70,000 Africans trained in Europe who have decided to stay there. This is in sharp contrast to the technical assistance being provided to Sub-Saharan African countries. With some 100,000 expatriates actually employed, the number is even higher now than at independence. The major source of technical assistance, France, which accounts for 16.5% of total technical assistance to Africa, currently employs some 3,000 professionals in the field of education and research in Sub-Saharan Africa, predominantly (i.e. 85%) in the (twenty) francophone countries (*Afrique Education*, 1993: 6; Berg, 1993: 80; Saint, 1992: 23).

It will be clear that if researchers from Sub-Saharan African countries are to play an increasing role in the much needed discussion with policy-makers from their own countries as well as from international organizations – and we all recognize the need for it – then we shall have to do more than just support existing institutions like the ACBI, based in Harare, CODESRIA, based in Dakar, AERC, based in Nairobi, or CIEREA, based in Ouagadougou. Policy-makers should also review their expenditure priorities and their development budgets, in particular the expenditures on technical co-operation in Sub-Saharan Africa which have now reached almost $4 billion a year, i.e. one fourth of the total aid to the region (Berg, 1993: 80; Bossuyt *et al.*, 1992: 78).

With research being essential to a better understanding of the mechanisms behind the adjustment process and of the impact of the adjustment policies which have been implemented, it will be obvious that it ought to be part and parcel of the adjustment programmes. Moreover, in our view structural adjustment measures should by no means impede or reduce research activities but rather enhance and increase them. And are not African researchers well placed to do this job, given their familiarity with the economic, social and political environment? We therefore want to make a strong plea for integrating research into these programmes, including also its financing, and for having this carried out by African researchers, thus reducing the current under-utilization of the available research potential in Sub-Saharan Africa, enhancing the local 'ownership' of SAPs, thereby giving an important impetus to African self-reliance, and reducing the dominance of researchers from the North over their counterparts from the South.

## Lessons for Policy-makers

A special comment seems to be warranted on the at times inconclusive nature of the discussions at the seminar. Three factors seem to be responsible for this. First, the actual conditions in the 48 different countries that constitute

Sub-Saharan Africa are highly complex. Situations differ strongly with respect to the countries' area, climate, natural resource endowment, size, composition and quality of the population and other socio-economic characteristics, in short their economic potential, as well as with respect to their recent economic history. Moreover, they differ with respect to their general history, colonial heritage, languages and other cultural as well as political characteristics. It is this great variety which imposes the need for both 'tailor-made' structural adjustment programmes, ably demonstrated by Toye, and for 'tailor-made' poverty alleviation programmes, clearly presented in their various forms by Seshamani. Secondly, there is only limited factual knowledge about these countries and their populations because of the frequent inaccuracy of the official data and the virtual absence of data with respect to the so-called informal sector. Moreover, the importance of the informal sector in the economies of Sub-Saharan Africa seems to be growing – ironically, often as a result of structural adjustment programmes. Azam rightly pointed this out in his paper. Thirdly, the seminar's discussions have made it abundantly clear that there is no generally accepted and applicable methodology to measure the impact of structural adjustment policies. Ajayi, Mosley and Azam all elaborated on this issue.

These factors may explain why researchers have at times come to different and sometimes even contradictory conclusions in so far as the impact of structural adjustment programmes is concerned. Improvement of the data base therefore stands out as one of the most urgent challenges facing policy-makers, both in governments in Sub-Saharan African countries and in donor and other financial organizations, as was repeatedly pointed out during the seminar. Policy-makers should be aware that in the meantime country-specific case studies seem to be the most appropriate way to investigate the intentional and unintentional effects of structural adjustment programmes.

National and international policy-makers would also be wise to take into account the six lessons from research mentioned by Ajayi. Chief among these lessons are his conclusions that there is no 'quick fix' and that the international environment has been very hostile to the smooth implementation of structural adjustment programmes.

Our discussions on the economics of structural adjustment programmes, both with regard to 'capacity', i.e. the productive capacity which has to be improved and the institutional capacity to implement the SAPs, and with regard to the social and poverty dimensions of these programmes, have been most instructive. They also contained several important lessons for policy-makers. It was very useful for them to listen to these discussions, in particular that on the issue – raised by Mosley – that it is not always necessary to aim at an overall system or approach with a fully fledged structural adjustment programme and a number of interrelated instruments, but that at times it might be sensible to concentrate on a number of individual, very specific instruments.

Another salient element for policy-makers is the emphasis which was laid by Mosley on the significance of catalysts. It is important to realize that instruments are only effective if there is policy stability, for example, or an adequate and growing level of domestic or international development expenditures, or, as far as the market mechanism is concerned, an adequate infrastructure in order to let the mechanism flourish rather than being jeopardized by inadequate infrastructural capacity. Policy-makers certainly have very often failed to take into account the fact that specific elements of the adjustment policy may affect certain catalysts in a counterproductive way.

A major issue discussed at the seminar was the relationship between structural adjustment and poverty alleviation. If we agree that structural adjustment, instead of aiming solely at enhanced economic growth, should rather aim at sustainable and equitable development, as was frequently stated by various seminar participants, then it is logical that the benefits of structural adjustment will only be sustainable if poverty reduction is fully integrated into the adjustment programmes, right from the outset. Poverty alleviation requires economic growth, but economic growth alone is not a sufficient tool to fight poverty. Also needed are investments in the social sectors (health, education). In reality, poverty alleviation and economic growth are inextricably interwoven since investments in human resources simultaneously constitute an effective means of fighting poverty and are the fulfilment of an important prerequisite for economic growth.

Along the same line of thought one can also argue that poverty alleviation is more than the safety net component of a SAP. Seshamani rightly explained this in his contribution. Poverty alleviation requires structural adjustment, provided that the adjustment leads to the integration of the poor into the economy, not to their exclusion. Failure to effectively reach the poor would debar them from the modern economy and keep them poor. Furthermore, it could risk the destabilization of society and incite the governments of adjusting countries which feel threatened by popular discontent with their policies to adopt a 'stop-go' policy with respect to the implementation of the programme.

Poverty alleviation requires investments in poor people's health and education that will increase labour productivity and improve their chances of employment. It also demands investments in poor people's second main asset, namely land. Therefore, what is needed is an investment policy which, on the one hand, concentrates on the agricultural sector, aiming at increasing its productivity and competitiveness – a position which was also taken by Husain – and, on the other hand, creates jobs for the unemployed, the poor, and civil servants in the urban centres who have been made redundant. A labour-intensive, gender-oriented employment policy will not only create the necessary purchasing power in the cities for the agricultural products from the rural areas but will also strengthen the political base for the reform programme by appeasing the most vociferous part of the population. This may prove essential for a smooth transition to greater democracy, a political process which in many Sub-Saharan African countries is taking place simultaneously with the economic reforms.

Adjustment programmes should also aim at preserving the quality of the environment and thereby enhance the prospects of truly sustainable development. Structural adjustment, on the one hand, and poverty reduction and environmental protection, on the other, are not conflicting aims, but reinforce each other. In this respect it was encouraging to listen to Husain, and we would like to urge the World Bank in particular to deepen its understanding of the impact of macroeconomic policies on poverty, employment, investment and the environment.

A final issue to be taken into account by policy-makers concerns the political considerations associated with structural adjustment programmes, which was briefly mentioned earlier. All participants seemed to agree on this subject. Morrisson and his colleagues made a laudable effort to integrate political variables, and hence political considerations, with economic variables in their model from the very outset. It may, however, be too early to arrive at definite conclusions, because the exercise is still in an early stage of modelling, and is being developed on the basis of simulation, rather than of specific variables in practice. But their work may indeed lead to enlightening results.

This brings us to the experience with structural adjustment programmes which Kasonde brought with him from Zambia, and more specifically to the conditions for success which he enumerated. Two of them deserve particular attention, since in a number of countries they may not be fulfilled so easily as the other conditions which he specified. The first is that there should be political stability in the country, which implies more than a belief on the part of the people in the government and a committed government. The second is that there should be a favourable international economic environment leading to adequate external financial resources to finance the structural adjustment programmes and the investments associated with them. This point was shared by others, for example the plea made in this regard by Husain.

These two conditions have a general validity, but they apply in particular to Africa. We are afraid that, with respect to Sub-Saharan Africa, they are not going to be met in the near future. This inevitably leads us to an important question which we need to answer now or in the years ahead, namely to what extent can we continue with structural adjustment programmes in nations which are getting weaker and weaker because of political instability resulting from other than economic causes? The answer to this question may have consequences for the way in which structural adjustment programmes need to be designed. The issue ought to be discussed in more depth in the near future. Furthermore, a second, maybe very alarming, political issue arises from the fact that increasingly there will be fewer external resources available for developing countries, irrespective of whether they are engaged in structural adjustment or not.

It is therefore strongly to be recommended, maybe just as a scenario, that future structural adjustment programmes should be designed and developed which depend much less on external funds in support of the policy changes and for the subsequent financing of the investments necessary to promote and realize sustainable and equitable economic growth. This may be alarming as a projection for some people, though not perhaps for others. Ignoring this particular possibility may create much more frustration than we already have. Given the external environment, this only adds weight to the pleas put forward by various participants for changes in international debt policy (Kasonde made this plea very strongly), changes in international trade policies (a plea made by several people, in particular Stewart) and changes in what might be called international good governance, with regard to international democratic decision-making on issues which are crucial for the developing countries. These changes now appear to be even more important than they were in the 1970s and 1980s when Sub-Saharan African countries were relying heavily on external financial resources.

# Economic Reforms, Political Transformation and Good Governance

The issues of good governance and of the relationship between economic reform and political transformation were raised by various participants, in particular by Harrigan in her comments on Wapenhans' paper. Harrigan highlighted the political dilemma very well. Even assuming that (i) we have a clear idea of what does constitute good governance in Sub-Saharan Africa and that (ii) a positive correlation exists between good governance and the macroeconomic balances of sustainable growth – assumptions which she admittedly accepted as open to dispute – she still found herself left with many pertinent questions for the international donor community. The answers to these questions are important since they determine the decision to give, to continue or to withhold foreign assistance to these related processes of economic reform and political transformation. Interestingly, on the basis of present experiences, for example in Malawi and Kenya, Harrigan came to the conclusion that there is a divergence between the bilateral donors and the international financial institutions that may be attributed to the fact that there is a difference of opinion between them on the relation between economic structural change and political transformation.

This may be a difference implicit in the point of view of these organizations. It may also be just a pretext on the part of the international donor community, which is no longer able or willing to provide adequate financial resources and for these reasons is currently using the issue of good governance in developing countries as an excuse. If that were not the case, Harrigan's plea for making resources available to help Sub-Saharan African countries to set up their own structural adjustment programmes, so-called 'home-grown' SAPs, and to facilitate political transformation, would, of course, have been addressed in a positive way much earlier. We share her plea, difficult and risky as it may be. Nevertheless, the vitally important political question she raised has to be answered: whether such administrative, legal and institutional reforms offer an appropriate enabling environment in the face of unaccountable political regimes. This question of last resort cannot be answered by researchers. It is a political question which must be answered by politicians. And here again the question is: Who is going to answer this specific question?

In this context of 'good governance' the following is important. It is a fact that the donor communities are either very reluctant to act or are self-oriented towards rents serving their own (perceived and often distinct) interests rather than those of the recipient countries. Wuyts rightly took issue with Wapenhans in this respect. Good governance in the widest sense of the word therefore has to be defined as a dynamic concept, not a static one. It has to be defined in a credible, neutral and democratic way, which means not by donors alone and not by the rent-seeking agencies themselves, but by donors *and* recipients together.

# The Role of the Bretton Woods Institutions

This brings us back to the role to be played by the international financial institutions. Despite the criticism of their approach during the difficult 1980s, we need them very much. This is precisely why these discussions between researchers and policy-makers have to be held and are being held, because in principle these organizations can act more credibly, more neutrally and more democratically than any bilateral donor could do. Political views held by individual politicians in donor countries will remain important, but they will have to be neutralized and isolated from rent-seeking behaviour by the donor countries themselves. This can only be done by the international organizations.

Thus the international financial institutions are much better placed provided (i) they do not act in a technocratic or arrogant way, (ii) they indeed take into account the specific social and political situations in the individual countries concerned and (iii) they define good governance and political transformation, in particular in terms of the consequences for people, as was requested by van der Hoeven, for example. The human rights issue then also becomes extremely important.

Despite criticism of the attitude of the Bretton Woods institutions in the 1980s, the transformation from the 1980s into the 1990s has demonstrated that the World Bank and the International Monetary Fund have increasingly been able to listen to criticism and to organize meetings favouring a dialogue, in particular at the higher levels of these organizations. To conclude, therefore, we want to appeal to these international organizations to continue to follow that open attitude of being listeners and to be real brokers, brokers between researchers and policy-makers, brokers between governments in the South and governments in the North and brokers between governments and their peoples.

## Note

* This chapter is mainly based on Minister Jan Pronk's Opening Address on 1 June 1993 and his speech on 3 June 1993 as well as on Fred van der Kraaij's summary view on the seminar's discussions, conclusions and possible recommendations as presented during the closing session of the seminar.

## References

*Afrique Education* (1993) 'France: Vers Une Baisse du Nombre de Coopérants en Afrique?', *Afrique Education*, Colombes, France; Imfrano TB Conseils, October/November.

Berg, Elliot J. (1993) *Rethinking Technical Cooperation – Reforms for Capacity Building in Africa*, New York: Regional Bureau for Africa, UNDP and Development Alternatives, Inc.

Bossuyt, J., Laporte, G. and van Hoek, F. (1992) *New Avenues for Technical Cooperation in Africa – Improving the Record in Terms of Capacity Building*, ECDPM Occasional Paper, Maastricht, The Netherlands: European Centre for Development Policy Management.

Saint, William S. (1992) *Universities in Africa – Strategies for Stabilization and Revitalization*, World Bank Technical Paper No. 194, African Technical Department Series, Washington DC: World Bank.

# APPENDICES

These three appendices were originally written in April 1993 for the pre-seminar Reader which was distributed to the participants in advance.

# APPENDIX 1

# A Review of Research Literature on the Impact of Structural Adjustment in Sub-Saharan Africa

# WILLEM VAN DER GEEST

## Introduction

This review of the literature on the impact of structural adjustment in Sub-Saharan Africa attempts to present the range of research results and conclusions reached. Research papers and publications may be distinguished in terms of:

(i) their stated objectives and the issues/cases studied;
(ii) the methods and techniques of analysis utilized;
(iii) the results and conclusions obtained; and/or
(iv) institutional criteria, such as, for example, the sponsoring institution.

Perhaps the best way of establishing the range and convergence, if any, of views and results reached is by organizing the literature into objectives and issues addressed. For this bibliographical review the following classification by subject themes has been adopted:

a) Research on the origins, progress and models of evaluation of Sub-Saharan Africa's structural adjustment experience;
b) Research on the macroeconomic impact of structural adjustment;
c) Research on the meso, sectoral and social impacts of structural adjustment;
d) Research on the political economy of structural adjustment;
e) Research on the long-term developmental impact of structural adjustment.

It may be noted that this classification follows the programme of the seminar and is neither complete nor mutually exclusive. Many publications included in the review contribute to one of the general and macro categories (a) and (b) above, but also add to the understanding of specific impact at the sectoral or household level. In principle, the research literature has been classified as specifically as possible; for example, if household or sectoral issues are the focus of the publication it is classified under that heading, even though it may include a discussion of the macroeconomic or long-term developmental impact as well. Finally, within each sub-section only a few significant publications are selected

**Appendix Table 1.1.** *Preliminary classification of research on the impact of SAPs by research method and level*

| Research Method \ Research level | Household or Micro level | Sector or Meso level | National or Macro level | Cross-Country Comparison | Multi-country aggregate/International |
|---|---|---|---|---|---|
| Sample survey of firm/farm or household | Bigsten and Kayizzi-Mugerwa (1992); Alessie et al. (1992) | Bevan et al. (1989) | Bevan et al. (1990) | Bevan et al. (1989, 1990) | |
| Systematic analysis of national or census data | Kakwani (1989); various LSMS; Christensen and Stack (1992) | | Jabara (1991); Chhibber and Fischer (1991); Chhibber (1992) | Duncan and Howell (1992) | World Bank (eg. 1992); Devarajan and Rodrik (1992) |
| Construction of consistent database or economic model | Sarris (1990b) | | Sarris (1990b) | | Evans et al. (1992) |
| Qualitative and/or quantitative analysis of programme objectives, design or implementation | Morgan (1988) | Commander (1989) | Ihonvbere (1993); Radelet (1992); Hadjimichael et al. (1992); Sahn et al. (1990) | Mosley et al. (1991) | Stewart (1991a); Cornia et al. (1987); Sahn (1990a) |
| Short-term and long-term assessment/projection of programme impact | Cornia et al. (1987) | | Cornia et al. (1992) | | ECA (1989); Stewart (1991b) |

NOTE: The selected literature is merely indicative; further elaboration of the classification and inclusion of all the literature would be desirable; some researches may appear in more than one cell.

and these are included in alphabetical order. Other publications whose subject is closely related are cross-referred; further publications on the same theme which are included in the Bibliography, but not separately reviewed, are identified at the end of each section.

Research is defined to include any analysis of primary data and observations; systematic and thorough review of secondary data and information; construction of a consistent database (eg. the social accounting matrix) or an economic model; qualitative and/or quantitative analysis of programme objectives, design or implementation, including 'with-and-without programme' and 'before-and-after programme' methods of research; and/or short-term and long-term assessment and/or projection of the programme's impact.

The various research methods used to determine the impact of structural adjustment may be applied to different objects of research, for example a village or a region, a sector of the economy, one or more countries, etc. Appendix Table 1.1 shows the possible permutations, using these two dimensions of research object and method; the publications which are reviewed below are classified.

Appendix Table 1.1 may serve as a starting point for identifying the limitations of the present research on the impact of structural adjustment; it could be expanded by providing a more detailed description of research methods as well as of the research object. For example, qualitative research publications on the intellectual origins of structural adjustment (Ferreira, 1992), the methods of programme design (Tarp, 1993), research on research methods (Scobie, 1989) or the politics of adjustment (Nelson, 1990; Haggard et al., 1992) are not easily accommodated in the classification of the table. A further definition and delineation of the categories of the research object would be desirable and would need to incorporate issues which manifest themselves at various levels; important examples include gender issues, the environmental impact of adjustment policies and civil service reform programmes.

The Bibliography at the end of this review includes references to research-based working papers, articles and books published within the last ten years, but it particularly emphasizes literature published since 1988. It is limited in a number of important respects:

(i)   it only includes studies focusing on Sub-Saharan Africa and hence excludes related research on North Africa, South Asia, Latin America, etc.;
(ii)  it focuses on macroeconomic adjustment under externally funded Structural Adjustment Programmes (SAPs) only and does not specifically look at literature on IMF-sponsored stabilization programmes; and
(iii) the links to and feedbacks from the SAPs on the agricultural sub-sector are examined, leaving out a review of the literature on industry and services (including public service reform). A review of the literature on African industry under structural adjustment is available in Appendix 2.

The coverage excludes 'grey cover' documents of governments and international organizations as well as operational documents pertaining to structural adjustment lending operations. Unpublished master and doctoral theses are not included. Only literature available in the English language is reviewed; references are listed alphabetically by the author's name, when given, and otherwise by the name of the sponsoring institution.

# SSA's Structural Adjustment Experience: Origins, Progress and Models of Evaluation

The *African Alternative Framework to Structural Adjustment Programmes for Socio-economic Recovery and Transformation (AAF-SAP)* by the Economic

Commission for Africa (1989) provides a perspective on Sub-Saharan Africa's adjustment which has been formulated and endorsed by African political leaders and senior policy-makers. It emphasizes the international economic reasons for Africa's external imbalances (collapsing primary commodity prices, reduced net flows of resources, etc.) and the weak and disarticulated structures of Africa's economies. The alternative framework attempts to shift the focus towards transformation, noting the structural weaknesses of SSA's economy.

The proposed policy instruments and measures under the AAF-SAP focusing on productive capacity include: land reform, enhancing the role of women, devoting more public investment to agriculture, focusing imports on vital inputs, increasing linkages between agriculture and industry, priority allocation of credit to the food sub-sector and the manufacture of essential goods, adopting investment codes tailored to small-scale industries, selectively reducing interest rates for productive activities, strengthening rural financial institutions, setting up an effective national maintenance system for infrastructure, and using multiple exchange rates to ensure the availability of essential imports. Cross references to the AAF-SAP are manifold. They include Please (1992) noting correspondences between ECA views and the World Bank's (1989) long-term perspective study; Cornia et al. (1992) attempting to formulate African recovery policies with similar objectives; see also Ihonvbere (1993) for a political analysis with similar premises to those of the AAF-SAP.

Ferreira (1992) offers a stimulating and comprehensive overview of the evolution of ideas generated by or within the World Bank on the macroeconomic analysis of adjustment as well as the microeconomic issues of allocative efficiency and equity. The current paradigm for adjustment analysis and advice draws on Dornbusch's early and influential review of stabilization policies (1982), which depicted the macroeconomics of adjustment as a combination of expenditure reduction and expenditure switching. The subsequent analytical development qualified these notions in a number of respects clarifying:

(i) the undesirable possible accelerator relationship between devaluation and inflation;
(ii) the need to sequence policy interventions in order to realize their potential without counter effects from other policy changes ('competition of instruments');
(iii) the alternative strategies of budget deficit reductions, given conditions at the time the programme was adopted;
(iv) the need to minimize the social costs of adjustment; and
(v) the politics of acceptance of adjustment conditionality.

Finally, the author notes (as does, for example, Tarp, 1993) that the new macroeconomic and strategic trade theory has not been used, partly because some of the outcomes predicted by this body of literature did not actually occur during adjustment programmes.

Allocative efficiency, a main objective of adjustment programmes, is to be obtained through appropriate microeconomic reforms of trade, prices and taxes; financial liberalization; privatization; labour market reform and institution building. Ferreira traces the history of increasing emphasis and advice on the need for these reforms, and notes instances where the microeconomic advice contradicts the objectives of equitable distribution, an area which has been receiving increasing attention since 1987. He concludes that the early thinking on adjustment (pre-1982) was based on an over-optimistic prediction of growth and that early adjustment practice (up to 1987) over-emphasized the internal public deficit as the cause of all economic instability. The World Bank was a 'follower' rather than an 'innovator' where macroeconomic analysis was concerned, although it did provide guidance in the formulation of microeconomic reform (on trade and tax reform, for example). It ignored the effects of adjustment on equity until 1987 when it was confronted with growing criticism from, *inter alia*, Cornia *et al.* (1987). Cross references for Ferreira's working paper include Tarp (1993); Taylor (1988, 1992) as well as Demery and Addison (1987) on the analytical basis of the macroeconomics of adjustment; Cassen in van der Geest (1994) and Please (1992) on the context in which the World Bank adopted the SAP approach.

*A Macro-Micro Framework for Analysis of the Impact of Structural Adjustment on the Poor in Sub-Saharan Africa* by Sarris (1990b) is an outline of a model which is 'designed to link macroeconomic policies with household-level outcomes' in order to execute counterfactual simulations. The computable general equilibrium (CGE) model, of the recursive dynamic type, places emphasis on:

(i) aggregation starting from micro-level features;
(ii) explicitly representing structural features;
(iii) maintaining stock-flow consistency through an updated social accounting matrix as well as an asset-liability balance sheet.

Extensions of the CGE framework, developed by Sarris and particularly relevant for SSA, include:

(i) disaggregation of the agricultural sub-sector;
(ii) the description of 'official' and 'open' markets for staple food and/or export crops;
(iii) the description of import rationing and the resulting parallel markets for goods and foreign exchange.

This Cornell Food and Nutrition Policy Program (CFNPP) monograph presents both a one-period static and a multi-period dynamic model and provides detailed elaboration of the specification of the extension. The analytical properties of the model are investigated. The author concludes with the observation that the fully specified CGE model may be too data-intensive to be capable of implementation in SSA at the present time. However, it provides the starting point for empirical work and may guide data-collection efforts as envisaged in the CFNPP programme. Cross references include Bourguignon *et al.* (1989) which outlines a comparable modelling framework for analysis of adjustment and equity relationships; the various publications by Bevan *et al.* (1989, 1990) have similar objectives, utilizing different modelling approaches; for the modelling of Africa's food marketing features see van der Geest (1991).

*Macroeconomic Adjustment and the Poor* by Scobie (1989) spells out the intellectual and methodological foundations for the extensive CFNPP programme of research, which includes a range of country-focused case studies of the effects of adjustment on the poor. The author takes the Salter-Swan open economy adjustment model as a starting point and discusses the extensions which are required to analyse the link between adjustment and distribution. He reviews the literature on various issues of:

(i) programme implementation (order, timing, mixing and interdependence of policies);
(ii) modelling approaches (sector models, the social accounting matrices and the computable/applied general equilibrium (CGE/AGE) models);
(iii) welfare indicators (poverty identification, measures of poverty and nutritional status).

Scobie concludes by summarizing the major elements of a research strategy, including formulating a theoretical framework, reviewing the evidence, making country case studies and, finally, cross-country comparative analysis. Cross references include Demery and Addison (1987) on the link between macroeconomic policy changes and income distribution and various Social Dimensions of Adjustment (SDA) publications as well as Sarris (1990b) and other CFNPP monographs, using the approach outlined by Scobie.

Stewart (1991a), in a sequel to Cornia et al. (1987), assesses the social and economic impact of SAPs. She discusses:

(i) the macroeconomic performance of the African countries which were involved in structural adjustment lending programmes with policy conditionality;
(ii) the change in the social conditions of low-income households during the programmes;
(iii) the change in World Bank and IMF policies in response to the macroeconomic and household evidence.

Measuring the impact of SAPs presents methodological problems, the author notes; in particular, it is very difficult to distinguish external factors, such as commodity price movements, and stochastic shocks from the impact of structural adjustment policies. The distinction, though academic for the low-income households concerned, does matter for the kind of policy reform adopted. Comparing the macroeconomic performance of countries with and without SAPs does not make the distinction. In particular, to note that those which adopted the SAP grew faster is unsatisfactory because it ignores the very different 'initial conditions' in which these countries adopted the SAPs. Moreover, the growth variation within the adjusting group is tremendous.

Stewart suggests examining household-level indicators, in particular:

(i) income, which is itself determined by levels of employment, self-employment and real wages;
(ii) exogenous prices, such as those for food obtained from the market, etc.;
(iii) public expenditure, especially on health and education; and
(iv) women's time usage.

Incomplete data for Africa about these indicators show falling per capita incomes. Only rural incomes have improved, in response to improved rural-urban terms of trade. However, the aggregation of food producers and food consumers in the rural areas ignores the food-deficit households. The rural differentiation has increased as richer farmers have emerged in, *inter alia*, Côte d'Ivoire, Malawi and Ghana. Public expenditure on health and education (in real terms) remained broadly constant in SSA as it was not as sharply reduced as overall expenditure. Women's changing time usage is unfortunately not well documented for Africa (unlike Latin America, where adjustment meant women working longer hours and relying on younger children for child care).

The Bretton Woods institutions differed in their policy responses in terms of redesigning SAPs; they either did not move, in spite of the attention paid to the issues by the executive director (IMF) or did not move enough (WB). The World Bank's SDA concept was designed to leave the macro and meso context of the policies unchanged. It focused primarily on the new poor and the compensation needed for them. Regressive meso policies included in the programmes were not eradicated. Finally, the SAPs' focus is too much on the internal policies of the deficit countries, ignoring the adverse external and international dimensions of adjustment problems. Cross references to Stewart include Sahn (1990a and b) and (1991) which differs in diagnosis and conclusion; Cornia *et al.* (1987); Stewart (1991b) and various World Bank reviews of adjustment lending.

Other related references regarding the origins, progress and models of evaluation of SSA's adjustment experience include Adam *et al.* (1992) contrasting privatization experiences; Bourguignon *et al.* (1989) on the modelling of macro-micro linkages; Davies *et al.* (1991) on a case of self-imposed adjustment; Delaine (1992) on the use of the Living Standard Measurement Survey household surveys to monitor adjustment effects; van der Geest (1994) on policy choices and dilemmas facing African decision-makers; Faini *et al.* (1991) on the experience of growth-oriented adjustment programmes; Ghai (1992) on the global context in which structural adjustment has been adopted; De Janvry *et al.* (1989) on the different welfare effects of adjustment policies; Levine and Renelt (1991) on the methodology of analysis of structural adjustment; Mosley (1992) on the assessment of adjustment policies in Nigeria, in the absence of reliable data; Patel (1992) on IMF policy perspectives for Africa; Please (1984) on the World Bank's positions and practices; Stewart *et al.* (1992) on alternative adjustment and development strategies; and World Bank (1986, 1989, 1990a, 1990b, 1991b and 1992) on adjustment experience.

# The Macroeconomic Impact of Structural Adjustment

*Economic Reform in Sub-Saharan Africa* edited by Chhibber and Fischer (1991) comprehensively covers issues of macroeconomic significance in its 22 chapters: exchange-rate policy, parallel markets, fiscal deficit and expenditure policy, financial sector policy, trade policy, regional integration, human capital and entrepreneurship and growth-oriented adjustment. The editors selectively draw out some seven lessons:

  (i) exchange-rate policy in SSA must match the competitive adjustments of East Asian countries; using the exchange rate to manage inflation leads to loss of export markets and of growth;

(ii) low returns to investment in SSA are a reflection of inefficient management of public capital;

(iii) trade diversification cannot be achieved by taxing primary commodity producers, but will require appropriate exchange rates, deregulation of the domestic economy and efforts focused on export promotion;

(iv) the role and functioning of informal financial systems needs to be recognized and financial sector policies should not disrupt well-functioning informal financial markets;

(v) illegal regional trade is under-recorded, showing that the current trade policy regimes hinder rather than foster regional integration;

(vi) incentive-oriented policy changes will need to be accompanied by the provision of infrastructure, as well as consumer goods where these are currently rationed through trade restrictions;

(vii) the low level of human development in SSA is largely attributed to colonial policies which did not encourage education, and this will take several decades to rectify.

Cross references to Chhibber and Fischer's volume are manifold. They include Bevan *et al.* (1989 and 1990); Devarajan and de Melo (1987); Goldin and Winters (1992) as well as Bourguignon, de Melo and Morrisson (1991).

*The Gambia: Economic Adjustment in a Small Open Economy* by Hadjimichael, Rumbaugh and Verreydt (1992) of the IMF, reviews recent economic performance and contrasts the situation of The Gambia in 1985/86 at the outset of the Economic Recovery Programme (ERP) with the economic indicators as available for May 1992, when the country was in the second year of the follow-up Programme for Sustained Development (PSD). The ERP and PSD programmes are evaluated in terms of changes in macroeconomic indicators, especially savings, investment and real GDP growth. The authors point to considerable growth improvements, though falling short of programme targets, and improved domestic savings, even when both the volume and the price of the country's principal export commodity (groundnuts) declined sharply. Specific attention is given to the impact of exchange-rate unification and the maintenance of a real effective exchange rate, supported by lowering average import duties; a positive relation with the increased export diversification is postulated. On the social impact of adjustment the authors note that 'the Government has been aware of the hardships faced by the poorest segments of the population and has been monitoring closely the social impact of the reform program' (p. 38). An SDA project currently being implemented, the National Population Policy, and a Women in Development project are mentioned as mitigating measures. The authors provide no analytical or empirical evidence linking the macro-economic indicators to specific SAP policies, nor do they provide any precise statement about changes in income distribution, food availability and security or improvements in social status, in response to the social dimension policies and programmes.

*Structural Adjustment and Stabilization in Niger: Macroeconomic Conse-quences and Social Adjustment* by Jabara (1991) of the CFNPP offers a descriptive account of the changes in Niger's economic and social system during the 1980s and identifies the effects of the SAPs in the context of:

(i) the up- and down-swings of uranium export earnings, in particular in the context of the withdrawal of favourable output price contracts;
(ii) macroeconomic policy changes including attempts at trade policy reform, given sizeable unofficial imports;
(iii) meso policy changes, including agricultural price and marketing reform;
(iv) microeconomic policy changes, including direct and indirect tax reform.

The social impact of Niger's SAPs is not at all well established; even summary base-line data, for example for pastoral groups, are not available. Niger's recorded real GDP *per capita* decline at 4.4% per annum for 1980–90 was among the severest for any developing country.

At the macroeconomic level, membership of the West African Monetary Union implies limited autonomy in controlling the money supply and credit; the CFA exchange rate is fixed to the French franc. Moreover, the informal trade with neighbouring Nigeria has caused a continuous outflow of 'hard' currency, evading both currency regulation and trade taxes. The resulting external imbalance was aggravated by the continuous decline of uranium spot prices in Europe and the (slowly) declining contract prices. The social indicators for Niger are incomplete; however, the example of the extremely low percentage of children immunized against DPT (13% for 1988–90) may be indicative.

A detailed year-by-year account of exogenous influences, foreign assistance, economic adjustment measures and economic outcomes provides an in-depth qualitative overview of the adjustment process (pp. 45–49, comparable to Jabara, 1990). The author concludes that the SAPs, supported by the rescheduling of external debts, have helped to 'cushion the impact of declining revenues on the economy and to stretch out the adjustment period'. The social effects are not well established because of a lack of data on the characteristics of the different income groups. Cross references include Komlev in van der Geest (1992), focusing on Niger's forestalled attempt at economic and trade diversification away from uranium.

*Stabilization and Structural Adjustment: Macroeconomic Frameworks for Analysing the Crisis in Sub-Saharan Africa* by Tarp (1993) is an exceptionally lucid presentation of the policy-oriented macroeconomic frameworks used for analysing the stabilization and structural adjustment issues of SSA. It sets out the basic macroeconomic accountancy framework and illuminates the absorption issue, contrasting demand-side policies which reduce aggregate public and private demand and policies emphasizing growth and the outward shift of the production possibility curve; it also discusses the various ways by which *ex ante* imbalances are reconciled.

The IMF's financial programming approach had started out as an 'empty model' without behavioural relationships. It was augmented by Polak in 1957 to include the relationships between domestic monetary supply and the economy's external account. Domestic credit expansion which creates demand beyond domestic productive capacity will lead to a deterioration of the balance of trade and a fall in international reserves. Hence, balance-of-payments crises will need to be remedied by domestic credit reductions. Tarp shows the next step in its intellectual development, i.e. the 'Chicago model' of Frenkel and Johnson, which considers the exchange-rate adjustment issue – which Polak had assumed as nominally fixed. Its policy conclusion is that a devaluation may be required to halt the reduction of international reserves; however, it needs to be complemented by limiting the excess of credit expansion over money demand. In practice, the financial programming approach treats reserves, inflation and additional credit to the private sector as targets, whereas real output, exports and net international financial flows are considered as exogenous. Hence, imports (and the balance of payments) are endogenous. If initial results for the balance of payments of the financial programming are within acceptable limits, the need for additional ESAF borrowing does not arise. However, if not, the programme considers devaluation and the reduction of credit expansion through cutting public expenditure as instruments for achieving an acceptable level of foreign reserves. It follows from the financial programming approach that performance criteria for the stabilization and adjustment programmes will include ceilings on domestic credit expansion and the fiscal deficit. Real variables and their determinants are ignored, as are uncertainty, risk, expectations and the results of the 'new' macroeconomics and the strategic trade theories.

Tarp includes a further detailed discussion of growth programming, the counterpart to financial programming, practised by the World Bank. The synthesis between the two approaches, as developed by Corbo et al. (1987), is discussed. Tarp notes that the merger of the approaches has reduced their transparency, but did not increase their explanatory power nor provide a basis for different policy advice. Cross references to Tarp's treatment of the macroeconomic frameworks include Taylor (1988, 1992) developing structuralist models for development policy analysis, as well as Chhibber and Fischer (1991).

Other related references on the macroeconomics of structural adjustment include Chhibber and Shafik (1990) on inflation and devaluation; Collier and Gunning (1992) on exchange-rate adjustment; Devarajan and de Melo (1987) on real effective exchange rates; Kapur et al. (1991); Koester et al. (1990) on international demand-side constraints on exports; López et al. (1991) on import dependence; Loxley (1989) on devaluation experience; Nashashibi et al. (1992) on public deficit reductions and Ndulu and Hyuha (1986) on inflation in the context of liberalization; Pinto (1988) on inflation and devaluation if parallel foreign-exchange markets exist, and Roe (1992) on the financial sector and policy instruments.

# The Meso, Sectoral and Social Impacts of Structural Adjustment

## Meso and Sectoral Impacts
*Peasants and Governments: An Economic Analysis* by Bevan, Collier and Gunning (1989) analyses both expenditure and savings-investment responses by 'peasants' to the economic shocks which resulted from unanticipated upward movements of agricultural commodity prices. The analysis contrasts two country case studies (Kenya and Tanzania) based on household surveys conducted in 1982 and 1983 respectively, using part of the sample frames constructed for earlier data collection by the countries' central statistical bureaux. The primary data focused

on farm households' assets, non-farm sources of income, changes in agricultural production patterns and the households' access to government services, health, education, water, wood and sewerage. The number of sampled households was 783 for Central and Nyanza Provinces of Kenya and 498 for the Dodoma, Iringa, Kilimanjaro and Ruvuma Provinces of Tanzania (see Putterman (1990) for a critique). The primary data are interpreted in the context of earlier descriptions of the farming sub-sectors as well as the different pricing and taxation policies followed by the two governments.

The descriptive Part I focuses on the structure of product and factor markets, the structure of, and the historical changes in, peasant incomes, and the responses during the extraordinary coffee price peaks which occurred in 1976/77 and 1979/80. Part II analyses peasant households' responses to the increased level (and volatility) of coffee and other related prices in Kenya, formulating a theory of production responses to temporary earning windfalls. This microeconomic theory accounts for the implications of:

(i) increasing returns to scale in coffee growing;
(ii) indivisibility of investment activities, in particular for livestock;
(iii) restricted access to investment capital; and
(iv) incomplete information and adaptive learning.

The empirical evidence for Kenya indicates that the recognition of the temporary nature of the earnings contributed to a high savings ratio. This enabled Kenyan peasants to overcome some of the entry barriers linked to the above characteristics.

Part III develops the microeconomic theory further for the case of Tanzania, where the publicly controlled marketing system did not pass on the increased coffee prices; moreover, the shortage of consumer goods persisted throughout the period of study. The authors develop the 'incentive goods' theory of peasants' supply, when consumer goods are rationed though perhaps available at high 'unofficial' prices. The theory, corroborated by empirical evidence, predicts that the increased availability of 'incentive goods' may generate a positive supply response of traded crops (such as coffee). The confluence of the rationing of consumer goods and the increased implicit taxation on foreign-exchange-earning crops did not generate investment and increased production, even when market opportunities existed.

The conclusions of this seminal treatment of the microeconomics of peasant responses are manifold, but policy-related ones include the propositions that:

(i) commodity price-stabilizing interventions underestimate the ability of peasants to plan investment through adaptive learning;
(ii) taxation which reduces the average relative prices of traded goods, complemented by import and price controls, tends to reduce foreign-exchange earnings and public revenues.

*Peasants and Governments* is compulsory reading for those engaged in the design of agricultural sector adjustment programmes, where the initial situation is characterized by mono- or oligopsony and foreign-exchange rationing is supported by import quantity and/or price controls. Cross references to this volume include the companion volume by Bevan *et al.* (1990) on controlled open economies, pointing out that governments often pursue incompatible policy regimes, where the intended effects of policy interventions cannot be realized as other interventions form an obstacle; Lundahl (1989) on incentives for the agricultural sector; Lundahl and Ndulu (1985) for an early formulation of the incentive good proposition; and Ndulu and Hyuha (1986) on the nature of inflation in a context of price control regimes.

*Structural Adjustment and Agriculture: Theory and Practice in Africa and Latin America* edited by Commander (1989) covers the design of adjustment programmes and their impact on agricultural households and the sector as a whole, complemented by case studies (Ghana, Zambia and Senegal in SSA) and an overview of the experience. Green's contribution to the volume outlines in considerable detail the elements of a programme design favourable to agriculture, including specific recommendations for exchange-rate reform, pricing policy, credit policy and fiscal policies. Cross references to Commander include Goldin and Winters (1992) on the inter-relationships between the macroeconomic policy and agriculture and Jaeger (1992) on the same but specifically for Africa.

*Structural Adjustment and the African Farmer* edited by Duncan and Howell (1992) traces the impact of structural adjustment policies on the incomes and welfare of Africa's peasant farmers, who currently operate at very low levels of productivity of both land and labour and are confronted with low household income and inadequate food security. The country case studies entitled 'Assessing the Impact of Structural Adjustment' cover Ghana by R. Pearce, Kenya by A. Bigsten and N. Nddung'u, Madagascar by A. Hewitt, Malawi by E. Cromwell and Niger by J. de Coninck and were initially sponsored by the International Fund for Agricultural Development (IFAD). They analyse and compare the links between national economic policies and the markets in which the smallholders operate, and the services and infrastructures which influence their productive capacities. Both positive and negative impacts of structural adjustment are observed and evidence based on national agricultural data is provided. The editors conclude by arguing for a more targeted, project-specific approach to small farmer development. Cross references to Duncan and Howell include the CFNPP monographs based on case studies for the same countries: Dorosh *et al.* on Madagascar (1990), Alderman on Ghana (1991), Sahn *et al.* on Malawi (1990) and Jabara on Niger (1991) as well as Commander (1989) on the design of agricultural programmes of adjustment.

*Open Economies: Structural Adjustment and Agriculture* edited by Goldin and Winters (1992) provides a state-of-the-art treatment of the inter-relationships between structural adjustment and agriculture, drawing on recent results from the open economy macroeconomic literature. Its twenty-two authors, brought together for the OECD/CEPR-sponsored conference, cover many different issues and areas in thirteen chapters, complemented by detailed discussion notes. A number of the chapters are devoted to SSA and most of the other chapters contain theory or analyses which are pertinent to adjustment and economic reform; three of the SSA-focused chapters are discussed below.

Devarajan and Rodrik analyse some of the benefits and costs of fixed exchange rates in the franc zone. They argue that the lower inflation of the franc zone has corresponded to a very much lower growth of output, if compared with other SSA countries.

Chhibber analyses the relationships between devaluation, inflation and supply response for SSA, excepting the franc zone. He argues that the causality between exchange-rate adjustment (henceforth ERA) and inflation is not singular: in a number of countries high inflation preceded ERA and was brought about by public finance deficits fuelling money and credit creation, though elsewhere inflation was aggravated by increased import costs. Chhibber classifies African economies into four prototypes, distinguishing macro-policy regimes as (i) with fixed exchange rates, an open capital account and few or no price controls, (ii) with fixed but adjusting exchange rates, a closed capital account and selective price controls, (iii) with dual/multiple exchange rates, a closed capital account and selective price controls, and (iv) with dual/multiple exchange rates, a closed capital account and widespread price controls. For each of these prototypes the relative importance of the sources of inflation (imported, cost-push effects of devaluation, wage-push inflation, demand-pull inflation and decontrol of prices) is discussed and estimated where possible (e.g. Zimbabwe and Ghana). The devaluation-inflation interaction and the supply response are examined with a small simulation model for Zimbabwe; it is observed that very low export responsiveness, combined with budget financing by monetary creation, may wipe out the effects of devaluation completely. However, devaluation may lead to a reduction of inflation, if it means a withdrawing of implicit foreign-exchange subsidies to importers and/or increased external budgetary support.

Evans, Goldin and van der Mensbrugghe analyse 'the possible consequences of the removal of the small country assumption from policy advice', noting the importance of SSA, in its totality, on the international tropical beverages markets. The Rural Urban North South (RUNS) model is adapted to explore structural adjustment and export tax policy issues and a baserun plus various scenarios cutting tree crop export taxes are explored. The tentative results indicate that the cutting of export taxes by African governments leads to both tax revenue and GDP losses. The authors argue that 'stabilization could be provided through continued use of trade policy instruments, such as export taxes, and this could enhance the possibility of success of other adjustment measures'. (p. 185). To distinguish their observations from any call for protectionist policy, they note that, since the benefits of export tax reductions partially accrue to consumers, compensatory measures (e.g. OECD import tariff reductions) should be considered. Cross references include Jabara (1991) for an examination of the fixed exchange-rate issue and adjustment; Chhibber and Fischer (1991) on exchange-rate reforms and supply responses; Chhibber and Shafik (1990) as well as Henstridge in van der Geest (1994) on the inflation-reducing impact of devaluation in the presence of sizeable parallel foreign-exchange markets.

Other related references to the meso and sectoral impact of structural adjustment, with a focus on agriculture, include Amani et al. (1992) on the emergence of private trade in liberalized food markets; Bloomfield and Lass (1992) on international cocoa markets; Booth (1991) on the sequencing of agricultural reform; Bourguignon and Morrisson (1991) on trade and income distribution; Cheru (1992) on the negative social and ecological effects of adjustment programmes; Cornia and Strickland (1990) on rural differentiation; Diop et al. (1991) on health sector development; Due (1991) for a careful quantitative account of female-headed agricultural households and the impact of structural adjustment on their economic position; Fontaine and Sindzingre (1991) on fertilizer policy; Gersovitz (1991) on pan-territorial pricing; Jaeger and Humphreys (1988) and Jaeger (1991, 1992) on the effect of general economic policies on agriculture; Lele and Meyers (1989) on agricultural performance; López and Thomas (1990) on import dependence; Migot-Adholla et al. (1991) arguing that limitations on the right to transfer land do not seem to impair land improvements and yields; Nunberg (1990) on public sector management reform; Sarris (1987, 1990a and 1991) on agriculture and structural adjustment; Smith and Spooner (1990) on the sequencing of agricultural policies; White (1992) on private investment responses; and Whitehead (1991) on rural women's role in African agriculture.

## The Social Impact

*Women and Adjustment Policies in the Third World* edited by Afshar and Dennis (1992) sets out a framework for critically examining the 'male bias in structural adjustment'. Can, and do, adjustment programmes incorporate the interests of women? Stewart in her contribution to the volume notes the multiple role of women as producers, managers, mothers and in the community and the negative impact which reduction of public services may have on effectively fulfilling that role (eg. having to restrict time for child caring). Winifred Weekes-Vagliani notes the role of women in the informal sector (e.g. in Côte d'Ivoire). Various contributors note that at the micro level of intra-household resource allocation insufficient systematic research has been conducted; data on, for example, the economic contribution of men and women to their household do not exist.

Bigsten and Kayizzi-Mugerwa's analysis of the adaptation to distress in Kampala households (1992) provides an unusually detailed insight into the 'coping strategies' of households exposed to war and civil disturbance followed by rehabilitation involving severe stabilization and structural adjustment policies. The survey intends to remedy 'the lack of current household data which has made all attempts at devising alleviation policies seem rather *ad hoc*' (p. 1423). The authors formulate a framework predicting that household strategies include, *inter alia*:

(i) income diversification including engaging in informal sector activities, in particular for households with fewer endowments;

(ii) extraction of illicit rents, in particular in response to a sharp reduction of wage income in the formal (public) sector;

(iii) urban to rural migration and reduced outward remittances.

The urban household survey, undertaken in 1990, included 239 households comprising 1,876 individuals. It focused on the structure of income, the different income-generating processes and the access to health and education services.

Bigsten and Kayizzi-Mugerwa conclude that income diversification responses to economic decline enabled urban dwellers 'to meet some of their most pressing needs: food, clothing and housing' (p. 1439), but could not prevent a sharp cut in living standards. The government sector's services declined and formal sector employees had to resort to the informal sector, which had previously been a pressure valve on urban unemployment. In effect, the competition for informal income opportunities reduced the earning potential of the urban low-income households. The two main elements of adjustment programmes – a relative price shift towards the tradeable goods sector and fiscal restraint – would not benefit Kampala's urban economy. The main tradeable sector for Uganda is agriculture – bypassing the urban areas – whereas fiscal restraint tends to reduce the demand for both formal and informal services. Cross references for this study include Bevan et al. (1989) for similar surveys but focusing on rural households, as well as a parallel study by Bigsten and Kayizzi-Mugerwa (1991).

Adjustment and Equity in Developing Countries: A New Approach by Bourguignon and Morrisson (1992) is the synthesis of a large-scale research project undertaken by the OECD Development Centre, which has involved some 20 researchers and covered Côte d'Ivoire and Ghana in SSA as well as Chile, Ecuador, Indonesia, Malaysia and Morocco. The authors of this synthesis volume set the context of the disequilibria and crisis in which stabilization and adjustment measures are adopted, and review the changes in employment, incomes, living standards and poverty during adjustment. The experience of building simulation models for the assessment and counterfactual evaluation of adjustment and its impact on income distribution is reviewed prior to the volume's summary and recommendations.

The initial conditions for adjustment differed, but generally included the need to adjust to a particularly strong external shock. This combined a deterioration in the terms of trade with an increase in interest rates on foreign debt, while no further access to foreign funds was granted. The need for adjustment may, in principle, be responded to by policies which do not change the distribution of income; however, the resulting growth rate may be below that feasible when a reallocation of income across households is introduced. Hence, evaluation of the income distributional changes during adjustment needs to analyse the long-run trade-offs between efficiency and equity. The synthesis of the distributional outcomes of adjustment is complicated by the different initial and external conditions for each country, and the lack of direct household-level observation during adjustment for most of the countries.

In summary, employment in the rural areas did not deteriorate, given the slower growth of labour supply, whereas unemployment increased in the urban areas (often reflected in the increase of informal sector activity). Agricultural incomes moved favourably, in contrast to the non-agricultural wage incomes; the extent to which total income declined depends on the level and distribution of non-wage factor incomes and the provision of government services. Hence, living standards do not necessarily fall during adjustment: improvement in the rural areas of Ghana was observed, but also sharp falls in the urban areas of Côte d'Ivoire.

Economy-wide models were used to study the impact of public expenditure cuts, monetary contraction, devaluation of the exchange rate and structural changes in the tax system (described in Bourguignon et al. (1989) and the relevant case studies). They were also used to study the magnitude of the impact of the adjustment measures, as well as counterfactual simulations; the most comprehensive modelling exercises were undertaken for Indonesia. The simulations indicated that devaluation is in general a more efficient and equitable instrument of stabilization than cutting public expenditure or the money supply: resulting in less output contraction and a favourable distribution of income towards the rural sector. It should be noted that 'optimal' adjustment sequences may often not be feasible, given the political context. One example is where an influential middle class resists measures exclusively targeted at the poorest in society (Ecuador). The social costs of adjustment are largest when public sector enterprises are reorganized. In such cases compensation programmes to aid the unemployed are indispensable. Cross references to other components of the OECD research study include the paper by Bourguignon, de Melo and Morrisson (1991) presenting a further overview, Lambert *et al.* (1991) for Côte d'Ivoire and Pyatt *et al.* (1991) for Ghana.

Christensen and Stack (1992) analyse household food insecurity in Zimbabwe over the period 1980–91, noting that it is widespead – an unexpected situation for a middle-income country. They estimate that 28% of the population (approximately 545,000 households) are chronically food-insecure, notwithstanding ample cereal production and food stocks. A further 400,000 rural households, comprising commercial farm workers, communal farmers and unemployed suffer from transitory food insecurity. Moreover, household food insecurity has increased since independence, due to weak macroeconomic conditions, growing unemployment, ineffective land reform, and inappropriate government policy. The structural adjustment programme is predicted to worsen household food insecurity, as maize consumer prices increase. The effects of Zimbabwe's SAP, adopted in 1991, on wage-earners will be direct, through increased unemployment; however, the impact on the grain-deficit communal farm households will depend on the precise pace and sequencing of the grain market liberalization. The authors point to the need to target any safety-net provisions, for example to food-insecure families with children under five years of age or nursing mothers. This proved to protect children during an earlier period of social disruption, as well as during prolonged drought. Cross references include Morgan (1988) on safety nets and Ahmad *et al.* (1991) on social security more generally.

*Adjustment with a Human Face: Protecting the Vulnerable and Promoting Growth* edited by Cornia, Jolly and Stewart (1987), undoubtedly the most cited publication on structural adjustment, reviews the evidence of recession and adjustment on child welfare (Part 1) and formulates an alternative approach of 'growth-orientated adjustment with a human face'. The human face 'indicates the need for the human implications of an adjustment policy to be made an integral part of adjustment policy as a whole, not to be treated as an additional welfare component' (p. 2). Evidence of the deterioration in the conditions of children during the early 1980s is presented, focusing on food availability and access to education and health services (through case studies of Botswana, Ghana and Zimbabwe in SSA, as well as Latin America and Asia).

The authors emphasize the long-term developmental impact of short-term stabilization measures such as cuts in government health expenditure, reduction in real food subsidies and increases in food prices. In response to these measures, low-income households devise strategies to:

(i) generate resources, such as increasing the labour supply or self production, increasing indebtedness or reducing assets and attracting more private transfers;

(ii) improve the efficiency of resource use, e.g. changing habits in food purchase and preparation; changing consumption and dietary patterns and changing

the intra-household food distribution, e.g. reducing the food available to women and young girls;
(iii) changing the household composition and/or migration (e.g. to rural areas).

The growth-oriented approach would involve the following distinct policy elements: more expansionary macro policies; meso policies prioritizing vulnerable groups; sectoral policies to restructure the productive sector; efforts to increase the equity and efficiency of the social sector; and frequent monitoring of the vulnerable during adjustment. Part II spells out these elements in greater detail, including alternative macro and meso policies, targeted social policies e.g. towards small farmers, support for productive employment among vulnerable groups, and health, education and nutrition policies and programmes. The questions of monitoring and international measures are also discussed. Cross references include Stewart (1991a and b), Stewart *et al.* (1992) and Cornia *et al.* (1992), all discussed in this review.

Demery and Addison's theoretical article (1987) on the trade-offs between income-distributive and stabilization objectives is among the early publications which contributed to (and coincided with) an intellectual reorientation of donor views of adjustment policies – i.e. towards inclusion of targeted poverty alleviation measures. The authors focus on the principal instruments of stabilization policies, namely exchange-rate depreciation, monetary/credit control and fiscal restraint. They analyse the links between the instruments and income distribution in the context of the Salter-Swan adjustment theory and contrast its predictions with observed outcomes.

Theories of devaluation are contrasted with observed supply and aggregate demand responses; various hypotheses are formulated regarding the possible micro household impacts of devaluation. Similarly, the effects of monetary and fiscal restraint on aggregate output, the tradeable and non-tradeable sectors and the mechanisms of labour market adjustment are identified. Specific hypotheses are formulated for the micro-level impact. The authors conclude that the precise relationships are essentially 'an empirical question', but they note some of the implications for empirical research; system-wide methods complemented by in-depth studies at the community and household level. Cross references include various SDA papers providing empirical evidence as well as Cornia *et al.* (1987) and Stewart (1991a) reviewed above, and Stewart (1991b).

*Economic Reform and Poverty in The Gambia* by Jabara (1990) provides an in-depth account of the effects of the ERP using the longitudinal 'before-and-after' comparative method. The specific objectives of the research are to identify:

(i) the reasons for the apparent success of the ERP on macroeconomic variables; and
(ii) the impact of the ERP on production and saving incentives, the shift in favour of rural income opportunities, consumer price changes and the urban formal and rural labour market conditions.

The CFNPP monograph provides an extensive description of the initial conditions of employment and incomes, a poverty profile for the mid-1980s drawing on an IFPRI/PPMU rural expenditure study (and further partial accounts), and the pre-ERP policy environment.

Jabara identifies, on a detailed year-by-year basis, the exogenous influences which co-determined the economic outcome of the ERP, such as, for example, the movements of world groundnut prices, the variations in official financial inflows, the late or timely rains, the time of arrival of grant fertilizer, etc. (pp. 52–54). The author offers cautious optimism on the effects of the ERP on rural incomes, but is less sanguine about its effects on investment and efficiency in the agricultural sector. The shift in public expenditure away from investment and the declining expenditure on health and education services are further indicators of the need to assess the precise impact of the ERP. In particular, the consequences of the ERP for the urban (semi) informal groups and low-income rural groups are not sufficiently documented. The monograph therefore concludes by noting the need for further household-level surveys to assess the impact of the ERP on poverty. Cross references include Hadjimichael *et al.* (1992), focusing on macroeconomic changes post-1985 and Radelet (1992), identifying the specific circumstances facilitating the acceptance of the ERP.

Kakwani (1989) is one of a number of LSMS working papers which are highly relevant to the question of monitoring the status of households during adjustment. The paper is based on the unique Côte d'Ivoire database gathered during the period of adjustment and sharply falling *per capita* incomes. The author reviews various measures of poverty and income inequality (see also Foster *et al.*, 1984) and decomposes the change in poverty into two components: (i) the impact of growth on poverty, given a particular distribution of income and (ii) the effect of income redistribution when the total income of the society remains unchanged. The methodology is applied to 1985 data for Côte d'Ivoire, and is complemented by projected *per capita* growth rates during the adjustment. Kakwani estimates that total poverty can be expected to increase during the adjustment programme but he shows that targeting can reduce the growth of poverty. The targeting would need to be focused on households with an agricultural occupation, living in one particular region and with the age of the head of household exceeding 65. Cross references include other LSMS working papers, *inter alia*, Glewwe and de Tray (1988) on Côte d'Ivoire living standards, Glewwe and van der Gaag (1988) on informational requirements for poverty-reducing policies, Alessie *et al.* (1992) on labour supply decisions and Kanbur (1990) on the targeting problem, as well as Grootaert (1992) noting the need for big samples, frequently repeated surveys using a transparent methodology and a relatively short questionnaire.

Morgan (1988), subsequently included in Ahmad *et al.* (1991), analyses the scope for protection of vulnerable groups in SADCC states through targeted social welfare programmes. These include programmes to broaden access to primary health care, education, water supply, agricultural programmes for enhancing the productivity of the poor, food and income support programmes for vulnerable groups and consumer pricing and subsidies. The author addresses the question of the choice of welfare strategy in the context of the limited impact of existing programmes on vulnerable households. He concludes, drawing on case studies of Botswana and Mozambique, that prevention of crises requires:

(i) development of institutional capacity for the design, implementation and monitoring of targeted assistance programmes;

(ii) multi-sectoral strategies which inform macroeconomic decision-making;
(iii) routine training for the designers of emergency programmes;
(iv) an increased degree of community responsibility for the operation and maintenance of programmes;
(v) systematic tests of cost efficiency to ensure programme sustainability; and
(vi) cross-country exchange of experience in the design of the programmes.

*Fiscal and Exchange Rate Reforms in Africa* by David Sahn (1990a) is a prelude to the various country case studies undertaken (or ongoing) by the CFNPP, Washington, funded by the Africa Bureau of USAID. The study gives only stylized facts and its limited objective is to provide insights into how the changes in some key variables (exchange rates, public expenditures, food production, real food prices and real wages) have impacted on the poor of Africa during the 1980s. Sahn notes the problems of cross-country comparisons, in particular in view of differences in the:

(i) initial position in the starting year of the programme;
(ii) external and domestic circumstances during the adjustment programme;
(iii) policies adopted; and
(iv) pace and sequence of programme implementation.

Within these limitations he tackles three questions central in the adjustment debate:

(i) did countries receiving policy-based adjustment loans reduce (real) government expenditure?
(ii) did the composition of public expenditure move away from capital expenditure, jeopardizing long-run growth prospects? and
(iii) did public expenditure move away from the human development sectors, in particular health and education?

Sahn's answers to these three questions are all negative, though with important caveats and qualifications for the second and the third. Reduction in government expenditure, where observed, 'generally pre-dated the beginning of donor-financed adjustment programs' (p. xi). The shares of recurrent relative to capital expenditures increased sharply in only two countries and were somewhat higher in 14 out of 22 countries during the SAPs; real public spending on wages did not change from its 1981–83 level. As for the third question, *per capita* public expenditure on health and education declined, but 'at the margin a relatively larger share of government expenditures was allocated to health and education in 1985–87 than between 1974–84' (p. xii). Regarding the effects of reduced food subsidies, the author notes the negative nutritional consequences among the urban poor, but argues that the most vulnerable households in the rural areas never benefited from the urban-biased food subsidy system.

Sahn's monograph (and the related Sahn, 1991 and 1992) was a distinct departure from the emerging progressive consensus that SSA governments were being over-squeezed under adjustment, with detrimental social and long-term consequences (e.g. Cornia *et al.* (1987) and Stewart (1991a). His study cautions against large-scale compensatory programmes as long as the precise identification of low-income losers from the SAPs is incomplete, especially given the 'extensive managerial and financial resources and social infrastructure that would be required' for compensatory efforts (p. xv). The study has met with substantive methodological criticism noting, *inter alia*, the arbitrary choice of base year and the differing time periods used for comparisons. It is argued that the inadequate database for assessing the impacts of adjustment programmes (or the absence of it) on low-income urban and rural African households allows only very tentative conclusions.

*Policy Reform and Poverty in Malawi: A Survey of a Decade of Experience* by Sahn *et al.* (1990) provides a comprehensive profile of poverty in Malawi for different social groups, in particular smallholders, wage labourers, tenant farmers, the urban poor and female-headed households. The authors characterize the economic situation before the start of the SAP and trace the changes over time of indicators relating to agricultural input and output markets, the industrial and service sectors, external indicators (balance of payments, exports, external debts) and internal indicators (money supply, inflation, credit, interest rates and public financial balances).

Sahn *et al.* note that the Malawian Government did adopt and, to a considerable degree, implement the reformist policies of the various SAPs. The results have been disappointing: economic growth stagnated, aggregate supply responses were weak or absent and output growth in the non-traded service sector outpaced that of the traded sectors. Food security, technological change in agriculture and social indicators did not improve, while real wage levels fell and land pressures continued to increase. The study concludes that 'the structural impediments to growth . . . have not been effectively addressed through the policy reform process' (p. 217). Poverty prevailed among households in all economic sectors prior to adjustment and 'few, if any, aspects of the reform programme can be held responsible for the poverty problem or be persuasively argued to have worsened the income distribution' (p. 218). The study notes the importance of increasing both access to land and the control of assets by smallholders, including measures to halt estate expansion into customary lands, and of lifting crop-growing restrictions for smallholders, as a requisite to halting the aggravation of the poverty problem.

Other references regarding the social impact of adjustment include Addison and Demery (1987) on income distribution; African Development Bank/UNDP/WB (1990) on formulating a joint policy agenda; Ahmad *et al.* (1991) on social security; Alderman (1991) with detailed nutritional information about Ghana; Boateng *et al.* (1990) on Ghana; Bourguignon (1991), Bourguignon, de Melo and Suwa (1991) and Bourguignon, de Melo and Morrisson (1991) on the methods and results of the OECD Development Centre project; Dorosh *et al.* (1990) on the experience of Madagascar; Foster *et al.* (1984) on poverty measurement; Glewwe and de Tray (1988) and Glewwe and van der Gaag (1988) on some of the results of the LSMS project; Heller *et al.* (1988) on public deficits; Heyer (1991) on rural poverty in Kenya; Iliffe (1987) on the history of poverty in Africa; ILO (1988) on promoting informal sector opportunities; Lambert *et al.* (1991) on the OECD study for the Côte d'Ivoire; Palmer (1991) on gender and population; Platteau (1991) on economic anthropological aspects of the African food crisis; Roe (1990) on the effects of structural adjustment in Malawi; Sahn and Sarris (1991) on welfare effects of SAPs; and the World Bank (1990c, 1990d and 1991a).

# The Political Economy of Structural Adjustment

Ihonvbere's (1993) analysis of political responses to the economic adjustment process in Nigeria notes the widespead agreement among labour representatives, manufacturers associations, students, other popular organizations and the media that the SAPs are 'not leading to economic recovery' (p. 141). The author argues that the design of the programme paid no attention to 'initial conditions' in terms of the 'legitimacy of the government, . . . the depth of institutional decay, available resources and so on'. The article, which consists of political analysis based mainly on secondary sources, reviews the background to the restructuring and examines how Nigeria fared from economic emergency to structural adjustment, and the pains and costs of that adjustment, with a final section on desirable improvements in SAP design and implementation. It underlines the need for adjustment in Nigeria but calls for (i) better programme design by the World Bank and the IMF, recognizing the specific conditions of the country, (ii) a serious attempt to protect the vulnerable groups, and (iii) the need for 'opening up of democratic spaces' requiring the withdrawal of the military from the political scene. Cross references include Cornia et al. (1987) and ECA's AAF-SAP (1989).

*Aid and Power: The World Bank and Policy-based Lending* by Mosley, Harrigan and Toye (1991) constitutes the most comprehensive analysis of the political economy of the conditionality of policy-based structural adjustment lending to date. Volume 1 covers the analysis and policy recommendations, focusing on the process of bargaining which lies at the heart of policy-based lending; Volume 2 presents nine supporting country case studies, including three from Africa (Ghana, Malawi and Kenya). The objective in examining the bargaining process is to spell out the nature of trade-offs which may exist, given the multiple goals and objectives of both the lending and the borrowing parties.

Volume 1 covers (i) the origins and progress of structural adjustment lending since 1970, (ii) the dynamics of policy reform, and (iii) an assessment of its effectiveness. The main theoretical contribution is the attempt to analyse the character of the bargaining process between governments ('offering' policy reforms) and the World Bank, drawing on game-theoretical concepts to outline potential strategies for donors and recipients. Assessing the effectiveness of the SAPs raises the question of the appropriate method(s) of programme evaluation, comparing simple tabular methods, regression techniques and simulation models. The authors observe (pp. 301–2) that SAPs:

(i) were 'almost always favourable to export growth and the external account';
(ii) negatively influenced aggregate investment;
(iii) had a positive national income response but only after a lag for the implementation of the conditions, whereas the negative responses due to demand compression were felt immediately;
(iv) had a neutral impact on income distribution, reflecting positive effects from increased farm prices and negative effects from (i) the withdrawal of food subsidies, (ii) the reduction in public expenditure and (iii) price reforms.

Part IV of Volume 1 summarizes the arguments and offers policy proposals, intended to improve the design of SAPs through the modification of existing practices. Some of these may benefit donors, while others may benefit recipients. The former include:

(i)   shortening the list of key conditions, tailoring it to genuine distortions only; and

(ii)  consistency in implementing the threat of refusing refinance or disbursement of a second tranche or even refusing refinance at random.

Proposals of benefit to recipients include:

(iii)  particularly for least developed countries, conditionalities should incorporate 'positive' state interventions, e.g. for infant-industry protection, credit for low-income groups, expansion of infrastructure, etc. in addition to measures to remove harmful state interventions;

(iv)  introduction of policy changes on an experimental or pilot basis e.g. in one province, to allow policy reversals if the desired impact is not obtained;

(v)   empirical models used for assessing the possible impact of policy conditions should be lodged with recipient countries for further assessment and sensitivity analysis;

(vi)  improving the use of 'local' information and expertise in programme design;

(vii) use of independently prepared forecasts of world commodity prices;

(viii) extending the use of Policy Framework Papers to middle-income countries which are currently not receiving the IMF's SAF or ESAF credits, the purpose being to improve co-ordination between the IMF and the World Bank, and incorporating covenants protecting real governmental development expenditure;

(ix)  increasing the linkage between sectoral policy conditionality and the implementing agency through, *inter alia*, offering loans in kind.

Measures providing benefits to both donors and recipients include the offer of compensation in a non-distortive way to losers from policy-based reform programmes. Cross references to Mosley *et al.* include van der Geest (1994) on the bargaining process of structural adjustment lending and Martin in van der Geest (1994) on debt rescheduling negotiations, and the World Bank's own reviews of adjustment lending.

Radelet's analysis of reform in The Gambia (1992) asks why economic reform was postponed for so long, why such a radical change of policy did take place in 1985 and why, once initiated, the SAP met with so little public opposition. The lessons drawn from the political analysis, based on in-depth interviews with senior decision-makers, are partly general and partly specifically related to The Gambia. In general, major policy shifts can be brought about within a democratic framework, though the status of, and public confidence in, political leaders matters a great deal. Moreover, for The Gambia, the agro-climatic conditions were favourable in the early years of the SAP, the pro-rural orientation appealed to the large rural constituency of the governing party and opposition groups were carefully 'managed' through consultations. Cross references to Radelet's analysis include Hadjimichael *et al.* (1992) on The Gambia's economic performance under adjustment post-1985 and Jabara (1990) comparing indicators before and after the ERP.

Other related references on the political economy of structural adjustment include Bade (1991) for a critique of the external control of Africa through structural adjustment; Callaghy (1990) on the politics of adjustment; Drèze and Sen (1989) on the importance of public action and accountability; Drèze and Sen (1991) on the nature of the food crises in Africa; Haggard *et al.* (1992) and Nelson (1990) on the politics of the distributive effects of adjustment, and Toye (1992) on the agricultural interests of the political elites in Kenya and Malawi as an impediment to adjustment policies.

# The Long-Term Developmental Impact of Structural Adjustment

*Africa's Recovery in the 1990s: From Stagnation and Adjustment to Human Development* edited by Cornia *et al.* (1992) with further contributions from, *inter alia*, Stewart and Helleiner, is perhaps best characterized as a sequel to *Adjustment with a Human Face*. It consists of three parts: in the first part Jespersen provides a comprehensive and up-to-date overview of the crisis of the 1980s, the second part reviews and contrasts the adjustment experiences of Burkina Faso, Niger, Tanzania, Zambia and Zimbabwe, while the third part focuses on outlining alternative approaches for the 1990s and beyond.

The overview of the long-term development strategy identifies three theoretical and practical motives for its formulation: (i) the persistent failure to achieve modification in SSA's production and trade structures, (ii) the fragility of growth, and (iii) the persistent neglect of the human factor in adjustment and development programmes. The long-term development strategy for Sub-Saharan Africa identified smallholder agriculture and small-scale industry, with manifold forward and backward linkages, as the engine of growth. The justifications for this recommendation are that these farms and firms are characterized by:

(i) a more equitable distribution of earnings;
(ii) higher microeconomic efficiency in the use of resources and labour;
(iii) the ability to accelerate food production and food security;
(iv) the ability to reduce food import requirements;
(v) more comprehensive agriculture to non-agriculture linkages;
(vi) a less capital-intensive choice of techniques; and
(vii) a higher degree of technological self-reliance.

International measures to support Africa's long-term recovery would include debt write-offs, increased aid levels and commodity price agreements. Cross references to Cornia *et al.* include Haggblade *et al.* (1989) and Bagachwa and Stewart (1990) on farm-non-farm linkages, as well as Adelman and Vogel (1991) on the relevance of agricultural development-led industrialization for SSA.

McMahon (1990) looks at the long-term distributional effects of the removal of tariffs, using a computable general equilibrium (CGE) model in the context of the Kenyan economy. He outlines the income distribution analysis, using a disaggregation of sixteen income classes and focusing on agricultural households in different agro-ecological zones and with different production patterns. Model simulations assess the impact of both comprehensive and selective tariff reduction. The results indicate that:

(i) the overall welfare gains of a comprehensive tariff removal policy may be positive and significant, though less than the gains if tariffs were removed on intermediate goods only;
(ii) in a dual economy with a skewed income distribution, the income distributional effects may be regressive, as poorer groups tend to consume fewer imported goods;
(iii) the lags of the effects of the tariff removal, partly through trickle-down effects, may be in the order of ten years;
(iv) the precise distributional impact will depend, *inter alia*, on employment and labour market policies.

Stewart (1991b) examines the trade-off between long-term economic development and short-term adjustment, pointing out that demand contraction at an early stage of the SAP is primarily oriented towards increasing efficiency in the short run, rather than on long-term economic growth. She emphasizes the need for:

(i) a focus on the agricultural sector;
(ii) economic diversification;
(iii) participatory development and institution-building, and
(iv) a focus on long-term development.

In 1987 in Sub-Saharan Africa, agriculture produced 34% of the GDP, engaged 70% of the population but was allocated only 7% of government expenditures. This 'under-investment' is reflected in the stagnant output indicators of the sector. Policies for the agricultural sector include:

(i) land reform (see Ghai and Radwan, 1983);
(ii) increase of the investible resources for agriculture;
(iii) price reforms to improve the agricultural terms of trade, to redress the heavy focus on export-crop price reform and to correct a bias in the allocation of agricultural investment to facilitate non-agricultural linkages.

Industrialization and economic diversification did not advance in the 1980s; on the contrary, considerable de-industrialization took place in SSA. The experience has been dubious: inefficient industries were set up and subsequently failed to produce for export markets. Neither multinationals nor joint ventures were successful, as case studies of Côte d'Ivoire and Tanzania show. Capacity utilization is low and there is a lack of transfer of skills and training of indigenous managerial capacity. Policy advice suffers from an 'aggregation mistake' with respect to the earning potential for primary commodities, especially as no efforts are undertaken to co-ordinate countries' experiences with SAPs.

Human capabilities tend to be perceived as an end of, rather than a means to, economic development. The social returns of programmes for women, for example, tend to be very high, particularly as they have important indirect productive effects through family health. Similarly, participation and institutional development are inputs to the development process. Low rates of political participation are observed all over Africa. Studies indicate the importance of 'participation' as a precondition for equitable, rather than overall, growth. References related to Stewart's discussion of the long-term development implications of structural adjustment include Ghai and Radwan (1983) on land reform in Africa; Cornia and Stewart (1990) on public deficits; ECA (1989) on African Alternatives; Mosley and Weeks (1992) on Africa's recovery and Stewart *et al.* (1992) on the alternative development strategies for Africa, setting out the major elements of a long-run development strategy.

## Bibliography

Adam, C., Cavendish, W. and Mistry, P. S. (1992) *Adjusting Privatization: Case Studies from Seven Developing Countries*, London: James Currey.

Addison, T., and Demery, L. (1987) *The Alleviation of Poverty Under Structural Adjustment*, Washington DC: World Bank.

Adelman, I. and Vogel, S. J. (1991) *The Relevance of ADLI for Sub-Saharan Africa*, Giannini Foundation Hall Working Paper No. 590, University of California at Berkeley, CA.

African Development Bank, UNDP and World Bank (1990) *The Social Dimensions of Adjustment in Africa: A Policy Agenda*, Washington DC: World Bank.

Afshar, H. and Dennis, C. (eds) (1992) *Women and Adjustment Policies in the Third World*, Basingstoke: Macmillan.

Ahmad, E. S., Drèze, J. Hills, J. and Sen, A. (eds) (1991) *Social Security in Developing Countries*, WIDER Studies in Development Economics, Oxford: Clarendon Press.

Alderman, H. (1991) *Downturn and Economic Recovery in Ghana: Impacts on the Poor*, Cornell Food and Nutrition Policy Program Monograph No. 10, Ithaca, NY: Cornell University.

Alessie, R., Baker, P., Blundell, R., Heady, C. and Maghir, C. (1992) 'The Work Behaviour of Young People in Rural Côte d'Ivoire', *World Bank Economic Review* 6 (1), 139–54.

Amani, H. K. R., van den Brink, R. and Maro, W. E. (1992) 'Tolerating the Private Sector: Grain Trade in Tanzania after Adjustment', Cornell Food and Nutrition Policy Program (draft), Ithaca, NY: Cornell University.

Bade, O. (1991) *A Future For Africa: Beyond the Politics of Adjustment*, London: Earthscan for the Institute for African Alternatives.

Bagachwa, M. S. D. and Stewart, F. (1990) *Rural Industries and Rural Linkages in Sub-Saharan Africa: A Survey*, L.d'Agliano-QEH Development Studies Working Paper No. 23. Turin: Luca d'Agliano.

Benjamin, N. C. (1992) 'What Happens to Investment under Structural Adjustment: Results from a Simulation Model', *World Development* 20 (11), 1335–44.

Bevan, D., Collier, P. and Gunning, J. W. (with A. Bigsten and P. Horsnell) (1989) *Peasants and Governments: An Economic Analysis*, Oxford: Clarendon Press.

Bevan, D., Collier, P. and Gunning, J. W. (with A. Bigsten and P. Horsnell) (1990) *Controlled Open Economies: A Neoclassical Approach to Structuralism*, Oxford: Clarendon Press.

Bigsten, A. and Nddung'u, N. S. (1992), 'The Impact of Structural Adjustment on Smallholders and the Rural Poor' in Duncan and Howell.

Bigsten, A. and Kayizzi-Mugerwa, S. (1991) 'Rural Sector Responses to Economic Crisis: A Study of Masaka District in Uganda', mimeo, Department of Economics, University of Gothenburg, Sweden.

Bigsten, A. and Kayizzi-Mugerwa, S. (1992) 'Adaptation and Distress in the Urban Economy: A Study of Kampala Households', *World Development* 20 (10), 1423–41.

Bloomfield, E. M. and Lass, R. A. (1992) *Impact of Structural Adjustment and Adoption of Technology on Competitiveness of Major Cocoa Producing Countries*, OECD Development Centre Working Paper No. 69, Paris: OECD Development Centre.

Boateng, E. O., Ewusi, K. Kanbur, R. and McKay, A. (1990) *A Poverty Profile for Ghana, 1987–88*, Social Dimension of Adjustment Working Paper No. 5, Washington DC: World Bank.

Booth, D. (1991) 'Timing and Sequencing of Agricultural Policy Reform, Tanzania', *Development Policy Review* 9 (4), 353–79.

Bourguignon, F. (1991) 'Optimal Poverty Reduction, Adjustment and Growth', *World Bank Economic Review* 5 (2), 315–38.

Bourguignon, F., Branson, W. H. and de Melo, J. (1989) *Macroeconomic Adjustment and Income*

*Distribution: A Macro-Micro Simulation Model*, OECD Development Centre Technical Paper No. 1, Paris: OECD Development Centre.

Bourguignon, F., de Melo, J. and Morrisson, C. (1991) 'Poverty and Income Distribution during Adjustment: Issues and Evidence from the OECD Project', *World Development* 19 (11), 1485–1509.

Bourguignon, F., de Melo, J. and Suwa, A. (1991) *Distributional Effects of Adjustment Policies: Simulations for Two Archetype Economies*, World Bank Policy Research and External Affairs Working Paper No. 674, Washington DC: World Bank.

Bourguignon, F. and Morrisson, C. (1991) *External Trade and Income Distribution*, Paris: OECD Development Centre.

Bourguignon, F. and Morrisson, C. (1992) *Adjustment and Equity in Developing Countries: A New Approach*, Paris: OECD Development Centre.

Callaghy, T. M. (1990) 'Lost Between State and Market: The Politics of Adjustment in Ghana, Zambia and Nigeria', in Nelson.

Campbell, B. and Loxley, J. (1989) *Structural Adjustment in Africa*, Basingstoke: Macmillan.

Cassen, R. (1994) 'Structural Adjustment in Africa', in van der Geest.

Cheru, F. (1992) 'Structural Adjustment, Primary Resource Trade and Sustainable Development in Sub-Saharan Africa', *World Development* 20 (4) 497–512.

Chhibber, A. (1992) 'Exchange Reforms, Supply Response, and Inflation in Africa', in Goldin and Winters.

Chhibber, A. and Fischer, S. (eds) (1991) *Economic Reform in Sub-Saharan Africa: A Symposium*, Washington DC: World Bank.

Chhibber, A. and Shafik, N. (1990) *Exchange Reform, Parallel Markets and Inflation in Africa: The Case of Ghana*, World Bank Policy Research Working Paper No. 427, Washington DC: World Bank.

Christensen, G. and Stack, J. (1992) *The Dimensions of Household Food Insecurity in Zimbabwe, 1980–1991*, Food Studies Group Working Paper No. 5, University of Oxford.

Collier, P. and Gunning, J. W. (1991) 'The Liberalization of Price Controls: Theory and an Application to Tanzania' in Chhibber and Fischer.

Collier, P. and Gunning, J. W. (1992) 'Aid and Exchange Rate Adjustment in African Trade Liberalizations', *Economic Journal* 102.

Commander, S. (ed.) (1989), *Structural Adjustment and Agriculture: Theory and Practice in Africa and Latin America*, London: James Currey for the Overseas Development Institute.

Corbo, V., Goldstein, M. and Khan, M. S. (1987) *Growth Oriented Adjustment Programmes*, Washington DC: World Bank and IMF.

Cornia, G. A., Jolly, R. and Stewart, F. (eds) (1987) *Adjustment with a Human Face: Protecting the Vulnerable and Promoting Growth*, Oxford; Clarendon Press.

Cornia, G. A. and Strickland, R. (1990) *Rural Differentiation, Poverty and Agricultural Crisis in Sub-Saharan Africa: Towards an Appropriate Policy Response*. UNICEF, International Child Development Centre, Innocenti Occasional Paper No. 4, Florence: Spedale degli Innocenti.

Cornia, G. A. and Stewart, F. (1990) *The Fiscal System, Adjustment and the Poor*, UNICEF, International Child Development Centre, Innocenti Occasional Paper No. 11, Florence: Spedale degli Innocenti.

Cornia, G. A., van der Hoeven, R. and Mkandawire, P. (1992) *Africa's Recovery in the 1990s: From Stagnation and Adjustment to Human Development*, Basingstoke: Macmillan.

Davies, R., Sanders, D. and Shaw, T. (1991) *Zimbabwe's Adjustment Without the Fund*, UNICEF, International Child Development Centre, Innocenti Occasional Paper No. 16, Florence: Spedale degli Innocenti.

Delaine, G. (1992) *The Social Dimensions of Adjustment Integrated Survey: a Survey to Measure Poverty and Understand the Effects of Policy Changes on Households*, Social Dimensions of Adjustment in Sub-Saharan Africa Working Paper No. 14, Washington DC: World Bank.

Demery, L. and Addison, T. (1987) 'Stabilization Policy and Income Distribution in Developing Countries', *World Development* 15 (12), 1483–98.

Devarajan, S. and de Melo, J. (1987) 'Adjustment With A Fixed Exchange Rate: Cameroon, Côte d'Ivoire and Senegal', *World Bank Economic Review* 1 (3), 447–87.

Devarajan, S. and Rodrik, D. (1992) 'Do the Benefits of Fixed Exchange Rates Outweigh Their Costs? The CFA Zone in Africa' in Goldin and Winters.

Diop, F., Hill, K. and Serageldin, I. (1991) *Economic Crisis, Structural Adjustment and Health in Africa*, World Bank Working Paper No. 766, Washington DC: World Bank.

Dornbusch, R. (1982) 'Stabilization Policies in Developing Countries: What Have We Learned', *World Development* 10 (9), 701–8.

Dorosh, P. A., Bernier, R. E. and Sarris, A. (1990) *Macroeconomic Adjustment and the Poor: The*

*Case of Madagascar*, Cornell Food and Nutrition Policy Program Monograph No. 9, Ithaca, NY: Cornell University.

Drèze, J. and Sen, A. (1989) *Hunger and Public Action*, WIDER Studies in Development Economics, Oxford: Clarendon Press.

Drèze, J. and Sen, A. (eds) (1991) *The Political Economy of Hunger*, WIDER Studies in Development Economics, Vols. I, II and III, Oxford: Clarendon Press.

Duncan, A. and Howell, J. (eds) (1992) *Structural Adjustment and the African Farmer*, London: James Currey for the Overseas Development Institute.

Due, J.M. (1991) 'Policies to Overcome the Negative Effects of Structural Adjustment Programs on African Female-Headed Households', in Gladwin.

Economic Commission for Africa (1989) *African Alternative Framework to Structural Adjustment Programmes for Socio-economic Recovery and Transformation* (AAF-SAP), E/ECA/CM.15/6/Rev. 3, Addis Ababa: ECA.

Edwards, S. (1992) *Sequencing and Welfare: Labor markets and Agriculture*, National Bureau of Economic Research Working Paper No. 4095, Cambridge, MA: NBER.

Evans, D., Goldin I. and van der Mensbrugghe, D. (1992) 'Trade Reform and the Small Country Assumption' in Goldin and Winters.

Faini, R., de Melo, J. Senhadji, J. and Stanton, J. (1991) 'Growth-Oriented Adjustment Programs: A Statistical Analysis', *World Development* 19 (8), 957–67.

Ferreira, F. (1992) *The World Bank and the Study of Stabilization and Structural Adjustment in LDCs*, Development Economic Research Centre/Suntory-Toyota Working Paper No. 41, London: London School of Economics.

Fontaine, J.M. and Sindzingre, A. (1991) *Macro-Micro Linkages: Structural Adjustment and Fertilizer Policy in Sub-Saharan Africa*, OECD Development Centre Working Paper No. 49, Paris: OECD Development Centre.

Foster, J., Greer, J. and Thorbecke, E. (1984) 'A Class of Decomposable Poverty Measures', *Econometrica* 52 (3), 761–6.

Geest, W. van der (1991) *Food Security: The Cereal Market Policy Model*, Food Studies Group Working Paper No. 3, University of Oxford.

Geest, W. van der (ed.) (1992) *Trade Diversification in the Least Developed Countries*, UNCTAD/LDC/GE/2, Geneva: UNCTAD.

Geest, W. van der (ed.) (1994) *Negotiating Structural Adjustment in Africa*, London: James Currey.

Gersovitz, M. (1991) *Agricultural Pricing Systems and Transportation Policy in Africa*, World Bank Working Paper No. 774, Washington DC: World Bank.

Ghai, D. (ed.) (1990) *The IMF and the South: Social Impact of Crisis and Adjustment*, London: Zed Books Ltd.

Ghai, D. (1992) *Structural Adjustment, Global Integration and Social Democracy*, United Nations Research Institute for Social Development Discussion Paper No. 37, Geneva.

Ghai, D. and Radwan, S. (1983) *Agrarian Policies and Rural Poverty in Africa*, Geneva: ILO.

Gladwin, C.H. (ed.) (1991) *Structural Adjustment and African Women Farmers*, Gainesville, FL: University of Florida, Centre for African Studies.

Glewwe, P. and de Tray, D. (1988) *The Poor during Adjustment: A Case Study of Côte d'Ivoire*, LSMS Working Paper No. 47, Washington DC: World Bank.

Glewwe, P. and van der Gaag, J. (1988) *Confronting Poverty in Developing Countries: Definitions, Information and Policies*, LSMS Working Paper No. 48, Washington DC: World Bank.

Goldin I., and Winters, L.A. (1992) *Open Economies: Structural Adjustment and Agriculture*, Cambridge: Cambridge University Press.

Grootaert, C. (1992) *How Useful are Integrated Household Surveys for Policy-Oriented Analyses of Poverty*, World Bank Discussion Paper No. 1079, Washington DC: World Bank.

Hadjimichael, M.T., Rumbaugh, T. and Verreydt, E. (1992) *The Gambia: Economic Adjustment in a Small Open Economy*, International Monetary Fund Occasional Paper No. 100, Washington DC: IMF.

Haggard, S., Kaufman, R.R. and Evans, P. (eds) (1992) *The Politics of Economic Adjustment: International Constraints, Distributive Conflicts and the State*, Princeton, NJ: Princeton University Press.

Haggblade, S, Hazell, P. and Brown, J. (1989) 'Farm-Nonfarm Linkages in Rural Sub-Saharan Africa', *World Development* 17 (8), 1173–1201.

Heller, P.S., Lans Bovenberg, A., Catsambas, T., Chu, K.Y. and Shome, P. (1988) *The Implications of Fund Supported Adjustment Programs for Poverty: Experiences in Selected Countries*, International Monetary Fund Occasional Paper No. 58, Washington DC: IMF.

Henstridge, M. (1994) 'Stabilization and Structural Adjustment Policy in Uganda: 1987-1990', in van der Geest.

Heyer, J. (1991) 'Poverty and Food Deprivation in Kenya's Smallholder Agricultural Areas', in Drèze and Sen.

Ihonvbere, J. O. (1993) 'Economic Crisis, Structural Adjustment and Social Crisis in Nigeria', World Development, 21 (1), 141-53.

Iliffe, J. (1987) The African Poor: A History, Cambridge: Cambridge University Press.

International Labour Organization (1988) Employment Promotion in the Informal Sector in Africa, Addis Ababa: ILO Jobs and Skills Programme for Africa.

Jabara, C. L. (1990) Economic Reform and Poverty in The Gambia, Cornell Food and Nutrition Policy Program Monograph No. 6, Ithaca, NY: Cornell University.

Jabara, C. L. (1991) Structural Adjustment and Stabilization in Niger: Macroeconomic Consequences and Social Adjustment, Cornell Food and Nutrition Policy Program Monograph No. 11, Ithaca, NY: Cornell University.

Jaeger, W. K. (1991) The Impact of Policy in African Agriculture: An Empirical Investigation, World Bank Working Paper No. 640, Washington DC: World Bank.

Jaeger, W. K. (1992) The Effects of Economic Policies on African Agriculture, World Bank Discussion Paper No. 147, Washington DC: World Bank.

Jaeger, W. K. and Humphreys, C. (1988) 'The Effects of Policy Reforms on Agricultural Incentives in Sub-Saharan Africa', American Journal of Agricultural Economics.

Janvry, A. de, Fargeix, D. and Sadoulet, E. (1989) Economic, Welfare and Political Consequences of Stabilization Policies: A General Equilibrium Approach, Giannini Foundation Hall, University of California at Berkeley, CA.

Kakwani, N. (1989) Poverty and Economic Growth with Applications to Côte d'Ivoire, LSMS Working Paper No. 63, Washington DC: World Bank.

Kanbur, R. (1990) Poverty and the Social Dimensions of Structural Adjustment in Côte d'Ivoire, Social Dimensions of Adjustment Working Paper No. 2, Washington DC: World Bank.

Kapur, I., Hadjimichael, M. T., Hilbers, P., Schiff, J. and Szymczak, P. (1991) Ghana: Adjustment and Growth, International Monetary Fund Occasional Paper No. 86, Washington DC: IMF.

Koester, U., Schafer, H. and Valdez, A. (1990) Demand-side Constraints and Structural Adjustment in Sub-Saharan Africa, Washington DC: International Food Policy Research Institute.

Komlev, L. (1992) 'Trade Diversification in Niger: Constraints and Prospects', in van der Geest.

Lambert, S., Schneider, H., and Suwa. A. (1991) 'Adjustment and Equity in Côte d'Ivoire: 1980-86', World Development, 19 (11), 1563-76.

Lele, U. and Meyers, L. R. (1989) Growth and Structural Change in East Africa: Domestic Policies, Agricultural Performance and World Bank Assistance, 1983-86, Managing Agricultural Development in Africa (MADIA) Discussion Paper No. 3, Washington DC: World Bank.

Levine, R. and Renelt, D. (1991) Cross-Country Studies of Growth and Policy: Methodological, Conceptual and Statistical Problems, World Bank Working Paper No. 608, Washington DC.

López, R., Ali, R. and Larsen, B. (1991) How Trade and Economic Policies Affect Agriculture: A Framework for Analysis applied to Tanzania and Malawi, World Bank Working Paper No. 719, Washington DC: World Bank.

López, R. E. and Thomas, V. (1990) 'Import Dependency and Structural Adjustment in Sub Saharan Africa', World Bank Economic Review, 4 (2), 195-207.

Loxley, J. (1989) 'The Devaluation Debate in Tanzania' in Campbell and Loxley.

Lundahl, M. (1989) Incentives and Agriculture in East Africa, Basingstoke: Macmillan.

Lundahl, M. and Ndulu, B. J. (1985) 'Market Related Incentives and Food Production in Tanzania: Theory and Experience', (mimeo), University of Lund.

Martin, M. (1994) 'Negotiating External Finance for Adjustment' in van der Geest.

McMahon, G. (1990) 'Tariff Policy, Income Distribution, and Long-Run Structural Adjustment in a Dual Economy: A Numerical Analysis', Journal of Public Economics 42, 105-23.

Migot-Adholla, S., Hazell, P., Blaral, B. and Place, F. (1991) 'Indigenous Land Right Systems in Sub-Saharan Africa: A Constraint on Productivity?', World Bank Economic Review 5 (1), 155-75.

Morgan, R. (1988) Social Welfare Programmes and the Reduction of Household Vulnerability in the SADCC States of Southern Africa, Suntory-Toyota/ Development Economics Research Programme Working Paper No. 25, London: London School of Economics.

Mosley, P. (1992) 'Policy-Making Without Facts: A Note on the Assessment of Structural Adjustment Policies in Nigeria, 1985-1990', African Affairs 91, 227-40.

Mosley, P., Harrigan, J. and Toye, J. (1991) Aid and Power: The World Bank and Policy-based Lending, Vols. 1 and 2, London: Routledge.

Mosley, P. and Weeks, J. (1992) 'Has Recovery begun? Africa's Adjustment in the 1990s Revisited', Annual Conference of Development Studies Association, University of Reading.

Nashashibi, K., Gupta, S., Liuksila, C., Lorie, H. and Mahler, W. (1992) *The Fiscal Dimensions of Adjustment in Low-Income Countries*, International Monetary Fund Occasional Papers No. 95, Washington DC: IMF.

Ndulu, B.J. (1991) 'Growth and Adjustment in Sub-Saharan Africa', in Chhibber and Fischer.

Ndulu, B.J. and Hyuha, M. (1986) 'Inflation and Economic Recovery in Tanzania: Some Empirical Evidence', mimeo, University of Dar-es-Salaam.

Nelson, J. (ed.) (1990) *Economic Crisis and Policy Choice: The Politics of Adjustment in the Third World*, Princeton, NJ: Princeton University Press for Overseas Development Council.

Nunberg, B. (1990) *Public Sector Management Issues in Structural Adjustment Lending*, World Bank Working Paper Series, Washington DC: World Bank.

Palmer, I. (1991) *Gender and Population in the Adjustment of African Economies: Planning for Change*, Series Women, Work and Development No. 19, Geneva: ILO.

Patel, I.G. (ed.) (1992) *Policies for African Development from 1980s to the 1990s*, Washington DC: International Monetary Fund.

Pearce, R. (1991) *Food Consumption and Adjustment in Zambia*, Food Studies Group Working Paper No. 2, University of Oxford and in van der Geest (1994)

Pinto, B. (1988) *Black Market Premia, Exchange Rate Unification and Inflation in Sub-Saharan Africa*, World Bank Working Paper No. 37, Washington DC: World Bank.

Platteau, J. (1991) 'The Food Crisis in Africa: A Comparative Structural Analysis', in Drèze and Sen.

Please, S. (1984) *The Hobbled Giant: Essays on the World Bank*, Boulder, CO: Westview Press.

Please, S. (1992) 'Beyond Structural Adjustment in Africa', *Development Policy Review* 10 (3), 289–307.

Putterman, L. (1990) 'Village Communities, Cooperation and Inequality in Tanzania: Comments on Collier *et al.*', *World Development* 18 (1), 147–53.

Pyatt, G., Roe, A. and Schneider, H. (1991) *Adjustment and Equity in Ghana*, Paris: OECD Development Centre.

Radelet, S. (1992) 'Reform without Revolt: The Political Economy of Economic Reform in The Gambia', *World Development* 20 (8), 1087–99.

Roe, A.R. (ed.) (1992) *Instruments of Economic Policy in Africa*, London: James Currey.

Roe, G. (1990) 'The Effects of the Structural Adjustment Programme in Malawi', Report of the Workshop, Centre for Social Research, University of Malawi, Zomba.

Sahn, D.E. (1990a) *Fiscal and Exchange Rate Reforms in Africa: Considering the Impact on the Poor*, Cornell Food and Nutrition Policy Program Monograph No. 4, Ithaca, NY; Cornell University.

Sahn, D.E. (1990b) *Malnutrition in Côte d'Ivoire: Prevalence and Determinants*, Social Dimensions of Adjustment in Sub-Saharan Africa Working Paper No. 4, Washington DC: World Bank.

Sahn, D.E. (1991) 'Has Policy Reform Hurt the Poor in Africa?' (mimeo), USAID Bureau for Africa, Special Programme of Assistance Meeting, Washington DC.

Sahn, D.E. (1992) 'Public Expenditures in Sub-Saharan Africa during a Period of Reform', *World Development* 20 (5), 673–93.

Sahn, D.E., Arulpragasam, J. and Merid, L. (1990) *Policy Reform and Poverty in Malawi: A Survey of a Decade of Experience*, Cornell Food and Nutrition Policy Program Monograph No. 7, Ithaca, NY: Cornell University.

Sahn, D.E. and Sarris, A. (1991) 'Structural Adjustment and the Welfare of Rural Smallholders: A Comparative Analysis from Sub-Saharan Africa', *World Bank Economic Review* 5 (2), 259–89.

Sarris, A. (1987) *Agricultural Stabilization and Structural Adjustment Policies in Developing Countries*, Policy Analysis Division Technical Paper, Rome: FAO.

Sarris, A. (1990a) *Guidelines for Monitoring, the Impact of Structural Adjustment Programmes on the Agricultural Sector*, Economic and Social Division Technical Paper No. 95, Rome: FAO.

Sarris, A. (1990b) *A Macro-Micro Framework for Analysis of the Impact of Structural Adjustment on the Poor in Sub-Saharan Africa*, Cornell Food and Nutrition Program Monograph No. 5, Ithaca, NY: Cornell University.

Sarris, A. (1991) *Ghana under Structural Adjustment: The Impact on Agriculture and the Rural Poor*, Studies in Rural Poverty No. 2, New York: New York University Press for IFAD.

Savadogo, K. and Wetta, C. (1991) *The Impact of Self-Imposed Adjustment: The Case of Burkino Faso, 1983–1989*, UNICEF, International Child Development Centre, Innocenti Occasional Paper No. 16, Florence: Spedali degli Innocenti.

Scobie, G.M. (1989) *Macroeconomic Adjustment and the Poor: Towards a Research Policy*, Cornell Food and Nutrition Policy Program Monograph No. 1, Ithaca, NY: Cornell University.

Smith, L. and Spooner, N. J. (1990) *Sequencing of Structural Adjustment Policy Instruments in the Agricultural Sector*, CDS Occasional Paper No. 6, Centre for Development Studies, University of Glasgow.

Stewart, F. (1991a) 'The Many Faces of Adjustment', *World Development* 19 (11).

Stewart, F. (1991b) 'Are Adjustment Policies in Africa Consistent with Long-Run Development Needs?', *Development Policy Review* 9 (4), 413–36.

Stewart, F., Lall, S. and Wangwe, S. (eds) (1992) *Alternative Development Strategies in Sub-Saharan Africa*, Basingstoke: Macmillan.

Tarp, F. (1993) *Stabilization and Structural Adjustment: A Macroeconomic Framework for Analysing the Crisis in Sub-Saharan Africa*, London and New York: Routledge.

Taylor, L. (1988) *Varieties of Stabilization Experiences: Towards Sensible Macroeconomics in the Third World*, Oxford: Clarendon Press.

Taylor, L. (1992) *Socially Relevant Policy Analysis: Structuralist Computable General Equilibrium Models for the Developing World*, Cambridge: Cambridge University Press.

Toye, J. (1992) 'Interest Group Politics and the Implementation of Adjustment Policies in Sub-Saharan Africa', *Journal of International Development* 4 (2), 183–97.

White, H. (1992) *The Impact of Structural Adjustment Policies on Private Investment*, Institute of Social Studies Working Paper, The Hague: Institute of Social Studies.

Whitehead, A. (1991) 'Rural Women and Food Production in Sub-Saharan Africa', in Drèze and Sen.

World Bank (1986) *Structural Adjustment Lending: A First Review of Experience*, Report No. 6409, Washington DC: World Bank, Operations Evaluation Department.

World Bank (1988) *Report on Adjustment Lending*, Document R88–199, Washington DC: World Bank, Country Economics Department.

World Bank (1989) *Sub-Saharan Africa: From Crisis to Sustainable Growth: A Long Term Perspective Study*, Washington DC: World Bank.

World Bank (1990a) *Report on Adjustment Lending II: Policies for the Recovery of Growth*, Document R90–99, Washington DC: World Bank.

World Bank (1990b) *Adjustment Lending Policies for Sustainable Growth*, Washington DC: World Bank, Country Economics Department.

World Bank (1990c) *World Development Report 1990*, New York: Oxford University Press for World Bank.

World Bank (1990d) *Making Adjustment Work for the Poor*, Washington DC: World Bank.

World Bank (1991a) *Structural Adjustment and the Poor*, Social Dimensions of Adjustment Working Paper, Washington DC: World Bank.

World Bank (1991b) *Economic Performance and Effectiveness of Bank Supported Adjustment Programs in Sub-Saharan Africa*, Washington DC: World Bank.

World Bank (1992) *Third Report on Adjustment Lending*, Washington DC: World Bank.

# APPENDIX 2

# A Review of Research Literature on Industry in Sub-Saharan Africa under Structural Adjustment
# PETER DE VALK

## Introduction

This paper will survey the literature on the impact of structural adjustment policies on the manufacturing sector in Sub-Saharan African countries. Structural adjustment programmes have dominated the economic policies of the 1980s in most African countries. Industry, and in particular manufacturing, has been seriously affected by the direct and indirect, intended and unintended, effects of these policies. Yet, apart from the general policies of trade liberalization and privatization, the development of explicit and coherent industrial policies has received little attention in the structural adjustment programmes, which were mainly focused on macroeconomic balances, the supply reaction of agriculture, and, of late, the social dimensions of adjustment (Ravenhill, 1988; Rodrik, 1992; Stein, 1992). Indeed, it seems justified to talk of the manufacturing sector as 'a forgotten dimension' in African development (Riddell, 1990a). The industrial sector is merely expected to adjust to the increased competition in the liberalized markets.

In the mid-1980s several technical studies were carried out which showed the static inefficiencies of many firms (applying the domestic resource cost criterion). Subsequent structural adjustment policies directly and negatively affected the industrial sector through trade liberalization, massive devaluation, and restrictive monetary policies, thereby exposing the degree of inefficiency. Costs of imported inputs and servicing of foreign loans shot up in line with devaluation. Liberalization of trade increased competition and suppressed the ability of firms to pass on their increased costs to the consumer. Tight monetary policies did not allow even the potentially viable firms to buy time for adjustment through increased borrowing from domestic banks. Later in the 1980s, the policy of privatization of public enterprises, which were now exposed, gained momentum. In the meantime, sub-sectoral restructuring plans (including rehabilitation) were formulated for many sub-sectors in various countries. Indirectly, structural adjustment policies have affected workers' morale through lower real wages, while reduced efforts in the provision of (technical) education and health will have far-reaching long-term consequences. Thus, while one cannot say that the industrial sector was off the agenda, the theme of its long-term development certainly was.

Research efforts in this crucial period were limited. Meier and Steel (1989) provide a collection of papers discussing a broad range of issues and cases in African industrial development and adjustment in the 1970s and early 1980s. Various writers have stressed the paucity of research as well as the need for more research on the impact of structural adjustment on industry in Africa (Mkandawire, 1988; Pack, 1988; Helleiner, 1990; Stein, 1992). This observation applies equally to firm-level and sector-wide performance with respect to the structural adjustment policies of trade liberalization and devaluation, and to the experience with privatization.

Small-scale enterprises, which are looked upon as having grown up without government support or even despite government regulation, are given much more positive attention by the World Bank (Webster, 1990). Moreover, research on various aspects of small-scale industries is more widely available.

Alternative policy approaches take a long-term view, realizing that there are no short cuts: industrial capability must be built up, including the physical and institutional support structure, the development of indigenous technological, managerial, and entrepreneurial capability, regional linkages, and appropriate macro and sectoral policies, including a moderate degree of (selective) protection and, where possible, an export orientation in particular market niches.[1] Entrepreneurs from successful ethnic minorities could play a role in local industrial development but governments generally regard them as antagonistic to national interests. Foreign investment is not seen as a viable route towards development since, in the first place, little is forthcoming (Ravenhill, 1988) and in the second place, little transfer of the various manufacturing capabilities takes place even in the case of joint ventures (Navaretti, 1992). Programmes linking local to foreign firms are quoted as means of supplying technology, markets, and information (Egan and Mody, 1992; Frenz, 1990). Small-enterprise development is viewed by many (including the World Bank) as part of the answer (Levy, 1990; Liedholm, 1992; Helmsing and Kolstee, 1993) but their potential for growing into larger firms is limited (van Donge, 1992).

To various degrees, all these approaches, including structural adjustment itself, beg the question to what extent the state is willing and capable of designing and implementing these policies. Privatization, for example, meets with only half-hearted implementation and even outright resistance (Adam et al., 1992; de Valk, 1992). Export development along the lines of the Asian NICs presupposes, inter alia, a state and a political economy in general that does not exist in Africa.

The following pages will discuss first the impact of structural adjustment policies on large-scale, and second the impact on small-scale industry. Third, the findings on the policy of privatization are reviewed. Fourth, some of the alternative proposals are summarized. Lastly, the final section draws some lessons about the gaps in published research on the impact of structural adjustment on industry in Africa, the political feasibility or requirements of the alternatives, and their time horizon.

# Large and Medium-scale Industry

Mkandawire (1988) traces the history of industrialization in Africa since 1914 over three major periods defined by important changes in the international division of labour, and argues that Africa is not able to capture the opportunities that arise from those changes. During the last period analysed, that of debt-financed industrialization (1973–82), the African industrial sectors also failed to grow strong enough to benefit from international trade as the NICs have done through a policy of export-oriented growth. 'Africa simply had no industrial products to export' (*ibid.*: 22).[2] This observation has important consequences for the export supply reaction of industry under more neutral (or even export-biased) trade policies.[3] Stein (1992) picks up from there with his analysis and criticism of the World Bank/IMF model and its implications for industrialization, arguing that this will lead to de-industrialization because it misses the underlying structural features and reveals internal inconsistencies (restrictive monetary policies in the face of the higher cost of production; difficulties of small enterprises in obtaining foreign exchange and credit). While acknowledging that 'there are problems with the structure of industry in Africa, hoping the market will solve the difficulties is no substitute for developing an industrial policy' (Mkandawire, 1988: 94).

Country-by-country assessments of industry under structural adjustment have been made by Riddell (1990a; 1990c; 1992),[4] and UNIDO (1989). According to Riddell (1990a) the 1980s saw a general slowdown in all seven countries surveyed compared to the quite favourable growth from 1965 to 1980, although with substantial individual variations.[5] The most important factor explaining growth in all these countries has been the expansion of domestic demand, in other words, 'the existence of an environment conducive to steady expansive growth outside the sector itself' (*ibid*: 11).[6] Country-specific factors responsible for this variation include the type and quality of management, engineering skills, (in)adequacy of infrastructure and of planning, the degree of political interference, and the degree to which industrialization was pushed beyond the level compatible with human resource endowments and the domestic market. Structural adjustment policies have depressed manufacturing even further. Riddell confirms the very poor and even declining export performance as observed by Mkandawire (1988). Where Mkandawire attributes this to the general low level of industrialization, Riddell points to the absence of adequate export-oriented trade policies. Riddell claims that in a number of industrial sectors international competitiveness was maintained despite rising protection, with large individual differences between firms in the same sector. Tinkering with tariff levels, opening up to international competition, and increasing domestic competition will not lead to improved export performance. UNIDO commissioned a series of African country case studies for a conference in 1989.[7] The findings basically confirm the picture described in the previous section of rising costs, more price and quality competition, and lack of credit. Moreover, most of these studies describe the (rather obvious) sensitivity of firms to devaluation as depending on the ratio of imported inputs to exported output, indicating the limited possibilities for input substitution and the low or non-existent export supply reaction.

Firm-level studies relevant to evaluating the impact of structural adjustment are Grosh (1990; 1992)[8] and De Valk (1992). Grosh examines public enterprises in the Kenyan manufacturing sector in 1984. She distinguishes public enterprises (public enterprises with politically appointed management) from quasi-public enterprises (non-politically appointed management). Her main conclusion is that the conventional wisdom that the performance of public enterprises is always and everywhere inferior to private enterprises is wrong. Quasi-public enterprises were mainly located in unprotected sectors where they performed efficiently by world standards and at par with private sector firms. Public enterprises were located in the moderately protected industries; private firms were one-third in unprotected and more than one-third in highly protected industries. Low levels of capacity utilization were the main cause of observed inefficiencies. Cook (1992) adds that many of the problems of public enterprises stemmed from inadequate funding at their start and problems of repaying foreign debts with high rates of depreciation. Inefficiency in the public sector was more due to the choice of investment (unviable without protection) than to public management. The implications of Grosh's findings would be that the quasi-public firms should have no difficulty in surviving structural adjustment policies, whereas public firms and at least one-third of the private firms would run into problems.

De Valk (1992) analysed various aspects of the performance of public and private enterprises in the textile sector of Tanzania, using explanatory factors from the micro, meso, macro, and international level. While the technical performance of even the best firms was well below international standards, no clear difference between the public and private sectors existed for the technical performance index and the export index. Large differences between the public and private sectors were found in organizational, financial, and investment performance. In spite of these large differences, public firms were amongst the highest performers in the private sector for each index. Differences in performance could be explained by differences in micro factors between firms. Changes over time were explained by macroeconomic variables such as the exchange rate, the national consumer price index, the overall balance of payments (as an indicator of the foreign-exchange constraint),[9] the rate of interest, and the average domestic price of textile products. The overall conclusion is that liberalization has gone too far and too fast. The tight monetary policy of the structural adjustment package has resulted in a credit constraint affecting most firms. The time has been too short to face the increased competition or to switch profitably to the export market. Additional evidence since the research was completed has shown that even the most successful firms have experienced serious problems in the period 1988–91.

## Small-scale Industry

Although small-scale enterprises receive more policy attention (from international institutions) and stimulate active research interest, systematic research along analytically useful dimensions is scarce. The literature on small-scale enterprises uses concepts such as size, location, legal status, and technology to distinguish between micro, small, and medium enterprises, rural and urban enterprises, formal and informal enterprises, and recently also technologically simple and complex enterprises (Stewart et al., 1990; Steel and Webster, 1992). However, most of these categories do not explicitly refer to analytical distinctions useful in analysing the implications of structural adjustment policy changes. Moreover, because of the high degree of heterogeneity of small-scale enterprises (Dawson, 1993; Mumbengegwi, 1993), the impact of structural adjustment policies is differentiated as well.

With a few exceptions (for example Van Donge, 1992), research in Africa has tended to focus on non-dynamic factors (Liedholm, 1992). Van Donge shows, in the case of agricultural traders in Tanzania, how the rise and fall of businesses is related to the risky environment of agricultural trade and the lack of trust of business partners or employees outside the immediate nuclear family. Liedholm talks of a 'standard' pattern of growth, relating per capita income positively to scale.

Small-scale enterprises face both demand- and supply-side constraints. Since small-scale enterprises are assumed to produce for the domestic market only (with the exception of traditional items such as baskets, special cloth and garments, and other handicrafts, and non-traditional items such as horticultural products), different demand-side constraints develop with declining agricultural and formal sector income. Structural adjustment policies have had, at least in the short run, a depressing effect on urban small-scale enterprises in Ghana (Dawson, 1988; Sowa et al., 1992), while the larger urban enterprises and the rural small-scale enterprises have grown (Sowa et al., 1992). Steel and Webster (1992) report on the higher growth of more technologically complex small-scale enterprises in Ghana. Kessous and Lessard (1993) confirm this in the case of Mali and add that these enterprises are also more export-oriented. The expansion of these dynamic enterprises is blocked by supply factors, whereas the growth of micro and medium to large-scale enterprises is blocked by demand factors. Sowa et al. (1992) report that after devaluation small-scale enterprises are better able to compete with those domestic large-scale producers that are more dependent on imported inputs. Small-scale (and large-scale) garment producers were driven out of the market by cheap imported garments and second-hand clothing as a result of liberalization in Ghana (Fischer-Quincke, 1990) and Tanzania (de Valk, 1992). This is most probably the case in most other African countries, given the vast quantities of second-hand clothing imported into the continent. In Ghana and Tanzania other branches like soap, nuts and bolts, and sandals have also suffered from imports (Bagachwa, 1993; Dawson, 1993). Mumbengegwi (1993) estimates that the short-term (negative) demand effects will dominate the uncertain long-run recovery effect of the economy. While some of this competition from the foreign sector seems unfair (as in the case of second-hand imports, although not from the consumers' point of view), for small-scale enterprises liberalization has exposed inefficiencies that had developed in protected markets.

With regard to supply factors, Liedholm (1992) predicts an expansion of output as a result of structural policies in general, based on the empirical observation that 'both the short- and long-run supply elasticities of firms *within* the micro enterprise category in Africa are quite high (*ibid*.: 207, italics added). Supply constraints are cited first and foremost in finance, but also in imported inputs, foreign exchange, and training in technical and entrepreneurial skills. Generally, for the countries with structural adjustment programmes, access to foreign exchange has improved (with the exception of the experiment of auctioning systems, as in Zambia reported by Ncube (1987)) and with it the supply of imported inputs.

With respect to finance and credit the situation is not at all clear, revealing different experiences for different countries and different types of small-scale industries. Levy (1990) has found that access to credit for small firms in Tanzania (where the banking system is not yet liberalized) was exceedingly cumbersome and a major constraint to their expansion. Fischer-Quincke (1990: 243) comments that potential small-scale industries have lacked support from the banking system. Sowa et al. (1992: 46) find that in Ghana 'there is no significant relation between credit and output performance though the majority of firms indicated that they had been constrained by lack of credit'. Others argue that the more dynamic firms are especially constrained by lack of credit (Dawson, 1990; Steel and Webster, 1992). Similarly, Kessous and Lessard (1993), surveying the impact of structural adjustment on the industrial sector of Mali find that only the dynamic enterprises in the small-scale category were affected by lack of credit, while the micro and medium-sized firms were demand-constrained. Also Obi (1991) found that small-scale enterprises using foreign technology and/or imported inputs can more easily benefit from credit assistance than those using indigenous technology and local inputs, whose credit requirements mainly stem from cash-flow problems as a result of structural adjustment policies. Oyejide (1991) shows that in Nigeria after financial liberalization the total volume of credit to micro and small-scale enterprises had increased as a result of increased market share and increased credit supply. Mwarania (1993), however, warns that the Nigerian experience may be short-lived and many banks may run into problems, as has been the case in Kenya. He makes a case for special government-supported financial institutions for the small-scale enterprises because of their hostile economic environment. Aryeetey (1993) demonstrates for Ghana how the financial institutions have reduced risk by lending to commercial activities rather than manufacturing small-scale enterprises. Finally, Aredo (1993) shows how in Ethiopia alternative financial institutions (saving and lending clubs) can provide in a sustained manner for the lack of access to credit of small-scale enterprises.

## Privatization and Public Sector Reform

Privatization is one of the main pillars of the World Bank's structural adjustment policy towards the industrial sector in Africa. Privatization can be understood as a continuum of possibilities ranging from (a) ownership measures, including sales of assets, joint ventures, and liquidation, to (b) organizational measures, such as restructuring and changing the structure of the holding company, and to (c) operational measures such as contract production and rationalization of government control (Ramanadham, 1989). Privatization is thus seen as a process by which market forces are used to enhance the performance of public enterprises. A wider definition would refer to 'a process by which the state's role within the economy is circumscribed while at the same time the scope for the operation of private capital is deliberately expanded' (Young, 1991: 50). Most privatization efforts in Africa are of type (a), although the slow progress caused by various problems such as lack of buyers and reluctant governments has shifted the policy attention to other forms as well. A systematic treatment of public sector reform and privatization would relate these different forms to the type and nature of sectors, to the level of economic development, and to differences in the political economy. Such research has not been conducted in Africa (or elsewhere, for that matter). Instead, one finds a mixture of detailed case studies comparing public and private performance (Grosh, 1990, 1992; de Valk, 1992), some rather general articles on privatization (Ndongko, 1991; Sandbrook, 1988; Young, 1991), and a few isolated case studies on the experience with privatization (Ramanadham, 1989; Adam et al., 1992). No studies seem to exist where the subsequent development of privatized enterprises has been analysed.

Sandbrook (1988) attributes the failure of parastatals to generic factors, such as the contradictory objectives of profitability, employment generation, regional development, and subsidized goods and services, and to factors specific to Africa or less developed countries in general, such as technical and managerial weaknesses, low wages and salaries, external shocks, foreign-exchange shortages, and the high degree of political interference.[10]

In his general overview of African experience with privatization, Young (1991) notes that the size of the public enterprise sector does not depend on the economic and political ideology of a country. Technical problems are related to the existing legal frameworks and investment codes, the valuation of assets, and the lack of local expertise. As a result, even where it is attempted, divestiture takes too much time and investors lose interest. Economic problems include the lack of a developed capital market, the depressed condition of most economies, the rather unhealthy financial condition of many parastatals, and the reluctance on the part of governments to sell profitable enterprises. However, political problems are of most overriding significance. Vested interests exist with ministries, managers, and patronage networks. Trade unions fight against job losses. Transfer of assets to foreign investors or ethnic minorities has become a sensitive issue for indigenous entrepreneurs, students and opposition groups.

Case studies focusing on the process of privatization from a public administration angle have appeared in Ramanadham (1989) for Ethiopia, Ghana, Kenya, Malawi, Nigeria, and Uganda. The general problems discussed do not deviate much from those identified by Young (1991) above. More detailed analysis, including the economic background and an assessment of the achievements of privatization, can be found in Adam et al. (1992) for the cases of Kenya and Malawi. 'Gradual private sector development will be the catalyst for successful privatization rather than vice versa' (ibid.: 374). Both Grosh (1992) and Adam et al. (1992) suggest that there is ample scope for improving efficiency through public enterprise reform. In this context Ndongko (1991) speaks of the commercialization of public enterprises as an alternative to privatization. The 'threat' effect of privatization has already done its job in halting further public sector expansion. Grosh and Adam *et al.* also stress the importance of regulatory policies, especially where privatization occurs in monopolistic sectors.

## Alternative Industrialization Strategies

The African Alternative Framework for Recovery and Transformation (AAF-SAP) points to the main elements of an alternative industrial strategy (ECA, 1989; Thisen, 1991). In general, industrial production will be stimulated by (a) administering imports to allow existing industries to survive by ensuring their vital import needs, (b) lower interest rates for industrial production than for other purposes, (c) a system of selectively used multiple exchange rates, (d) better access to credit and legal enfranchisement for informal enterprises, (e) promotion of small-scale, easily mounted industries manufacturing essential goods through appropriate investment codes and national credit policies, and (f) the creation of special funds for loans at subsidized interest rates to strategic enterprises. In addition, better forward and backward linkages between industry and agriculture should be encouraged. The general trade policy proposed has a mildly regional, inward-looking orientation: regional co-operation should rationalize production structures and promote areas of specialization; exports (outside Africa) are only envisaged after satisfying local and regional demand. Technological capability is addressed through the promotion of a technologically focused educational and research system.

Four broad concerns of the AAF-SAP (technological capability, small-scale industries, regional co-operation, continued protection) have received wider attention in the literature. Firstly, the issue of technological capability has been addressed by Lall (1992) and Pack (1993). Both see the entrepreneurial problem as the most important one for Africa. While indeed most African industries have been able to survive because of the protective environment and 'industrial productivity in Africa might be improved by the typical macroeconomic *cum* liberalization policy package, the magnitude of the gain is not likely to be particularly large given the scarcity of industrial managers and the paucity of general industrial experience' (Pack 1993: 4, italics added). Pack places question marks behind the 'orthodox' alternative strategies such as stimulating linkages, resource-based industrialization, and basic industries. He analyses the actions necessary to increase productivity at the national level (sectoral strategies should be developed, building on the available skills while further developing the skill base through technical training), the industry level (improving total factor productivity of the sector and reducing the differences between firms), and the firm level (for existing firms: temporary, 3 to 5 years, management assistance contracts; for new firms: foreign investment by multinationals). He does not consider subcontracting to small-scale industries as a feasible option for large-scale enterprises. Lall (1992) focuses more on the development of indigenous capabilities both in terms of the individual as well as the national dimension. In this way Lall is much closer to the AAF-SAP than Pack.

Secondly, promotion of small-scale industries is seen as one of the means to develop entrepreneurial skills and as the starting point for the small-scale sector to mature and diversify towards larger-scale and more technologically complex sectors (Liedholm, 1992). Clearly, this has to be one of the elements of future African industrial development. However, the questions are: how much emphasis should be placed on it, how does it relate to other strategies, how many resources should be devoted to it in relation to other efforts, and above all how can this effectively be done. The section on small-scale industries above showed that the discussion of small-scale enterprises should be differentiated according to the type of small-scale enterprise in order to make a meaningful contribution to the debate on the future of African industrialization. Thirdly, the potential for and problems of regional co-operation are extensively discussed (see, for example, Adedeji et al. (1991)). Fourthly, the overnight liberalization has shocked the industrial sector to the extent that many contend that it has proceeded too rapidly and argue for continuation of protective policies, albeit in a different form from those practised in the past (Pack, 1993; Helleiner, 1990; Rodrik, 1992; Yahaya, 1991).

Parastatal restructuring and reform has been discussed as an alternative to full-scale privatization by Adam et al. (1992), Cook (1992), Grosh (1992), and Mihyo (1993). The lessons learned from the past are that government interference should be kept to a minimum, industrial parastatals should have a more commercial orientation, and subsidies should be eliminated gradually.

Linkage programmes (often donor-supported) are seen as alternatives to market-led joint ventures for both large-scale enterprises (Egan and Mody, 1992) and small-scale enterprises (Frenz, 1990; Carlsson, 1990; Mramba, 1990). They can take many different forms depending on the actual requirements of the co-operating firms and ranging from supply contracts to joint ventures. These linkages can ensure the provision of technology, market information, foreign market outlets, foreign exchange, and management advice.

## Conclusions

This survey has put forward a wide range of issues but, because of the nature of the paper, none of them has been treated with sufficient depth to do it justice. Yet, some general conclusions can be drawn. Firstly, serious research on the impact of structural adjustment on industry in Africa is scarce. This applies in particular to impact studies of medium and large-scale industries and to a systematic study of the various aspects and forms of privatization. Small-scale industry research is more substantial but a systematic differentiation of types of industries has not yet emerged. Secondly, most alternative strategies will have only long-term effects. A quick dynamic response in African countries cannot be expected for a long time to come. Gradual capability building through a mixture of various strategies is the long, winding road that industrialization in Africa will have to travel.

Thirdly, most alternative strategies are formulated under a different conception of state-society relations. What is most urgently needed is a state (government and its administration) with internal discipline, able to design and implement policies from a national rather than an individual or group perspective.

Finally, some form of action must be undertaken to save the industrial sectors of most Sub-Saharan African countries. Liberalization has come too fast and has gone too far. On the other hand, the continuation of past pre-structural adjustment policies would have killed off the industries as well, whatever the blame put on external circumstances. For the survival and increased efficiency of most industrial sectors all possible efforts must be mobilized, including controlled forms of foreign investment (if forthcoming at all), establishment of foreign and regional linkages, improved applied technological education at all levels, the employment of entrepreneurial talents whatever their ethnic origin, selective and declining protection, sectoral industrial and trade strategies, and support for dynamic small-scale enterprises. Most of these policies are not conflicting. It is high time to put the industrial sector back on the agenda and to develop the industrial strategy that structural adjustment policy currently lacks.

## Notes

1. See Stewart *et al.* (1992) for a recent collection of papers dealing with alternatives to structural adjustment policies in industry and other sectors. Several chapters are referred to separately in the text.
2. Meijer (1990) discusses the causes and problems of export diversification in Zambia. More positive results are reported from the relatively more industrialized African countries, Kenya (Stevens, 1990) and Zimbabwe (Riddell, 1990b), while the success story of Mauritius is described in McQueen (1990).
3. Singh (1988) stresses the export problems of industry by focusing on the foreign-exchange costs (rather than earnings) of exports.
4. Riddell (1990a) is a summary in article form of Riddell (1990c). Riddell (1992) is an article primarily based on two chapters of Riddell (1990c) but adding a comparison of Côte d'Ivoire and Zimbabwe as two relative successes as industrializers in Africa.
5. These countries were: Botswana, Cameroon, Côte d'Ivoire, Kenya, Nigeria, Zambia, and Zimbabwe.
6. Shaaeldin (1988) estimates sources of growth from the supply side for Kenya, Tanzania, Zambia, and Zimbabwe. He concludes that, with the exception of Zimbabwe, rates of total factor productivity growth have been negative and that increases in factor inputs account for most industrial growth in all four countries. Causes are given in terms of capacity underutilization, market size, import-substitution policies, market structures, external and scale economies, and technological development, but no strong evidence of direct causation is provided.
7. Countries included were: Côte d'Ivoire, Ghana, Kenya, Nigeria, Senegal, Zaire.
8. The article (Grosh, 1990) is a forerunner to the book (Grosh, 1992).
9. See Mbelle and Sterner (1992) for a firm-level analysis of the foreign-exchange constraint in Tanzania.
10. See de Valk (1992) for the case of political interference in Tanzania. For an overview of issues of the political economy of the state in relation to industrialization in Africa see: Beckman, 1991; Bienen, 1990; Colclough and Manor, 1991; Evans, 1989; Gereffi and Wyman, 1990; Killick, 1990; Lal, 1989; Shapiro and Taylor, 1990; de Valk, 1992.

## References

Adam, C., Cavendish, W. and Mistry, P.S. (1992) *Adjusting Privatization: Case Studies from Developing Countries*, London: James Currey.

Adedeji, A., Teriba, O. and Bugembe, P. (eds) (1991) *The Challenge of African Economic Recovery and Development*, London: Frank Cass.

Aredo, D. (1993) 'The Iqqub and its Potential as an Indigenous Institution Financing Small Enterprises in Ethiopia', in Helmsing and Kolstee.

Aryeetey, E. (1993) 'Sectoral Credit Allocation Policy and Credit Flow to Small Enterprises in Ghana', in Helmsing and Kolstee.

Bagachwa, M.S.D. (1993) 'Impact of Adjustment Policies on Small-Scale Enterprise Sector in Tanzania' in: Helmsing and Kolstee.

Beckman, B. (1991) 'Empowerment or Repression? The World Bank and the Politics of African Adjustment', *Africa Development* 16 (1), 45–72.

Bienen, H. (1990) 'The Politics of Trade Liberalization in Africa', *Economic Development and Cultural Change* 38 (4), 713–32.

Carlsson, J. (1990) 'The Sister Industry Programme in Tanzania and the Zambian Alternative', *Small Enterprise Development* 1 (2), 34–40.

Colclough, C. and Manor, J. (eds) (1991) *States or Markets? Neo-liberalism and the Development Policy Debate*, Oxford: Clarendon Press.

Cook, P. (1992) 'Privatization and Public Enterprise Performance in Developing Countries', *Development Policy Review* 10 (4), 403–8.

Dawson, J. (1988) 'Small-Scale Industry Development in Ghana: A Case Study from Kumasi', *ESCOR* (mimeo), London: Overseas Development Administration.

Dawson, J. (1990) 'The Wider Context: The Importance of the Macroeconomic Environment for Small Enterprise Development', *Small Enterprise Development* 1 (3), 39–46.

Dawson, J. (1993) 'Impact of Structural Adjustment on the Small Enterprise Sector: a Comparison of the Ghanaian and Tanzanian Experiences' in Helmsing and Kolstee.

Donge, van J.K. (1992) 'Waluguru Traders in Dar es Salaam', *African Affairs* 91, 181–205.

Economic Commission for Africa (1989) *African Alternative Framework to Structural Adjustment Programmes for Socio-economic Recovery and Transformation*, E/ECA/CM.15/6/Rev.3, Addis Ababa: ECA.

Egan, M.L. and Mody, A. (1992) 'Buyer-Seller Links in Export Development', *World Development* 20 (3), 321–34.

Evans, P.B. (1989) 'Predatory, Developmental, and Other Apparatuses: A Comparative Political Economy Perspective on the Third World', *Sociological Forum* 4 (4).

Fischer-Quincke, G. (1990) 'Small Enterprises for the Needs of the People? Ghana's "Small-Scale Industrial Take-Off"', in *African Development Perspectives Yearbook 1989, Vol. 1: Human Dimensions of Adjustment*, Berlin: Schelzky & Jeep.

Frenz, A. (1990) '"Twinning" Programmes for Assistance to Small Enterprise – A Review of the GTZ Experience', *Small Enterprise Development* 1 (1), 32–7.

Gereffi, G. and Wyman, D.L. (1990) *Manufacturing Miracles*, Princeton, NJ: Princeton University Press.

Grosh, B. (1990) 'Public, Quasi-Public and Private Manufacturing Firms in Kenya: the Surprising Case of a Cliché Gone Astray', *Development Policy Review* 8 (1), 43–58.

Grosh, B. (1992) *Public Enterprises in Kenya*, Boulder, CO and London: Lynne Rienner.

Helleiner, G.K. (1990) 'Trade Strategy in Medium-Term Adjustment', *World Development* 18 (6), 879–97.

Helmsing, A.H.J. and Kolstee, T. (1993) *Small Enterprises and Changing Policies: Structural Adjustment, Financial Policy, and Assistance Programmes in Africa*, London: Intermediate Technology Publications.

Kessous, J., and Lessard, G. (1993) 'Industrial Sector in Mali: Responses to Adjustment', in Helmsing and Kolstee.

Killick, T. (1990) *A Reaction Too Far, Economic Theory and the Role of the State in Developing Countries*, London: Overseas Development Institute.

Lal, D. (1989) 'The Political Economy of Industrialization in Primary Product Exporting Economies: Some Cautionary Tales', Chapter 12 in N. Islam (ed.), *The Balance between Industry and Agriculture in Economic Development, Vol. 5*, New York: St Martin's Press.

Lall, S. (1992) 'Technological Capabilities and Industrialization', *World Development* 20 (2), 165–86.

Levy, B. (1990) 'Obstacles to the Development of Indigenous Small and Medium Enterprises: An Empirical Assessment', Background Paper to: *Tanzania: Country Economic Memorandum*, Washington, DC: World Bank.

Liedholm, C. (1992) 'Small-scale Industry in Africa: Dynamic Issues and the Role of Policy', Chapter 6 in Stewart *et al.*

Mbelle, A. and Sterner, T. (1991) 'Foreign Exchange and Industrial Development: A Frontier Production Function Analysis of Two Tanzanian Industries', *World Development* 19 (4), 341-7.

McQueen, M. (1990) *ACP Export Diversification: The Case of Mauritius*, ODI Working Paper 41, London: Overseas Development Institute.

Meier, G. M. and Steel, W. F. (eds) (1989) *Industrial Adjustment in Sub-Saharan Africa*, Washington DC: Economic Development Institute, World Bank.

Meijer, F. (1990) 'Structural Adjustment and Diversification in Zambia', *Development and Change* 21 (4), 657-92.

Mihyo, P. B. (1993) *Non-Market Controls and the Accountability of Public Enterprises in Tanzania*, Aldershot: Avebury.

Mkandawire, T. (1988) 'The Road to Crisis, Adjustment and De-Industrialization: The African Case', *Africa Development* 8 (1), 5-31.

Mramba, B. P. (1990) 'Technology Transfer through the Sister Industry Programme in Tanzania – an Alternative View', *Small Enterprise Development* 1 (2), 41-7.

Mumbengegwi, C. (1993) 'Structural Adjustment and Small-Scale Enterprise Development in Zimbabwe', in Helmsing and Kolstee.

Mwarania, K. M. (1993) 'Financing Small and Micro Scale Enterprises in Kenya Under Conditions of Liberalized Financial Markets', in Helmsing and Kolstee.

Navaretti, G. B. (1992) 'Joint Ventures and Autonomous Industrial Development: The Magic Medicine? The Case of Côte d'Ivoire', Chapter 15 in Stewart *et al.*

Ncube, P. D. (1987) 'The International Monetary Fund and the Zambian Economy', in K. J. Havenik (ed.), *The IMF and the World Bank in Africa*, Uppsala: Scandinavian Institute of African Studies.

Ndongko, W. A. (1991) 'Commercialization as an Alternative to Privatization: Prospects and Problems', *Africa Development* 16 (3/4).

Obi, A. W. (1991) 'Prospects for Small-scale Industries Development Under a Structural Adjustment Programme: The Case of Nigeria', *Africa Development* 16 (2), 33-56.

Oyejide, T. A. (1991) 'Structural Adjustment and its Implications for Financing Small Enterprises', *Small Enterprise Development* 2 (4), 31-9.

Pack, H. (1988) 'Industrialization and Trade', in H. Chenery and T. N. Srinivasan (eds), *Handbook of Development Economics*, Vol. 1, Amsterdam: North Holland.

Pack, H. (1993) 'Productivity and Industrial Development in Sub-Saharan Africa', *World Development* 21 (1), 1-15.

Ramanadham, V. V. (ed.) (1989) *Privatization in Developing Countries*, London: Routledge.

Ravenhill, J. (1988) 'Adjustment with Growth: A Fragile Consensus', *The Journal of Modern African Studies* 26 (2), 179-210.

Riddell, R. C. (1990a) 'A Forgotten Dimension? The Manufacturing Sector in African Development', *Development Policy Review* 8 (1), 5-27.

Riddell, R. C. (1990b) *ACP Export Diversification: the Case of Zimbabwe*, ODI Working Paper No. 38, London: Overseas Development Institute.

Riddell, R. C. (1990c) *Manufacturing Africa: Performance and Prospects of Seven Countries in Sub-Saharan Africa*, London: James Currey for the Overseas Development Institute.

Riddell, R. (1992) 'Manufacturing Sector Development in Zimbabwe and the Côte d'Ivoire', Chapter 7 in Stewart *et al.*

Rodrik, D. (1992) 'Conceptual Issues in the Design of Trade Policy for Industrialization', *World Development* 20 (3), 309-20.

Sandbrook, R. (1988) 'Patrimonialism and The Failing of Parastatals: Africa in Comparative Perspective', Chapter 7 in P. Cook and C. Kirkpatrick (eds), *Privatization in Less Developed Countries*, Hemel Hempstead: Harvester Wheatsheaf.

Shaaeldin, E. (1988) 'Sources of Industrial Growth in Kenya, Tanzania, Zambia, and Zimbabwe', *Eastern Africa Economic Review* 4 (2), 21-31.

Shapiro, H. and Taylor, L. (1990) 'The State and Industrial Strategy', *World Development* 18 (6), 861-78.

Singh, A. (1988) 'Industrial Policy in Developing Countries: The Foreign Exchange Cost of Exports', *Industry and Development* 23.

Sowa, N. K., Baah-Nuakoh, A., Tutu, K. A. and Osei, B. (1992) *Small Enterprises and Adjustment: The Impact of Ghana's Economic Recovery Programme*, London/Accra: Overseas Development Institute/University of Ghana.

Steel, W. F. and Webster, L. M. (1992) 'How Small Enterprises in Ghana Have Responded to Adjustment', *The World Bank Economic Review* 6 (3), 423-38.

Stein, H. (1992) 'Deindustrialization, Adjustment, the World Bank and the IMF in Africa', *World Development* 20 (1), 83-95.

Stevens, C. (1990) *ACP Export Diversification: Jamaica, Kenya and Ethiopia*, ODI Working Paper No. 40, London: Overseas Development Institute.

Stewart F., Lall, S. and Wangwe, S. (eds) (1992) *Alternative Development Strategies in Sub-Saharan Africa*, Basingstoke: Macmillan.

Stewart, F., Thomas, H. and de Wilde, T. (1990) *The Other Policy*, London: IT Publications.

Thisen, J.K. (1991) 'The Design of Structural Adjustment Programs: The African Alternative Framework', *Africa Development* 16 (1), 115–64.

UNIDO (1989) *Conference Papers on the Impact of Structural Adjustment Policies on Industry in Africa: Côte d'Ivoire, Ghana, Kenya, Nigeria, Senegal, Zaire*, Vienna: UNIDO.

Valk, P. de (1992) 'A General Framework for Evaluating the Performance of Textile Enterprises in LDCs: With an Application to Tanzania under Structural Adjustment, PhD Thesis, Vrije Universiteit, Amsterdam.

Webster, L. (1990) 'Fifteen Years of World Bank Lending for Small and Medium Enterprises', *Small Enterprise Development* 1 (1), 17–26.

Yahaya, S. (1991) 'State Intervention versus the Market: A Review of the Debate', *Africa Development* 16 (3/4), 55–74.

Young, R.A. (1991) 'Privatization in Africa', *Review of African Political Economy* No. 51 July, 50–62.

# APPENDIX 3

# Background Notes on Sub-Saharan Africa
# FRED VAN DER KRAAIJ

## Current Economic Situation[1]

Any economic overview of the countries of Sub-Saharan Africa must focus on the following: what their economies have in common; the differences between them; problems confronting national economies and societies; the extent and seriousness of poverty in these countries, and the marginal international position of SSA.

However, we shall not attempt to tackle these issues in this paper. Not only is the subject too extensive, but it can be assumed that those participating in the seminar have sufficient prior knowledge of the matters in question. Our intention is therefore not to give a comprehensive view of the above issues but to present a number of selected data which serve to illustrate them and which should shed some light on SSA's problems and performance. It should be noted, however, that, for a variety of reasons, the data may not always be regarded as reliable. The lack of reliable institutions in the countries concerned, the absence of recent population or other, such as agricultural, censuses, difficulties in charting the growing informal economies in many of these countries,[2] ongoing or recently terminated civil wars and armed rebellion form obstacles to the collection of reliable data.

*Some basic general data*
Appendix Table 3.1 contains some general data. Column 1 of the table shows one of the most significant differentiating factors between the countries of SSA and their economies, i.e. population size. While Nigeria has a population of 88.5 million (its estimated population in the years prior to 1992 being 115 million), there are 8 countries with a population of less than 1 million. Population density also varies considerably, both between countries and from area to area within countries, Botswana, Mauritania and Namibia having as few as 2 persons/km$^2$ and Rwanda 280 persons/km$^2$ (column 3).

Column 4 shows the high fertility rates common to the countries of SSA. In combination with other factors, these high rates[3] contribute to the annual 3% population growth. If the population continues to grow at this rate, the overall population of SSA – now 500 million – will double within 22 years. However, growth rates may even increase in the near future if the infant mortality rate continues to fall (column 5). The overall SSA infant mortality rate fell from 139 to 99 per thousand in the years 1980–90 and the mortality rate of children under the age of five fell from 199 to 162 over the same period. The socio-economic, political and environmental impact of this demographic trend may reach disastrous proportions in those countries that are already overpopulated if measures are not taken to diversify the national economy, create more off-farm employment and develop a population policy. It is interesting to note the falling infant mortality rates, as this may be important in considering the effects of structural adjustment programmes on the health situation in SSA.

Though agricultural production has shown an annual growth of 2% since 1960, per capita food production fell due to the discrepancy between population growth and growth in agricultural production. As agriculture forms the main economic activity of the great majority of the population (see Appendix Table 3.2, column 2), it is hardly surprising that around 50% live below the poverty line[4] (column 7 of Appendix Table 3.1 gives the details.) Calorie intake per capita (column 8 of the table) is thus low. In addition to being indicative of the degree of poverty of the population, it also gives rise to concern in view of the relationship that has been established between malnourishment and productivity.

32 of the 47 countries classified as least developed in 1992 are to be found in SSA, the per capita GNP of the combined population of 285 million being US$ 360. Average life expectancy at birth is 49.6 years, the average adult literacy rate is 39.5% and the manufacturing sector contributes an average of only 10.6% to GNP (least developed countries only). Columns 9–11 of Appendix Table 3.1 give the details for each of the SSA countries.

*Some basic economic data*
Appendix Table 3.2. contains some basic macroeconomic data. In all but 12 countries the single most important economic activity is agriculture in terms of the contribution of the primary sector to GNP (see column 2), but in terms of employment and income only a few countries form an exception.[5] However, the contribution of the primary sector to GNP varies considerably. Countries with a relatively large industrial or mining sector, such as Botswana, Congo, Gabon and the Republic of South Africa, and Djibouti with its service sector, derive 10% or less of their GNP from the agriculture sector. Agriculture contributes more than 50% to GNP in 10 countries (Burundi, Chad, Equatorial Guinea, Guinea Bissau, Mali, São Tomé and Principe, Somalia, Tanzania and Uganda and, nowadays, Liberia). The figure is between 10% and 50% in the remaining 32 countries.

Some countries have considerable mineral resources (e.g. copper, diamonds, gold, iron ore, natural gas, oil, phosphates and uranium), but since the nineteenth century these countries have been exporters of unprocessed primary products, the prices of which are beyond their control and subject to extreme fluctuations. In 1980 exports from developing Africa totalled some US$93 billion, but this figure had fallen to US$63 bn by 1990, the region's share in world trade thus falling from a low 4.7% in 1980 to an even lower 2% ten years later (ECA, 1991). This example clearly illustrates the marginalization of SSA in international economic affairs.

**Appendix Table 3.1** *Sub-Saharan Africa: General data, 1991*

| Country | Population (millions) | Area 1000 km² | Popul. density pers/km² | Fertility rates | Infant mortality rates | | Under 5-yr mortality rates | | GNP per capita (US$) | Calorie intake per capita | Life expectancy at birth | Adult literacy rate (%) | Value added to GNP by manufacturing sector (%) |
|---|---|---|---|---|---|---|---|---|---|---|---|---|---|
| | | | | | 1980 | 1990 | 1980 | 1990 | | | | | |
| | (1) | (2) | (3) | (4) | (5) | | (6) | | (7) | (8) | (9) | (10) | (11) |
| Angola | 10.0 | 1247 | 7 | 6.4 | 160 | 137 | 261 | 292 | 750 | 1807 | 46 | 42 | 10 |
| Benin* | 4.9 | 113 | 43 | 7.0 | 108 | 90 | 176 | 147 | 426 | 2305 | 47 | 23 | 12 |
| Botswana* | 1.3 | 582 | 2 | 6.3 | 82 | 67 | 110 | 85 | 2200 | 2375 | 60 | 64 | 5 |
| Burkina Faso* | 9.2 | 274 | 33 | 6.5 | 162 | 138 | 261 | 228 | 360 | 2288 | 48 | 18 | 22 |
| Burundi* | 5.6 | 28 | 201 | 6.9 | 137 | 119 | 225 | 192 | 205 | 1932 | 49 | 50 | 15 |
| Cameroon | 12.2 | 475 | 26 | 5.9 | 111 | 94 | 175 | 148 | 1000 | 2217 | 54 | 54 | 19 |
| Cape Verde* | 0.3 | 4 | 84 | 5.2 | 70 | 44 | 92 | 56 | 880 | 2706 | 67 | 53 | 18 |
| Central Afr. Rep.* | 2.7 | 623 | 4 | 5.6 | 122 | 104 | 213 | 169 | 410 | 2036 | 50 | 38 | 9 |
| Chad* | 5.9 | 1284 | 4 | 5.3 | 154 | 132 | 254 | 216 | 202 | 1743 | 47 | 30 | 14 |
| Comoros* | 0.6 | 2 | 258 | 7.0 | 120 | 99 | 150 | 125 | 490 | 1960 | 55 | 61 | 13 |
| Congo | 2.3 | 342 | 7 | 6.9 | 85 | 73 | 132 | 110 | 1060 | 2590 | 54 | 57 | 10 |
| Côte d'Ivoire | 12.1 | 322 | 38 | 7.4 | 116 | 96 | 167 | 136 | 670 | 2577 | 54 | 54 | 17 |
| Djibouti* | 0.4 | 23 | 18 | 6.6 | 170 | 117 | 350 | 164 | 1300 | | 48 | 49 | 12 |
| Equatorial Guinea* | 0.4 | 28 | 13 | 5.6 | 149 | 127 | 243 | 206 | 310 | | 46 | 50 | 5 |
| Ethiopia* | 51.0 | 1222 | 42 | 6.1 | 149 | 137 | 260 | 220 | 110 | 1667 | 46 | 66 | 18 |
| Gabon | 1.2 | 268 | 4 | 4.8 | 122 | 103 | 287 | 164 | 3300 | 2383 | 53 | 61 | 12 |
| Gambia* | 0.9 | 11 | 78 | 6.4 | 166 | 143 | 340 | 238 | 260 | 2370 | 44 | 27 | 11 |
| Ghana | 15.4 | 239 | 65 | 6.4 | 103 | 90 | 166 | 140 | 415 | 2248 | 55 | 60 | 26 |
| Guinea Bissau* | 1.0 | 36 | 28 | 5.4 | 176 | 151 | 290 | 246 | 160 | 2506 | 43 | 37 | 9 |
| Guinea* | 6.0 | 249 | 24 | 6.2 | 167 | 145 | 275 | 237 | 480 | 2132 | 44 | 24 | 10 |
| Kenya | 25.9 | 583 | 44 | 8.1 | 88 | 72 | 133 | 108 | 370 | 2163 | 60 | 69 | 20 |
| Lesotho* | 1.8 | 30 | 60 | 5.8 | 123 | 100 | 161 | 129 | 520 | 2299 | 57 | 78 | 33 |

| | | | | | | | | | | | | |
|---|---|---|---|---|---|---|---|---|---|---|---|---|
| Liberia* | 2.7 | 111 | 24 | 6.6 | 167 | 142 | 245 | 205 | 250 | 2382 | 55 | 40 | 10 |
| Madagascar* | 11.5 | 587 | 20 | 6.6 | 150 | 120 | 216 | 176 | 200 | 2158 | 55 | 80 | 15 |
| Malawi* | 8.6 | 118 | 72 | 7.7 | 177 | 150 | 299 | 253 | 216 | 2139 | 48 | 47 | 18 |
| Mali* | 8.3 | 1240 | 7 | 6.7 | 191 | 169 | 325 | 284 | 295 | 2314 | 45 | 32 | 11 |
| Mauritania* | 2.1 | 1031 | 2 | 6.5 | 149 | 127 | 249 | 214 | 488 | 2685 | 47 | 34 | 7 |
| Mauritius | 1.1 | 2 | 574 | 2.3 | 38 | 23 | 42 | 28 | 2420 | 2887 | 70 | 86 | 30 |
| Mozambique* | 16.0 | 802 | 20 | 6.4 | 160 | 141 | 268 | 297 | 90 | 1680 | 48 | 33 | 30 |
| Namibia | 1.4 | 824 | 2 | 6.1 | 126 | 106 | 202 | 167 | 1377 | 1946 | 58 | 40 | 11 |
| Niger* | 8.0 | 1267 | 6 | 7.1 | 157 | 135 | 259 | 221 | 280 | 2308 | 46 | 28 | 12 |
| Nigeria | 88.5 | 924 | 96 | 6.6 | 124 | 105 | 198 | 167 | 300 | 2312 | 52 | 51 | 7 |
| Rep. of South Africa | 38.8 | 1221 | 32 | 4.5 | | | | | 2810 | 3122 | 62 | 70 | 33 |
| Rwanda* | 7.4 | 26 | 280 | 8.5 | 140 | 122 | 231 | 198 | 230 | 1971 | 50 | 50 | 22 |
| São Tomé and Príncipe* | 0.1 | 1 | 124 | 5.4 | 97 | 43 | 150 | 55 | 380 | 2419 | 66 | 63 | 5 |
| Senegal | 7.3 | 196 | 37 | 6.4 | 112 | 87 | 232 | 185 | 650 | 2369 | 48 | 38 | 24 |
| Seychelles | 0.1 | 1 | 155 | 3.2 | 20 | 18 | 24 | 21 | 4670 | 2335 | 70 | 89 | 15 |
| Sierra Leone* | 4.3 | 72 | 59 | 6.5 | 179 | 154 | 300 | 257 | 155 | 1799 | 42 | 21 | 6 |
| Somalia* | 7.5 | 638 | 12 | 7.4 | 149 | 132 | 247 | 215 | 150 | 1906 | 46 | 24 | 10 |
| Sudan* | 25.5 | 2506 | 10 | 6.5 | 131 | 108 | 210 | 172 | 150 | 1974 | 51 | 27 | 15 |
| Swaziland | 0.8 | 17 | 43 | 6.5 | 140 | 118 | 206 | 167 | 850 | 2591 | 57 | 72 | 27 |
| Tanzania* | 26.4 | 945 | 28 | 7.1 | 125 | 106 | 202 | 170 | 140 | 2206 | 54 | 65 | 7 |
| Togo* | 3.6 | 57 | 65 | 6.6 | 117 | 94 | 184 | 147 | 410 | 2214 | 54 | 43 | 15 |
| Uganda* | 17.0 | 236 | 72 | 7.3 | 114 | 103 | 186 | 164 | 210 | 2153 | 52 | 48 | 4 |
| Zaïre* | 36.7 | 2345 | 16 | 6.1 | 103 | 83 | 163 | 130 | 150 | 1991 | 53 | 72 | 8 |
| Zambia* | 8.3 | 753 | 11 | 7.2 | 94 | 80 | 146 | 122 | 420 | 2077 | 54 | 73 | 24 |
| Zimbabwe | 9.6 | 391 | 26 | 6.5 | 86 | 66 | 116 | 87 | 680 | 2299 | 60 | 67 | 31 |

Note: Least developed countries are marked with an asterisk.

Sources: Cambessédès, 1992; ECA, 1993; UNDP, 1992; World Bank, 1992a.

**Appendix Table 3.2** *Sub-Saharan Africa: Economic data, 1990/91*

| Country | GNP US$m. | Contrib. primary sector to GNP (%) | Contrib. secondary sector to GNP (%) | Contrib. tertiary sector to GNP (%) | Total ext. debt US$m. | Total ext. debt as % of GNP | Debt service ratio 1990 | Average Growth Domestic 1965–80 | Annual Rate of Gross Investment 1980–90 |
|---|---|---|---|---|---|---|---|---|---|
| | (1) | (2) | (3) | (4) | (5) | (6) | (7) | (8) | (9) |
| Angola | 7500 | 13 | 55 | 32 | 7710 | 103 | 7.1 | | −4.4 |
| Benin* | 2080 | 36 | 16 | 48 | 1427 | 69 | 3.4 | 10.4 | 0.4 |
| Botswana* | 2750 | 3 | 55 | 42 | 516 | 19 | 4.4 | 21.0 | 10.3 |
| Burkina Faso* | 3300 | 38 | 24 | 38 | 834 | 25 | 6.4 | 8.5 | 3.2 |
| Burundi* | 1150 | 56 | 15 | 29 | 906 | 79 | 43.4 | 9.0 | −3.5 |
| Cameroon | 12200 | 24 | 31 | 45 | 6023 | 49 | 21.5 | 9.9 | |
| Cape Verde* | 300 | 15 | 18 | 67 | 138 | 46 | 8.0 | | |
| Central Afr. Rep.* | 1250 | 41 | 19 | 40 | 901 | 72 | 12.5 | −5.4 | 6.6 |
| Chad* | 1240 | 54 | 14 | 32 | 492 | 40 | 4.8 | | |
| Comoros* | 230 | 37 | 13 | 50 | 200 | 87 | 1.5 | | |
| Congo | 2500 | 10 | 38 | 52 | 5118 | 205 | 20.0 | 4.5 | −11.7 |
| Côte d'Ivoire | 8470 | 29 | 17 | 54 | 17956 | 212 | 39.8 | 10.7 | −11.6 |
| Djibouti* | 550 | 3 | 12 | 85 | 258 | 47 | 4.5 | | |
| Equatorial Guinea* | 130 | 60 | 5 | 35 | 184 | 142 | 11.2 | | |
| Ethiopia* | 6000 | 42 | 18 | 40 | 3250 | 54 | 33.0 | −0.1 | −7.5 |
| Gabon | 3900 | 9 | 51 | 40 | 3647 | 94 | 7.6 | 14.1 | |
| Gambia* | 229 | 35 | 11 | 54 | 354 | 155 | 26.0 | | |
| Ghana | 6300 | 37 | 30 | 33 | 3498 | 56 | 34.9 | −1.3 | 7.7 |
| Guinea Bissau* | 160 | 60 | 9 | 31 | 530 | 331 | 45.2 | | |
| Guinea* | 2760 | 30 | 35 | 35 | 2497 | 90 | 8.3 | | |
| Kenya | 8950 | 31 | 20 | 49 | 6840 | 76 | 33.8 | 7.2 | 0.6 |
| Lesotho* | 910 | 18 | 34 | 48 | 390 | 43 | 4.1 | 17.8 | 5.6 |

| | | | | | | | | |
|---|---|---|---|---|---|---|---|---|
| Liberia* | 700 | 35 | 30 | 35 | 1870 | 267 | 44.5 | 6.4 | 4.8 |
| Madagascar* | 2250 | 41 | 15 | 44 | 3938 | 175 | 22.5 | 1.5 | -2.4 |
| Malawi* | 1850 | 37 | 18 | 45 | 1544 | 83 | 11.5 | 9.0 | 9.8 |
| Mali* | 2420 | 53 | 13 | 34 | 2433 | 101 | 13.9 | 1.8 | -5.4 |
| Mauritania* | 1000 | 38 | 19 | 43 | 2227 | 223 | 8.6 | 19.2 | 10.0 |
| Mauritius | 2590 | 20 | 30 | 50 | 939 | 36 | 14.4 | 8.3 | 1.8 |
| Mozambique* | 1450 | 40 | 30 | 30 | 4718 | 325 | | | -7.0 |
| Namibia | 1960 | 16 | 30 | 54 | | | | | |
| Niger* | 2250 | 47 | 17 | 36 | 1829 | 81 | 25.4 | 6.3 | -6.0 |
| Nigeria | 33000 | 32 | 25 | 43 | 36068 | 109 | 20.4 | 14.7 | -10.2 |
| Rep. of South Africa | 109000 | 5 | 44 | 51 | 19000 | 17 | 14.5 | 4.7 | -4.3 |
| Rwanda* | 1700 | 37 | 23 | 40 | 741 | 44 | 34.0 | 9.0 | 1.7 |
| São Tomé and Príncipe* | 50 | 70 | 5 | 25 | 250 | 500 | 20.4 | | |
| Senegal | 4850 | 22 | 26 | 52 | 3745 | 77 | 8.2 | 3.9 | 2.8 |
| Seychelles | 318 | | | | | | | | |
| Sierra Leone* | 650 | 40 | 19 | 41 | 1189 | 183 | 15.9 | -1.0 | -1.0 |
| Somalia* | 946 | 64 | 10 | 26 | 2350 | 248 | 11.7 | 12.1 | -2.6 |
| Sudan* | 4000 | 37 | 15 | 48 | 15383 | 385 | 5.8 | 6.4 | |
| Swaziland | 660 | 27 | 29 | 44 | 277 | 42 | 6.7 | | 0.3 |
| Tanzania* | 3270 | 54 | 7 | 39 | 5866 | 179 | 25.8 | 6.2 | -1.9 |
| Togo* | 1500 | 30 | 23 | 47 | 1296 | 86 | 14.1 | 9.0 | |
| Uganda* | 3680 | 81 | 4 | 15 | 2726 | 74 | 54.5 | -5.7 | -1.7 |
| Zaïre* | 7000 | 38 | 17 | 45 | 10115 | 144 | 15.4 | 6.6 | -3.6 |
| Zambia* | 3390 | 14 | 39 | 47 | 7223 | 213 | 12.3 | -3.6 | -0.8 |
| Zimbabwe | 6750 | 14 | 41 | 45 | 3199 | 47 | 23.3 | 0.9 | |

Note: Least developed countries are marked with an asterisk.

Sources: ibid.

Appendix Table 3.3. Sub-Saharan Africa: Economic growth rates, 1965-91

| Country | Average annual GDP growth (%) | | | | | | Average annual GNP growth per capita (%) | | | | |
|---|---|---|---|---|---|---|---|---|---|---|---|
| | 1965-73 | 1974-80 | 1981-85 | 1986-89 | 1990 | 1991 (est.) | 1965-73 | 1973-80 | 1980-89 | 1990 | 1991 (est.) |
| Angola | | | | 7.1 | | | 1.1 | -9.8 | -1.8 | 0.9 | |
| Benin* | 2.5 | 2.8 | 3.1 | 0.2 | 3.9 | 3.0 | 0.0 | -0.3 | 6.2 | 7.4 | 7.7 |
| Botswana* | 14.0 | 11.2 | 11.0 | 11.5 | 5.7 | 8.8 | 9.3 | 7.3 | 2.2 | -1.1 | 1.0 |
| Burkina Faso* | 2.5 | 4.2 | 3.4 | 2.7 | 1.3 | 6.0 | 1.2 | 2.5 | 1.6 | 0.8 | 2.2 |
| Burundi* | 10.8 | 4.0 | 3.2 | 4.1 | 3.6 | 4.9 | 3.2 | 1.9 | 0.6 | -5.8 | -5.1 |
| Cameroon | 2.2 | 9.6 | 6.1 | -6.1 | -2.5 | 0.5 | -0.4 | 5.7 | 3.2 | -0.8 | 0.6 |
| Cape Verde* | | 8.2 | 7.2 | 6.6 | 2.1 | 3.6 | | 7.3 | -1.5 | -1.8 | -4.3 |
| Central Afr. Rep.* | 3.3 | 1.2 | 2.8 | 0.4 | 0.7 | -1.9 | 1.5 | -0.5 | 3.9 | -3.6 | 3.1 |
| Chad* | 0.6 | -3.4 | 10.8 | 6.9 | 0.7 | 8.3 | -1.3 | -3.5 | -0.6 | -2.8 | -1.7 |
| Comoros* | | | | 1.1 | 0.8 | 1.8 | | | | -2.3 | 5.6 |
| Congo | 6.5 | 4.2 | 9.0 | 1.2 | 1.0 | 7.9 | 4.2 | 1.1 | 0.4 | -6.8 | -6.2 |
| Côte d'Ivoire | 9.1 | 5.4 | 0.6 | -1.3 | -2.6 | -2.1 | 4.5 | 1.2 | -3.0 | | -0.3 |
| Djibouti* | | | | 0.3 | 1.2 | 1.6 | | | | | |
| Equatorial Guinea* | | | | 3.3 | 3.1 | -1.0 | | | | 5.2 | -7.0 |
| Ethiopia* | 4.1 | 2.4 | -0.2 | 4.0 | -1.6 | -0.6 | 1.1 | -1.2 | -1.1 | -4.8 | -0.4 |
| Gabon | 7.4 | -1.1 | 2.4 | -0.9 | 4.7 | 2.6 | 4.9 | 0.2 | -2.8 | 2.7 | 0.9 |
| Gambia* | 4.5 | 2.6 | 2.6 | 4.2 | 1.5 | 4.0 | 1.7 | -2.1 | -0.6 | 1.1 | 1.8 |
| Ghana | 3.2 | 0.0 | 0.8 | 5.1 | 3.0 | 5.0 | 1.0 | -4.2 | -0.8 | 0.4 | -1.3 |
| Guinea Bissau* | | 0.4 | 2.4 | 5.9 | 3.0 | 3.1 | | 1.3 | 1.5 | -3.4 | -0.4 |
| Guinea* | | | | 4.8 | 4.1 | 1.9 | 1.2 | | | 2.0 | |
| Kenya | 8.7 | 5.9 | 2.2 | 5.6 | 4.3 | 1.7 | 4.7 | 1.3 | 0.0 | 0.6 | -2.4 |

| | | | | | | | | | | | |
|---|---|---|---|---|---|---|---|---|---|---|---|
| Lesotho* | 8.7 | 5.6 | 1.8 | 10.2 | 4.4 | 5.3 | 4.2 | 6.6 | −0.5 | 0.5 | 1.3 |
| Liberia* | 2.5 | 5.4 | −1.7 | 2.9 | 3.0 | −6.9 | 2.4 | −0.7 | −5.3 | 2.5 | −10.2 |
| Madagascar* | 1.3 | 3.6 | 0.6 | 3.2 | 4.7 | 7.8 | 1.1 | −1.5 | −2.7 | 1.3 | 4.0 |
| Malawi* | 5.6 | 5.6 | 4.2 | 1.5 | 3.4 | −0.2 | 4.3 | 1.4 | −0.1 | 0.2 | −2.7 |
| Mali* | 6.4 | 3.1 | 0.1 | 3.4 | −1.5 | 2.3 | 1.2 | 4.3 | 1.3 | −4.2 | −3.1 |
| Mauritania* | 1.5 | 3.2 | −0.7 | 9.5 | 5.3 | 4.1 | 0.8 | −0.6 | −1.8 | 4.3 | 3.5 |
| Mauritius | 4.8 | 2.2 | 4.1 | 5.5 | 1.9 | 2.7 | | 3.9 | 4.9 | 0.7 | −1.0 |
| Mozambique* | | | −5.7 | 0.1 | 3.1 | 1.9 | −3.7 | 2.6 | −5.6 | −5.4 | −1.0 |
| Namibia | | | | | | | | | | | |
| Niger* | 6.0 | −1.4 | −5.6 | 5.1 | 5.7 | 6.5 | 5.3 | 1.2 | −2.6 | 1.4 | −2.2 |
| Nigeria | 2.9 | 6.5 | −1.2 | 2.9 | −0.9 | 1.0 | 3.2 | 2.2 | −5.0 | 4.9 | 2.6 |
| Rep. of South Africa | 2.6 | 4.7 | 0.6 | −1.9 | −1.7 | −1.5 | 2.3 | 7.2 | −3.6 | −4.3 | |
| Rwanda* | 7.4 | 5.6 | 1.3 | 0.8 | 2.5 | 1.5 | 0.1 | −0.5 | −1.8 | −4.9 | −6.7 |
| São Tomé and Príncipe* | 9.5 | | 1.0 | 2.7 | 4.5 | 1.2 | −1.7 | 4.5 | −4.7 | −5.6 | −1.0 |
| Senegal | 1.9 | 1.8 | 3.0 | 4.9 | 6.6 | −1.1 | 5.8 | −0.8 | 0.0 | 2.3 | −2.2 |
| Seychelles | 7.9 | 6.4 | 3.4 | 3.4 | 3.0 | 0.7 | 2.0 | 4.6 | 1.8 | 5.6 | 0.1 |
| Sierra Leone* | 0.7 | 4.5 | −0.9 | 1.2 | −1.6 | 2.5 | 2.0 | 3.5 | −1.1 | 0.1 | 1.0 |
| Somalia* | 8.2 | 3.5 | 0.4 | 1.0 | −1.5 | 3.7 | 0.7 | 0.3 | −1.3 | −6.3 | |
| Sudan* | 5.3 | 0.9 | 0.2 | 6.5 | 9.8 | 0.0 | 0.3 | −0.9 | −1.6 | −6.4 | |
| Swaziland | 3.1 | 8.9 | 3.3 | 4.6 | 4.1 | 4.1 | −0.5 | 1.5 | 0.6 | 13.1 | 4.2 |
| Tanzania* | 2.2 | 5.9 | 1.4 | 3.6 | −0.5 | | 2.6 | −6.2 | −1.2 | −5.1 | 1.4 |
| Togo* | 4.1 | 5.1 | 0.0 | 9.0 | 4.3 | −1.8 | | | −2.3 | −2.7 | −3.9 |
| Uganda* | | | | | | | | | 0.7 | 0.8 | |
| Zaïre* | −2.5 | 4.9 | 2.1 | 0.4 | −1.9 | | 0.3 | −4.7 | −1.6 | −6.8 | 0.5 |
| Zambia* | −0.3 | 2.5 | −1.1 | 2.9 | | | −0.5 | −2.2 | −3.6 | −5.8 | |
| Zimbabwe | −0.7 | 9.5 | 1.7 | | −1.4 | | 2.6 | −2.0 | −1.1 | 0.1 | 2.6 |

Note: Least developed countries are marked with an asterisk.

Sources: Jaycox, 1992; Osunsade and Gleason, 1992; World Bank, 1992a.

The persistently unfavourable situation on international commodity markets has severely affected SSA economies. Export earnings have plummeted – as a result of low commodity prices and other factors such as political unrest and economic mismanagement. This has had a negative effect on individual countries' debt-service capacity, investment behaviour and public deficits. In some countries poor management had already led to fiscal deficits, which, in turn, had had devastating effects on the national economy – worsening of the external debt position, reduction of the credits available to the private sector, and inflation – and these were exacerbated. It should also be noted that the adverse conditions on the international commodity markets presented an obstacle to the implementation of structural adjustment programmes. In some cases, gains made as a result of the successful implementation of economic reforms were lost. Columns 5 to 8 of the table give further information on these trends.

The need to service external debts led to a considerable reduction in the amount of foreign exchange available to finance investments. Gross domestic investment rates in SSA decreased overall in the 1980s from 20% to 16.4% of GDP in 1987, with the exception of Nigeria where investment remained stable. A considerable percentage of these investments were financed by foreign sources (the international donor community and commercial banks). Prospects in most SSA countries for the external financing of gross investments (foreign savings in the form of direct foreign investment and official development aid) are not very promising. In the late 1980s direct private investment from foreign sources in non-oil-exporting countries amounted to less than US$500 m a year (Pfefferman and Madrassy, 1992); for the record, this is a further illustration of SSA's marginal position in international economic affairs. This situation is not likely to improve in the near future, given the uncertainties prevailing in SSA. Furthermore, aid to SSA is more likely to decrease than to increase. Gross domestic investment will therefore largely be determined by the level of domestic savings. In view of the past economic performance of the SSA countries (see Appendix Table 3.3 for the economic growth in the 1965–91 period), few will be able to generate substantial savings internally. Capacity is therefore unlikely to grow in these countries and governments will be left with only one option, namely to improve the utilization of existing capacity. Within this context, structural adjustment programmes play an important role.

# Political Context[6]

Political stability is as important a precondition as, for example, a good macroeconomic policy for social and economic development. In addition, emphasis is increasingly being laid on greater involvement of the population in development, particularly in the light of the failure of the state apparatus in the SSA countries to act as a positive force in this respect. As a result of this failure democratization of the social and political decision-making structures was inevitable. For these reasons, attention is paid here to certain significant political factors in the SSA countries. Politically speaking, Sub-Saharan Africa presents a very varied picture, as can be seen from Appendix Table 3.4, which illustrates a number of the political characteristics of the now 48 SSA countries.

*The past*
In the first half of the 1960s a great many SSA countries gained independence. This was largely followed, sooner or later, by the introduction of one-party states. Three of the presidents who came to power during this period are still there: in Côte d'Ivoire, The Gambia and Malawi.[7]

The 1965-85 period was one of military coups, with the military taking power by force at least once in 27 countries, i.e. in more than 50% of the SSA countries. However, many of the remaining 19 countries[8] had to deal with failed attempts at military takeovers.

Many of the heads of state who came to power as a result of a military coup later legitimized their positions, frequently by holding 'elections' in which only the government party took part. Two notorious examples are the Presidents of Zaïre and Rwanda, who have held power since 1965 and 1973 respectively and who have so far resisted all pressure from both within and outside their countries to call multi-party elections. A large number of their 'legally' appointed counterparts, i.e. those who came to power legitimately (in some cases after the resignation or death of their predecessors), were until recently no more enthusiastic about free elections. Countries from both categories were ruled by authoritarian regimes until the 1990s. This also applies to a number of other SSA countries where, for various reasons, no reasonable perspective exists nor has a firm date for the holding of presidential or legislative elections yet been announced; these include Chad, Equatorial Guinea, Eritrea, Ethiopia, Liberia, Malawi, Sierra Leone, Somalia, Sudan, Swaziland, Tanzania and Uganda.

In fact, until recently, there were only 4 democratic exceptions to the authoritarian rule in Sub-Saharan Africa: Botswana, The Gambia, Mauritius and, to a certain extent, Senegal.

*The present*
*Multi-partyism.* Democratic presidential elections, i.e. involving more than one party (though in some cases not more than two, e.g. in the Comoros and Côte d'Ivoire) have been held in 25 SSA countries since 1989. This number also includes the 1993 legislative elections in the Kingdom of Lesotho. Power has since changed hands in 12 countries: Benin, Burundi, Cape Verde, Central African Republic (after French pressure), Congo, Lesotho, Madagascar, Mali, Niger, Nigeria (though not to the winner), São Tomé and Príncipe and Zambia. In 13 countries the elections were won by the sitting president, in some cases without opposition: Angola, Burkina Faso, Cameroon, Comoros, Côte d'Ivoire, Djibouti, The Gambia, Ghana, Kenya, Mauritania, Senegal, the Seychelles and Togo. However, in 2 countries the non-acceptance of the elections outcome by one of the major parties had serious political consequences, varying from a resurgence of the civil war in Angola to the spectre of an emerging civil war or another military takeover in Nigeria.

As a result of these elections, there are now 25 'democratic' countries south of the Sahara,[9] inasmuch as they have leaders elected through multi-party elections – although many of these regimes have retained their authoritarian characteristics. Experience clearly shows that introducing a multi-party system or lifting the ban on opposition parties does not automatically lead to democracy or greater respect for human rights.

**Appendix Table 3.4** *Sub-Saharan Africa: Political data (as at 31 October 1993)*

| Country | Year independence gained | Name current head of state | When and how power initially gained | Current political system[b] | Number of heads of state since independence[c] |
|---|---|---|---|---|---|
| Angola | 1975 | Jose Eduardo Dos Santos | Constitutional '79[a] | 1 | 2 |
| Benin | 1960 | Nicephore Soglo | Elections '91 | 1 | 13 |
| Botswana | 1966 | Quett Masire | Constitutional '80[a] | 1 | 2 |
| Burkina Faso | 1960 | Blaise Compaore | Coup d'état '87 | 1 | 6 |
| Burundi | 1962 | | | 1 | 6 |
| Cameroon | 1960 | Paul Biya | Constitutional '82[a] | 1 | 2 |
| Cape Verde | 1975 | Antonio Monteiro | Elections '91 | 1 | 2 |
| Central Afr. Rep. | 1960 | Ange Félix Patasse | Elections '93 | 1 | 5 |
| Chad | 1960 | Idriss Deby | Civil war '90 | 1 | 7 |
| Comoros | 1975 | Said Mohamed Djohar | Constitutional '89[a] | 1 | 3 |
| Congo | 1960 | Pascal Lissouba | Elections '92 | 1 | 6 |
| Côte d'Ivoire | 1960 | Félix Houphouët Boigny | Constitutional '60[a] | 1 | 1 |
| Djibouti | 1977 | Hassan Gouled Aptidon | Constitutional '77[a] | 2 | 1 |
| Equatorial Guinea | 1968 | Teodoro Obiang Nguema | Coup d'état '79 | 1 | 2 |
| Eritrea | 1993 | Issayas Afeworki | Liberation war '93 | 4 | 1[d] |
| Ethiopia | Antiquity | Meles Zenawi | Civil war '91 | 1 | 6[d] |
| Gabon | 1960 | Omar Bongo | Constitutional '67[a] | 1 | 2 |
| Gambia | 1965 | Sir Daouda Diawara | Constitutional '65[a] | 1 | 1 |
| Ghana | 1957 | Jerry J. Rawlings | Coup d'état '81 | 1 | 9 |
| Guinea | 1958 | Lanzana Conte | Coup d'état '84 | 1 | 3 |
| Guinea Bissau | 1974 | Jao Bernardo Vieira | Coup d'état '80 | 1 | 2 |
| Kenya | 1963 | Daniel Arap Moi | Constitutional '78[a] | 1 | 2 |

| Country | Year | Head of State | Status | System | No. |
|---|---|---|---|---|---|
| Lesotho | 1966 | Ntsu Mokhehle | Elections '93 | 1 | 4 |
| Liberia | 1847 | Amos Sawyer | Interim Pres. '90 | 1 | 21$^d$ |
| Madagascar | 1960 | Albert Zafy | Elections '93 | 1 | 6 |
| Malawi | 1964 | Hastings Kamuzu Banda | Constitutional '64$^a$ | 1 | 1 |
| Mali | 1960 | Alpha Oumar Konare | Elections '92 | 1 | 4 |
| Mauritania | 1960 | Moawiya Ould Taya | Coup d'état '84 | 1 | 5 |
| Mauritius | 1968 | Anerood Jugnauth | Elections '82 | 1 | 2 |
| Mozambique | 1975 | Joachim Chissano | Constitutional '86$^a$ | 1 | 2 |
| Namibia | 1990 | Sam Nujoma | Constitutional '90$^a$ | 1 | 1 |
| Niger | 1960 | Mahamane Ousmane | Elections '93 | 1 | 4 |
| Nigeria | 1960 | Ernest Shonekan | Interim Pres. '93 | 2 | 9$^a$ |
| Rep. of South Africa | 1961 | Frederik De Klerk | Constitutional '89$^a$ | 1 | 5$^d$ |
| Rwanda | 1962 | Juvenal Habyarimana | Coup d'état '73 | 1 | 2 |
| São Tomé and Príncipe | 1975 | Miguel Trovoada | Elections '91 | 1 | 2 |
| Senegal | 1960 | Abdou Diouf | Constitutional '81$^a$ | 1 | 2 |
| Seychelles | 1976 | Frans-Albert René | Coup d'état '77 | 1 | 2 |
| Sierra Leone | 1961 | Valentine Strasser | Coup d'état '92 | 4 | 6 |
| Somalia | 1960 | | | 4 | 4 |
| Sudan | 1956 | Omar Hassan el Beshir | Coup d'état '89 | 4 | 7 |
| Swaziland | 1968 | King Mswati III | Constitutional '86$^a$ | 3 | 2 |
| Tanzania | 1964 | Ali Hassan Mwinyi | Constitutional '85$^a$ | 1 | 2 |
| Togo | 1960 | Gnassingbe Eyadema | Coup d'état '67 | 1 | 3 |
| Uganda | 1962 | Yoweri Museveni | Civil War '86 | 3 | 8 |
| Zaïre | 1960 | Mobutu Sese Seko | Coup d'état '65 | 1 | 5 |
| Zambia | 1964 | Frederick Chiluba | Elections '92 | 1 | 2 |
| Zimbabwe | 1980 | Robert Mugabe | Constitutional '87$^a$ | 1 | 2 |

Notes: a) The term 'Constitutional' does not imply any value judgement.
b) 1 = multi-party system; 2 = limited number of parties allowed; 3 = one-party system; 4 = no political parties allowed/existing.
c) Heads of State serving for two distinct periods interrupted by another incumbent – Benin, CAR, Ghana, Liberia, Uganda, Zaïre – were counted twice.
d) Ethiopia since 1900; Liberia since 1847 and Rep. of S. Africa since 1961.

At the end of 1993, Sub-Saharan Africa was composed as follows:

* 4 countries with no political parties, or in which they are banned (Eritrea, Sierra Leone,[10] Sudan and Somalia);
* 2 countries with a one-party system (Swaziland and Uganda);
* 2 countries in which a limited number of political parties are permitted (Djibouti and Nigeria);
* 40 countries with an official multi-party system.

The following should be noted with respect to the last category:

(i) In many countries, political parties based on religious or ethnic origins are not permitted.
(ii) In a large number of countries, the freedom to form political parties is little more than a formal legal right.[11] This explains the preponderance of 'multi-party systems' in Appendix Table 3.4.

*Political instability.* In an increasing number of SSA countries political stability has disappeared or is threatened to a greater or lesser extent by anarchy, where, the central government has ceased to function effectively or at all (Burundi,[12] Liberia and Somalia), civil war, where the central government only functions 'normally' in parts of the country (Angola and Sudan; Mozambique is in a transitionary phase) and rebellion, which, to a greater or lesser extent, prevents the central government from functioning normally (Djibouti and Sierra Leone). Furthermore, ethnic conflict is also rife in many countries, while a number are considered high-risk states where open or potential conflict threatens to make them ungovernable. The situation is highly unstable in Chad, Mali, Niger, Rwanda and Senegal, where on various occasions agreements concluded proved too fragile to provide lasting peace. Clearly, it is impossible or well-nigh impossible to conduct an efficient macroeconomic policy in these countries.

Ethnic conflicts occur sporadically but persistently in many other SSA countries. In addition to the 13 countries mentioned above, where the conflict is primarily tribal in character, these include Ghana, Guinea, Kenya, Mauritania and Nigeria. In addition, the following countries can be considered high-risk: the Republic of South Africa, Zaïre and, albeit to a lesser or much lesser extent, the Central African Republic, Congo, Côte d'Ivoire, Ethiopia, Madagascar, Malawi, Nigeria and Togo. Any classification, of course, risks being rendered out of date by new events. The unpredictable character, as well as the vulnerability, of African societies is well illustrated by the Burundian example.

This political instability, fragility and variability in SSA is further illustrated by the two countries having no Head of State as at 31 October 1993, Burundi and Somalia, by the existence of interim Presidents in two countries, Liberia and Nigeria, and by two other countries, Côte d'Ivoire and Malawi, where for health reasons the President was expected to be replaced in the near future, all situations which may give rise to serious political strife.

*SAPs*
It is important to note that one or more structural adjustment programmes are being conducted in many of these countries. Examples are Burundi, the

Central African Republic, Chad, Côte d'Ivoire, Ethiopia, Ghana, Kenya, Mali, Mauritania, Mozambique, Nigeria, Rwanda, Senegal and Togo. These 14 countries account for more than 50% of the group of 25 SSA countries in which general or sectoral SAPs are in progress.[13] It is clear that political stability is crucial for the successful implementation of an economic reform programme.

# Stabilization and Structural Adjustment Programmes Supported by the IMF and the World Bank 1980–93

The Bretton Woods institutions' involvement in stabilization programmes and structural adjustment programmes is shown in Appendix Tables 3.5 and 3.6a and b.

**Appendix Table 3.5.** *IMF assistance to Sub-Saharan Africa: SAFs and ESAFs, 1986–93*

| Country | SAF I | SAF II | SAF III | ESAF I | ESAF II | ESAF III | ESAF IV |
|---|---|---|---|---|---|---|---|
| Benin | 87–88 | 91–92 | | 93–94 | | | |
| Burkina Faso | 91–92 | | | | | | |
| Burundi | 86–87 | 88–89 | 89–90 | 91–92 | 92–93 | | |
| Central Afr. Rep. | 87–88 | 88–89 | 90–91 | | | | |
| Chad | 87–88 | 89–90 | 90–91 | | | | |
| Comoros | 91–92 | | | | | | |
| Equatorial Guinea | 88–89 | 91–92 | 93–94 | | | | |
| Ethiopia | 92–93 | | | | | | |
| Gambia | 86–87 | 87–88 | | 88–89 | 89–90 | 90–91 | |
| Ghana | 87–88 | | | 88–89 | 89–90 | 91–92 | |
| Guinea | 87–88 | 89–90 | | 91–92 | | | |
| Guinea Bissau | 87–88 | 89–90 | | | | | |
| Kenya | 88–89 | | | 89–90 | 90–91 | 91–92 | |
| Lesotho | 88–89 | 89–90 | 90–91 | 91–92 | 92–93 | | |
| Madagascar | 87–88 | | | 89–90 | 90–91 | | |
| Malawi | | | | 88–89 | 89–90 | 90–91 | 91–92 |
| Mali | 88–89 | 90–91 | | 92–93 | | | |
| Mauritania | 86–87 | 87–88 | | 89–90 | 92–93 | | |
| Mozambique | 87–88 | 88–89 | 89–90 | 90–91 | 91–92 | '93 | |
| Niger | 86–87 | 87–88 | | 88–89 | 90–91 | | |
| Rwanda | 91–92 | | | | | | |
| São Tomé and Príncipe | 89–90 | | | | | | |
| Senegal | 86–87 | 87–88 | | 88–89 | 89–90 | 91–92 | |
| Sierra Leone | 86–87 | | | | | | |
| Somalia | 87–88 | | | | | | |
| Tanzania | 87–88 | 88–89 | 90–91 | 91–92 | 92–93 | | |
| Togo | 88–89 | | | 89–90 | 90–91 | 92–93 | |
| Uganda | 87–88 | 88–89 | | 89–90 | 91–92 | '93 | |
| Zaïre | 87–88 | 89–90 | | | | | |
| Zimbabwe | | | | 92–93 | | | |

Source: IMF, 1993.

## The IMF
The International Monetary Fund finances stabilization programmes by means of (i) stand-by arrangements, (ii) the Structural Adjustment Facility (SAF), and (iii) the Enhanced Structural Adjustment Facility (ESAF).

Stand-by arrangements provide recipient countries with foreign exchange to deal with short-term balance-of-payments problems. These arrangements do not therefore serve exclusively for the purpose of stabilization. Reimbursement to the Fund takes place within a period of three to five years. The need of countries involved in adjustment programmes for assistance in the longer term led to the creation in 1974 of the Extended Fund Facility (EFF). However, a disadvantage attached to the stand-by arrangements – the interest rate – continued to apply. This led to the creation of the Structural Adjustment Facility (SAF) and the Enhanced Structural Adjustment Facility (ESAF), both of which provide for concessional financial aid, with recipient countries paying an annual interest rate of only 0.5%. The loans have a 5-year grace period, the principal being repayable over a period of 5.5 to 10 years. IMF assistance under the terms of the SAF and the ESAF requires an agreement between the IMF and the recipient country which is laid down in a Policy Framework Paper (PFP). The World Bank is closely involved in negotiating this PFP.

As Appendix Table 3.5 shows, the SAF was first introduced into SSA in 1986 when 6 countries benefited from this arrangement (Burundi, The Gambia, Mauritania, Niger, Senegal and Sierra Leone). Since then a total of some 30 countries have benefited from SAFs, the most recent recipients being Burkina Faso (1991), Rwanda (1991), Comoros (1991), Ethiopia (1992) and Zimbabwe (1992). However, a considerable number of countries discontinued IMF aid after one or two years. The Enhanced Structural Adjustment Facility, which was first introduced in 1988, has been granted to 18 countries, Malawi being the only country to apply successfully in four consecutive years.

*The World Bank*
Appendix Tables 3.6a and b show the countries of SSA with past or present Structural Adjustment Programmes (SAPs) financed by the World Bank. The overview (World Bank, 1992b) shows that in the past:

* a total of 35 countries have implemented or are currently implementing structural adjustment programmes;
* the first SAPs were introduced in 1980 in Kenya, Malawi, Mauritius and Senegal; programmes are still being implemented in Kenya and Senegal;
* the World Bank has co-funded 55 general programmes and 67 sectoral programmes in these 35 countries since 1980;
* the 67 sectoral programmes related to:
  * the agriculture sector[14] (15 countries);
  * the industrial sector (9 countries);
  * the trade sector: import and export (7 countries);
  * the human resources sector[15] (7 countries);
  * the financial sector (6 countries);
  * the infrastructure sector[16] (2 countries);
  * other.

The situation in early 1993 was that:

* 24 countries were implementing a SAP: 17 a general SAP and/or 13 one or more sectoral SAPs;
* 13 countries were implementing 22 sectoral SAPs;

**Appendix Table 3.6a.** *World Bank adjustment loans to Sub-Saharan Africa: SALs 1980–93*

| Country | First year SAL | First year ongoing SAL | Number of SALs |
|---|---|---|---|
| Benin | 1989 | 1991 | 2 |
| Burkina Faso | 1991 | 1991 | 1 |
| Burundi | 1986 | 1992 | 3 |
| Cameroon | 1989 | 1989 | 1 |
| Central Afr. Rep. ⌐ | 1987 | 1990 | 3 |
| Comoros | 1991 | 1991 | 1 |
| Congo | 1987 | | 1 |
| Côte d'Ivoire | 1982 | | 3 |
| Gabon | 1988 | | 1 |
| Gambia | 1987 | | 2 |
| Ghana | 1987 | | 2 |
| Guinea | 1986 | 1988 | 2 |
| Guinea Bissau | 1987 | 1989 | 2 |
| Kenya | 1980 | | 2 |
| Malawi | 1981 | | 3 |
| Mali | 1991 | 1991 | 1 |
| Mauritania | 1987 | | 1 |
| Mauritius | 1981 | | 2 |
| Mozambique | 1988 | 1989 | 2 |
| Niger | 1986 | | 1 |
| Rwanda | 1991 | 1991 | 1 |
| São Tomé and Príncipe | 1987 | 1990 | 2 |
| Senegal | 1981 | 1990 | 4 |
| Tanzania | 1987 | | 1 |
| Togo | 1983 | 1991 | 4 |
| Uganda | 1988 | 1992 | 3 |
| Zaïre | 1987 | | 1 |
| Zambia | 1986 | 1991 | 2 |
| Zimbabwe | 1992 | 1992 | 1 |

Source: World Bank, 1992b.

* 6 countries were implementing both a general and one or more sectoral SAPs (Burkina Faso, Burundi, Guinea Bissau, Mali, Togo and Uganda);
* the political unrest in at least 25% of the 24 countries in which SAPs were being implemented adversely affected the conduct of government (see Political Context above.)

*Regional structural adjustment programmes.* These have not, as yet, been initiated, although the World Bank is currently investigating the scope for doing so in Central Africa among the member states of UDEAC, the Customs Union of Central African States. These programmes are based on a relatively new concept, i.e. that national SAPs tend only to address internal problems and take no account of the regional factors which are frequently crucial to their success. Regional structural adjustment programmes could provide a solution and also enable the co-ordination or monitoring of macroeconomic policy in the countries concerned.

**Appendix Table 3.6b.** *World Bank adjustment loans to Sub-Saharan Africa: SECALs, 1980-93*

| Country | Number of SECALs | First year of SECAL | Agric. sector | Industr. sector | Finan. sector | Commercial sector | Public sector | Infrastr. sector | Human resources | Other | Number of ongoing SECALs |
|---|---|---|---|---|---|---|---|---|---|---|---|
| Burkina Faso | 2 | 1985 | 1985 | | | | | | | | 1 |
| Burundi | 1 | 1989 | 1989 | | | | | | | | 1 |
| Central Afr. Rep. | 1 | 1988 | 1988 | | | | | | | | |
| Chad | 2 | 1989 | | | 1989 | | | 1989 | | | 1 |
| Côte d'Ivoire | 6 | 1990 | 1990 | | 1992 | | | 1990 | 1992 | 1992 | 3 |
| Ghana | 9 | 1983 | | 1986 | 1988 | 1983 | | | 1987 | 1991 | 3 |
| Guinea | 1 | 1990 | | | | | | | 1990 | | 1 |
| Guinea Bissau | 1 | 1985 | | | | 1985 | | | | | |
| Kenya | 6 | 1986 | 1986 | 1988 | 1989 | 1988 | | | 1992 | 1992 | 3 |
| Madagascar | 4 | 1985 | 1986 | 1985 | | 1987 | 1988 | | | | |
| Malawi | 3 | 1983 | 1983 | 1988 | | 1988 | | | | | |
| Mali | 3 | 1988 | 1990 | | | | 1988 | | 1989 | 1990 | 3 |
| Mauritania | 4 | 1985 | 1990 | | | | 1985 | | | | 1 |
| Mauritius | 1 | 1987 | | 1987 | | | | | | | |
| Niger | 1 | 1987 | | | | | 1987 | | | | |
| Nigeria | 4 | 1984 | 1984 | | | 1987 | | | 1990 | | 1 |
| Senegal | 1 | 1990 | | | 1990 | | | | | | |
| Sierra Leone | 1 | 1984 | 1984 | | | | | | | | |
| Somalia | 2 | 1986 | 1986 | | | | | | | | |
| Sudan | 2 | 1980 | 1980 | | | | | | | | |
| Tanzania | 4 | 1981 | 1990 | 1989 | 1992 | 1981 | | | | | 2 |
| Togo | 2 | 1991 | | | | | | | 1991 | | 1 |
| Uganda | 2 | 1983 | 1983 | | | | | | | | 1 |
| Zaïre | 1 | 1986 | | 1986 | | | | | | | |
| Zambia | 3 | 1984 | 1985 | 1986 | | 1984 | | | | | |
| Zimbabwe | 1 | 1983 | | 1983 | | | | | | | |

Source: *ibid.*

# Notes

1 Including the Republic of South Africa, but excluding the Western Sahara, despite its recognition by the majority of African States and the OAU. Also excluding Eritrea which became independent on 24 May, 1993. Figures for Ethiopia reflect the situation prior to Eritrea's independence.
2 Including the, frequently underestimated, contribution made by women engaged in nonmonetarised economic activities.
3 The average 6.5 SSA fertility rate is considerably higher than those in other parts of the developing world, 4.8 (Southern Asia), 3.9 (South-East Asia), 2.3 (East Asia), and Latin America 3.7.
4 i.e. a per capita annual income of less than US$370 – 1985 purchasing power parity.
5 We do not elaborate on the fact that many individuals in SSA engage in more than one economic activity as part of their survival strategy.
6 This section includes the Republic of South Africa but excludes the Western Sahara, despite its recognition by the majority of African states and the OAU. These political background notes have been updated and reflect the situation as at 31 October, 1993.
7 President Banda of Malawi has declared himself 'President for Life'.
8 In addition to the three countries mentioned above, these were: Angola, Botswana, Cameroon, Cape Verde, Gabon, the Gambia, Kenya, Mauritius, Mozambique, the Republic of South Africa, São Tomé and Principe, Senegal, Swaziland, Tanzania, Zambia and Zimbabwe. Given the time period 1965–85, Eritrea and Namibia are not included.
9 Two countries, where elections have recently been held, have been excluded: Burundi because of the killing of the democratically elected president in the (failed) coup d'état of October 1993 and Nigeria because of the (disputed) annulment of the result of the June 1993 presidential elections. Two 'traditionally' democratic countries, Botswana and Mauritius, have been added.
10 Sierra Leone was the last country to date in which a military coup was successfully carried out.
11 One of the most striking examples of this is Equatorial Guinea, where the ban on political parties was lifted in January 1992 but the restrictions on freedom of assembly remained in force.
12 The situation as at 31 October, 1993, following the bloody failed coup d'état in which the recently installed and democratically elected President was killed and there was a resurgence of traditional tribal violence.
13 Ethiopia which concluded a SAP in the course of 1993 has been added to the 24 countries presented in the following background note on IMF and World Bank-supported programmes.
14 Including fertilizer loans.
15 Embracing human resources development in general and the education sector in particular.
16 Comprising the transport sector, the water supply and sewerage sector and the energy sector.

# References

Cambessédès, Olivier (1992) Atlaseco 1993, Paris: Editions du Sérail.
Economic Commission for Africa (1993) African Socio-Economic Indicators 1990/91, Addis Ababa: Economic Commission for Africa.
Economic Commission for Africa (1991) Foreign Trade Statistics for Africa – Direction of Trade, Series A, No. 34, Addis Ababa/New York: United Nations.
International Monetary Fund, (1993) Operational Modalities and Funding Alternatives for an ESAF Successor – Preliminary Considerations, EBS/93/32, Washington DC: IMF.
Jaycox, Edward V.K. (1992) 'Africa: From Stagnation to Recovery', Statement to the Board of Executive Directors, World Bank, Washington DC, February.
Osunsade, F.L. and Gleason, Paul (1992) IMF Assistance to Sub-Saharan Africa, Washington DC: International Monetary Fund, External Relations Department.
Pfeffermann, Guy P. and Madrassy, Andrea (1992) Trends in Private Investment in Developing Countries 1993, Statistics for 1970–91, Discussion Paper No. 16, Washington DC: International Finance Corporation, World Bank.
United Nations Development Programme (1992) Human Development Report 1992, New York: Oxford University Press for UNDP.
World Bank (1992a) World Development Report 1992 – Development and Environment, New York: Oxford University Press for World Bank.
World Bank, (1992b) Third Report on Adjustment Lending: Private and Public Resources for Growth, R92-47, IDA/R92-29, Washington DC: World Bank.

# List of Participants

Prof. S. Ibi Ajayi, University of Ibadan, Ibadan, Nigeria
Dr Hans–Henning Andresen, Kreditanstalt für Wiederaufbau, Frankfurt am Main, Germany
Prof. Brian van Arkadie, Africa Capacity Building Fund, Harare, Zimbabwe
Prof. Jean–Paul Azam, Université d'Auvergne, Clermont-Ferrand, France
Prof. Boubacar Barry, Institut de Recherche pour l'Intégration sous-Régionale, Dakar, Senegal
Dr Anupam Basu, International Monetary Fund, Washington DC, USA
Dr Jacques Bugnicourt, Environmental Development Action in the Third World, Dakar, Senegal
Mr Moustapha Deme, Societé d'études et d'applications techniques, Bamako, Mali
Mr Lionel Demery, The World Bank, Washington DC, USA
Prof. Diane Elson, University of Manchester, Manchester, UK
Mr Cheikh-I. Fall, African Development Bank, Abidjan, Côte d'Ivoire
Prof. Valpy FitzGerald, Institute of Social Studies, The Hague, The Netherlands
Mr Michael Foster, Overseas Development Administration, London, UK
Dr Jane Harrigan, University of Manchester, Manchester, UK
Mr Kunio Hatanaka, Overseas Economic Cooperation Fund, Paris, France
Dr Bert Helmsing, Institute of Social Studies, The Hague, The Netherlands
Dr Rolph van der Hoeven, ILO, Geneva, Switzerland
Dr Ishrat Husain, The World Bank, Washington DC, USA
Mr Michel Jacquier, Caisse Française de Développement, Paris, France
Mr Emmanuel Gabriel Kasonde, Century Holdings Ltd, Lusaka, Zambia
Dr Ad Koekkoek, Ministry of Foreign Affairs, The Hague, The Netherlands
Dr Fred van der Kraaij, Ministry of Foreign Affairs, The Hague, The Netherlands
Mr Marnix Krop, Ministry of Foreign Affairs, The Hague, The Netherlands
Mr Karl Larsson, Swedish International Development Association, Stockholm, Sweden
Mr Klaus Lidy, Bundesministerium für wirtschaftliche Zusammenarbeit und Entwicklung, Bonn, Germany
Prof. John Loxley, University of Manitoba, Winnipeg, Canada
H.E. Prof. Kighoma A. Malima, Ministry of Finance, Dar es Salaam, Tanzania
Prof. Stefaan Marysse, University of Antwerp, Antwerp, Belgium
Mr Leon Mazairac, Ministry of Foreign Affairs, The Hague, The Netherlands
Mr Henk Meilink, Africa Studies Centre, Leiden, The Netherlands
Mr Taye Mengistae, Addis Ababa University, Addis Ababa, Ethiopia
Dr Percy S. Mistry, Oxford International Associates, Oxford, UK
Mr Abdul Mohammed, Inter-Africa Group, Addis Ababa, Ethiopia
Dr Christian Morrisson, OECD Development Centre, Paris, France

Prof. Paul Mosley, University of Reading, Reading, UK
Mr Harris Mule, TIMS Ltd., Nairobi, Kenya
Mr Harouna Niang, Prime Minister's Office, Bamako, Mali
Dr Achola Pala Okeyo, United Nations Development Fund for Women, New York, USA
H.E. Jan Pronk, Ministry of Foreign Affairs, The Hague, The Netherlands
Mr Wouter Raab, Ministry of Finance, The Hague, The Netherlands
Prof. Jorn Rattsoe, University of Trondheim, Dragvoll, Norway
Prof. Alexander Sarris, University of Athens, Greece
H.E. Jacques Sawadogo, Ministry of Planning, Ouagadougou, Burkina Faso
Prof. Venkatesh Seshamani, University of Zambia, Lusaka, Zambia
Mr Gerard Steeghs, The World Bank, Washington DC, USA
Dr Frances Stewart, International Development Centre, Oxford, UK
Mr Haruo Suzuki, Japan International Co-operation Agency, Paris, France
Dr Finn Tarp, University of Copenhagen, Copenhagen, Denmark
Prof. John Toye, Institute of Development Studies, University of Sussex, Brighton, UK
Mr Ruud Treffers, Ministry of Foreign Affairs, The Hague, The Netherlands
Dr Peter de Valk, Institute of Social Studies, The Hague, The Netherlands
Prof. George Waardenburg, Ministry of Foreign Affairs, The Hague, The Netherlands
Dr Jumanne H. Wagao, University of Dar es Salaam, Dar es Salaam, Tanzania
Prof. Samuel M. Wangwe, United Nations University – Institute for New Technologies, Maastricht, The Netherlands
Dr Willi A. Wapenhans, Gaithersburg, USA
Mr Wim Wessels, Ministry of Foreign Affairs, The Hague, The Netherlands
Prof. Marc Wuyts, Institute of Social Studies, The Hague, The Netherlands
Prof. Joseph Yao, Centre Ivoirien de Recherches Economiques et Sociales, Abidjan, Côte d'Ivoire
Mr Jürgen Zattler, Commission of the European Communities, Brussels, Belgium

# Index